Pitt Series in

POLICY AND INSTITUTIONAL STUDIES

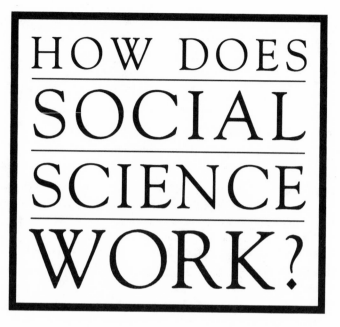

HOW DOES SOCIAL SCIENCE WORK?

Reflections on Practice

PAUL DIESING

UNIVERSITY OF PITTSBURGH PRESS

Published by the University of Pittsburgh Press, Pittsburgh, Pa., 15260
Copyright © 1991, University of Pittsburgh Press
All rights reserved
Baker & Taylor International, London
Manufactured in the United States of America

Library of Congress Cataloging-in-Publication Data

Diesing, Paul.
   How does social science work? : reflections on practice / Paul Diesing.
     p.   cm—(Pitt series in policy and institutional studies)
   Includes bibliographical references.
   ISBN 0-8229-3661-5 (cloth)
   1. Social sciences—Philosophy.   2. Social sciences—Research.
 I. Title. II. Series.
 H61.D535   1991
 300—dc20
                                        90-41706
                                          CIP

For Paul Feyerabend

CONTENTS

INTRODUCTION

THIS BOOK is intended for the practicing social scientist or social science student. It is concerned with actual research, and focuses on three main questions: (1) What are the actual goals of the various current research methods? Call the goals "truth" or "knowledge"; then what characteristics does achieved truth have in the various methods? (2) What social, cognitive, and personality processes occur or should occur during research, and how do they contribute to the outcome? (3) What persistent weaknesses and dangers appear in research, and what can we do about them?

Brinberg and McGrath (1985, pp. 78–86) would call this book *applied philosophy of science,* since it focuses on the practical problems and processes of research. Indeed, its spirit is very similar to that of Brinberg and McGrath, and to the various writings of McGrath and associates. They describe their validity network schema as a schema for raising consciousness about research (p. 161), and that is the aim of the present book as well. I am trying to get at the actual practices and influences, conscious and unconscious, that lie behind the official procedures and rules that people are taught to follow. The official procedures are not wrong, but they don't tell the whole story.

The reader who works through this material should develop a greater self-awareness, and also an understanding of alternative approaches to research. I am not arguing for one philosophy and one research method as the best way to truth; I leave that decision to the reader.

Pure philosophers of science will find little or nothing to interest them in the present work; they can stop reading right here. It does not deal with issues that epistemologists have disputed for decades and centuries: the justification of induction, the relation between universals and bare particulars, the nature of causation, the relation between reasons and causes, the logical structure of explanation, the transcendental a prioris of science. Such issues have little or no relevance to the practice of research, at least in the terms that philosophers have debated them. Nor do I wish to get involved in debates about such subjects. (For my ideas on reasons and causes, see Diesing, 1986; 1982, pp. 329–36.)

More recently some philosophers of science have come to think that they should know what they are arguing about, and have immersed themselves in some sector of the social sciences. I welcome these philosophers as readers; they will be able to understand my argument. But they will probably miss my main point, which is not to *argue* except incidentally, but to promote greater self-awareness among social scientists. Also I hope they will forbear from the usual philosophical tactic of putting the work in some "old error" category—relativism, idealism, irrationalism, objectivism, historicism, or whatever—and then misrepresent it. I want to stay out of that verbal boxing game.

Part I surveys some philosophical traditions that have been influential in the social sciences. The purpose here is to collect proposed answers to our first two questions: What is truth, and how ought we achieve it? The philosophers have answers aplenty to these questions, but the answers conflict. We can try the proposed answers against research practice (part II) and see which ones seem to fit best, in general or for specific methods. I have included Kuhn in part I, although he is not officially a philosopher, because he has suggested an influential answer to question 2.

Part I also has the secondary purpose of enabling some social scientists to reexamine their own philosophy of science, their own conception of what they are doing. If researchers are taught only one philosophy of science in a methods or philosophy course and are told, "That's it. That's what philosophy of science teaches," they will have to come to terms with that philosophy, and will unavoidably include much of it in their own philosophy of science. The availability of several alternative philosophies and their variants should free researchers from this dependence.

The main dependence for decades has been on one philosophy, logical empiricism or *positivism*, as its opponents call it. Too many researchers have learned in methods courses that the aim of science is to discover universal laws, and the method is to deduce causal hypotheses from more general theories and test them against masses of observable data. This teaching has had a dogmatic certitude—that's what science *is*; philosophers of science say so, and they know—that has not been present in many of the logical empiricists themselves. The methods textbooks also fail to mention the problems that have come up in the philosophy that have led to its continual transformation and virtual abandonment by 1980.

Accordingly, chapter 1 traces the development of logical empiricism, including the main problems that have come up, the main transformations, and the retrospective modest evaluation of its achievements by later logical empiricists. Chapters 2–5 present alternative philosophies, arranged by increasing distance from the doctrines of logical empiricism. Researchers are invited to pick whatever philosophy best fits their practice and use it to think about their work. They should notice, however, that whatever philosophy they choose has its own problems or weaknesses; they will have to deal with these problems somehow if they think the philosophy is sound.

I do not mean to claim that logical empiricism is totally wrong. What is wrong is the dogmatic, simplified, problem-free version that has come down on social scientists. Once one escapes from servitude to that doctrine, one can find helpful ideas and warnings even in "positivism," though not many. This will be more true in some areas of social science than others.

Part II summarizes social studies of science of the last two decades or so. Since social research is a social and cognitive activity, it can in principle be studied like any other social activity, and has been. Here we can see ourselves through the eyes of other social scientists. Here, looking through their eyes, we can examine our own unconscious cognitive processes, political commitments, economic exchanges, social class location, expressions of personality, and see how they have affected our research.

Part II, the heart of the book, embodies the principle of reflexivity: any knowledge of social practices is also knowledge of the practices of social scientists. Accordingly, part II provides tentative answers to questions 2 and 3: "What social, cognitive, and personality processes occur during research?" and "What persistent problems and weaknesses occur?"

I know from experience that some social scientists will strongly resist the material in one or another of these chapters. They will vehemently deny that they have any political or ideological commitments at all, or will angrily reject the thought that their personality affects their research in any way. Indeed, they will assert that the mere suggestion of "ideological bias" or personality influences is insulting and improper. I assume these people are correct about themselves. However, these same people will readily find ideological biases or personality influences or cognitive biases in other scientists. In such cases, I suggest, the material of chapters 6–10 can be used to understand the research practice of *other* social scientists, though not of oneself. It is easier to see the mote in the other fellow's eye.

Part III synthesizes the material of the other two parts to provide proposed answers to our three questions: "What is truth?" "How is or should it be achieved?" and "What major problems or weaknesses come up along the way?" The weaknesses are presumably the areas where improvement is most needed. Or, conversely, perhaps the pragmatist's unbounded faith in the possibility of improvement is a delusion here. Perhaps all we can learn from self-study is the need for humility, a recognition of our own limits and the limits of science. Perhaps the best we can do is to avoid the most serious errors, the descent into pseudo-science, propaganda, self-delusion, aimless disputes, mindless routines. Of course, readers are free to draw their own implications, and can use the material of part III as a foil or starting point for their own interpretation of science.

This work, like all my writings, is a product, or perhaps a by-product, of the continuing conflict between two sides of my nature: the one that strives for order, system, clarity, neatness, and above all punctuality, and the other that enjoys empirical complexity, change, commotion, chaos, and a bit of tomfoolery. We both like Whitehead's proposed motto for science: Seek simplicity and distrust it. Over the years, the two of us have gotten to know each other well and have even learned to cooperate fruitfully in Whiteheadian fashion—or so the orderly one deludes himself, until he finds that he has once again been tricked by the other fellow. I remain caught on the horns of McGrath's "dilemmatics" (see chapter 4).

The reader may notice the continuing counterpoint of these two voices in what follows, and may want to add her own voice, especially in part III. Three-part counterpoint is better than two-part.

The final result before you has been much improved by the detailed criticisms of Ben Agger, Fred Dallmyer, H.C.B. Denber, John Kearns, Joseph Masling, William Mishler, Ian Mitroff, and Jan Swijtink. In particular, some of them and some referees have vigorously insisted that I should simplify, systematize, and clarify the argument. I am also grateful to Sara Abosch, Brenda Major, David Phillips, Lionel Lewis, Lynette Spencer, Frank Zagare, and others for showing me materials that brought my overly simple, abstract argument closer to empirical reality.

I

PERSPECTIVES FROM THE
PHILOSOPHY OF SCIENCE

1

Logical Empiricism, 1922–1970

LOGICAL EMPIRICISM was the dominant movement in twentieth-century philosophy of science until about 1965. During its prime in the 1950s it dominated the field so totally that philosophers regarded it as identical with philosophy of science itself. Its basic definitions and distinctions were regarded as self-evident, and anyone who questioned them was contemptuously ignored as simply not a philosopher of science. After about 1958, it was increasingly on the defensive against newer movements, and by 1970 all the innovation was occurring in the newer movements. By 1980 it had almost completely disappeared from philosophy of science convention programs in the United States. The general approach or mood continues among some philosophers of science such as Ayer (1987), but the specific doctrines are no longer asserted, except in social sciences textbooks.

The movement declined and disappeared because its internal difficulties were insurmountable. It was not overthrown; it slowed, stopped, and died out. Yet it remains important historically, in part because of its positive achievements and in part because all later movements defined themselves in opposition to one or more of its doctrines. In philosophy of science after 1950, it was the thesis; all other movements were antitheses. They were all, in part, negations. As Popper observed, if the logical empiricists were positivists, then he was a negativist (1962, p. 229). However, each movement negated a different set of doctrines, so they disagreed with one another as well as with the received philosophy. Stockman (1983) contrasts three of these antipositivist movements. Of course, logical empiricism too began as a negation and it too must be understood as an attempt to correct "old errors." By 1950 the negative program of logical empiricism had been pretty well completed and people thought of it as simply positive philosophy of science, so we must go back to the 1920s to recover the original meaning of this movement.

I begin with 1922 because this was the year in which the Vienna

Circle began to form around the newly appointed Professor Schlick at the university. The earliest members included Carnap, Neurath, Feigl, Waismann, Gödel, and Kraft (Kraft, 1968, pp. 1–2). Other early members were Gustav Bergmann and Philipp Frank (B. Smith, 1987, p. 36). Popper distinguished himself from the Vienna Circle but was regarded by them as part of the movement; he was a dissenting member. Some writers regard the Vienna Circle as the original logical empiricists (or logical positivists), while others regard the Circle as the predecessors of true logical empiricism. In either case, the movement soon spread to include such people as Reichenbach and Hempel in Berlin and Ayer in London.

The Vienna Circle made a sharp distinction between science and metaphysics, identifying themselves with science and against metaphysics. By *science* they meant primarily physics, and especially Einstein's theory of relativity. They also meant mathematics, which was an essential part of physics and astronomy. Some of the Vienna Circle were mathematicians or physicists, and all the others had studied physics and especially relativity theory or some other science (Carnap, 1963, p. 21). Carnap's thesis was titled "Raum" (space), and Schlick's thesis was on the physics of light, under Max Planck (Schlick, 1938, p. viii).

By *metaphysics* they did not mean study of the general characteristics of the real world. They meant the study of a reality beyond appearance, a supersensible reality. They meant primarily Kant, with his thing-in-itself; Bradley, with his Absolute; Spinoza; Schopenhauer, with his Will and Idea, and the like. Schlick begins his *Problems of Philosophy* (1933–34) with the "pernicious" appearance-reality distinction and devotes several chapters to theories about ultimate reality, the thing-in-itself, the essence of things, the external world. His *Allgemeine Erkenntnislehre* (1925) also devotes several chapters to the *Ding an sich*, appearance and reality, and the like.

The science-metaphysics distinction provided two tasks for the Vienna Circle: explain what science is, and expose the errors of metaphysics. They called the first task an "explication" or "rational reconstruction" of science. There was no doubt that physics exists and does provide knowledge. The task of the scientific philosopher was to clarify just how physics does this. Science seeks truth; philosophy seeks clarity (Schlick, 1933–34, pp. 48–49). Each needs the other; both tasks go hand in hand (pp. 51–53). The explication of a science includes stating the general principles any science has to follow to get knowledge (Schlick, 1925, p. 7), and also the logical or mathematical structure of some particular science. Thus for Carnap the philosophy of a science is a syntactical analysis of the language of that science (1935, p. 88 and *passim*).

In order to explicate a science, one has to know the science, of course. "Philosophy is at home in all sciences, and I am convinced that one can only philosophize successfully from within science" (Schlick, 1925, p. 7)—especially natural science (p. 8). "All philosophical work is bound to be unproductive if it is not done in close cooperation with the special sciences" (Carnap, 1937, p. 332). "The philosopher who does not wish to fall into empty speculations must be master of the scientific mode of procedure" (Schlick, 1933–34, p. 52).

Metaphysical questions about ultimate reality can be exposed as pseudo-questions resulting from misuse of language (Waismann, in Schlick, 1938, pp. xxi–xxiii). Thus "Das Nichts nichtet" (the nothing nothings—Heidegger) gets its apparent profundity from the syntactic misuse of "nichts," adding a "das" to it (Kraft, 1968, p. 29). The question, "Do numbers exist or did we invent them?" is exposed as a pseudo-question when we talk instead about numerical expressions, words (Carnap, 1935, pp. 78–82). If we ask, "Do numerical expressions exist?" the puzzle has disappeared.

The most important antimetaphysical task was to recover mathematics for science. Kant had declared Euclidean geometry to be our a priori way of perceiving the world; it was a transcendental condition of all experience, a metaphysical truth about the world of appearance. Non-Euclidean geometries could be dismissed by Kantians as human inventions; but when the theory of relativity used Riemannian geometry, the picture changed. A human invention had fit the world better than an a priori truth. The Vienna people declared that all forms of mathematics, including that of Euclid, were human inventions for dealing with the world. They were languages, ways of expressing scientific hypotheses. Consequently, the way to clarify science was to study scientific languages, and especially the formal, mathematical one that physicists used. The study of language would also help in exposing metaphysical misuse of language.

Scientific languages had three aspects: syntax, semantics, and pragmatics. The syntax rules (L-rules) specified how to construct a sentence; for example, it had to have a subject and a predicate. Other rules of syntax told how to transform a sentence into an equivalent sentence, how to make deductions from sets of sentences, how to deduce predictions, boundary conditions, equilibrium conditions, and so forth, and also how to find inconsistencies. Philosophical clarification of a language through syntactical analysis would help the scientist avoid errors in these processes. The semantic rules, as they were later called, showed how to find the meaning of terms and sentences, and thereby reduce misunderstandings due to differences of meaning in scientific discussion. Pragmatics was concerned with how scientists actually work, but since this was practice, not logic, logicians could have nothing to say about it. Philosophical clarification was limited to syntax and semantics.

Formal languages can range from the most general to the most specific. The most general one would be a unified mathematical logic suitable for expressing and transforming any scientific sentence. The basic example for the Vienna Circle was Whitehead and Russell's *Principia Mathematica* (1915), which had just swept through the world of philosophy in 1920 and which had also inspired Wittgenstein (Toulmin, in Achinstein and Barker, 1969, pp. 26–27). Scientists could invent more particular languages to express their special theories. According to Carnap, anyone could make up a formal language with its own rules (1963, p. 55) and could change the rules when necessary for making changes in a scientific theory (1937, p. 318).

Between 1922 and 1930, the Vienna people developed a basic explication of science that carried out the above program in general terms. They thought of science, physics, as a set of sentences that were (1) true, (2) known to be true, (3) expressed or potentially expressible in a formal or artificial logical language, and (4) related to one another in some sort of structure.

1. There were two kinds of true sentences in science, analytic and synthetic. Analytic sentences are true by definition; they are tautologies saying nothing about the world. Examples: "2 + 2 = 4"; "All oculists are eye doctors"; "The total quantity of money in circulation is the sum of the money in circulation in each Federal Reserve district, each Thursday at 5:00 P.M." Carnap called this sort of truth L-truth. Such sentences are useful in science for making deductions, such as deducing the total quantity of money. That is, if (1) total M = the sum of the M in each district, and (2) M in district 1 = $50 billion; (3) M in district 2 = $39 billion; (4) 50 + 39 = 89; then (5) total M = $89 billion. The first and fourth sentences are analytic, true by definition; two, three, and five are synthetic, empirical.

Synthetic or empirical sentences are not true by definition; they say something about the world. They are synthetic in that the predicate is not contained in the subject. Thus in "All ravens are black," "black" is not contained in the definition of "raven." It adds something new. Some ravens in western Manitoba could conceivably have a green head or bars on their wings, and still be ravens, just as western flickers have red rather than yellow underwings. The assertion "Some ravens in western Manitoba have green heads" is not false by definition, in the way that "2 + 2 = 5" is.

"Empirically true" had already been defined by Wittgenstein in his *Tractatus Logico-Philosophicus* (1922, secs. 2.2, 4.06, 4.4, 5.1, etc.) and again by Tarski (1944, originally 1933; cf. Schlick, 1933–34, p. 53). Wittgenstein's *Tractatus*, along with ideas of Mach, Bolzano, and others, inspired the Vienna Circle and provided many of its early ideas. According to Wittgenstein and Tarski, empirical truth is correspondence with reality. Thus "All ravens are black" is true if all ravens are black. What else could it be?

2. The second characteristic of science was that its statements were known to be true. That is, they had been tested and verified. Anyone could construct sentences that might happen to be true, but to know and to prove that they were true was a much more difficult enterprise. Testing was thus an important scientific activity, perhaps the most important one.

We test the truth of analytic statements by substituting equivalent symbols until we get an identity, $A = A$ (Schlick, 1925, pp. 189–90). Empirical or synthetic statements are about the world, so we have to test them there. If empirical truth is correspondence with reality, then testing consists of examining reality to see whether some statement corresponds to it. For example, Einstein's theory of relativity had been tested in 1919 when some astronomers observed a star during an eclipse. "Examining reality" consisted of observing the star, and the observation was expressed in a sentence. Thus the correspondence was between two sentences, one by Einstein, "Star x will appear in space-time line y" and one by the observer, "Star x appeared in space-time line y." If the x's and y's and their relation are identical, the theory has been verified (Schlick, 1938, p. 225). Carnap called the observer's sentence a *protocol sentence* to distinguish it from the sentence in the theory (Carnap, 1937, p. 317).

3. Carnap's *Der Logische Aufbau der Welt* (the logical structure of the world, 1928) was the first sketch of a formal language for describing the whole physical and psychocultural world. The language was modeled on the logical language of Whitehead and Russell's *Principia Mathematica*. The elementary terms of the language referred to elementary experiences

such as "red" or a musical chord; the terms could not be defined, but their meaning could be given by pointing to the experiences (ostensive definition). There was a single primitive relation, a recalled similarity between two experiences. Other concepts were defined in terms of this relation, and still others in terms of those concepts. For example, a *part similarity* is a similarity between parts of two experiences; a *similarity circle* is all the experiences that have a part similarity relation to each other. The musical chord C-E-G belongs to three similarity circles.

Carnap's *Abriss der Logistik* (1929) claims to be an instruction manual for explicating the formal language of any science. It is again based on *Principia Mathematica* (PM). The analyst is instructed to define actual concepts of the science in terms of other concepts of the science, and so on until ultimate concepts such as "red" or "similar" are reached. Syntactic rules can be set up as needed for the task. The analyst can pick whatever ultimate concepts are convenient for defining the others, as in PM. Note that the *Abriss* analysis runs in the opposite direction from the *Aufbau* construction.

One of Carnap's examples is physics. Here the elementary terms refer to space-time points in world-lines. There are two basic relations between points: K, coincides with; and Z, in the same world-line at different times.

4. The sentences of a science have to be related in some deductive fashion, so that particular sentences can be deduced for testing purposes. According to Carnap (1929, p. iii), this means that each science has some basic axioms from which the others are deduced. The axioms cannot be directly compared with protocol sentences for testing, but low-level sentences deduced from them can. Conversely, the definitions of the low-level concepts are provided by more abstract ones, so that the whole set is a system (Schlick, 1925, p. 87).

We now shift from syntax to semantics. In the 1920s the Vienna Circle advanced their attack on metaphysics by applying Wittgenstein's (1922) definition of meaning. There are two kinds of meaning, logical and empirical, corresponding to the two kinds of truth. Logical meaning is simply definition, that is the equivalent words and sentences. The empirical meaning of a proposition is what it says about the world—that is, what about the world would be different if it were true rather than false. "All ravens are black" says they're not white, green, or mottled; they're black. But this is precisely what we look for when we test the proposition. Consequently, Wittgenstein asserted, we know what a proposition means when we know how to test it. "All ravens are black" means (1) instructions on how to identify a raven, for instance by showing two or more pictures and saying, "Any experience similar to that one but different from that or those is a raven," and (2) instructions on how to identify black, using a hairpin and a tomato, or a color chart (cf. Schlick, 1933–34, p. 129; Carnap, 1963, p. 45; Ayer, 1936, p. 35: "We say that a sentence is factually significant to any given person if, and only if, he knows how to verify the proposition which it purports to express").

The delicious consequence of this concept of meaning is that metaphysical propositions are not only misused language; they are meaningless. Consider "The Absolute is perfect," Hempel's favorite example. What instruction does the metaphysicist[1] give for locating this Absolute? Does he have a photograph of it, or directions on where to go to find it? How would one recognize it—does it sneeze or bark? And what would "perfection" look like? What color is it? What temperature? Bradley's theory does not answer these questions, so the statement is empirically meaningless. Similarly, all metaphysical statements about ultimate reality are meaningless.

The simplest, most dogmatic account of the logical empiricist program was Ayer's *Language, Truth, and Logic* (1936), written in a burst of youthful enthusiasm for the new philosophy, at a time when that philosophy was already being changed. Ayer concentrated on truth, verification, and meaning, and had little to say about the formal-mathematical language of science that so concerned Carnap and the Vienna Circle. Ayer belonged to the British empiricist tradition of Hume rather than to the mathematical tradition of Frege, Hilbert, Whitehead, and Russell that inspired the Vienna Circle.

Ayer enthusiastically applied the verification rule for empirical meaning to metaphysical statements, such as "The Absolute is lazy." (Bradley never actually said that.) However, he also applied the rule to ethical statements. He observed that they are not only untestable and therefore nonscientific; they refer to no possible observables and thus have no meaning. Ayer's assertion was immediately challenged by Stevenson in his *Ethics and Language* (1938). Stevenson argued that a typical ethical statement like "Honesty is right" does indeed have no cognitive meaning, as Ayer correctly asserted, because "right" refers to nothing. But it has emotive meaning. It means "I approve of honesty, and you should, too." Ayer later agreed with this. Stevenson's argument opened a whole new field of philosophic inquiry, since if there were emotive meanings there could be other kinds of noncognitive meanings, too, such as imperative meanings, and there might be various kinds of emotive meanings. There could even be metaphysical meanings.

DIFFICULTIES AND CHANGES

Even in the 1920s there was discussion and disagreement in the Vienna Circle over some of the foregoing points, and the discussion expanded as the new ideas caught on. Between 1931 and 1938 the Vienna Circle spread all over Europe and America. In part they made contact with like-minded thinkers and held annual conferences that drew 100 to 150 participants; in part they accepted university appointments, chiefly in the United States (Kraft, 1968, sec. 1). The new American audience called for a shift of emphasis. For one thing, the metaphysical philosophies of Europe were scarcely known to American philosophers, and when known were rejected. Thus philosophers who sought to distinguish science from metaphysics were speaking to the already convinced. For another thing, U.S. philosophic schools and especially pragmatism seemed to agree with logical empiricism in part and so were potential collaborators.

The result was a gradual dropping of the original "combat metaphysics" program and a concentration on the "explicate science" program. This program was also redefined as a program to provide a logical foundation for empirical science. The foundation, by clarifying what science is, would help scientists avoid errors and blind alleys.

Neurath's *Encyclopedia of Unified Science* project, begun in 1935, embodied this new self-definition of logical empiricism. The first two volumes were supposed to provide the logical foundations of science in general, plus mathematics and logic, and later volumes would analyze the methodological problems of special sciences and the degree of unity that they had achieved. The project also afforded an opportunity to draw pragmatists into collaboration: Charles Morris, already collaborating with Carnap at Chicago, wrote the *Foundation of the Theory of Signs*, and John Dewey wrote *Theory of Valuation* (1939). Dewey's work attacked emotivist ethics, including the work of Ayer and Stevenson, by arguing that valuation in the sense of appraisal was certainly a rational process, therefore cognitively meaningful, since it involved estimation of costs and consequences, comparisons, predictions, correction of estimates, and so on.

The new aim of providing a logical foundation for science brought with it some additional tasks. It was not enough to clarify what truth, meaning, and verification were; other scientific activities needed clarification as well. These included theory building, model building, explanation, and prediction. Since the old tasks were thought to be pretty nearly completed by 1936, at least by Ayer, the new tasks were welcome. However, not all activities of scientists were to be clarified, as Reichenbach emphasized in his distinction between discovery and justification (1938). Discovery was a creative process of inventing new hypotheses; it had no logic to it, since one could not use logical calculation to make a new idea pop into one's head. It just happened. But justification, the testing of hypotheses, had a logic to it, the logic of verification. Only the logical activities of scientists could have a logical foundation; the other activities belonged perhaps to psychology but certainly not to philosophy.

During the following thirty years, the discussions, difficulties, and changes continued to appear, until the original doctrines had either been changed beyond recognition or abandoned. (See Manicas, 1987, p. 243, for a list of abandoned doctrines, though there may be disagreement on some of them.)

We begin with Carnap's project of explicating the language of science—that is, its syntax and semantics—and of specific sciences. In the mid-twenties he had discussions with Neurath and others on what the elementary terms of the language should refer to, and gives several possibilities in paragraphs 62–67 of the *Aufbau* (1928). They include electrons, space-time points, atomic sensations, and whole experiences. Carnap chose the latter, based on Gestalt psychology, but later was convinced by Neurath to shift to physical elements; he used space-time points in his *Abriss der Logistik* (1929). Empiricists like Ayer (1936) thought that space-time points were mighty abstract; Ayer preferred atomic sensations, sense data. If one asked, "What does 'space-time point' mean?" the physicist could not answer by pointing to one; he would have to give a theoretical definition. We would still be operating in theory, not in direct experience. But an empirical science should be based on experience, and preferably the simplest. Since observables were the locus of testing and therefore of empirical meaning, they should really be observable, like "red," and unlike space-time points or electrons.

Sense data, however, are private; I do not experience yours. What then does it mean to me when you say, "I see a raven and it's black!" How can I test this sentence? That is, how can I see whether you are telling the truth about your sense data? Of course, I can look in the same place, but suppose I see a crow there? Now, there are two assertions to be tested and thereby get some meaning on them, and the same problem recurs. The problem is that I can test my own assertion by looking again—I know what I mean—but I cannot test yours because I do not have your sense data. All observation reports are untestable and meaningless except for the person who utters them. Science is founded on nearly meaningless statements.

Ayer in 1987 asserted that he had no solution to this problem, which he did not appreciate in 1936 (1987, pp. 30–31). Presumably he rejected Schlick's solution (1933–34, chap. 16), which located empirical meaning in formal relations of similarity and ordering of colors, not in colors or sounds. Schlick in turn rejected sense data as too positivistic; he rejected the positivism of Hume, Mill, and Comte (p. 182).

We can solve Ayer's problem in practice, pragmatically, by discussing, pointing out characteristics, asking questions, checking our instruments—or by using rhetoric: "Stupid! That's a crow!" But practice is not logic and does not solve the logical problem. The basis of practice is intersubjectivity; but what we share is language, not sense data. And, as Carnap observed, if we study the language of scientists when they discuss observations, they speak about things with attributes and relations, not sense data. Consequently, he and Neurath argued in 1931–34 that the elementary terms of scientific languages should refer to things (Carnap, 1928, 2d ed. 1961, p. viii).

Both Carnap's physicalist position and Ayer's phenomenalist position were held by some logical empiricists for a time; in the 1950s some philosophers were still talking about red patches, while others scorned them. Still others preferred to drop the whole problem and assume that it is solved in practice by discussion among scientists. Once it is solved, what comes out of the discussion is a sentence, an observation report, not sense data. Consequently, meaning is a relation between sentences, not between a sentence and sense data, electrons, or world lines. The generalization "All crows are black" refers to observation reports like "Black crow observed on 9/4/84 at 11:15 A.M. in the Murphys' corn patch." We can imagine these reports to be made by a standard observer, or an ideal, honest, and infallible observer, or certified as correct by a panel of scientists. Thus meaning, being a relation between sentences, is similar to confirmation, which is a relation between hypothesis (sentence) and evidence (sentences).

Sense data were real in the highest degree for Ayer in 1936 and for

Hume; but when they were no longer needed for the logic of confirmation and for meaning, they were neglected and scorned, until for some philosophers they no longer even existed. "I don't happen to believe that there are such objects as 'sense data,' " wrote Putnam (1962, p. 362).

Theoretical terms, at the opposite end of the language from the elementary observation terms, presented a more serious problem. The idea of a tree of definitions running from the most abstract concepts like electrons and intramolecular forces right down to elementary things proved to be too complex to work out. In any case, physicists use many terms that do not refer to or mean anything observable or conceivably observable, such as curved spaces or space-time points. Yet physicists know what they mean, because they can use these terms in theorizing. The terms are defined by reference to other theoretical terms, not by reference to observables. The whole chain of theorizing, however, eventually leads to some empirical prediction.

In other words, physicists do not have a tree of definitions in which every theoretical term eventually is defined in terms of elementary observables. Instead they have a network of concepts connected at a few points to observation. The concepts are partly defined in terms of each other, and partly defined by some indirect observable consequences (Kraft, 1968, p. 103).

This means that all current sciences are expressed in two languages, logically: a theoretical language which may be mathematical or symbolic or highly technical and assumes nothing about existence; and an observation language for reports of pointer readings and Commerce Department statistics (Carnap, 1956). Carnap had already developed the idea of two languages in 1936 (1963, p. 78), and by the mid-1940s it was well established among logical empiricists, such as Margenau at a 1944 Yale colloquium. The two languages are connected at some points by "rules of correspondence" (Margenau, Carnap), or "interpretative sentences" (Hempel, 1965, p. 184). The correspondence rule connects some theoretical term with observation reports but does not define the theoretical term. Definitions stay within the theoretical language, so that any theoretical term has additional meaning beyond any observation report.

Empirical meaning now is a relation between two languages, not two sentences. This implies that the unit of meaning is a whole theory and its language, not a sentence or a term. Terms and sentences get their theoretical meaning within the theory, and the theory gets its empirical meaning from the occasional connections to observation sentences. Similarly, we test a whole theory, not one hypothesis, because the whole theory is needed to connect to some observation sentence (Carnap, 1937, p. 318).

As a consequence, the empirical meaningfulness of a theory varies according to the number of correspondence rules that have been established. A new and abstract theory may be mainly a mathematical exercise with few empirical interpretations—for instance, game theory as of 1944—while an old and well-established theory may have developed many empirical interpretations. Complete lack of meaning is the limiting case of a completely uninterpreted theory.

A further consequence is that the distinction between scientific and metaphysical terms can no longer be maintained. One can no longer ask of a suspected metaphysical term or sentence: to what possible observation reports does this refer? The answer can be that this term or sentence functions as part of a scientific theory that has meaning as a whole. And indeed, argues Hempel, the supposedly metaphysical term may have a heuristic value for the scientist, suggesting theoretical constructions and implications that eventually lead to empirical predictions. For instance Einstein's metaphysical belief that God does not depend on chance was important in influencing his arguments in quantum mechanics.

Even whole metaphysical theories can no longer be sharply distinguished from scientific theories. Any metaphysical theory, even one about the Absolute, can work out some few interpretive sentences and thus have some empirical meaning. It would be hard to imagine a theory with no meaning at all. "There must be some rudimentary sense in which all terms actually in use have meaning" (Rozeboom, 1962, p. 352). The difference between science and metaphysics can at most be one of degree, if indeed there is any difference. Presumably scientists control their observations more carefully than metaphysicians, but that is a pragmatic difference, not a logical one.

The reluctant readmission of metaphysics into science in the 1950s was not nearly as shocking as it would have been in 1935. In 1937 Carnap observed that eliminating metaphysics from science was not so easy after all (1937, p. 322). About 1948 a student at Chicago asked Carnap whom he had in mind when he described metaphysics as meaningless. He answered immediately, "Heidegger!" "What about Whitehead's metaphysics?" Pause. Silence. "That would be a very difficult question." By 1950 it was not news that any scientific language and any logic expressed some metaphysical commitments, in the sense of what is real, not in the sense of what is beyond all experience. Bergmann (1954) even began to investigate the metaphysical implications of symbolic logic and basic logical empiricist concepts. Others like Craig, however, continued to try to eliminate metaphysics from science, in principle at least; and Ayer (1987) still insists that Heidegger and Derrida at least are meaningless.

Unfortunately, once the two languages had been distinguished, it proved difficult to keep them apart. Some philosophers argued that most scientific observations nowadays are made through instruments, and the instruments embody a theory by which we interpret the observed fuzzy lines and patches as moons of Jupiter, microbes, or Brownian motion. Thus even "observation terms are themselves for the most part theoretical terms whose credentials we have come to accept at face value" (Rozeboom, 1962, p. 339). Consequently, there could be no pure and distinct observation language.

We turn next to problems with the central concept of verification. It was clear from the start that complete verification of an empirical proposition was impossible, because things might always change (Schlick, 1925, p. 193; Carnap, 1937, p. 321, crediting Popper). Logically, any universal hypothesis such as "All crows are black" requires an infinity of observations to verify it, because new crows keep getting born. Since complete verification is impossible, all we get in science is confirmation, supporting evidence. This in turn implies that no scientific law is absolutely certain; even a highly confirmed one might someday be disconfirmed. The same point is true of protocol sentences; here Carnap and others accepted Popper's arguments (Carnap, 1963, p. 32). A further consequence is that complete falsification is also impossible, since the protocol sentence might itself be mistaken (Carnap, 1937, p. 318). All we can get is disconfirmation.

However, as Schlick later observed, this does not discredit scientific knowledge. "No theory which has been at all verified by experience was ever entirely overthrown" (1938, p. 233). Confirmed theories have been made more accurate, more detailed, or have been absorbed into broader theories (like Newton's theory), but have not been completely falsified.

The philosophical problem then is to provide an explication of the logic of confirmation, not verification. Confirmation is the relation between a hypothesis h, or a whole theory, and a finite set of protocol sentences or observation reports e, such that e provides favorable evidence for the truth of h, but not conclusive evidence. Hempel reviewed the various proposed definitions of *confirmation* in 1945 (1965, chap. 1) and proposed his own definition: e confirms h if h is true for the set e. This definition does not accomplish much, as Hempel recognized. Suppose we have only one observation report that confirms h; is this as good as many reports? Obviously we need a concept of the degree of confirmation, either cardinal or ordinal. This further problem is the one that Carnap worked on for many years, and we will examine it presently.

However, Hempel, notes that we always have much more than one observation report, and in fact e is always very large. Observation reports about ravens are relevant to "All ravens are black," but reports on non-black objects are also relevant. Since "All ravens are black" is logically equivalent to "If it's not black it's not a raven," anything that confirms the second hypothesis confirms the first as well. Consequently, any non-black object that's not a raven confirms both versions of h, and a non-black raven disconfirms both. "Consequently, any red pencil, any green leaf, any yellow cow, etc., becomes confirming evidence for the hypothesis that all ravens are black" (Hempel, 1965, p. 15). By similar reasoning, all nonravens also confirm h. In short, all possible observations about anything are relevant to any hypothesis; e is always infinite in number. To be sure, the class of nonravens and nonblack objects is larger than the class of ravens, but this is a mere empirical fact, Hempel observes, and thus is irrelevant to the logic of confirmation.

The above argument is known as "the paradoxes of confirmation" or *Hempel's paradoxes* and was the subject of much discussion among logical empiricists in the 1950s and 1960s, without any solution. More recently, the paradoxes seem to have been quietly ignored.

We turn now to Carnap's problem, how to measure the degree of confirmation of h by e. This is a problem in the logic of a priori probability, not in methodology. Carnap did not want to tell scientists what sort of evidence would be most relevant for confirming h—and indeed by Hempel's paradoxes any sort of evidence would be equally relevant, logically. He wanted only to get a number between zero and one for $C(h, e)$. To simplify the problem, he worked with a simple formal language, hoping to eventually extend any results there to actual science. Even so, the problem was difficult.

Goodman (1955) pointed out one basic difficulty. He argued that any e that confirms h_i also confirms an infinite set of alternative h_j, all contradicting h_i somewhat. Thus any degree of confirmation of h_1 applies also to

h_2 . . . and since the h's are infinite and the degrees sum to 1, $C(h, e) = 0$. Any e provides zero confirmation for any h; confirmation is as impossible as verification. This is known as *Goodman's paradox*.

Goodman's example was unfortunate because it directed discussion in the wrong direction. He argued that any e that confirmed h_1 "All ravens are black" also confirmed h_2 "All ravens are blite," where "blite" means "being black until, say, 1991 and white after that." By varying the date, one can get an infinite series of hypotheses.

Unfortunately, the philosophers of science argued over the example and forgot the problem. They exclaimed, "Whoever heard of *blite*? If scientists would stick to familiar concepts, i.e., those in daily life, such odd problems would not come up." Others argued over whether *blite* even is a real color, or only a schmoller. Color, schmoller. But if scientists had stuck to familiar concepts we would never have discovered neutrons or the galvanic skin response, an observable.

Goodman pointed out a real problem, as Hempel has observed (1965, pp. 70–71). Any evidence that confirms (is consistent with) one hypothesis may also be consistent with somewhat different hypotheses. Thus it is a mistake to accept h, even if a great deal of evidence supports it, until we have ruled out, disconfirmed, some of the alternatives. How many alternatives must we rule out? Who knows? This in turn means that we must know some of the alternatives before we can test h. Testing is always a comparative process. Friedman's neglect of this point is one error in his "methodology of positive economics" (1953, chap. 1)—an error that he could not have known of in 1953, of course. In terms of significance tests, finding a significant correlation does not confirm a hypothesis that predicted the correlation, because a variety of other theories might also predict the same correlation. And worse, still other theories that define and measure the variables somewhat differently might produce still better correlations. In addition, we can never conclusively rule out any alternative theory, because the disconfirming observation reports might be mistaken.

Hempel's proposed solution to the problem takes us in a different direction. He argues that the acceptance of h_1 rather than h_2 is a pragmatic process that involves estimating the epistemic utility of the two and choosing the one with greater utility, not the true one. However, he does not explain how epistemic utility is measured.

Finally, the most fundamental distinction in the logical empiricist armory weakened and perhaps disappeared. This is the distinction between logical or analytic truth and meaning, and empirical or synthetic truth and meaning. Quine published the basic objection to the distinction in 1953. He did not question mathematical statements like "2 + 2 = 4," but focused rather on empirical entities like ravens and oculists. If all oculists are eye doctors by definition, who made the definition? If it's in the dictionary, where did the dictionary writer get it? Presumably he looked at common usage and practice, and decided that *oculist* and *eye doctor* meant the same thing.

Turning to science, then, we decide whether a sentence is analytic by looking at the meaning of its terms. According to logical empiricist doctrine, the meaning of a statement is its mode of verification; so we can compare terms by putting them into two statements and seeing whether they are tested in the same way. But by 1950 logical empiricists had agreed that a scientific theory is tested as a whole, not statement by statement, so we cannot perform the tests on two individual statements.

Nor can we by-pass meaning and just look at the definitions. Scientists make the definitions, not the dictionary writer, and scientists can change the definitions as a theory develops. If the data do not confirm a theory, the scientist has a range of freedom to decide which propositions or correspondence rules he will declare falsified and subject to change. The others then have been immunized from falsification by redefining them; they have been treated as analytic, since analytic sentences cannot be empirically falsified. The scientist will probably treat the basic propositions as immune and the auxiliary ones as falsifiable; but he has leeway to choose.

For example, a theoretical statement like "The ratio of permanent consumption to permanent income is a constant" ($Cp/Cy = K$) takes its meaning from the associated theory, which is connected at some points to possible observations. The statement cannot be tested directly, since neither permanent consumption nor permanent income is observable; they are defined within the theory, by auxiliary hypotheses and tentative operational definitions. These hypotheses and tentative definitions are used to estimate Cp and Cy.[2] Then the two sets of estimates are compared over time to see whether the ratio is a constant. But if the ratio varies erratically, such puzzling results can be corrected by reestimating on the basis of improved definitions. At some point, the ratio becomes approximately a constant. Does this mean that the statement has been treated as analytic, so that Cp/Cy will be operationally defined by whatever way it equals K? Or has one discovered the empirically correct definitions of Cp and Cy so that the empirical K is now observable? It's hard to say which it is, analytic or synthetic.

In the decade after 1953, others worked out variations and compromise positions. (See Putnam, 1962, for a clear statement and development of Quine's argument, and Suppe, 1977, pp. 67–80, for a summary of later arguments.) For instance, Feigl (1956) argued that the analytic-synthetic distinction is useful for clarity of thought, and it does apply to the artificially fixed languages that logicians invent. However, he agreed with Quine that it does not apply to growing and changing natural languages, like the language of actual science. In a growing language, a sentence that once was synthetic can become analytic as our definitions change. Thus actual scientific sentences do not fit into either category, analytic or synthetic.

THE IDEAL LANGUAGE

By the mid-1950s, all the original distinctions of the Vienna Circle had become unclear, and all the original certainties had collapsed. The distinctions between logical and empirical, analytic and synthetic, theory terms and observation terms, meaningful and meaningless, even science and metaphysics, had become differences of degree, circumstance, interpretation. The problem of meaning had become quite complex, and the problem of defining "confirmation" and "degrees of confirmation" for theories rather than for statements about ravens seemed insoluble. And worse, disputes over all these issues divided the originally unified logical empiricist school into many different positions. Some of the differences appeared in the contrasts between various units of the *Encyclopedia of Unified Science*, whose publication had almost ceased by 1955. The last unit of volumes 1–2 was assigned to a historian of science, Thomas Kuhn, and plans for additional volumes were dropped. Of course, when Kuhn's essay appeared in 1962 it was a disaster for the idea of a unified science built on logical empiricist foundations.

Carnap's proposed solution to these problems, from the 1930s on, was to design the language or languages of science in such a way as to avoid them. His original purpose in the 1920s had been to explicate the actual language of physics, and then other sciences, along the lines of *Principia Mathematica*. This proved difficult—impossible, in fact—and gradually his attention became focused on the difficulties philosophers had brought up, and away from the actual language of physicists.

By the 1950s Carnap and others were trying to construct simplified formal languages in which the problems did not occur (Scheffler, 1963, pp. 160–82). If one could solve a problem in a simple language, this might reveal a solution for the more complex languages of science (Hempel, in Hintikka, 1975, p. 10). Thus ideally any sentence that followed the rules of the desired language would have meaning in the language and would be either analytic or synthetic; the built-in correspondence rules would ensure that synthetic sentences were testable in principle; observation terms and theoretical terms would be clearly distinguished; and the degree of confirmation of a hypothesis by given observations could be exactly measured. Meaning would come directly from following the rules of the language; if the rules were followed, no metaphysics could sneak in. A further possibility considered in the 1950s was to build in some ethical terms, thus conferring cognitive meaning on selected ethical theories as well.

Some philosophers called this projected problem-free language the "ideal language" for science, though Carnap apparently did not use that term.

The logical foundations of science were now to be constructed some distance away from the actual practice of science. However, Carnap and associates hoped that once the foundations had been solidly constructed, some science at least could be moved over and set upon the new foundation. This would be accomplished by developing a more complex language based on the ideal language and then reformulating the theories, quasi-theories, and models of the science into it. Some portions of the old science would not translate, and these would be exposed as metaphysical, incoherent, untestable, or otherwise defective. The result would be a purified science that could advance free of the trouble and confusion that plagued existing science, including physics.

The construction of the ideal language proved to be a slow and difficult task (Radnitzky, 1970, pp. 30–36). Most philosophers of science were too involved in various ongoing disputes to lend a hand, and those who did take an interest contributed further criticisms and disagreements. Carnap did succeed in providing a way to measure the degree of confirmation of a simple hypothesis, according to Hempel, though Popper disagreed (1963, p. 220). Eventually Carnap died and the project stopped. With its end, the larger project of constructing a sound logical foundation for science also came to an end.

However, philosophers of science continued their previous activities; the previous means became the new end. They now defined their activity as the analysis and clarification of concepts having to do with science, concepts like those of explanation, prediction, theory, law, observation, test, truth. Such clarifications presumably would help scientists think more clearly. Thus Bergmann observed in a 1958 colloquium I attended, "Let's face it; these scientists need our help in thinking; they are confused."

For example, Hempel and Oppenheim in 1948 clarified the concept *explain* (Hempel, 1965, chap. 10). They argued that in a well-formed theoretical language a factual or lawlike statement is explained when it is deduced from a more general law or laws. The laws would have to be true, of course, and the empirical conditions of applicability would also have to be stated. This became known as the deductive-nomological model of explanation, or the D-N model. Actual scientific explanations could be rearranged and interpreted as approximations to the D-N model. They fell short insofar as the explaining laws were not known to be true, or were not all stated explicitly, and because the conditions of applicability of the laws were not all stated. Actual explanations were "explanation sketches" that would be gradually filled in as our knowledge expanded.

Philosophers then attempted to reduce various kinds of explanation to the D-N model, including functional explanations, teleological explanations, explanations by reasons, motives, intentions, dispositions, causes, and so forth (Nagel, 1961). It wasn't easy. A breakthrough occurred when Hempel constructed an inductive-statistical (or I-S) model, and this led to further discussion (Salmon, 1971). Historical explanations received much attention. As late as 1969, Rudner argued with great vehemence and conviction in a colloquium that historical explanations were *necessarily* deductive; they logically *had* to appeal to (unknown) laws of human behavior and state (unknown) circumstances of applicability. All historical explanations are deductive, and there are no historical explanations.

Another topic was whether explanation and prediction are logically the same; some said yes, some no.

By the 1960s, the original aim of explicating or rationally reconstructing science had moved far into the background. The central topic now was not the activities of physicists, but the puzzles and paradoxes of the received philosophical doctrine. Philosophers of science were no longer expected to be thoroughly at home in physics or some other science; indeed, they hardly seemed to know much science, other than a few stereotyped examples they picked up from other philosophers. They were at home in the ever expanding philosophical puzzles and disputes. When they came across some bit of social science, they tried to squeeze it into the received philosophical categories, as Rudner and Nagel did; if it didn't fit, they criticized the science, not their categories. One exception was Nagel (1961, pp. 503–20) on the ideal line of development of some discovered statistical generalization, a perceptive analysis.

Thus a philosophy of science that began with the intention of explicating, clarifying, the logic of a well-known science ended by issuing prescriptions to largely unknown sciences.

These philosophers who analyzed and disputed are most properly called *analytic philosophers* (Pap, 1949). The earlier name *logical empiricists* was less suitable by 1960 because the logical-empirical or analytic-synthetic distinction was by no means clear anymore. *Positivist* suggested tired old arguments about sense data and theoretical terms, where it referred to one of the various positions and not the others. *Analytic* was the only term that covered all the various schools and positions by 1960.

There were two kinds of analytic philosophers, the "ideal language" or IL and the "ordinary language" or OL kinds. The IL were descended from the Vienna Circle logical empiricists, and some still hoped for results from Carnap's "ideal language" enterprise. They analyzed a concept by examining the characteristics of some ideal or constructed symbolic language, and their arguments depended heavily on a machinery of postulates, axioms, definitions, theorems, and symbolic notation. The OL were followers of the later Wittgenstein, followers who suddenly appeared about 1950 as a compact and enthusiastic new school and who steadily made converts from the IL ranks during the 1950s. These people analyzed a concept by examining its ordinary use in some ordinary language like English. They argued, with later Wittgenstein, that the language of science grows out of ordinary language, not out of symbolic logic or Boolean algebra, and the confusions of scientists result from misuses of ordinary language. They would clarify a concept like *explain* by listing the uses of explain-words in OL and then seeing which of these uses appear in science. (Brown, 1960, found nine uses in OL and seven in science.) They proposed to dissolve philosophical puzzles like sense data and how we can know other minds by examining typical OL sentences like "I cannot have your toothache" (Bouwsma). They pointed out the errors of behaviorism by distinguishing the uses of "itching" and "scratching." They argued that all such problems had long ago been worked out in daily practice by users of OL, so that if scientists could only be brought to return to the ordinary uses of OL, their puzzles would dissolve.

The IL analysts ridiculed the whole OL program, arguing that science is different from OL and that in any case OL lags far behind science and gradually absorbs the new concepts scientists invent, so it cannot be an arbiter of scientific practice (Hempel, 1965, pp. 485–86). Much of the dispute in the period of about 1958–65 was between IL and OL analysts; in the IL works of these years the main opponent is OL analysis, not metaphysics. Heidegger was long since forgotten. After about 1964 the IL people also began to criticize newer movements in philosophy of science, beginning with Kuhn (Scheffler, 1967).

In the 1950s and 1960s, the main argument between IL and OL analysts was about causes and reasons. Adherents to IL argued that the goal of the social sciences necessarily was to state confirmed causal laws, because that was what science was, laws. OL defenders argued that the goal of the social sciences necessarily was to find reasons for actions, because human beings act for reasons, not causes; they have free will. Thus the free will versus determinism argument got mixed in; philosophers had forgotten Schlick's solution to this metaphysical argument, namely, that laws just describe what usually happens (1933–34, chap. 15). For example, Flew (1956) praised Freud for extending the study of reasons into the unconscious, and for inventing a talking cure that used OL, while IL people condemned Freud for not finding causes. Flew called psychoanalysis a particularly rational enterprise, an educative force of liberation and enlightenment (p. 168) because it looks for reasons, while von Eckhardt (1982) called it unscientific because it didn't conclusively test any true causal laws (cf. also Diesing, 1985b). Some IL proponents said that reasons *were* causes; others distinguished different kinds of causes and reasons, looking for a compromise.

This analytic and critical activity continued, aimlessly, through the 1970s, the only noteworthy change being the breakup of OL analysts into various groups. Some IL advocates, including Cunningham (1972) and Leinfellner (1983), became Marxists or pro-Marxists, and used their logical skills to analyze and "clarify" various concepts in the Marxist literature.

The continuation of an activity after the official reason for it has disappeared is a familiar phenomenon of bureaucratic politics. Thus Kharasch observes that the real purpose of an organization is to continue its regular activity, and its official aims are pretexts or official justifications (1973, pp. 13, 24). If the official aim is achieved, or becomes completely unachievable, the organization will continue its activity, either by adopting a new goal or by emphasizing the preliminary nature of its work. For instance, suppose Congress were to decree that a replica of Mount Vernon should be constructed out of cottage cheese (1973, p. 112). The implementing agency would never report that the assignment is impossible; no, it would make endless "preliminary" studies of curds and whey, textures, and design specifications, all officially preparing for the great day when Mount Vernon would rise curd on curd. Or, in this case, when the Logic of Science would rise word on word.

The analytic philosophers continued their "clarifying" activity long after projects to "explicate science," "eliminate metaphysics," and "construct logical foundations" had ended, *because that was what they knew how to do.* Of course, they justified this activity, vaguely, as being helpful to science, but that was a pretext. That it was a pretext was clear from the fact that they did not seek feedback from science to see whether they had indeed been helpful. They did not check to see whether the scientists using some "confused" term were actually in trouble and needed help (Achinstein, in Achinstein and Barker, 1969, pp. 268–69, 290–91). Had they checked, I believe they would have found that their activity was of almost no relevance to the social sciences. Or had they actually collaborated in research, as Frederic Fitch did in the late 1930s in a learning theory project (Hull et al., 1940), they might have found something that needed clarification. Instead, if they noticed that some scientific activity did not fit their specifications, they simply condemned it as immature or unscientific. One exception to the above is the recent Sneed-Stegmüller structuralist school, which will be discussed in chapter 3.

PRELIMINARY EVALUATION

At this point, the only basis we have for evaluating logical empiricism is the basis provided by the movement itself. We can record the judgments analytic philosophers have made on their own past, their estimates of achievements and failures. Where their judgments disagree strongly, we must suspend judgment. Later chapters will provide perspectives that yield new insights, interpretations, and judgments. Though these later judgments are almost uniformly negative, we must remember that every negation is also an affirmation insofar as it builds on the negated material.

This movement approaches science from far above, from the ideal of perfect knowledge. Thus the treatment of testing begins with the ideal of complete verification, moves down to confirmation, and then gets tangled in Hempel's and Goodman's paradoxes. It never does get to the real problem of how one constructs an alternate hypothesis relevant to some test; that belongs to discovery, not logic. Explanation is defined first as deduction from true, verified laws with all relevant circumstances specified; then the analysis moves down to partial explanation, involving some well-confirmed generalizations and some circumstances, and ends with explanation sketches involving a somewhat confirmed hypothesis and unknown circumstances. *Theory* is defined first as a fully axiomatized structure of axioms, postulates, definitions, and theorems. All concepts are defined first for a fully mathematical-symbolic IL and later, if at all, extended to current scientific languages.

Actual sciences are interpreted as approximations to the ideal. Consequently the movement downward encounters first the most advanced science, physics, in its most advanced practitioners, Einstein and Newton. Physics has a theoretical language, concepts, laws, and some fairly complete partial explanations. As we move down the scale to the more imperfect sciences, we find that they resemble the ideal less and less. Thus political science, according to Isaak (1975), has no theoretical concepts, no theory, of course no laws, and consequently no explanations, though it has explanation sketches, prototheories, and a great deal of heuristics.

This approach to science brings with it a ready-made conception of scientific change: real change consists in moving up the ladder closer to the ideal. The immature social sciences should move up through economics toward physics, and physics should become more fully axiomatized and its laws should become more general and simpler. There was some attempt in the 1950s to argue that physics had actually done this in the move from Galileo to Newton to Einstein (Nagel, 1949); Galileo's laws were a special case of Newton's laws for objects near the earth's surface, while Newton's laws were a special case of Einstein's laws for objects in the solar system. However, Feyerabend's argument (1962) demolished this attempt. In general, the treatment of scientific change is normative—science ought to develop toward the ideal if it is to be real science—and analytic philosophers have avoided the study of actual change in science. The history of science is distinct from the philosophy of science for them.

Scientific practice is also outside the analytic philosopher's domain.

Logical empiricism deals with the logic of science, its syntax and semantics, not its pragmatics. It is not just the context of discovery that is excluded from philosophy; the context of justification as it actually occurs also belongs to pragmatics. All that is included is the logic of justification—that is, what structure a confirmatory argument must have to confirm a theory.

The ideal of science is derived from Hume and from early Russell's atomistic metaphysics, as embodied in the symbolic logic of *Principia Mathematica*. If reality consists of many entities with attributes and dispositions, then knowledge must consist of the regularities that connect attributes and dispositions to various kinds of entities. The typical scientific sentence therefore is "All ravens are black." For Hume, *regularities* was another name for *causes*, so science consisted of causal laws. This identification was unsatisfactory for many of his twentieth-century followers, who tried to distinguish causal laws from regular coexistence or succession in time. The regular blackness of ravens might be an accidental coexistence rather than a true causal law. However, this topic remained unsettled.

Since the ideal is a statement of what knowledge must necessarily be (given an atomistic metaphysics), it is not derived from scientific practice. If practice and ideal differ, the practice is deficient. However, in the intermediate area between ideal and practice, there is some tendency to compromise. A treatment of confirmation, or partial explanations, or nonaxiomatized proto-theories might try to reconcile the logical analysis and the practice. The argument is that the better physicists are already approximating the ideal, so the logical structure of their theories and tests should be a guide to the philosopher in his reconstruction of the logic of the intermediate area. Of course, the immature sciences are no guide to logic at all because they are so deficient in it.

The early logical empiricism of Wittgenstein's *Tractatus* (1922) and Ayer's *Language, Truth, and Logic* (1936) is now entirely discarded as too simple and abstract. Ayer recently asserted, partly in jest, that it was all false (1987, p. 27). It pointed the way, but its sharp distinctions have softened or disappeared, and its naive certainties have given way to problems and complexities. As Hempel observes, the successive changes in Neurath's originally bold and simple doctrine of physicalism have made the doctrine increasingly cautious, elusive, and weak (in Achinstein and Barker, 1969, p. 190). The reasons why people needed those simple distinctions and certainties have been forgotten; they are merely historical circumstances, not logic.

The newer analytic philosophy comes from the 1940s and early 1950s. In place of the naive analytic-synthetic, logical-empirical, meaningful-meaningless, observation-theory distinctions, there is a vague, unsatisfactory distinction between theory language and observation language, with theory connected to observation sentences by occasional rules of correspondence. Theoretical terms, including probably some metaphysical ones, get their meaning mainly from other terms in the theory, and ideally from the theory's axioms, postulates, and definitions. As a theory develops, its empirical meaning increases through increased connections to observations. Many observation terms, conversely, have some theory built into them or into the instruments producing the observations.

The big achievement of the newer analytic philosophy is Hempel's work on explanation, including the D-N, D-S, and I-S models and also Salmon's R-S model. (For a recent statement, see Van Fraassen, 1980.) The D-N and D-S models were not developed empirically from scientific practice but were derived from the ideal of perfect knowledge, with some heuristic guidance from examples. If science consists of laws and if laws are deduced from axioms, postulates, and other laws in a theory, then a scientific explanation must have a law and a deduction in it somewhere, or it is not even science. When analytic philosophers look at an actual explanation, they try to find a law or generalization in it somewhere. If they find one, the explanation is deductive; if they do not, it is no explanation at all, but only a description. The I-S model was developed later, in the early 1960s, for the intermediate region between advanced real science and the ideal science, so it combines inductive logic with some reference to scientific practice.

The unsolved and perhaps unsolvable problems include the logic of confirmation, the process of observation, the meaning of meaning, and the quest for an ideal scientific language. *Confirmation* can be defined, but there is no measure of the degree of confirmation, and Goodman's and Hempel's paradoxes bar the way to ever getting a measure other than zero. Nor is there any logical procedure for testing a hypothesis. By Hempel's paradoxes, absolutely any observation is equally relevant to testing any hypothesis, so logic offers no guidance here. Testing must be regarded as a pragmatic process. The simplified versions of logical empiricism such as Isaak (1975) and Payne (1975) either go back to the early logical empiricists and talk of sense data, or dodge the problem by asserting that there *must* be *some* valid process of induction (Isaak, 1975, pp. 94–97). "If there is any way to know the world, it is by induction" (p. 97; cf. also Feigl, 1971: If anything works, then induction does). Carnap never completed his inductive logic project, even for the ideal language. Isaak, however, agrees that induction and therefore testing is a pragmatic process.

The related issue of how scientists produce valid observation reports has also been consigned to the realm of practice; that is, scientists seem to do it somehow. Here, again, if there were no valid observations, there could be no science, so scientists *must* somehow have some. Ayer's early certainty that the red patch before me really is a red patch has been discarded as inadequate to the complexity of actual scientific observation, or even to the observation "This is a raven," but no other certainty has replaced it.

The issue of meaning that once seemed so simple has gotten lost in the complexities of scientific theories and their varied relations to observation. As for the ideal language, the attitude seems to be that it would be good for logic if we had one, but nobody seems to be constructing it and it probably is too difficult to be worth doing.

These insoluble problems plus other disputed issues like the relation of explanation to prediction do not suggest to analytic philosophers that they are on the wrong track, since they know of no other track. Rather, they suggest that there is yet much work to do. However, each of these difficulties except the ideal language one has served as a point of departure for some other movement. In addition, the omitted realms of history, practice, and the growth of science have been central to other movements. Thus the failures and omissions of the logical empiricist-analytic movement have had a double effect; internally they have captured IL analysts in a net of endless, aimless dispute, and externally they have given impetus to the growth of antithetical movements.

What do recent analytic philosophers have to offer to social scientists? Basically they offer a clarification of concepts like *explain*, *theory*, *law*, *confirm*. But since social scientists do not have any of these things, the clarifications are not exciting. The main message is, "You have no science. But keep trying."

2

Popper and His Followers

FOR THE LOGICAL empiricists, Popper was simply one of the Vienna Circle, a member who made valuable contributions to analytic philosophy of science. He was a dissenting member who had pointed out some of the difficulties that led to early revisions of doctrine. His most valuable contribution was to emphasize that testing could involve falsification as well as verification. The two kinds of testing are symmetrical (Hempel, 1965, pp. 39–40). An existential statement like "Some ravens in western Manitoba have green heads" could be conclusively verified by going there and finding two or three of them, but could never be falsified because those three ravens might have flown north to Flin Flon the day before. Consequently, failure to find them would not prove anything. The same holds for statements about the Loch Ness monster; we cannot disprove the hypothesis that there is one down there somewhere. Conversely, universal statements like "All ravens are black" can be falsified by finding a green-headed one in Manitoba, but cannot be verified because we cannot check all of them. Thus scientific testing can involve either confirmation or disconfirmation or a combination of the two, depending on what is being tested.

However, Popper went too far in claiming that only falsifiable statements are scientific, since this would expel all existential statements from science as unfalsifiable. Science would consist only of universal laws (Hempel, 1965, pp. 45–46). It would be better to recognize scientific practice and admit all kinds of statements, both verifiable and falsifiable, into science.

Popper also contributed to the early discussion of protocol sentences, observation reports, by observing in 1935 that even observation reports contain universals, like *raven* and *crow*; they are not just sense data reports. Thus the observation report "Black crow observed 12/2/84 in the garbage bin" could be mistaken; it could have been a small raven. Thus we cannot even be sure that a hypothesis is confirmed by a set of observation reports, let alone conclusively verified; the reports might be mistaken. The implication, Popper asserted, was that induction is a logically defective method; and Schlick, Kraft, and other Vienna people were convinced by Popper's argument and agreed with it (Kraft, 1968, pp. 113–21).

This logical empiricist interpretation of Popper completely misses the point, as Popper has often complained. He was not pointing out minor difficulties that could be corrected by shifts of doctrine; he was trying to overthrow the whole logical empiricist enterprise. He was never a member of the Vienna Circle, dissenting or otherwise, though he held many discussions with Carnap and Feigl. He was not trying to exclude metaphysics from science by devising a falsifiability criterion of meaning; he was not concerned with meaning at all and had no objection to metaphysics, in or out of science.

Popper's concern was not to work out a logic of science—what science must be—nor to describe scientific practice—what science is. He wanted to propose a method for science—what science ought to be. By logical empiricist principles of 1922–36, statements about what science ought to be are meaningless, since *ought* refers to nothing observable, so it is not surprising that Carnap and others interpreted Popper's arguments to make them meaningful. Since there are only two kinds of meaningful statement, logical and empirical, and since Popper did not seem to be describing scientific practice, he must have been talking about the logic of science. Consequently, his remarks about falsifiability must have been about the logic of testability-and-meaning. The alternative interpretation would have been to regard Popper's arguments as meaningless, but Carnap and Feigl were too kind and tolerant to do this; by Popper's own account they welcomed his criticisms, accepted them, and changed their views accordingly—thus frustrating Popper terribly.

Popper's proposed method is based on a conception of science as something that grows. He begins with science as it is now, imperfect, fallible, fragmented, probably false, and asks, "What should science do to get better, to improve itself?" In contrast, the logical empiricists began with a conception of an ideal science, a set of true propositions or theories. They invented the logic of this ideal science and then applied that logic to actual science to understand it. Actual science is remote from the ideal: its hypotheses are not known to be true, its theories are not fully axiomatized, its explanations are mere sketches. From this perspective, the path of science is clearly laid out: it should become more like the ideal, at least in the emotive sense of *should*. How it can do this, however, is a matter of pragmatics and heuristics, not logic, so the logical empiricists had nothing to say about that.

Both Popper and the logical empiricists thought of science as statements, words, not people, in contrast to later conceptions of science.

For Popper the distinguishing mark of science is not that it is true; we cannot know for sure that any general law is true, and the ones we have are probably false. The distinguishing mark is rather that we can move closer to the truth by correcting errors and inventing better theories. Popper's method is intended to tell scientists how to do that, how to improve their theories in a rational way.

A proper science ought to begin with theorizing, not with observation. If we begin by looking around, we will not know what to look for and will not notice much. We should begin by inventing a hypothesis, and then use observation to test it. The hypothesis will assert something empirical, and this assertion will guide our observations, leading us to look for quite specific things or devise quite specific experiments.

Testing for Popper means trying to falsify our hypothesis, not trying to confirm it. Testing means to specify what facts would refute the hypothesis and then looking for those facts. If we succeed, our knowledge grows in two ways: we know that some part of our theory is false and in need of correction, and we have some unexpected observations that can suggest a correction. If we take the other tack and try to confirm our hypothesis, we will get nowhere. We can always find confirming evidence for a hypothesis if we look hard enough, Popper argues; the reason is that our observations always involve some selection and interpretation of facts in the light of our theory. Observations are theory-laden, as Norwood Hanson has argued (1958). As a result, it is easy to see facts that fit the theory and hard to see those that do not fit. If we look for facts that fit, we will find them; and this confirming evidence will convince us that we were right all along. As a result, we keep our original hypothesis even more tenaciously, and we get no unexpected observations and therefore no cues for how to improve it. The result is no growth.

In other words, only unexpected facts can shake us loose from our previous ideas and force us to develop new ones.

It may happen that our best efforts will not succeed in falsifying the original hypothesis. In this case the hypothesis is corroborated by the tests, not confirmed; that is, it is not yet falsified. It still has empirical support. We should retain a corroborated hypothesis until a better one comes along, meanwhile trying to falsify it when we get a chance.

These are the two main steps in Popper's scientific method, proposing a hypothesis and testing it; in short, conjecture and refutation. These two steps should distinguish a proper science from myths and oracles as well as from pseudo-sciences like astrology and psychoanalysis. The difference is not that the laws of science are true and the statements of oracles and pseudo-science are false. Some prophecy of an oracle or astrologer may be exactly correct, and some analyst's interpretation of a patient's problems may be entirely correct, while the laws of science are probably false, for all we know. The difference is that the pseudo-sciences and nonsciences have no way of improving their knowledge. Pseudo-sciences look only for confirming evidence, and this convinces people that they were right all along. When a prophecy fails or a case does not work out as expected, they can always explain this away; something interfered, the circumstances were not right, the analyst overlooked something he should have noticed. A proper scientific method forbids all such ad hoc protection of a hypothesis, and enjoins scientists to look for refutations and accept them.

Let us examine each of these two steps, conjecture and refutation, in more detail.

A hypothesis or conjecture generally grows out of a problem. Perhaps an old hypothesis has just been refuted by unexpected facts; here are puzzling facts to be explained in a way consistent with older facts. Or there may be a domain of facts which an old theory does not deal with, and we wish to extend the theory into this new domain. Another sort of problem occurs when two unrefuted theories conflict in a particular area and we wish to reconcile the theories or choose between them. Or we may find an unexpected inconsistency in our theory and wish to remove it. In all these cases, we look for a hypothesis that will reconcile or sort out the conflicting material and resolve the theoretical problem. However, the hypothesis must be testable or it is useless.

It may happen that more than one testable hypothesis is available to solve a theoretical problem. In that case, Popper asserts that we should choose the more easily falsifiable one—in other words, the more easily testable one, the one that makes the clearest, most specific empirical assertions. Popper calls such a hypothesis "bold." This rule is a corollary of the basic principle that science grows by refutation, not by confirmation. If refutation is more useful than confirmation, then the more easily refutable hypothesis is more useful than the timid one that is so qualified and vague that we cannot easily find out what is wrong with it.

Testing consists of producing observation reports and comparing them with the hypothesis. But if the two conflict, we should not directly conclude that the hypothesis is refuted; the observation report may be mistaken. That is, observation reports should be tested too, since nothing in science is infallible. We test observation reports by replicating the test that produced them, that is, by trying to falsify the observation report. If several replications in different circumstances or by different observers agree, the observation report is corroborated (not confirmed), and we should declare the hypothesis refuted.

How many replications do we need? There is room for judgment here, since we are comparing two fallible statements and either one may be wrong. It is equally wrong to give up a hypothesis too soon, since the test may be deficient in some unsuspected way, and to hold on to it too long, since the refuting observation may be correct. Popper forbids the first error with his rule of tenacity: do not give up a hypothesis too readily. A corollary is that one should not test a hypothesis too soon, but should wait until it is thoroughly worked out and clearly understood. The second error is forbidden by the opposite rule: do not hold on to a hypothesis too tenaciously.

Popper observes that these two rules correspond to two universal human tendencies, dogmatism and the critical attitude. Both tendencies are useful for science, in moderation, though the critical attitude is the more important one.

If the replications fail and the observation reports disagree, we should declare the observation report refuted, or suspect a deficiency in the testing process. Here again there is room for judgment, and for subsidiary testable hypotheses that will reconcile conflicting observation reports.

The above summarizes Popper's views as of 1935, omitting several details and many criticisms of the logical empiricists. Popper then shifted to political theory and constructed a theory of the open society and its enemies (1945). The open society is one in which political policies are based on rational discussion among opposed viewpoints. Its enemies as of 1945 were the Marxists. Marxists are opposed to rational discussion because they believe they know the laws of history and wish only to carry out these laws; their preferred society is totalitarian. In 1947 he added that there are also other opponents who love violence rather than discussion (1962, chap. 18).

In the 1950s Popper returned to philosophy of science and supplemented his earlier theory. First, he provided a measure of scientific growth, which he called verisimilitude. This was a solution to a problem that Popper had noticed (1962, pp. 231–36): if we do not know what the truth is, how do we know that we are getting closer to it? Perhaps all the changes resulting from refutations merely substitute new falsehoods for old ones, so that science changes but does not progress. How do we know that a new hypothesis is closer to the truth than the refuted hypothesis it replaces?

Popper gives a semantic answer to this question; he defines the term *verisimilitude*. Imagine first all the possible statements that can be deduced from a hypothesis; these are its *content*. Some of those statements (we don't know which) are true and constitute its truth content. Others are false and constitute its falsity content. The degree of verisimilitude of a hypothesis is its truth content minus its falsity content. This degree cannot be known, of course, but hypotheses about it can be tested. In practice, we conjecture that hypothesis A has greater verisimilitude than hypothesis B if deductions from A pass some test that deductions from B fail. We test this conjecture by trying to find a test that B can pass but not A. If we cannot find any, our conjecture about verisimilitude is corroborated.

The second supplement that Popper provides is more interesting (1935, trans. 1959, p. 16). He observes that in practice very few scientists actually follow his rule of trying to falsify their own hypotheses. Instead, they act like psychoanalysts and look for confirmation. However, he says, the refutation can be provided by other scientists. In this second-best method, scientist A can produce a hypothesis and scientist B can provide a refutation. Then A can replicate B's test to look for weaknesses in it, and so on.

This version is important because it connects Popper's political theory and his philosophy of science: rational discussion is central both to the open society and to science. In both cases, the purpose of rational discussion is to criticize and refute. In the open society, discussion focuses on government policy, and its purpose is to refute the government, persuade people to vote it out of office and put in a new one. Democracy is defined as a system in which governments are removed by discussion rather than by violence. In science, discussion focuses on a theory, and its purpose is to defend or refute the theory and work out a new one.

There are two conditions for rational discussion, readiness and variety of opinion. Variety provides the content for discussion; the more that people disagree, the more easily they can refute each other's ideas and set up the problems that can lead to better ideas. Readiness is a willingness to be refuted and to change one's mind. "All that is needed is a readiness to learn from one's partner in the discussion, which includes a genuine wish to understand what he intends to say" (1962, p. 352). Given this willingness, Popper thinks it is not difficult for people to understand one another. By 1954, when he wrote this, he seemed to have forgotten the difficulty the logical empiricists had in understanding him twenty years earlier.

However, he adds, critical debate is more likely to be fruitful if it is focused on clear, specific problems. Ideally, debaters should be in tentative agreement on most issues, so they can concentrate on one issue. Later they can open discussion on other issues, but only one at a time. In science, this means that attempted refutations should be of only one small part of a theory, for which an alternative hypothesis is already available. If one successfully refutes a whole theory, this is an ineffective way to work out a better one because one does not know what part of it to correct. In politics it means that discussion should focus on specific problems and aim at piecemeal reforms rather than grand changes of the whole social order; revolutionary changes always get out of control and usually make things worse.

In the 1960s Popper further developed his theory of verisimilitude with elaborate arguments written in symbolic logic. He declared that the aim of science is verisimilitude, not truth, since we cannot know the truth. Consequently, his measure of verisimilitude provided a logical foundation for scientific method; it provided a clear definition of what scientists ought to aim for and a hypothetical measure of how well they had achieved it.

Popper also put his rules of scientific method into a larger evolutionary setting, which he called evolutionary epistemology. All living organisms adapt to their environment by trial and error; those that successfully learn from their mistakes survive and pass on their learning ability in their genetic code. Human beings develop higher mental functions through language and pass on their corroborated theories and techniques in libraries rather than in a genetic code. In human beings trial and error takes place mainly at the level of ideas, in imagination and discussion, rather than by bumping into things and getting eaten up. Human beings try to describe their situation, criticize the description to make it more adequate, and devise plans of action to try out. Trial and error becomes conjecture and refutation. Science is the highest form of conjecture and refutation, at least if scientists followed Popper's rules, since it works on very general, abstract, and long-range problems and thus enables us to deal with our day-to-day problems more effectively.

Popper also developed a metaphysical theory of the realm of scientific ideas and theories (1972, chaps. 3, 4). He called this realm the *third world*, or later World 3, to distinguish it from the physical world of dust balls and spiders (World 1) and the psychological world of consciousness, the world of Will in Schopenhauer's sense (World 2). World 2 includes all the processes of thinking, inventing, criticizing, interpreting, describing; World 3 includes all the products of these processes. It includes ideas, numbers, all mathematics and logic, all theories true or false, descriptions, arguments, works of art, tools and techniques. World 2 is subjective and private, World 3 is objective and public. It exists in libraries, museums, computer memories, and archives. World 3 also contains the undiscovered implications of our ideas: potential theories, arguments, problems, and errors; undiscovered mathematical and logical theorems; potential techniques. The thought processes of World 2 operate on the products of World 3, criticizing them, drawing implications, interpreting, correcting, and also inventing new products. Thought process also apply World 3 objects to World 1 by measuring, counting, devising experimental apparatus and instruments. Thus World 2 mediates between 1 and 3. World 3, however, is largely autonomous in the sense that the logical implications and arguments are there in the theories whether or not someone discovers them or thinks about them today. There are numbers that no one has ever thought of, but they are just as real as 2 1/2, which we use every day.

The interactions among the three worlds and especially between 2 and 3 are the basis for the evolution of mankind. Individual minds develop their capacities by learning the techniques and theories in World 3. Also, any productive process involves a constant feedback from the unfinished product and its logical possibilities. "Everything depends on the give-and-take between ourselves and our work; . . . the incredible thing about life, evolution, and mental growth, is just this method of give-and-take . . . by which we constantly transcend ourselves, our talents, our gifts" (1972, p. 147).

Popper claims that his World 3 is similar to Plato's Ideas and Hegel's Objective Mind, though I do not recommend Popper as an interpreter of either philosopher.

Since the contents of World 3 are objective, public, and logical, they are more knowable than the subjective, private processes of World 2. World 2 is the subject matter of psychology, an infant science riddled with fashions and dogmas (1970, pp. 57–58), while World 3 is studied in logic, mathematics, and philosophy. Consequently, Popper asserts, the best way to study the thought processes of scientists and other people is indirectly through their products. Each stage in an intellectual process has a product, and if one can assemble a series of products one can easily see the process that led from one to the next. Thus one can study the successive sketches of a movement in Beethoven's notebooks to see the creative process at work.

This argument has direct implications for how to study the history of science. To understand Galileo's thinking one must first reconstruct the problem situation that faced him, including the conflicting theories and observations and also the conceptual and mathematical resources he had available. These are all third world objects. Then one can interpret his new theory as a rational response to that situation, whether or not he succeeded. This response set a new problem for him, one he dealt with in later writings. "History of science should be treated not as a history of theories but as a history of problem situations and their modifications" through attempts to solve them (1972, p. 177). The historian of science can learn to reconstruct problems and their solutions by first practicing on live scientific problems himself, so he sees how it is done. In contrast, a psychological interpretation of Galileo's thinking in terms of ambition, jealousy, or aggressiveness is inevitably superficial.

The history of science, in turn, is essential to understanding science, since each scientific work is an attempted solution to an earlier problem using materials from earlier theories. This recent emphasis on the history of science is a considerable change from Popper's early views, and the emphasis has continued in the work of his followers, who have become experts in the history of physics and chemistry.

Popper's last important change occurred about 1975, when he dropped the theory of verisimilitude in response to criticisms of it by David Miller (1974, 1975). Miller argued that the verisimilitude of two theories might possibly be compared and tested if the two theories are very similar, so that their content overlaps—that is, if they deal with the same things but make conflicting predictions. But most conflicting theories deal with different objects or aspects, or define their objects differently, so comparison fails. He also demonstrated that even for similar theories, if A is more accurate than B on one constant or variable, we can always define another constant or variable for which B is more accurate. In short, of two false theories neither is closer to the truth in Popper's sense than the other. See also Tichy, 1974.

Popper commented (1976) that Miller's and Tichy's arguments "have had a somewhat shattering effect on the situation of the theory" of verisimilitude. He felt that scientists should still try to get closer to the truth, but admitted that he no longer knew what that meant. Perhaps science does not progress after all, but only changes.

See also Andersson (1978) and Watkins (1978), who agree that Miller's argument is fatal to Popper's theory. "Without the possibility of content-comparison between logically incompatible theories, this philosophy of science would be in total disarray" (Watkins, 1978, p. 356). Radnitzky (1979) suggests that perhaps scientific progress consists of a shift to deeper problems; we do not know what "deeper" means either, but perhaps we can work out a definition someday.

PRELIMINARY EVALUATION

How can one evaluate a proposed method? If we compare it with practice and the two differ, a Popperian could simply respond that the purpose of the method is to improve practice, so of course it will differ from practice. It might be possible to compare an episode from the history of science that follows Popper's method and an episode that does not, to test the hypothesis that the method will improve practice. Perhaps one episode would involve attempts to falsify and the other would involve attempts to confirm. However, for the test we would need a measure of improvement, and with the discarding of "verisimilitude" in 1975 we do not have a Popperian measure of improvement.

One relevant consideration is the fact that Popper has never followed his own proposed method at all. This suggests at least that there is a problem somewhere. By this I mean that he has never tried to refute his own theories by experiment or argument. Of course, his own theories are not scientific but epistemological and metaphysical, so the proper method of refutation would be argument rather than empirical tests. He may have considered some negative arguments in private, but by his own principles we should look at World 3 products, not World 2 processes, and I find no arguments against his views in his published works. In his *Conjectures and Refutations* (1962), the conjectures are his own theories and the refutations are of others' theories.

Popper has admitted that almost no one follows his proposed method and has offered a substitute in which people can refute others' theories, not their own. However, he has not followed this method either. The substitute method relies heavily on rational discussion, which in turn depends on a readiness to be convinced by others and a genuine wish to understand them. If we rely again on Popper's products, not his subjective wishes, we find no such readiness and no such wish. He describes his many "enemies" in highly emotive terms, as lovers of violence, totalitarians, advocates of tyranny, irrationalists, pseudo-scientists. He, however, is a rationalist, a believer in freedom, in humility, and open-mindedness. But between violence and reason, or tyranny and freedom, there can be no dialogue, by definition.

Nor is there evidence that Popper has tried to learn from his "enemies"; at least if he did try, he failed. He gives absurd, unsympathetic misrepresentations of Plato, Hegel, Marx, Mannheim, the existentialists. There are exceptions, including a doubt that he has fully understood Plato (Popper, 1945) and an assertion of agreement with Marx on several points, but mostly his tone is that of the oracle or prophet rather than the discussant. When Kuhn in discussion asserted the value of studying the psychology of scientific communities, Popper did not reply, "Good! One of my conjectures is being refuted! Now we will learn something!" No, he expressed disappointment, saying, "All I have said . . . was in vain" (Lakatos and Musgrave, 1970, pp. 57–58). He did, however, learn from a friend, David Miller, on the topic of verisimilitude.

One of Popper's rules is that discussion should concentrate on small problems and limited hypotheses, within an agreed-on background, rather than ranging vaguely over whole theories. His refutations do just the opposite: he condemns psychoanalysis, Marxism, historicism, existentialism, and logical empiricism as a whole, and his criticisms of the Vienna Circle on, say, sense data were designed to overthrow the whole theory. Indeed, Carnap followed Popper's rules much better than Popper did; he welcomed criticism, accepted and learned from it, and changed his views several times. Conversely Popper has over the decades entrenched his original theory of 1935 in a vast system of metaphysics, epistemology, and political philosophy, so that it is difficult to change one part without disturbing the whole fabric.

Popper was a grand system builder urging piecemeal reconstruction on his followers. He was a founder of a school, an oracle, who urged his followers to break out of received frameworks and think for themselves;

yet when Feyerabend did just that, he would have nothing more to do with Feyerabend.

Note that this criticism, if it is correct, illustrates the value of Popper's proposed method. I have been following the method: I have suggested an apparent inconsistency between Popper's behavior and his teaching, and this sets up a problem that should allow one to revise Popper's theory and possibly improve it. Conversely, Popper has refuted his own theory by showing how much forty years of dogmatic system building can achieve.

POPPER'S CRITICAL FOLLOWERS

I do not call this section "The Popperian School" because Popper's followers disagree with each other as much as with their teacher Popper. They have carried out their teacher's method, and especially its critical spirit, much more than he has.

Popper's students began publishing in the late 1950s, and their publications have increased in volume and variety since then. In 1980 some of his followers formed an organization, The Open Society and Its Friends, to carry on Popper's teachings, although by then they had changed the original doctrine almost beyond recognition. Popper's influence is still substantial, though his 1935 theory has been transformed.

Agassi

The early writings of Agassi, mostly collected in his *Science in Flux* (1975), are searching attempts to criticize particular doctrines of Popper, without departing from the basic problem-conjecture-refutation scheme. Agassi uses extensive examples from the history of natural science, especially physics, to test Popper's rules of method. He selects episodes in which some rule was followed to see how the rule might work in practice. He also induces, tentatively, additional rules from some of these episodes. The result is a more complex picture in which rules have exceptions and counter-rules, or do not work in the way Popper intended. In particular, Agassi argues that scientific dogmatism, the main tendency that Popper's rules were designed to control, will find a way around any rule. Agassi, unlike Popper, has no use for dogmatism; his spirit is critical through and through.

Here are the changes Agassi suggests in Popper's rules:

1. According to Popper, if we try our best to refute a hypothesis and fail, if the hypothesis passes all our tests, the hypothesis is corroborated rather than confirmed. That is, it is not yet falsified, and we are stuck with it until we can find a better hypothesis to substitute for it. Agassi wonders whether corroboration is worth anything at all. He suggests that corroboration is really confirmation in Hempel's sense, and that Popper is sneaking a bit of positivism into his theory here, disguised by a name change. Popper seems to say that confirming evidence supports a hypothesis, but only if it happens by accident, that is, only if we are not looking for it. A positivist would accept this qualification and go on to define *degree of confirmation* as positive minus negative evidence. Popper's contribution to logical empiricism would be a rule forbidding the *search* for positive evidence.

Corroboration is valuable, according to Popper, because it reassures us that our hypotheses are actually increasing in verisimilitude, getting closer to the truth, whatever that means. If all our hypotheses immediately failed their first test, one after the other, it would be hard to argue that the last was better than the first, no matter how simple, general, or fruitful it was. Somewhere we would like a hypothesis finally to pass a test, to know we were not completely dreaming. But Agassi cites many instances in which already falsified hypotheses were later corroborated. That is, the presumed falsification was falsified. This sort of corroboration is worthless, according to Popper, because we have already rejected the hypothesis. But why should it make a difference whether the positive evidence comes before the negative evidence (good) or after it (bad)? Popper seems to be inconsistent here.

2. Popper passes too superficially over the problem of replicability. He asserts quite properly that no observation is infallible and that all tests must themselves be tested by replication. If the replication fails we should declare the experimental observation an error and reject it; if it succeeds, we should declare the observation corroborated and reject the hypothesis being tested. There is room for judgment here, Popper admits, but if scientists did not normally succeed in their replications science would be impossible.

Note that this is not too different from the logical empiricists' later position on observation reports, which is that scientists must solve the problem of confirming them somehow, in practice, so we need not worry about it.

Against this, Agassi emphasizes the utter unreliability of observation, including self-observation. He also points out that tests depend on subsidiary hypotheses about how our instruments work and how the material reacts, and these can be falsified much later. Consequently, even replicated tests can be mistaken, and our rejection of the tested hypothesis therefore also mistaken. For example, one chemist, after the most careful measurement, declared the atomic weight of chlorine to be 35.5, thus refuting the prediction that all atomic weights are whole numbers. This measurement was replicated. Sometime later isotopes were invented, and it was decided that ordinary chlorine was a mixture of chlorine 35 and chlorine 37 in a three to one ratio, weighing in aggregate 35.5. Thus the replicated observation did not falsify the atomic weight hypothesis after all; the presumed falsification was falsified.

Agassi also cites instances in which corroborating evidence was later found to be in error. In fact, he asserts, hypotheses have often been corroborated again and again, until they were finally refuted by new test procedures. This again shows the unreliability of corroboration.

3. Given the thorough unreliability of observations and tests, even replicated ones, we can sympathize with scientists who rejected replicated tests that seemed to refute their favorite hypothesis. Sometimes the rejected tests were later found to be in error and the scientist's tenacity was vindicated; in other cases the test results continue to be corroborated, thus far. Were the scientists justified in ignoring the seemingly negative evidence? If so, should they continue to ignore corroborated refutations, especially if corroborations are worthless? In any case, how long should they hold out in hope of eventual vindication by new tests? Or in general, when should we ignore evidence that seems to refute a hypothesis? (1975, chap. 6). If we always ignore it, hypotheses can never be refuted; if we never ignore replicated evidence, following Popper's rule, science will accumulate mistaken facts and misleading testing procedures, and lose some hypotheses prematurely. Plainly the area of judgment has gotten very large now; nothing is reliable anymore. Agassi's answer, that we should accept whatever rejection is more testable (1975, p. 149), seems circular because the same question returns: since tests are so unreliable, should we believe the results of that test?

Science is indeed in flux, in this version of Popper. The little certainties that Popper retained—replicated experiments, corroborated hypotheses, rules for choosing among hypotheses—are swept away, and we are left with the criticism of all against all.

W. Bartley, another Popperian, has developed a very similar theory, calling it "comprehensive critical rationalism," to contrast with Popper's "critical rationalism."

Lakatos

Like Agassi, Lakatos "tests" Popper's rules against episodes in the history of physics and chemistry, and finds that some of them do not fit. He then tries to induce other rules that scientists could have been following in those episodes. His goal is to construct a set of rules that the best natural scientists *could* have been following to get the results that they actually got. He follows Popper's advice not to speculate about World 2 processes—that is, how the scientists were actually thinking—but instead to look at World 3 products and make up rules consistent with those products. Lakatos initially called these rules *sophisticated methodological falsificationism.* Popper's rules are mainly naive methodological falsificationism, with some sophisticated rules mixed in, according to Lakatos.

Lakatos argues that his rules should also be used in writing the history of science. His rules specify how a rational scientist should act; historians ought to assume that scientists were rational, that is, that they were intuitively following Lakatos's rules. In cases where their actions contradict the rules, historians can conclude that this particular scientist was irrational and acted out of jealousy or some other psychological motive. Of course, if the best scientists did not follow some rule, the rule would be wrong, not the scientists.

According to Lakatos, the science he has studied has not progressed by isolated conjectures and refutations, but by the working out of long-range research programs. A research program is based on some very general conception of the world, such as: All of society must somehow be reducible to the actions, beliefs, and desires of individual human beings, because society is made up of individuals. Or: The economic institutions of society must somehow be more basic or more important than other institutions, because they are the locus of work, the essential human characteristic. In physics and chemistry the general conception may be metaphysical—for instance, the belief that reality consists of atoms interacting in complex ways, or consists of fields of unevenly distributed electromagnetic and other forces. Agassi too has argued that much of the driving force of progress in the natural sciences has come from very general metaphysical ideas. Stephen Pepper's "root metaphors" (*World Hypotheses*, 1938) are other examples of guiding metaphysical ideas.

Metaphysics has now become essential to science.

The general conception that inspires a research program is called its *hard core*. The core is not really testable because it is so vague and general. Any seemingly contradictory facts can be explained away, or simply set aside as puzzles that will be understood someday. Lakatos's rule is: Protect the core against refutation by adding or changing subsidiary hypotheses. These are called the protective belt.

Scientists embody their hard core beliefs in a series of theories. These theories are the main substance of the research program. For instance, if the core belief is that economic institutions are somehow more basic than others, scientists who believe this should draw up a list of the kinds of institutions and then develop theories about how they affect one another. Out of each theory will come some specific hypotheses, for instance, that a change from plantation agriculture to small production for export using local raw materials will shift the balance of political power from planters to small businessmen and thereby produce or support certain political changes. These hypotheses can be tested, but not the general theories that produced them.

A research program need not rush to test hypotheses, however; testing and empirical work can be postponed for a long time. Research programs are moved ahead not by empirical tests, but by their *positive heuristic*, which lays out a path of theorizing that will embody the core beliefs more and more precisely, systematically, and clearly. For instance, when Talcott Parsons set up his four-functional-prerequisites scheme in 1950–53, its positive heuristic was: If there are four basic subsystems of society, use the best-known one, the economy, as a model to clarify the others (Parsons and Smelser, 1956). Apply the four economic subsystems first to the polity (Parsons, 1969, pt. IV, chap. 9) then to the integrative system or societal community (1969, chaps. 7, 11), then to the socialization system. Apply it also to parts of a society, like formal organizations (1960, chaps. 1, 2). Then study the six interchanges among the systems. Clarify the four media of interchange, using money as the model for the other three. Eventually relate society to culture and to personality and see whether the same schemes will work there. Sooner or later apply the scheme to specific societies, starting with the United States (Robin Williams, 1951). This program kept Parsons and associates busy for twenty years. Similarly, a program focused on the mutual influences of economic and other institutions should work out more precise interactions between economic and political structures and processes, distinguish different kinds of influence, and clarify the exact ways in which economic institutions are more basic and the ways in which they are not.

Sooner or later there must be empirical tests of specific hypotheses. However, refutations are almost irrelevant, contrary to Popper. Every theory is born refuted and continues to be refuted, since they are all somewhat false anyway; but if we give up a theory at the first sign of imperfection we will never profit from its heuristic power to produce better theories. Agassi also has criticized Popper on this point (his point 3, above). Indeed, it is the occasional *verifications* that keep the program going (Lakatos, 1970, p. 137). They show not that the theory is true, but that the research program is onto something and is moving in the right direction. For instance, Rock's discovery about 1955 of one-trial learning, the Rock effect, showed that his program of relating learning to mental images rather than to behavioral rewards and punishments had real promise. Rock's work suddenly became important.

A program that produces occasional verifications, like the Rock effect, is a *progressive* program. It is going somewhere. It can afford to postpone or forget the negative facts and anomalies that come up in empirical tests; presumably some later version of the theory will take care of them. Eventually it can adjust its theories to these facts or even reinterpret them as positive for a revised theory. But a program that never gets empirical support from new facts is in trouble. Somehow it must come to terms with the continuous refutations it encounters. It can explain some away—something interfered, the data were from unreliable farm samples, the experimenters were poorly trained. Or it can reinterpret the data as positive—the lag was unusually long, but the expected effect finally appeared; the correlations with the *rate* of change are significant, at least. Or it can adapt the theory to the data: Lenin believed that once the world chain of capitalism was broken at its weakest link the whole chain would drop right off; but this did not happen, so now we must look for the next weakest link in the chain, and the next and the next (Althusser). If the expected response did not occur, we can assume a stimulus sampling process in which the subject responds to other stimuli beside the experimenter's and the desired response occurs once in a while. Or the theory's range can be narrowed in hopes of finding cases to which it does apply.

Progressive programs can and do use all of these devices to deal with refutations; but if a program is forced by constant refutations to concentrate on such devices it can no longer move forward to new facts. It becomes a *degenerating* program. However, a degenerating research program can turn progressive at any time, if a group of bright young scientists invent a new theory whose predictions are corroborated, or a new testing instrument. Conversely, a progressive program can run out of steam and get stuck for a time, trying to explain away refuting facts.

Consequently, there is no rule that says scientists ought to abandon a degenerating research program and shift to a progressive one. Two or three rival programs may develop side by side for a long time, each striving to produce the novel facts that mark it as progressive, and their fortunes may fluctuate several times. The only rule Lakatos suggests is that each program should keep an honest score, and the followers of a degenerating program should admit their poor score and their dwindling prospects.

Lakatos shifted his thinking on this topic several times. Originally he wanted a rule that a degenerating program ought to be given up as soon as a better one was available. But he could not specify any sufficient degree of degeneration, and since the fortunes of research programs do fluctuate, he had to give up the rule. Eventually he suggested only that editors ought not publish papers coming out of degenerated programs, but this curious rule would soon have been discarded too.

Marxism and psychoanalysis are examples of degenerating research programs, according to Lakatos. They do not predict new facts or produce new theories, but concentrate on adjusting their theories to fit events after they have happened. Most of the social sciences, in contrast, are simply infant sciences in a preresearch program state. They do not have guiding core beliefs, but simply pick up theories and facts in a seemingly aimless fashion. Lakatos was quite ignorant of the social sciences, as well as quite prejudiced, so his views here need not be taken seriously.

Thus for Lakatos science does not consist of true or probably true laws, and certainly not of trivial statements like "All crows are black." Nor is it a series of conjectures and refutations. Rather, it is a set of research programs, some progressive and some degenerating for a time, each guided and driven by deep metaphysical beliefs. Lakatos asserts that his "research program" is a World 3 version of Kuhn's World 2 "paradigm." Research programs are rational, since they are guided by Lakatos's rules, while paradigms are maintained by institutions and ideologies, that is, social and psychological forces. Kuhn's revolutions are simply mob psychology, while for Lakatos there is a rule for rational revolutions: a degenerated research program should only be discarded, if at all, when there is a rival progressive program that can incorporate the successful parts of the degenerate program. Also for Kuhn a mature science is one that is united by a single paradigm, while for Lakatos, "The history of science has been and should be a history of competing research programs (or, if you wish, paradigms)" (1970, p. 155). Scientists should feel free to start a new program at any time if they do not like the existing ones.

Lakatos's views are now being promoted and criticized by his critical followers in the London School or LSE School, including Urbach, Worrall, and Zahar.

Feyerabend

Feyerabend's first major work was an argument that pluralism was essential to the growth of science. This argument appeared in his "Explanation, Reduction, and Empiricism" (1962) and earlier articles, and also in "Problems of Empiricism" (1965) and "Linguistic Arguments and Scientific Method" (1969). It was based on Popper's teachings (1962, pp. 31–32; 1965, pp. 152, 153), though Feyerabend later denied this, and it also expressed agreement with Agassi (1965, p. 231). The opponents were Popper's opponents the analytic philosophers, both IL and OL. In 1965 the main opposed position was logical empiricism, and in 1969 the opponent was ordinary language philosophy.

By *pluralism* Feyerabend meant a plurality of Kuhn's "paradigms" or Lakatos's "research programs" or Stephen Pepper's "world hypotheses," not simply a plurality of low-level theories that agreed on basics. A corollary of the argument was that physics had in fact progressed through a clash of incompatible paradigms, through revolutions, not through the deduction and testing of hypotheses and the linear development of ever more general laws. The logical empiricist history of science was as false as its philosophy of science.

The argument was based on two of Popper's basic ideas. One was that science progresses by falsification. The second was that observation reports are fallible because observations embody theories and expectations, which may be mistaken. There are no pure sense data or pure observation languages.

The second point occupied almost all of Feyerabend's attention. If it is correct, it follows that a world hypothesis or metaphysic will so structure people's observations and their ordinary language that nearly all their observations, casual or controlled, will agree with the metaphysic and seem to confirm it. Confirmations are easy to produce, as Popper argued. To falsify a world hypothesis, we need an alternate world hypothesis that criticizes some observations as illusions, reinterprets others, and produces new observations that expose the weakness of the old paradigm. "We invent theories in order to criticize observational results" (1965, p. 152). If a metaphysical theory disagrees with all observation and ordinary language, this is an encouraging sign that it may be useful for criticizing entrenched scientific dogmas—if it is worked out in technical detail, provided with measuring instruments, and applied to accepted observational results. In short, metaphysics is essential to science.

Feyerabend uses three tactics to support the thesis that observation reports are fallible: abstract argument, evidence from the psychology of perception, and evidence from the history of science. The many abstract arguments include the assertion that the positivists' sense data theory is itself metaphysical, coming from the metaphysics of Locke and Descartes. It is not based on observation of how human beings perceive—it is not scientific—but on a metaphysic of atoms in motion impinging on passive sense organs and transmitting kinetic energy to nerves and muscles. Current (1960) psychology of perception gives a very different account of observation and experience. It asserts that observation is an active process of organizing a mass of stimuli into a coherent situation, based partly on beliefs and expectations and partly on inherent Gestalt processes (1965, pp. 219–20n8). Thus in the days of belief in witchcraft people really experienced possession by the devil, bewitchment, voices, even phantom pregnancies. A paradigm shift reinterprets the experiences as eruptions of a disguised id into consciousness, and the evidence for witches disappears (ibid.; cf. 1979, p. 121).

The main evidence is from the history of astronomy, and especially the history of the paradigm shift from Aristotle to Galileo and Newton. Aristotelian metaphysics, in which the heavenly bodies orbited around a stationary earth, was based solidly on observation, and Copernicus and Galileo attacked these observations as misleading and misinterpreted. Their own theory, and Newton's, was refuted at every point, but they insisted on reinterpreting the evidence as confirmatory. For instance, projectiles were observed to trace a parabola to earth as they lost momentum and not to travel a straight line as Newton would predict; a ball dropped from a tower fell directly to earth, though if the earth had moved and carried the tower with it as Galileo imagined, the ball would have appeared to move away from the (moving) tower. Galileo also produced new observations with his homemade telescope; yet when he invited critics to look for themselves, they could not see what he saw, and other homemade telescopes got different results. Galileo's observations could not be replicated (cf. Feyerabend, 1975, pp. 104–08, 123–24; 1965, p. 229).

The Galileo-Newton and later episodes were thoroughly misrepresented by scientists themselves, who reinterpreted their actions to fit their empiricist, Baconian theory of science, and who claimed as a result to have been guided by induction from direct observation. Historians of science, who were also empiricists, believed these accounts, and logical empiricist philosophers referred to them as evidence for their philosophy of science. Here again, an adequate history of science must be pluralistic, employing alternate world views to criticize and reinterpret primary and secondary historical sources (1965, p. 236n45).

After 1965 Feyerabend continued to extend and deepen his pluralist theory, publishing it finally as *Against Method* (1975) and, in an expanded version, *Wider den Methodenzwang* (1976). More than half of the 1975–76 book is a detailed account and interpretation of the Galileo-Aristotle episode referred to above. The basic argument is still that alternative world views are needed to criticize data that seem to confirm a theory, and that a theory is corroborated only if the alternatives themselves have failed. But now Feyerabend brings out additional implications of this argument. First, it is not enough to have two alternative world views in science, because they both could agree on something and have mutual blind spots while criticizing each other within a narrower range. Pluralism means having several, many, more and more world views. In his more extreme moments, he might even have approved the wild chaos now current in the social sciences, where new schools, new paradigms, new journals, and neo-this or that pile up faster than anyone can count them.

Second, pluralism is not just a temporary expedient to set a new science on the right track, after which the correct paradigm should take over and expel the losers, as in political revolutions. It is a permanent requirement for the advance of science. Any world view that has achieved monopoly tends to become dogmatic about its fundamentals, as the logical empiricists did in the 1950s. Since no one questions the fundamentals, they are felt to be true, even true a priori, and science stagnates into preoccupation with detail, epicycles. But if pluralism is always valuable, it is desirable for scientists to actively maintain it, by ensuring that their graduate students are exposed to multiple conflicting world views. "The best protective device against being taken in by one particular language is to be brought up bilingually or trilingually" (1979, p. 91). Moreover, each world view or research program should be maintained in the best possible condition; the degenerating ones should be strengthened, not abandoned. For instance, the national research funding agencies could seek out discredited and offbeat theories for funding and reduce funding for mainstream research. Feyerabend might even call the recent revival of the decrepit Austrian school of economics a gain for science; the Austrians can point out difficulties in the treatment of uncertainty in the neoclassical general equilibrium model. Similarly, creationism is useful as a critique of an evolutionary theory grown dogmatic (1975, p. 30). Gergen (1982, chap. 3), agreeing with Feyerabend, suggests several other ways in which offbeat theories can be strengthened.

Third, another reason to revive falsified theories and degenerate research programs is that they may have some unexpected truth in them. Feyerabend's main example is the ancient Pythagorean myth that the earth itself moves—totally discredited as false by Aristotle and Ptolemy, but revived by Copernicus to advance science beyond Aristotle (1975, p. 49). Psychoanalytic theory and psychosomatic medicine have brought out an element of truth in voodoo, witchcraft, and demonology by reinterpreting these real phenomena in psychosomatic terms. Remember Erik Erikson listening to an old California shaman telling how she cured some children bewitched by relatives, and feeling a kinship between his method and theory and hers (1950, pp. 146–50; 1964, p. 55). The shaman told of familial tensions and a rigid, disapproving, punitive grandmother who had "gotten under the child's skin." Lloyd Warner used to tell in class how he was cured of a chronic leg ailment by an Australian witch doctor, in a big, friendly community ceremony, and he made the cure intelligible in psychosomatic terms. Acupuncture has recently become scientifically respectable with the advance of physiology (Feyerabend, 1975, p. 305). Perhaps other discredited old myths—astrology or dancing for rain (1976, p. 77)—that today seem as absurd as supply-side economics will some day reveal a core of truth. "The knowledge of today may become the fairy-tale of tomorrow and the most laughable myth may eventually turn into the most solid piece of science" (1975, p. 52).

But how often?

Fourth, pluralism is not just good for truth but also for the development of individuality. It forces scientists to think for themselves, forces them to question their own beliefs and maneuver through a continuous cacophony of criticism. Here I must interject that many social scientists do not appreciate the Feyerabend-type paradise in which they live; they quickly join some school, attack and misrepresent a few opponents, and ignore the rest.

Feyerabend follows the argument of Mill's *On Liberty*, of which he asserts, "It is impossible to improve on Mill's argument." Chapter 2 of Mill gives the argument for freedom of thought and discussion as the basis of science; chapter 3 extols individuality as the end product of liberty. Feyerabend's whole theory appears in these two chapters. Also like Mill he argues that discussion among a plurality of views is basic to democracy (1965, p. 217).

Fifth, the truth toward which science moves is itself plural for the foreseeable future. The insights and empirical discoveries of psychosomatic medicine, behavior theory, game theory, world system theory, interaction process analysis, ethnomethodology . . . are incommensurable, though not necessarily contradictory. "Knowledge . . . is not a series of self-consistent theories that converge towards an ideal view; it is not a gradual approach to the truth. It is rather an ever increasing ocean of mutually incompatible alternatives, each single theory . . . forcing the others into greater articulation and all of them contributing via this process of competition, to the development of our consciousness" (1975, p. 30). Note that science is now in part people, not sentences, and the progress of science is in part an increase of individual sensitivity and awareness.

Finally, Feyerabend extends his pluralism to methods. The history of science shows that scientists, including the best ones, did not all follow the same method. Aristotle began his study of politics by collecting data about 158 political systems of his day; then he classified them according to various typologies and attempted to find empirical regularities in each type. Newton was reported to have proceeded mathematically, by abstract definitions and deductions that moved from the simple to the complex, and to have used data mainly as illustrations of some theorem. Consequently, the Popper-Lakatos attempt to prescribe a universal scientific method, either the method of conjectures and refutations or the method of progressive research programs, becomes a tyranny of method over science. The tyranny operates by expelling from science whole research programs like psychoanalysis and fields like empirical sociology for not following Lakatos's or Popper's rules. Yet Freud based his theories on evidence, discussed evidence carefully, accepted criticism and changed his views several times (Feyerabend, 1979). Lakatos's rules would expel Aristotle from science because Aristotle predicted no novel facts; yet that was not the method he used (Feyerabend, 1978). Nor did Copernicus predict new facts (Harris, 1972).

Scientists have developed different methods to fit the requirements of their world view, to deal with particular problems in their theories, and perhaps to suit their personal preferences (Feyerabend, 1980a). Sometimes particular circumstances called for an unusual, creative solution: Galileo, Feyerabend's favorite example, felt compelled to use even trickery and deception ("propagandistic machinations," 1975, p. 89; "lies," p. 106) to open the closed minds of his dogmatic Aristotelian listeners (1975, chaps. 6–12; p. 194) and thereby advance science beyond Aristotle.

Feyerabend is *not* proposing a rule that scientists ought to lie; he is reporting that they have used many different methods and tactics in different circumstances, and many though not all of these tactics were appropriate in the circumstances. Nor is he saying "Anything goes," in the sense that people can use any method they please and get equally good results. This is a common misinterpretation of Feyerabend by people who take the "Anything goes" out of context. Rather, Feyerabend means that the method to be used should be appropriate to the research situation, including subject matter, theory, audience, and personality of the scientist (Feyerabend, 1980a). "Anything goes" is not his rule at all; it is, he claims, the only rule a Popperian or Lakatosian historian can find that has no exceptions (1980b, chap. 6). Agassi would probably agree. It would have been just as inappropriate for Aristotle to imitate Galileo's trickery with the telescope, given Aristotle's audience, as for Galileo to collect case studies of each planet before beginning to generalize. "The only way of finding out whether a certain feature is necessary for science is to carry out a *functional study* of this feature (in the sense of modern anthropology) that examines its role in the growth of science" (1975, p. 184). The philosopher of science should become an anthropologist, studying particular methods in their total cultural context to understand their function in that context (1975, pp. 249–52). I agree.

I cannot claim that the above is the only true interpretation of Feyerabend's views. Feyerabend's work has different facets from different perspectives, and indeed he warns us not to take some of his arguments too seriously (1975, pp. 32, 189). It may be that in part Feyerabend wanted us to work it out for ourselves. He did not want to set up a new doctrine that would become the dogmatic foundation of a new school, just as Popper's originally stimulating insights and errors had ossified into the dogma of the Popperian School.

A POPPERIAN SCHOOL?

The above three writers are only a small selection from the people who studied with or were influenced by Popper. Do these critical followers have anything in common that would constitute the distinguishing mark of a Popperian school? They are all interested in how an imperfect science grows, in contrast to the logical empiricist interest in the logic of a perfect, completed science or at least the universal logical character-istics of any possible science. However, they share this interest with Kuhn, Toulmin, and the pragmatists, among others, and they have not provided any criterion or even definition of growth, to replace the departed "verisimilitude."

A corollary interest is in the history of physics and chemistry, as well as for Feyerabend physiology and medicine, as a basis for studying the growth of science. Again they share this interest with many non-Popperians. Also they continue Popper's interest in providing rules that scientists can follow to promote scientific growth—or in criticizing rules that other Popperians have offered.

Perhaps most important, they (like quarreling siblings) share a history of studying and discussing Popper's teachings, a familiarity with each other's work, and an easy personal communication. They are in part each other's audience, and one must understand the writings of each as in part a continuing dialogue with the others, as evidenced by the frequent footnote references. To be sure, the dialogue has gotten ever more acrimo-nious. Feyerabend needled Lakatos by dedicating his 1975 *Against Method* to Lakatos, "friend, and fellow-anarchist," knowing that Lakatos ab-horred anarchism. Lakatos earlier had commented, "Feyerabend seems now to have joined the enemy camp" (1970, p. 115) of irrationalism and anarchism (p. 178). Agassi begins a review of Feyerabend's *Against Method* by blurting out, "How do you read a book which extols lies?" (1976, p. 165). Elsewhere he describes Lakatos as a Stalinist, an advo-cate of oppression and violence, knowing that Lakatos abhorred Stalin-ism (Agassi, 1981, pp. xviii–xx). Radnitzky declared that since Feyer-abend could not define scientific progress, his views are destructive of a free society and a forerunner of totalitarianism, knowing that Feyerabend abhorred totalitarianism and knowing that he himself, like Popper, could not define scientific progress either (Radnitzky, 1981, p. 280). These friendly enmities show that the Popperians are at least a family, though not a school.

3

Kuhn and Stegmüller

KUHN'S THEORY of scientific revolutions swept through the social sciences in the early 1970s with enormous effect. One theorist after another announced that the social sciences were in crisis, that the old paradigm was collapsing under the weight of its anomalies, and that the new paradigm had just appeared. If we are to believe all these announcements, the social sciences experienced a revolution every six months, on the average, in those years. In each case, all the social sciences were included in the old paradigm except for a few anticipations and predecessors of the theorist making the announcement. His work, of course, was the new paradigm.

Kuhn had provided social scientists with a flashy rhetorical device. By his rules, all social scientists ought to abandon their outdated old paradigm work and flock to the new paradigm; those who did not would be left behind by history.

There were several difficulties, though. Most important, the device didn't work. All those preparing their own new paradigm for announcement and publication of course would refuse to take the other imposters seriously; and those working within "old paradigms" had not yet discovered that there was any crisis to worry about.

Next, the rhetoric misinterpreted Kuhn. Kuhn was not proposing rules for scientific progress as the Popperians were; he was a historian of science attempting to interpret natural science theories and understand how they developed and changed. His task was hermeneutic, not prescriptive (Kuhn, 1977, p. xiii). Out of the resulting historical understanding one might induce some institutional characteristics that were functionally necessary to science, but not rules for individuals to follow.

Next, Kuhn was writing about the natural sciences, not the social sciences. The social sciences seemed to be very different to him. He had the impression, based on casual observation, that they were mainly in a "preparadigm" state, one in which a great variety of theories and paradigms coexisted (1970a, pp. viii, 15; 1970b, p. 244; 1977, pp. 221–22). If they were, no revolution of the sort he described could even occur. One of the would-be revolutionaries, Arthur Staats (1983), bases his case on the "preparadigm" idea, arguing that until psychology agrees on a single paradigm, preferably his own social behaviorism, it has not started to be a true science by Kuhn's argument. Ritzer (1975) makes a similar claim for sociology.

Finally, Kuhn might have been mistaken about the "preparadigm" characterization. Its main implication was a prediction that the social sciences in the future would imitate the past history of the natural sciences; but Kuhn had no basis for such a prediction, and in his view historians should not make predictions anyway. Perhaps the social sciences were different from the natural sciences—for instance, in their relation to "external" circumstances—and would therefore have a different history.

In order to derive implications for the social sciences from Kuhn's work, therefore, it is necessary to go beyond the flashy initial message and get at the underlying ideas about science. I shall first summarize the argument of *The Structure of Scientific Revolutions* (1962, rpt. 1970), including changes and clarifications Kuhn added later; then I shall interpret his argument to find ideas that will help us understand the social sciences.

I should warn the reader that there are varying interpretations of Kuhn in the literature, and not just because Kuhn changed his views several times. I have come across over twenty-five different versions of Kuhn, each related to the interpreter's own position. Kuhn's theory has been and could be a good projective test. Psychologists of science should list the themes in the theory, collect the interpretations of each in the literature, devise a scoring system, and start testing it.

HISTORY OF A TYPICAL SCIENCE

Kuhn found that natural sciences usually went through several distinct stages.

1. First, there is a *protoscientific* or preparadigm stage in which a new field of study is just getting started. This is a stage of relatively random fact gathering, mainly of readily accessible data. From a later perspective, the result is a morass of interesting, trivial, irrelevant, and even mistaken observations. There are a variety of theories, mainly derived from philo-

sophical speculation, that collectively provide little guidance to data gathering. There is some theory testing and correction, but the main efforts of theorists are devoted to criticizing each other. Disputes range all the way from fundamental principles, through methods and techniques, to the classification and interpretation of data. There is no agreement on anything. Newly arrived scientists frequently announce their appearance with a whole new theory, complete with philosophical assumptions, methods, and program of study. Others take up an existing theory and join the school that has formed around it.

2. Eventually one theory comes to dominate and displace all the others. The losers either die out or are declared to be unscientific, or their remaining adherents redefine themselves as philosophers and withdraw from competition. A school of perhaps twenty-five to a hundred people forms around the winning theory and its founder, whether or not he is still alive. The members of the school treat the founder's work as an *exemplar* of what science should be, and they try to imitate it in their work. Thus the school establishes a *discipline*—that is, a clearly defined subject matter and a way of dealing with it. The founder's teachings plus later interpretations are codified as a *disciplinary matrix*. This includes the founder's basic laws or equations or categories, a more general conceptual scheme or analogy that describes the basic nature of the subject matter (for example: Society is composed of individuals with resources, tastes, and information), values, methods, and the example provided by the founder's work.

3. The disciples teach this matrix to their students as the way to do science. The task of science is to apply the founder's basic laws or equations or insights to one specific topic after another, and sometimes to extend them to new areas. The topics are those that were in dispute in the previous, protoscientific stage; the purpose is to demonstrate that this theory can actually explain all these phenomena in a consistent way. Failure to account for or explain some specific phenomenon does not show that the theory is wrong; it shows that the student or disciple has not yet fully understood the theory and method. But repeated failure by many people suggests that this phenomenon is a puzzling, unusually difficult one, and it is laid aside for future study.

Kuhn calls this stage *normal science*. It is a stage of solving detailed puzzles on the basis of a given theory and following a given pattern or exemplar. Fundamentals have been settled, and the scientist is a narrow specialist or technician.

Since the members of the school are in agreement on the disciplinary matrix, they can communicate readily, and they do—through letters, exchange of manuscripts, a specialized journal, conferences and conventions. The constant exchange of ideas and results allows them to build on each other's research. This is how science progresses, in contrast with the first stage when nothing is ever settled. Also in contrast with the previous stages, the school mostly ignores other schools and disciplines, though sometimes two schools carry on a dispute within a single field.

Part of the progress of normal science is the invention of data-gathering and measuring instruments, which produce refined or esoteric data adapted to the theory. The result is more esoteric laws and equations that deal with hidden structures and processes and explain better-known phenomena as surface manifestations. Some of these newer concepts and laws overturn earlier explanations of the phenomena.

4. Some phenomena persistently refuse to act according to the theory, and even according to later, more refined versions of the theory. These are the *anomalies* for the school. The attempts to explain these puzzling phenomena produce new, more widely divergent theories. One theory may explain an anomaly but only at the cost of upsetting accepted explanations of other phenomena. The increased theory conflict and/or persistence of anomalies produce a sense of uneasiness and a questioning of fundamentals. This is the *crisis* state, which repeats some characteristics of the protoscience stage (1977, pp. 202–08).

5. Eventually some scientist declares a new conceptual scheme that one way or another establishes a new school. An example would be the Keynesian revolution in 1936, whose appeal lay in its explanation of the anomaly of mass unemployment in Britain from 1925 on; the previous dominant theory had proved that such a phenomenon could not occur. (Or so the Keynesians asserted). The stubborn adherents of the old disciplinary matrix gradually die out and the discipline returns to stage 3, normal science.

Sometimes the crisis stage is skipped and a new and better conceptual scheme appears for other reasons. Sometimes a crisis does not end in revolution; either a new variant of the old theory succeeds in explaining some anomaly, or the anomaly is set aside as unknowable, beyond the scope of the science, or belonging to an area that ought not be studied.

Revolutions come in all sizes, big and small. The rare big ones like the Copernican revolution change a discipline's way of perceiving the world almost completely; the commoner little ones produce partial changes in perception. An example of a little one was the assertion that Uranus was a planet, not a star or comet; this changed the concept *planet* from "one of a set of six bodies like the Earth that orbit the sun" to "anything that orbits the sun in an Earthlike orbit." This set astronomers to looking for more planets, and they presently found twenty more (asteroids) (Kuhn, 1970a, pp. 115–16).

The essential characteristic of a revolution is not that it resolves or follows a crisis, since some revolutions happen without crises. It is rather that a redefinition or rearrangement of concepts produces a new way of looking at the world. This calls into question old facts, laws, and analogies, and suggests new empirical investigations. The Keynesian revolution, for example, consisted in part of adding radical uncertainty about the future to the investment equation, and in part of seeing an economy as a mainly closed system within which commodities and money circulate, in which some channels of circulation go through banks and government, and in which the latter two are variable reservoirs of credit and money (Keynes, 1937; cf. also Samuelson, 1948, pp. 263–64; Patinkin, 1976, chap. 8). This replaced a neoclassical view of the economy as a mainly unbounded aggregate of individuals who exchanged their resources in markets, and in which government was separate from the economy though it supplied a medium of exchange and enforced the rules. The economy was unbounded in the sense that individuals could leave it at any time, shifting from work to leisure, and could return at any time. On this view, unemployment was normally voluntary and consisted of individuals collecting information about the jobs available, and leaving the economy if they found no suitable job. The Keynesian conception enabled economists to conceive of massive involuntary unemployment due to irregular circulation of resources and money. Conversely, the neoclassicist could readily conceive of government interference in the economy, while for the Keynesian this concept was meaningless because government was an integral part of the economy.

The switch from the old way of looking at the world to the new way is a kind of conversion experience. It is not something you are persuaded to do or decide to do; it is something that happens. Kuhn likens it to a gestalt switch, in which an ambiguous figure like a cube reverses itself while you are looking at it (1977, pp. xiii, 308–18). It happens to some people and not to others; thus there are still neoclassicists who cannot see things the Keynesian way and believe that government interference caused the Depression of 1929, that unemployment is voluntary, and that

Keynes's main contribution to economics was curiosities like absolute liquidity preference.

Note that by providing an example from economics I am suggesting that Kuhn's assignment of the social sciences to the protoscientific stage is not correct. For some decades the followers of Keynes did have a discipline, an disciplinary matrix, and of course an exemplar. A good deal of what they did could be interpreted loosely as normal science, working out the details and extending the applicability of Keynes's vision. In chapter 5 we will consider a different interpretation of the work of Keynes's followers.

It is essential to understand Kuhn's account of a typical history *in contrast* to a position he was opposing. The opposing position was that there was only one revolution in a field, the shift from protoscience to science. Before this revolution, people speculated and argued; then the founder of the science taught them to look for themselves, and science got under way. Once people started studying the facts without prejudice, they no longer needed to argue, but could readily agree on simple generalizations and discard their earlier mistaken conceptions. With more careful observation the initial generalizations could be refined, corrected, and made more precise. Thus science progresses in a linear or cumulative fashion, moving on to the next decimal place or the next deeper level of observation.

Against this view of science, Kuhn argues, like Popper and Feyerabend, that perception of facts is an active process in which our perceptual categories and expectations shape and organize stimuli into facts. The prerevolutionary scientists did observe the world, but with a different set of concepts and categories. The Copernican or Galilean revolution was not simply a decision to start looking at the facts but was a conceptual gestalt shift that made the old observations look queer, misleading, or mistaken. The postrevolutionary school did not know about the psychology of perception; they thought they were simply observing nature and that their predecessors could not have been, and they wrote their histories of science accordingly. Positivist philosophers who shared the seventeenth-century categories of a mechanistic external world found these histories intelligible and accepted them as fact.

Since it is hardly possible that any one conceptual framework perfectly imitates the real structure of nature—if indeed there is any clear structure—the progress of science requires a series of revolutions in which the blind spots or distortions of one set of concepts are corrected by a later set. However, the revolutions cannot be arbitrary, but must rise out of perceived deficiencies of a previous conceptual framework. These deficiencies are brought to light through the careful, detailed work of normal science. Thus scientific progress requires an alternation of normal science and revolution in a discipline, not permanent revolution (Popper and Feyerabend) and not permanent normal science (logical empiricism).

Kuhn thought that his view of the growth of science was very similar to Popper's and especially to that of Lakatos (Kuhn, 1970b, 1971) except for his greater emphasis on the importance of normal science. Consequently he was disappointed when they called him names in response—relativist, irrationalist, believer in mob psychology. He thought that careful presentation of a few historical examples might induce them to make a gestalt switch from their categories to his. Once they had learned to see things his way it would be easy to set up rules of translation—for instance, Kuhn's "crisis" is Lakatos's "degenerating research program" and Kuhn's "normal science" is Lakatos's "progressive research program"—and then it would be possible to discuss their few differences of emphasis. However, the gestalt switch never occurred and the name calling continues (see, for example, Newton-Smith, 1981.

Kuhn reminds us several times that his history is deficient in one important respect. He has focused attention only on *internal* factors in science, factors within scientific communities. But science is not separate from society; political, economic, and social institutions constantly influence the history of science. Some crises are produced or intensified by social influences; some conceptual shifts, revolutions, come from outside of science; and scientific values are influenced by the larger culture. Kuhn has not studied these *external* factors systematically, and indeed an external history of science would be a very different and much more difficult task, calling for the genius and broad scope of a Fernand Braudel. But the result is a partial view of science. We shall consider external studies of science in chapter 6.

NECESSARY CHARACTERISTICS OF A SOCIAL SCIENCE

From the above generalized history, we can induce several characteristics that seem to be needed for any halfway decent science. First, to deal systematically with anything we need a conceptual scheme that will organize our perceptions and guide our dealings with our subject matter.

Kuhn is not saying that if you do not have a conceptual scheme you will make a poor scientist, so you ought to get yourself one next week. No, he is saying that everyone deals with the world in an organized fashion and that this is part of being human. Kuhn's lesson is rather that we should be aware that we make our own data. They are not sense data that come to us directly from nature. Kuhn emphasizes direct perception, but he could easily have added measuring instruments and experimental apparatus constructed according to the specifications of our conceptual scheme— also statistical techniques for adjusting raw data, and data quality control criteria. We cannot make data as we please, but nature is flexible enough to fit into many different conceptual schemes, more or less.

Awareness that we have a conceptual scheme should presumably help us deal with troubles more effectively; we can suspect that the source of the trouble might be our own preconceptions, rather than unknown interfering forces, chance, or poor data collecting techniques. We might also become more tolerant or at least more understanding of the weird theorizing and tricky data manipulation of other schools. However, Kuhn does not draw these implications.

Next, science is a social enterprise lasting over centuries, so we need a community to carry on scientific work. Community means communication, and communication is based on a shared language. To work together we must understand each other—that is, we must share the same conceptual scheme, and conceptual schemes are embodied in languages. Community also means shared values, so that we do not work at cross purposes even though we understand each other. In short, community requires a disciplinary matrix. The matrix does not produce uniformity, since values can be applied in very different ways and we can communicate disagreement as well as assent. The matrix produces understanding and thereby collaboration.

Note that science is now being treated as people, communities, not sentences.

The early logical empiricists thought scientists could simply collect protocol sentences that described the facts of nature—"Black crow observed pecking at some carcass 6/3/85, 11:10 a.m." Consequently, they did not appreciate the problem of communication and the need for community, for shared conceptual schemes. They believed that since scientists shared a common set of sense data or real objects or world lines, they could merely refer to these to resolve disagreements; and since philosophers and scientists shared a common reason they could check a line of argument for error to get true reasoning. Today's analytic philosophers still believe in a common reason, which if exercised carefully enough will produce valid argument, and they are distressed at all the errors philosophers continually make. They attribute these errors to stupidity and carelessness. Kuhn's denial of direct access to the real external world seems to them to be a form of relativism, an ancient error that would make science impossible (for example, Scheffler, 1967).

Third, since all of our scientific communities sooner or later come to grief in their efforts to adapt nature to their own conceptual scheme, we need multiple conceptual schemes to capture more aspects of the truth. However, Kuhn hastens to add that the multiplicity should be sequential, not simultaneous as a rule, and that each new scheme should appear only when the inadequacies of its predecessor have become apparent. A further implication is that science needs both convergent and divergent personalities in Liam Hudson's sense (Mitroff and Kilmann, 1978; see also chapter 10, below). Convergent people are those who are impatient of loose speculation but like to isolate a small problem that can be solved by exact work and an attention to detail; they are suited to Kuhn's normal science. Divergent thinkers are those who see connections and analogies, and whose problems and thinking get larger and larger, crossing boundaries readily; they are suited to times of crisis (Kuhn, 1977, chap. 9).

Kuhn later qualified his 1962 insistence that each community in the natural sciences usually has one and only one disciplinary matrix. There are many overlapping communities in the natural sciences, some larger and some smaller, each with a different conceptual scheme, so overall the situation may look rather ramshackle and incoherent (1970a, p. 49). There may even be two or more communities in the same large field, say, chemistry, though each community defines its subject matter and problems in its own way, so there is little actual overlap (1970a, pp. 177–181). However, the real work is done within a community, and here there is little or no pluralism.

Since there are multiple overlapping communities even in the natural sciences and of course in the social sciences, another necessity is for individuals to be able occasionally to communicate across conceptual schemes. This requires patience and a tolerance of ambiguity (Kuhn, 1970b, pp. 276–77), a willingness to try to look at a situation through another's conceptual scheme and to learn a new way of perceiving. Once such a gestalt switch has occurred it is possible to set up translation rules ("Oh! By ——— you mean what I call ——— mostly") and communicate after a fashion. Scientists who participate in two or more communities—Kuhn claimed to be in three (1977, chap. 1)—can, like anthropologists, gain facility in cross-communication.

One thing science does not need is rules of method, especially rules laid down by Popperian philosophers. Here as elsewhere Kuhn agrees with Feyerabend. Rules are necessarily abstract and general, while scientific problems are specific, complex, and varied. If a proposed rule is relatively specific, such as Popper's rule that in choosing between hypotheses one should choose the boldest one that makes the most specific claims, as it is the easiest one to falsify, such rules do not fit scientific practice. If a rule is more general, such as Lakatos's rule that a degenerating research program should not be abandoned (if at all) until a better one is available, it is too vague to give guidance.

In normal science, rules are unnecessary because scientists have exemplars (paradigms) that show them how to go about researching some puzzle. In times of crisis, the exemplars do not seem to work any more, or need to be changed, so then it is appropriate to appeal to more general rules and values in the disciplinary matrix for guidance and argument. But even these rules and values will not help in a revolutionary situation.

KUHN AND FEYERABEND

The similarities between Kuhn and Feyerabend are obvious and important, but the differences will teach us something too. They both base their thinking on the history of natural science, and both emphasize the importance of conceptual schemes and reject general rules of method. They both reject Popper's World 3 (Feyerabend, 1974). The third world is not an impersonal public world; it is Popper's conceptual scheme dogmatically universalized. The second world is not private; it is the habits learned by socialization into a community. There is only one world, the social world. They also agree that multiple incompatible conceptual schemes both coexist and succeed one another over time.

But where Feyerabend emphasizes the pluralism in science and thinks it should sometimes even be increased, Kuhn looks for small communities that exclude pluralism from their disciplinary matrix. Kuhn emphasizes the communal aspect of science, while Feyerabend emphasizes the individual aspect, as Mill did before him. For Kuhn communication and shared values are crucial so that people can collaborate and build on each other's work. Feyerabend, and Mill before him, assumes that communication is no problem, and emphasizes the importance of individual creativity in science. He does not mean the creative genius, to be set on a pedestal and worshipped, like Einstein for the Vienna Circle, but just ordinary independent thinking (Feyerabend, 1987). Feyerabend (1970a) is horrified at the shrunken, narrow-minded specialists with their mindless routines that Kuhn seems to be praising as "normal science." He argues that Kuhn has gotten his history wrong and that progressive revolutions have come, not from the narrow specialists, but from the independent critical thinkers who could work with multiple paradigms and invent new ones. "It is not the puzzle-solving activity that is responsible for the growth of our knowledge but the active interplay of various tenaciously held views" (1970a, p. 209). Kuhn in contrast assumes that creativity is no problem, but it needs discipline and patient attention to detail, convergent thinking, to make it pay off. It also needs communication and collaboration to produce cumulative results over time. A bunch of egotistical individualists talking past each other is a good scene for the social sciences, which are nowhere in any case, but will not do in the advanced sciences (Kuhn, 1977, p. 231n3). Feyerabend, like Mill before him, emphasizes that individuality is an element in well-being, and asserts that scientific activity should produce human development as well as theories.

The difference of emphasis is also apparent in the style of Feyerabend's and Kuhn's published debates, so it must express personality differences as well. Kuhn has always emphasized the points of agreement with critics despite differences of conceptual scheme. He has shrugged off the name calling and tried to get critics to see things his way—experience a temporary gestalt shift—to improve communication and facilitate a discussion of differences. Feyerabend has emphasized and even exaggerated disagreement. He has consciously praised and supported views that he assumed would be unpopular with his audience—Leninism, dialectic, psychoanalysis (for a Popperian audience), astrology, witchcraft, creationism (for an evolutionist audience). His purpose has been to open the closed minds of his audience a bit, just as Galileo did with his trickery. He was agitating for pluralism.

We can easily (perhaps too easily) conclude that both the community aspect and the individual aspect are essential to social science, and that neither can be taken for granted. We need both creativity and communication.

STEGMÜLLER

In Germany analytic philosophy has taken a new turn in the work of Wolfgang Stegmüller and associates (1976, 1977, 1979, 1982, pp. 17–22, 1986; Hands, 1985). These people, calling themselves structuralists, continue the analytic project of clarifying or explicating or rationally reconstructing science; but they accept the arguments of Kuhn, Lakatos, and Feyerabend against earlier analytic philosophy. In particular, Stegmüller regards Kuhn's work as a definitive refutation of both logical empiricism and Popper.

Stegmüller's early work was a Carnap-type IL analysis, dealing with the serious problems that had come up in the ideal language project. He also criticized the critics of analytic philosophy such as Kuhn. Then about 1973 he experienced a "paradigm shift" and decided that Kuhn was right and the IL analysts were wrong (1976, p. ix). If Kuhn's history of physics is correct, then physicists have not at all acted like the analytic explication of their work. Nor have they followed Popper's rules at all. Consequently, if the philosophers of science wish to explicate or rationally reconstruct actual scientific work, they must start over in a very different direction.

The analytic philosophers made several fundamental mistakes (1976, intro; 1977, pp. 153ff.).

1. They used the mathematical logic of the sort found in Whitehead and Russell's *Principia Mathematica* (1915) as their model of a scientific language. Stegmüller calls this, half-seriously, the Hilbert-Gödel-Tarski myth (1976, p. 2), referring to three mathematical logicians. This sort of mathematics consists of equations—that is, sentences—arranged deductively. First there are one or more axioms and postulates; then other equations are deduced from them. The deductions add nothing new; they only make explicit what was already contained in the premises.

If one follows this model, one thinks of a scientific theory as a set of sentences or equations. First there are one or more laws or hypotheses, and second there are theorems deduced from them for empirical testing. If the tests are successful, the laws are confirmed; if a test is unsuccessful, one or more laws are disconfirmed. But Kuhn's history shows that natural scientists have not constructed their theories in that fashion.

2. Deductive logic is static in the sense that it tries to preserve constancy of meaning between premises and conclusions. But this makes a rational reconstruction of the history of science difficult or impossible.

In the history of science, meanings change (as Kuhn has reported and Quine also has emphasized), so that old theories cannot be deduced from new or vice versa. Consequently, one cannot a give a rational account of scientific progress using deductive logic. In the 1930s Carnap allowed scientists to change their language and meanings with change of theory, but gave no rational reconstruction of such a process. In the 1950s some logical empiricists tried to describe scientific progress as the substitution of more general, simpler axioms from which the old ones could be deduced as special cases, but Stegmüller agrees with Feyerabend's 1962 criticism of this attempt.

3. The analytic philosophers focused on the general language of science rather than on particular theories and theory change, as Kuhn did. Consequently, for the IL analysts this language had to be very general and formal, to accommodate any possible theory (1976, pp. 3, 9). Though linguistic considerations are sometimes relevant to science, the pursuit of the ideal language took philosophers ever farther away from the physical theories with which they started before 1920. Eventually they were left with a metascience of science fiction (1976, pp. 267, 269).

4. Popper's attempt to make falsification and falsifiability central to science has no relation to the practice of physicists, as Kuhn has shown (Stegmüller, 1977, p. 166). Not only have physicists not tried to falsify their theories, they have not even specified what facts would falsify them. Indeed, theories in science are not falsifiable in Popper's sense (1976, p. 13). Falsification does occur in normal science but not in revolutions, contrary to Popper (1986, p. 118f.).

A proper philosophy of science would avoid these errors by developing a quite different conception of scientific rationality based on Kuhn's historical work. "For me Kuhn has *revealed new and different dimensions of rationality*" (Stegmüller, 1976, p. 7). This new rationality cannot be found in the work of Kuhn, Feyerabend, Hanson, and Toulmin (1961). Stegmüller accepts the negative arguments of these critics of IL analysis, but feels that they failed to break away from deductive logic to a new conception of rationality. Kuhn was explicitly sociological and psychological, and this is appropriate for a historian of science, but not for a philosopher. Lakatos tried to give a rational version of Kuhn, but his rules remain vague and fairly useless, as Feyerabend has argued (Stegmüller, 1986, pp. 118–24; 1976, pp. 20–21). Instead, Stegmüller finds the necessary building materials in the set-theory logic of J. D. Sneed.

For Stegmüller and associates, a theory is not one or more laws or hypotheses about the world; it is not an empirical statement. He calls this the *nonstatement* view of theories. Instead, it is a network or structure of concepts—hence, "structuralism" (1986, chap. 1; 1977, chaps. 6, 7; 1976). The concepts may define or qualify or supplement other concepts, and may combine with still other concepts in specific ways.

The network develops over time. Unlike the logical empiricists' science fiction, scientific theories have a history, as Kuhn has shown. Historically, a theory has a core structure that stays the same, and various expansions that change, develop, or grow organically. Thus a Kuhnian community of researchers all have the same theory in the sense that they share the same core over time; but they develop different extensions over time and in that sense are divided.

Consider for example the Hotelling-Downs theory, or game theory, or Keynesian theory, or recent Marxism. The core of the Hotelling-Downs theory is an n-dimensional space in which customers, or voters' opinions, are distributed; and two or more businesses or political parties that locate themselves in the space in such a way as to maximize the number of customers or voters that they attract. Expansions include specific dimensions: liberal-conservative in economic policy, bilingual-monolingual in cultural affairs, libertarian-authoritarian in government power. Expansions also include electoral or credit rules such as proportional representation that affect the ease of entry of additional parties or businesses; varying degrees of foresight on the part of party leaders; varying degrees of party unity; and varying changeability of opinions or customers' tastes.

The core of game theory is an n-dimensional payoff matrix in which each cell specifies the payoff to each player of that outcome. A player is any entity that can choose among $2+$ strategies, and whose choice affects the outcome. Each dimension of the matrix is divided into $2+$ rows or columns, which together specify the strategies available to one player. A play of the game consists of each player choosing one strategy; the set of choices uniquely determines one outcome. Expansions include the various games; also game trees, expanded and extended games, supergames, metagames, sequential choice, preplay communication, probabilistic outcomes, and so forth.

The core of Keynesian theory is a circulation in a closed economy. Goods and services cycle in one direction and money in the other direction, with banks and the central bank a variable reservoir of money and credit, and government a variable reservoir of demand. Concepts include wages, prices, consumer demand, capital goods demand, investment, uncertainty, animal spirits, bullish and bearish propensities, interest rates, the multiplier, and so on. Each of these variables except the multiplier is located at one point in the cycle and pulls or pushes the circulation along, expanding or contracting it. The value of each variable except animal spirits depends on the value of other variables in a complex structure of influences and feedbacks. Expansions include additional variables in the banking system (such as H. Minsky, 1986), multiple wage and price variables, additional multipliers, variable lags in the influence of one variable on another, the equilibrium rate of growth, opening the closed economy to international circulation of various sorts, etcetera.

The core of orthodox Marxism, according to Lukács (1923, chap. 1), is not any theory at all, but a method, the dialectical method of locating developing contradictions within the social totality. However, it turns out that this totality has a Stegmüller-type structure: capital circulates in a Keynesian fashion in an economy, gradually accumulating in some locations and draining from others; the conflicting interests and varying distribution of power among participants in the circulation process express themselves in politics; the different experiences of participants express themselves in thought and science; the structures of politics and of culture reshape these inputs; and the variable outputs feed back on the circulation of capital and redirect it.

As structures, scientific theories are neither true nor false. "A theory is not . . . the sort of entity of which 'falsified' [can] sensibly be predicated" (Stegmüller, 1976, p. 13). How could one test the game of Chicken? Theories make no empirical claims; they are not statements about the world, but mathematical structures: matrices, spaces, networks, digraphs, cycles, Markov chains, Poisson processes, and so on. What does have truth value is a statement applying the theory to some empirical situation: Britain in 1930 was a Keynesian economy; the Cuban missile crisis was a Chicken game (false); Canadian politics of the 1970s moved in a two-dimensional Hotelling-Downs space. In such statements the theory is a predicate.

The empirical situation to which a theory is applied is called a *model* of the theory by Stegmüller—not the normal social science use of the term. Each theory is intended to apply to a class of empirical situations— capitalist economies, interpersonal interdependence, oligopolistic competition, attitude structures (cognitive balance theory, a signed graph), communication networks. This class is called the class of potential models of the theory (see Stegmüller et al., 1982, pp. 17–22 for further detail). Expanded theories can be applied to additional classes of models; thus Hotelling applied his theory to downtown banks and businesses, while Downs expanded it to apply to party politics. In Marxist theory David Harvey (1985b) and others have developed the concept of a second circuit of capital, in applying the theory to recent urban political economy in the United States. The world system people (Wallerstein, 1979) observe that the circulation of capital is worldwide, so that the social totality is the world system, not one country.

The inventor of the theory, Hotelling or von Neumann-Morgenstern or Keynes or Marx, develops it by reference to one model. This is the Kuhnian paradigm or exemplar. For Keynes it was Britain of about 1925–35, as formalized in Kalecki (1939); for Hotelling it was the main street of a small one-horse town, a one-dimensional space; for Marx it was mid-nineteenth-century Britain. Game theory does not fit Kuhn's history; the original interest was in oligopoly theory, not in any specific case. Applications came later.

The community that develops around a theory attempts to apply it to other instances in the class of possible models—the U.S. economy, the British economy of the 1950s, etcetera, in the Keynesian case. The new models require new concepts, expansions: for French politics of the 1980s, a libertarian-authoritarian dimension not important in Canadian politics, and in West German politics of the 1950s a Catholic-Protestant-secular dimension. Researchers can also try to develop an improved, more detailed application to the paradigm case or some other model, and this also requires new concepts. For example, Shubik (1959), refines the original von Neumann-Morgenstern treatment of oligopoly considerably, adding such concepts as K-R stability. Finally, researchers can explore new classes of potential models: in game theory shifting from oligopoly to U.S.-Soviet relations, international crises, committees (Duncan Black), or political coalitions (William Riker).

All of the above constitute Kuhn's "normal science." During normal science, specific expansions of the theory can be tested for their fit with the data, and new expansions can be developed. What is tested, however, is not the theory component but its application to the case: if the Cuban missile crisis was not a game of Chicken, it is not Chicken that is falsified but the sentence applying it to Cuba in 1962. In this case, the new expansion is the game of Called Bluff, which applies to some cases previously thought to be Chicken. The new game brings out characteristics of these cases that were distorted or hidden by the application of Chicken.

If the application to a class of models consistently encounters trouble, and if suitable expansions cannot be devised, then the theory does not apply to that class of models. For instance, if various samples of light do not act according to the predictions of Newtonian particle mechanics, this does not falsify Newton's theory; one merely concludes that the theory does not apply to light (Stegmüller, 1976, p. 200; Hübner, 1978, p. 300).

The effect of several decades of normal science is a great expansion both of the theory and of its empirical models. Different expansions apply to different models or classes of models; but sometimes different expansions seem to apply to the same model, and this produces conflict in the community. Thus the Keynesians long ago divided into left, right, and center groups, among others, each developing different variants of the theory. Marxists and game theorists similarly developed many variants; Hotelling-Downs has not developed much.

The above examples show that normal science is not a mindless routine carried on by shrunken, narrow-minded specialists, as Popper and Feyerabend supposed. It involves plenty of creativity and independence.

Normal science can also produce persistent puzzles in a class of intended models: in the Keynesian case, the stagflation of the 1970s. If the community does not want to exclude those models from the theory, and if no suitable expansion can be devised, the theory is in trouble. For a simple example, consider the Phillips curve, an expansion of part of Keynesian theory. Phillips described and explained a curvilinear relation between unemployment and inflation in Britain before 1954. As unemployment went down, inflation went up, at first very slowly, then at a rapidly increasing rate. This curve worked fine through the 1960s, then encountered data that were way off the curve. The solution was to declare that the curve had shifted, and—sure enough—the data now fit the new curve nicely. But a few years later the curve shifted again, and maybe even a third time. By now the question was, "What causes those shifts?" Whatever it was, the Phillips concepts did not predict their occurrence, so new concepts within or outside of Keynesian theory were called for.

This is an instance of Kuhn's "revolution," though the Phillips case is a very tiny revolution indeed. Stegmüller is very concerned to argue that revolutions *can* be rational and lead to scientific progress; mob psychology and conversions are not the whole story. A revolution is progressive if the new theory explains what the old theory does, and more. The successor to the Phillips curve would have to explain the "shifts," but also the inflation-unemployment function that Phillips did explain. The explanation may well be different, and the shifts may disappear in the process, but that does not matter. The old theory need not be a special case or a part of the new one. However, the new theory should be able to explain why the old one worked for a while or in some cases (Stegmüller, 1977, pp. 196–202, 169; 1976, pp. 215–16.) Of course, if the new theory does not explain more than the old one, the revolution was not progressive.

Besides the above two kinds of progress, normal and revolutionary, Stegmüller sketches a third kind or aspect of progress (1976, pp. 202–12). In normal science, a theory develops variants, extensions including new concepts and empirical models; in some revolutions, theories of greater explanatory power appear. Running through both kinds of science is a long-run process of gradual refinement of concepts, measuring techniques, and indicators of depth variables. Thus Newton depended on several centuries' work of transforming qualitative phenomena into quantitative data (p. 207). In economics, such concepts as velocity, the multiplier, the accelerator, and their variants; techniques for describing and comparing business cycles; and techniques for measuring the rate of profit, are now the common property of all current economic theories.

Stegmüller recognizes that his conception of scientific progress is vaguely similar to that of Lakatos (Stegmüller, 1976, pp. 220ff.; 1986, pp. 118ff.); indeed, they both drew inspiration from Kuhn's work. However, he rejects the concepts that Lakatos drew from Popper. He notes that Lakatos tried to develop a *falsification* concept that would apply to a research program, and argues that "sophisticated falsification" is not falsification at all. He also rejects Lakatos's Popperian attempt to devise rules that scientists ought to follow to insure progress. He agrees with Feyerabend's criticism of Lakatos's vague rules, and, most important, also agrees that philosophers have no business dictating rules of method to scientists anyway. The whole Popperian normative project is wrong.

Recently Stegmüller and associates have turned their attention to the social sciences. In accordance with Stegmüller's original project, they define their task as one of clarifying or explicating specific theories, not some general or ideal language. The explication is intended to be useful to social scientists: it should reduce verbal disputes based on misunderstanding of vague concepts, should bring out possible ambiguities and contradictions for correction, and should facilitate application by distinguishing the empirical and theoretical parts of the theory.

Their first such project was to formalize mathematical theories in economics, especially general equilibrium theory (Stegmüller et al., 1982). Since these theories are already mathematical, there is very little vagueness in them, and the main task is to specify the empirical models, intended models, partial possible models, constraints, and presupposed axioms. However, Stegmüller has recently formalized Freudian theory, a more ambitious undertaking (1986, chap. 14.4). According to Stegmüller, Freud's core theory is that in all people there are constant unconscious processes (*Akten*) that push toward consciousness and action. If the acting out of an unconscious process gets associated with a very unpleasant experience, it can happen that the process is kept from consciousness and is expressed as sick symptoms (p. 416; my paraphrase). The symptoms vary in different cultures (p. 419). There are two variants of the theory, in which "is expressed as sick symptoms" is replaced by "is sublimated" or "is expressed in dreams." This theory is formalized in about a page and a half of logical symbols, including time subscripts and spans, sets of possible experiences, painful experiences, and unconscious processes; and expression in consciousness. There is also an axiom, a constraint, and a set of intended models (all human beings). The paradigmatic models are Freud's early cases; later analysts followed these models in adapting the theory to new cases. The result was a considerable amount of new empirical material, which analysts used to produce expansions of the theory. These results, according to Stegmüller, show that Freud's theory is unquestionably scientific.

Unfortunately, Hands (1985) concludes that structuralist formalizations have been of almost no help to economists, who can do their own formalizing. In particular, general equilibrium theory has no intended empirical models; no one claims that any economy is ever in general equilibrium. The structuralist treatment is thus misleading; Stegmüller has missed the point of the theory. As for Freudian theory, I cannot see that Stegmüller's "clarification" is of any use to anybody. Perhaps he meant it as an example of what structuralists can do. Perhaps in the future structuralists will use their clarification techniques to cut through useless disputes based on misunderstanding, and possibly facilitate empirical application. That would be helpful.

For example, Stegmüller shows that philosophical objections to the term *unconscious mind* as logically self-contradictory are mere verbal fussiness. One can always call the Unconscious something else.

We can treat these two initial formalizations as illustrations of what the structuralists can do, and as learning experiences for them. As they get more familiar with areas of social science, we can expect more useful, relevant clarifications, which we surely need. Also the new set of intended models may produce expansions of the structuralist core logic.

4

Pragmatism

PRAGMATISTS TREAT SCIENCE as a process of inquiry or search for truth. The emphasis is on process, method, correction, change, not definitive and permanent results. Inquiry begins with a question or a problem, and is directed to answering the question or solving the problem. Problems are initially practical ones: How can we resolve or tone down family quarrels? How can we reduce the inflation rate, or compensate for its more harmful effects without causing trouble elsewhere? However, the search for solutions brings up more abstract problems: What is a good measure of inflation? What is the relation between the quantity of money and the inflation rate? How important is credit? What other factors might affect money, credit, and inflation? These problems in turn produce more technical problems of method and theory: How should we define *money*? How can we get a more accurate count, a more representative sample, a more valid and detailed report? Scientific methods and theories are the accumulated results of previous problem solving, available for trying on new problems.

Thus science is not sharply distinct from common-sense problem solving—what time should we leave in the morning?—or even from pseudo-science, which also answers questions after a fashion. Presumably scientific problem solving is more careful and controlled, and thus more likely to arrive at better solutions and answers. But the important thing about science is that it tries to improve its methods of question-answering and problem solving (Ackoff et al., 1962, pp. 1–4). It is self-reflective. It questions its own methods, its own theories, its own standards of evaluating solutions, its own standards for evaluating its methods. In Dudley Shapere's words, science consists of *learning to learn* (1984).

Thus science is not just careful, controlled inquiry; it also includes methodology, or inquiry into inquiry (Bentley, 1954). Methodologists study the problems researchers have, and sometimes the problems they don't realize they have. For example, Ackoff reports some questions he asked about a survey intended to find the number of occupants per room in certain dwelling units: "What is a room? . . . Does that include walk-in closets? . . . Does the size of the room matter? The height of the ceiling?" (1962, pp. 147–48). He could have asked similar questions about *occupants*. Here the accuracy of the measurement depended on the validity of the definitions, which depended on the intended uses of the data. That is, the objective meaning of *room* and *occupant* depends on the problem. If we are studying living space, the size of the room and the time spent there are very relevant; if we are studying transportation needs, room size is irrelevant, and occupation becomes important. Similarly, what *money* objectively is—M_1, M_2, M_3, etc.—depends on what problem we are studying. As typical problems are recognized, defined, and solved, our methods, techniques, concepts, awareness, aggregate data improve, and the quality of research improves. For example, the discovery of the response set, the tendency of some respondents to answer yes on a questionnaire and of others to answer no, led to an improvement in questionnaire construction: questions are now so worded that a respondent cannot consistently answer yes or no to all of them. If one respondent does, he is responding to the questioning process itself rather than to the content of the questions, and the scoring procedure will discover this.

As the methodologist studies a series of such problems, he finds implicit criteria for a good method and makes them explicit. For example, from problems such as the above we can induce that a good questionnaire is one that controls variables other than the ones being studied. Response set is one such contaminating variable. Then, having stated the principle, we can question it in turn. Is it always good to control variables? Can there be too much control? Would it perhaps be better to study some variable that keeps coming up, instead of controlling it away? Do the controls themselves contaminate the data? (Argyris, 1980, chap. 3). At some point in this bothersome questioning process, people start calling us philosophers of science. This kind of philosophy, however, is *very* different from analytic philosophy, both IL and OL. For a pragmatist, methodology and philosophy of science begin with scientific practice and attempt to improve practice. The criteria for improvement are found in practice and in the uses of science, and can themselves be questioned and improved. The pragmatist's approach is the opposite of the analytic philosopher's approach to science. The analytic philosopher begins with an ideal, perfect science and evaluates actual science by its distance from the ideal. But, objects the pragmatist, the ideal may not be the relevant one for some problem or method. The precise definitions and cardinal numbers appropriate for measuring the number of occupants per room would be inappropriate for a questionnaire on conservatism, where an ordinal Guttman scale or factor analysis would be more appropriate. The replicability appropriate for perception experiments would be inappropriate for a study of the British economy of the 1970s. The criteria for a good research design should come from the subject-matter and problem, not from an ideal of perfect knowledge. However, pragmatists do not object to a relevant, moderate ideal, one implicit in and derived from practice. Pragmatists do object to philosophical arguments that become self-sustaining, feeding on themselves and losing any connection to scientific practice (Handy, 1964, pp. 4–6, 12–13). Here the Stegmüller school is an exception within analytic philosophy; its intent is pragmatic.

JOHN DEWEY

John Dewey's philosophy of science, which reached its apex of development in the 1930s, had the misfortune to be obliterated by the new logical empiricism that was just then reaching America. When Dewey's last book appeared in 1949, it was ignored as simply not philosophy of science. Even the basic concepts of instrumentalism and pragmatism were replaced by logical empiricist concepts with the same name but very different content, and people forgot that there had ever been a Deweyan instrumentalism.

Philosophy of science was not a separate subject for Dewey; it was closely related to ethics, social psychology, metaphysics, politics, and esthetics. Dewey's social psychology (1922) described the typical structure of practical problems, his ethics was the general theory of problem solving, and his philosophy of science dealt with problems in scientific practice. The task of science, in turn, was to provide knowledge that would help us deal with our practical problems. Thus philosophy of science should indirectly contribute to solving the "problems of men" in society, not the artificial problems of philosophers.

An example of such an artificial problem was Russell's (and Descartes's) question, "How do we know that the external world exists at all, and we aren't imagining it?" This question was nonsense for Dewey. There is no *external* world *separate* from us. Through evolution human society has become *more or less* adapted to the natural world and has adapted that world to its needs. We are in the world and the world is in us, in our habits and physiology; we have made each other. Our sense organs are adapted to the physical world, and our thoughts, desires, and habits are adapted to our society through socialization (Dewey, 1916, chap. 11).

Similarly, Hume's problem of induction, "How do we know the sun will rise tomorrow, just because it has always risen in the past?" is nonsense. If the solar system were so erratic that the sun might not rise, the human species would not have survived. And similarly, if social processes were so erratic that they might change drastically at any time, society would not have survived. Analytic philosophers might reply, "But that's in the past. What about tomorrow?"—thus showing that they miss the point.

Underlying these artificial problems of philosophers is the spectator theory of knowledge, which Dewey frequently attacked (cf. Max Fisch, 1951, pp. 28–29; R. Bernstein, ed., 1960, chap. 2). The spectator theory assumes a separation between us and the object to be known, nature or society, so that our efforts to know it do not affect the object. We are spectators. Against this Dewey asserted that since we participate in our "object," society or nature, knowing involves interaction with the known. The spectator theory also assumes an unchanging truth out there, a truth that can in principle be known with certainty. Such a truth would exist in Popper's World 3. Against this Dewey asserted that the aim of social science is not to contemplate timeless laws but to help us deal more intelligently with the current problems of our changing society. We cannot achieve certainty in this enterprise, but should strive for as much empirical support or "warranted assertibility" for our diagnoses as we can get with limited time and resources. As the errors show up, we try to learn from them to improve our methods. And as our society changes, our earlier diagnoses also become outdated and must be corrected. In this sense, Dewey was an objective relativist (A. Murphy, 1927; A. Kaplan, 1964, p. 392).

Truth for Dewey could not be the correspondence of theory to reality. The correspondence definition assumes an external, unchanging world separate from us; it is part of the spectator theory of knowledge. But we are in the world, in a changing world, and we want to participate in those changes to make it a better world. Thus we want to know what changes are possible as well as what changes are occurring. We want to know how actual social process constrains, redirects, or prohibits possible changes, and what possibilities remain open. Nor do we need eternal truth; we need temporary truth about our present society, including the past and the possible futures it carries with it.

The real scientific process for Dewey is very different from that imagined by Russell, Hume, and Ayer. They wanted an unquestionable bedrock of fact on which we could construct our knowledge of the external world, and they came up with sense data as the bedrock. Given sense data, we could construct objects and could test hypotheses about those objects. But for Dewey we start with problems in a public, social world— problems of conflict or blocked action or confusion. In our attempts to define and redefine these problems, we sometimes question our own habits, modes of thinking, assumptions, perceptions, and even sensations, treating them as part of the problem. Thus sense data, and data in general, are abstracted from the ongoing experienced world; they are products of inquiry, not the starting point of knowledge, and they can themselves be questioned and corrected. Induction for Dewey was simply a process of noticing some feature of a case, some regularity or structure, and then seeing how far that feature could be generalized to other cases. It made no claim to certainty or universality. Thus there is no problem of induction. Nor do scientists simply collect observations. Scientists (typically experimenters for Dewey) act, in carefully controlled ways, and watch how people respond.

Social problems, the subject matter of social science, take several characteristic forms. (Here I extend Dewey's ideas a bit.) Economic problems involve a conflict of ends, so that we cannot achieve them all with given resources. Solutions involve "adapting means to ends, and ends to means," choosing an optimum mix of ends to fit these resources, and choosing or finding optimum resources for these ends. Social problems involve conflict within a personality, family, organization, community, and so forth; they can be managed by modifying conflicting forces, improving communication, improving self-awareness to facilitate self-adaptation and flexibility. Legal problems involve a conflict of legitimate expectations, and can be managed by legalistic extension of agreed-upon principles to this dispute.

Finally, political problems involve deficiencies in the decision-making structure that deals with social or economic or legal problems—the family council, the city council, the board of directors, the labor-management committee. Deficiencies include inadequate information channels to the problem, inadequate understanding of the problem, maldistribution of power among participants, a too strong or too weak central decision maker, and so on. Political problems are most fundamental because they prevent adequate solution of all other problems, including problems of improving the political structure. But, conversely, solving other problems can, by reducing conflict, improve the political structure.

Dewey calls the health of political systems *intelligence*. The long run goal of practical action is not to eliminate problems, which is impossible, but to increase our intelligence, our ability to solve more and more complex problems. *Democracy* is a closely related notion, almost synonymous with intelligence; it means participation, with adequate power, by all organizations affected by a problem-solving process. It means people solving their own problems through their own representatives.

Social science ought to be intimately involved in politics, since it supplies the information, diagnoses, and techniques a decision-making structure needs to do its job. Improved social science thus means increased intelligence. The ultimate aim of science and of political action is not truth or even warranted assertibility, but increased intelligence, increase in a society's ability to understand its own dynamics, diagnose its own problems, and solve them. Here Dewey agrees with Feyerabend.

In the 1920s and 1930s, Dewey came to believe that many of our social problems are not isolated and haphazard, but are a product of the dynamics of capitalism. He described capitalism as a regime of accident, waste, and distress—accident because production and distribution depended on the combats among captains of industry rather than on planning or market forces; waste because of the continuous destruction of capital in competition, planned obsolescence, conspicuous consumption, artificially induced needs; distress because of the maldistribution of resources, unemployment and poverty, and the combination of agricultural overproduction and widespread hunger of the 1930s. Most important, capitalism concentrated political power in the capitalist class, so that social problems were defined and solved primarily in terms of the interests and perceptions of that class. Capitalism is necessarily undemocratic. Consequently, the long-run goal of science, education, and political action was to gradually transform capitalism into a democratic socialism. The task of the social sciences was not just to solve particular problems like unemployment and delinquency as they happened to come up, but to work out the connections between these problems and the underlying economic system, and then solve them in such a way as to move toward a self-managing society. In particular it was necessary to create a scientifically informed public (*The Public and Its Problems*, 1927) that would set up the community councils and workers' councils and planning agencies of socialism. The task of education was to develop cooperative problem-solving ability in the future council members. The task of political action was to build and elect a socialist party that would break up the inter-locked corporation-government power structure and make room for community and workers' councils to have a voice in politics. A recent example of Dewey's type of social science based on community councils and trade unions is the work of Bluestone and Harrison (1980, 1982).

Dewey's grand synthesis came apart almost immediately. Some of his followers turned to technical philosophy of science and tried to combine the sharp distinctions of logical empiricism with Dewey's very different logic. Others concentrated on ethics, the theory of problem solving, and treated it as a neutral discipline for learning to solve any practical problem that happened to come along. Dewey's socialist organization, the League for Industrial Democracy, later set up a student branch that became Students for a Democratic Society (SDS) in 1960, aiming at social-ist revolution but without "bourgeois" science to guide it. Dewey had no use for revolution at all. Progressive education lost its democratic vision, became aimless, and was replaced by a "back-to-basics" movement. Dewey's union, the American Federation of Teachers, became dominated by fervent anticommunists who supported the cold war, U.S. militariza-tion, the South African bulwark against communism in Africa, and aid to the contras in Honduras. The AFT still proudly asserts that Dewey held its membership card no. 1, but says nothing about his socialist ideas.

Dewey himself moved away from social concerns in the 1940s. His later work on value (Lepley, 1945) and philosophy of science (Dewey and Bentley, 1949) is more technical and abstract than his earlier work. It can be read against the background of his 1930s social concerns, or apart from that background, as Bentley does.

We must conclude that Dewey's radical socialist synthesis of theory and practice was false; it was refuted by events. He had underestimated the power of capitalism. There was no Fabian path to socialism through scien-tific experimentation, trade unions, and progressive education in the 1930s. The social sciences have not been a liberal instrument of reform and social self-knowledge, but have divided into conservative, liberal, and radical wings with different aims, methods, and political connections. Whether Dewey's vision can be revised and revived remains to be seen.

Dewey's participatory socialist vision had provided a long-run ideal that could guide and constrain the short-run problem-solving process.

The pragmatist is normally absorbed in the immediate problematic situation, theoretical or practical. He tries to sort out the various entangled factors, estimates their flexibility or changeability, and works out a set of adjustments that will restore or enhance social action. In any problem, some factors are more flexible, some are slightly changeable with difficulty, and some are given. Yet Dewey insisted (Dewey and Bentley, 1949) that seemingly given factors also change in the long run, and it was also necessary to take the long-run direction of changes into account. To move toward greater social intelligence, that is, toward a socialist society, it could be advisable to reject the easy adjustments, the small problems, and work on longer run modifications of some seemingly inexorable constraints. This might involve questioning apparent constants such as available political resources and official policies, redefining a problem to bring in more factors, even stirring up trouble to loosen some fixed situation. Without a long-run vision, pragmatists have no particular reason to do this, to make a difficult situation still more difficult, and will prefer to adjust the flexible factors to the given ones. That is, they become servants of power.

In the social sciences, such short-sighted pragmatists will accept all social science methods as equally valid in their own way, and concentrate on the immediate tendencies, weaknesses, and possibilities of each method. They will not ask where they came from or why; they exist and can be improved. Nor will they ask where the problems come from or why; they exist and can be solved.

ABRAHAM KAPLAN

Kaplan opens the Conduct of Inquiry (1964) with an assertion of the autonomy of inquiry, which he credits to John Dewey (see, for example, Dewey and Bentley, 1949, p. 318). Kaplan begins: "It is one of the themes of this book that the various sciences, taken together, are not colonies subject to the governance of logic, methodology, philosophy of science, or any other discipline whatever, but are, and of right ought to be, free and independent." Kaplan emphasizes that this applies to the scientific community as a whole, not to individual sciences.

Kaplan's declaration of independence is directed against logical empiricism or analytic philosophy. The logical empiricist position was that there is a logic of science, or a logical foundation to science, that must characterize any theories that claim to be scientific rather than metaphysical. This logic is not yet known in detail, and the foundation has not yet been securely constructed. The proper task of the philosopher is to state this logic, or in Carnap's version to construct a language for science. Once this logic or language has been established, scientists will know what they have been doing and what they have to do to be scientific. For instance, the empiricist criterion of meaning would enable them to eliminate cognitively meaningless elements from their theories, such as value judgments, and the ideal of an axiomatic-deductive science would point the direction their theories must take to become fully scientific.

The OL analysts similarly argued that there is an ordinary language that scientists must use properly to avoid insoluble puzzles and errors. The logic of this language is known to philosophers and constitutes the logical foundation of social science, though not of natural science.

Kaplan, as a good pragmatist, is sensitive first to the political implication of the analytic philosopher's claim: it is a claim of authority over social scientists. The philosophers of science are the rule makers and judges; they set the standards of good science and evaluate particular theories for defects. One thinks for instance of Roger Buck's critique of general system theory for not following logical empiricist rules (1956) or Hempel's critique of functionalism for not this and not that (1965, chap. 11). They can even use the science-metaphysics distinction or Popper's falsifiability criterion to declare a whole school to be unscientific. Thus Hook (1959) elaborates on Popper's ruling that psychoanalysis is unscientific because it has never specified the possible observations that would totally refute it. And though the logical empiricist program has long since been abandoned, analytic philosophers still criticize particular works or schools for not following their version of the logic of science— for instance, by not supplying deductive explanations or not trying to axiomatize their theories, or not testing some causal hypothesis. Scheffler asserts that we already know what science is: "Science explains particulars by bringing them within the scope of appropriate general principles" (1963, preface). Then he criticizes various actual theories for not doing that.

Against this position Kaplan asserts that over the centuries scientists have developed their own procedures through trial and error, long before logical empiricism was invented. A procedure that successfully solved some theoretical or data-gathering problem would be used again and elaborated; a procedure that got nowhere would eventually be dropped. The simplest criterion for success was whether or not the problem continued to appear and make trouble; but over time more elaborate criteria could be inductively derived—does it solve one problem but create a worse one? These criteria in turn could be checked to see whether at some point they had gotten too rigid and impeded the growth of science. Kaplan calls these procedures and criteria the *logic-in-use* of science.

The social sciences have similarly developed their own logics-in-use over time, adapted to their own subject matter; their methods may or may not be similar to those of the natural sciences as a result. Note that Kaplan is neutral on the IL-OL dispute over whether the social sciences and the natural sciences ought to be (or logically are) the same or different.

Kaplan's declaration of independence reminds us that the social sciences *have* been colonized by logical empiricist philosophy through a host of methods textbooks (such as Isaak, 1975) that tell the student how to do science. Social scientists accept this foreign domination meekly because they feel inferior to the natural sciences; by comparison, they are soft, immature, preparadigm. So they try to carry out the methods of true, natural science somehow in their research. Or at least when they report their research tactics in interviews they try to use the proper language, mixed with more practical accounts of particular tactics and problems. Sometimes the proper language—postulates, hypotheses, deduced predictions, operational definitions, crucial experiment—appears in the early part of the work as routine homage to the authorities, and then is tacitly ignored. Even rebels like Merle Turner (1967) who struggle to throw off the yoke are unable to think differently and cannot get beyond negations. Turner asserts that "the terminology adopted by the theoretical behaviorists shows such diversity that we know it is impossible to separate the language of fact from that of a theory" (1967, p. 28). He asserts that the deductive-nomological (D-N) model of explanation works only with simple, complete, perfect hypotheses and data, and that no such things exist in psychology. Yet the only alternative he can conceive is the mythical *verstehende* (cf. chapter 5, below), which is obviously unscientific.

Thus it is not enough to simply declare the social sciences autonomous, though that is a good first step. The philosopher should also encourage autonomy by calling attention to the actual methods of social scientists, their logics-in-use. He can do this by observing, listening, reading, and questioning: "What do you mean by 'analyze the model'? Why do you need to do that? Are there different ways to analyze it?" To be sure, the philosopher will most probably not notice or understand everything and will not ask all the right questions. The result is an interpretation that is more or less faithful to some variant logic-in-use. Kaplan calls the philosopher's interpretation a *reconstructed logic*.

The purpose of reconstructing a logic-in-use and making it explicit, apart from encouraging autonomy, is to enable philosophers and scientists together to examine it and improve it. Each method has characteristic weaknesses that can lead to unreliable results and plain errors. Some weaknesses, like response set, have been known and studied for decades and already have standard solutions; others are known to methodologists but continue to make trouble.

For example, historians and ethnographers frequently go through three distinct stages in writing a history of a short episode or an ethnographic report. In the first stage, facts come in rapidly from several sources, but the sources conflict and produce a puzzling or inconsistent overall picture. The facts are puzzling, too. The meaning of a practice, or some central actor's intentions, are unclear; or three accounts of an episode disagree. Then a few key facts come in and everything suddenly falls into place and makes sense. The remaining task is to fill in the details by searching for missing facts, and cross-checking accounts of secondary incidents.

The weakness here is the tendency to accept the pattern that suddenly appears in the second stage as correct, and to concentrate thereafter on checking and filling in details. But a different order of fact collecting might have produced a slightly different but equally convincing illumination. Consequently, it is necessary to check the overall pattern as well as the details, and this can be done by trying to imagine a different overall picture and looking for the missing facts that would sustain that picture. (Popper would have approved that.) The philosopher of science can point out this tendency, having experienced it in his own research and having heard other researchers report the same experience, and can suggest ways of counteracting its effects.

Another example of a troublesome weakness is experimenter effects, which have been studied since about 1960 and occur in experimentation, survey research, and clinical interviews. The problem is that experimenters, surveyors, or clinicians unconsciously convey their expectations to the subjects and bias the results. A well-known problem in work using aggregate data is data massaging or data adjustment. The problem is that data collected by the census, the Commerce Department, or the National Bureau of Economic Research were either collected according to definitions and assumptions that researchers believe are false, or they obscure the effect researchers are studying because they fail to control for some variable or they combine two variables researchers want to distinguish. Thus Commerce Department data on labor productivity in the 1970s assume that service jobs do not increase in productivity, which is false (Block, 1985). Hence such data must be adjusted, corrected. The problem is that the researcher may legitimately adjust data that when unadjusted seem to disconfirm a hypothesis, while carelessly failing to adjust data that seem to confirm it.

Another task for philosophers of social science is to speak for the whole scientific community in relation to particular schools. Since philosophers are not specialists, they can rummage around in all sorts of scientific fields and bring back reports to others on how those scientists out there are doing. They can also bring into play the concepts and techniques of a wide variety of disciplines in understanding the logic-in-use of some group— sociometric analysis, cognitive styles, learning theory, power structure analysis, or whatnot. As Toulmin asserts in a preface that reads very much like Kaplan, "The rational appraisal of human understanding has involved many disciplines, without being in or of any one of them" (1972, p. 6). Of course, the use of a technique should be based on intimate acquaintance with it, and reports on the practices of other fields should be based on first-hand observation as well as interviews and written statements by scientists. Kaplan shows his familiarity with a number of fields in his examples, though his deepest acquaintance and most numerous examples come from psychoanalytic theory.

The logics of science are logics of discovery (E. Harris, 1970). They are rules of procedure, heuristics, search processes, strategies (A. Kaplan, 1964, pp. 15–18), since science is a process of searching for truth. The more empirical methods deal with how to find the important facts and connections; the more formal methods deal with how to construct and use a good model. Testing is a step in a research process, a check to see whether we are moving in the right direction. A significance test, or correlation measure, chi-square or r^2 or lambda, is a way of seeing whether we are on the trail of some correlation. It never guarantees success, but measures the risk that we are wasting our time looking in that direction against the risk that we will miss something if we shift direction. It never says that we have captured the truth to a significance of .001, since the correlation we are testing can be a mask for a great variety of similar connections and influences. (This is the pragmatic version of Goodman's paradox.) It never stops the search process with a "true" or "false," but merely redirects it. Redirection in turn is based on the *difference* between data and expectations. Thus the philosophical discussions about the relative importance of confirmation, disconfirmation, corroboration, and verisimilitude are irrelevant to the (pragmatic) logics of science.

This argument reverses Popper's assertion that the logic of science deals solely with testing and that discovery is a creative act following no rules.

The reconstructed logic offered us by logical empiricism deals with the products of science, not the process. It deals with the structure of a completed scientific theory, all folded and tied up with a ribbon. But science is never complete; its products are recycled into the process. The positivists' hypothetico-deductive model captures one aspect of some science, since science does have products, but it leaves much more out. It "presents the dénouement, but we remain ignorant of the plot" (1964, p. 10).

Similarly, the epistemological problems discussed by analytic philosophers come from philosophy, not from the actual problems of scientists. The problem of induction was set up by Hume, not by survey researchers, and the problem of whether the ideal language of science is physicalistic or phenomenalistic should not be a problem for social scientists, who use both languages (Diesing, 1966).

Diesing (1971) carries out part of Kaplan's program of reconstructing the logics-in-use of social scientists. The method of this work is participant-observation; it is an ethnography of science.

As of 1971, I found three groups of methods in use, as follows:

Quantitative methods: experimentation, survey research, aggregate data analysis;
Case study methods: participant observation, history, case histories, clinical research;
Formal methods: computer simulation, multiple small models, a single basic model with variants.

The aim of quantitative methods is to find variables and their connections, and the methods proceed by endless reformulation of variables and connections, and the endless subtraction (control) and addition (multivariate) of more variables. In experimentation, the controls are designed into the experiment; in survey research, some controls are designed into the survey and statistical controls are used on the data; in aggregate data research, the controls are mainly data adjustment techniques, such as controlling for seasonal variations. The aim of case study methods is to understand the structure and dynamics of a single case, ranging from an individual through a family, a town, a small culture, the U.S. political economy, to the capitalist world system. The methods proceed by end-lessly filling in and rearranging pieces as they come in, like a vaguely patterned jigsaw puzzle with pieces of flexible shape. The aim of formal methods is to capture a bit of logic that is exemplified in many varied empirical instances, and they proceed by first setting up the simplest

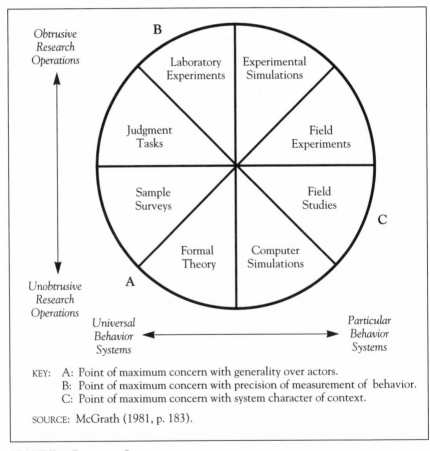

KEY: A: Point of maximum concern with generality over actors.
       B: Point of maximum concern with precision of measurement of behavior.
       C: Point of maximum concern with system character of context.

SOURCE: McGrath (1981, p. 183).

FIGURE 1. RESEARCH STRATEGIES

possible skeleton and then adding complications and qualifications; or sometimes by constructing component modules and connecting several in various ways.

Joseph McGrath has worked out a somewhat similar scheme (McGrath, 1981; Runkel and McGrath, 1972; Brinberg and McGrath, 1985, pp. 42–46). McGrath distinguishes eight research strategies in behavioral science, which can be classified in two dimensions: particular to universal, and obtrusive to unobtrusive research (figure 1). These eight strategies vary in their ability to achieve the three conflicting goals of behavioral research: precision, generality, and concreteness or faithfulness to a real situation. It is impossible to maximize more than one of these goals at a time, so together they constitute a three-horned dilemma for any research strategy. In McGrath's words, "*Every* research strategy either avoids two horns by an uneasy compromise but gets impaled, to the hilt, on the third horn; or grabs the dilemma boldly on one horn, maximizing on it, but at the same time 'sitting down' (with some pain) on the other two horns" (1981, p. 184).

Hypothesis testing is a part of most methods, but a relatively minor part. Thus Kaplan distinguishes "a dozen or so" types of experiment, including hypothesis testing as one type (1964, sec. 17). Experiments can be used to test a technique or apparatus; test a research design (pilot study); explore a topic and generate ideas (exploratory study); collect data; find boundaries of empirical processes or the range of applicability of a law; do a trial run on a small field sample; and so on. I have argued that in Milton Friedman's numerous publications from 1945 to 1982 I find only two very weak, almost useless tests (Diesing, 1985). The rest of his publications include much policy advice and argument, data collecting (such as Friedman and Kuznets, 1945), pure theory (such as Friedman and Savage, 1948), adjusting data to fit his theory, and most of all interpreting data (illustrated in Friedman and Schwartz, 1963, 1982). Most of Friedman's empirical work proceeds through the adjustment or interpretation of data without any testing, and I suspect this is not an uncommon practice in economics.

Abraham Kaplan distinguishes two types of theories, concatenated and hierarchical (1964, pp. 298–302).

> A concatenated theory is one whose component laws enter into a network of relations so as to constitute an identifiable configuration or pattern. Most typically, they converge on some central point, each specifying one of the factors which plays a part in the phenomenon which the

theory is to explain. . . . A hierarchical theory is one whose component laws are presented as deductions from a small set of basic principles. (1964, p. 298)

Similarly, there are two types of explanation: pattern explanations and deductive explanations (1964, secs. 38, 39). There are variations in each type, and perhaps a continuum of some sort. I find pattern explanations occurring in case study methods and computer simulations, while deductive explanations occur in quantitative methods and some formal models. A good number of formal models can be interpreted either way; they have both pattern and deductive components (Diesing, 1971). (For pattern explanations in history, see Kuhn, 1977, pp. 17–18; Stretton, 1969, chap. 3; in psychoanalytic theory, see Michael Sherwood, 1969; in world systems analysis, see Bach, 1980; in institutional economics, see Benjamin Ward, 1973, and Wilber and Harrison, 1978.)

Social science methods, and the theories and explanations associated with them, are obviously plural. In this context, the commotion over Feyerabend's *Against Method* (which could read "against a uniform method" or "against a Popperian-imposed method") seems quaint and irrelevant. Feyerabend has merely repeated Kaplan's assertion of the autonomy of science from any philosophically imposed method. There is no one scientific method or goal. If the philosopher's concern is rephrased as "What characteristics do all valid methods share?" the pragmatist will reply that they all have weaknesses and shortcomings, and all can be improved. Some social scientists will agree with this, and then add, "But my method has the least weaknesses." Well, OK. If the philosopher asks, "What characteristics must any method necessarily have to be scientific at all?" then that is a would-be umpire speaking, not a coach. Methods are not scientific or unscientific, they are improvable.

Similarly, the incommensurability that Feyerabend and Kuhn emphasized obviously exists; it is a constant problem of communication across methods and theories. A mathematical model builder and a clinician think very differently and have very different empirical sensitivities, and unless two such people are aware of their differences and try to translate or empathize with each other they will communicate very little. The theoretical debates between elitists and pluralists, or Keynesians and neoclassicists, or Parsons and Homans and their followers, have been exercises in poor or partial communication. Kuhn's concern with community and communication is very relevant.

The pragmatist's main criticism of logical empiricism and analytic philosophy is that it obscures, denies, or rejects the actual pluralism of methods and goals in the social sciences. It recognizes only one goal of science, the formulation of universally valid causal laws, and concludes that there must accordingly be one scientific method. In terms of McGrath's scheme (figure 1), it chooses the "universal" extreme on one dimension and ignores the other dimension. The result is to misrepresent all social science methods and to fasten alien requirements on them.

Case study methods are most thoroughly misrepresented. For the logical empiricist, one can "know" an "instance" only by subsuming it under a general law; and since we do not "yet" have the laws, case methods must test causal hypotheses too, and this requires control groups, quantification, and impartial administration of the independent variable. Nonsense. Formal methods are also misrepresented, since most mathematical models cannot be tested empirically—they are abstract structures making no empirical claims—and the requirement of empirical testing misdescribes them as empirical hypotheses. And worse, focusing on laws, linear connections, blinds one to the concept of structure, network, digraph, matrix, space, which is so essential in formal modeling. Models describe structures that constrain, shape, limit, redirect action, rather than linear forces that determine it. Quantitative methods come closest to the logical empiricist scheme, if one does not take "universality" seriously, so experimenters and survey researchers are the ones most likely to be taken in by the logical empiricist scheme. After all, it says that they are more scientific than the case study people, the simulators, and the model builders, and people like to hear that sort of praise. The fine print about what they are not doing right they can overlook or postpone. The result is to intensify the problem of communication across methods.

To reject the relevance of the logical empiricist scheme does not mean to reject the goal of achieving valid general laws; it means that there are other goals as well and that generality is a matter of degree. Generalizations about U.S. voting behavior can be valid even though they apply only between 1948 and 1972 and only to Americans. Truth does not have to be timeless. Logical empiricists have a derogatory name for such changing truths (relativism); but such truths are real, while the absolute, fully axiomatized truth is imaginary.

Alexander Rosenberg (1980) has taken the logical empiricist goal of universally valid laws to its absurd extreme. He argues that the social sciences can never establish any universally valid laws, never have any truth at all, because they have only a single case, the human species. Thus they can never set up any control groups, which require many comparable cases; therefore they can never test any hypotheses; therefore they can never assert any universal laws. His advice is to abolish the social sciences as a fraud and replace them with sociobiology. Sociobiologists are now reading Rosenberg, probably with enthusiasm. I imagine they are thinking "We are more scientific than they are." Rosenberg forgets that the sociobiologists too have only a single case, the planet Earth.

Once we accept the relative generality and relative validity of social science results, we can learn useful things from the logical empiricists, especially for quantitative methods, without having to make them the authorities on science.

Abraham Kaplan expresses the pragmatic conception of relative, partial, improvable truths as follows:

> We must avoid the blunders both of claiming that today at last science has arrived at the truth and claiming that science never does get at the truth. . . . I should prefer to think of truth as a matter of degree—not the ever-receding horizon but the ground beneath our feet as we traverse it. (1964, p. 321)

This is Kaplan's version of Dewey's "warranted assertibility." The eternal, certain truth of which logical empiricists dreamed is rejected as impossible and irrelevant. Instead, we give our assertions, factual and theoretical, general and particular, as much empirical support and error control as we can with given resources. What we learn in the process about better search techniques and error control should enable our successors to reach a truth for their time that will both falsify and build on ours.

Note, however, that Kaplan does not comment on where our feet are taking us. His concern remains short-run, unlike Dewey's.

THE CHURCHMAN SCHOOL

C. W. Churchman's early interests combined ethics, operations research (OR), and philosophy of science. Since for a pragmatist ethics is the general theory of problem solving or decision making, and since OR deals with industrial and organizational problems, OR is a branch of ethics or at least its close relative. Scientists too engage in problem solving with theoretical problems, and OR is a type of applied science, so the three fields are the same or closely related (Haworth and Minas, 1954). The unity of the three was manifested in the journal *Management Science* which Churchman and, later, his students edited, and which contained articles on OR, ethics, and philosophy of science. Consider also the title of one of Churchman's books: *Prediction and Optimal Decision: Foundation of a Science of Values* (1961).

The practical problem-solving experience of Churchman and his students the industrial engineers gave a characteristic slant to their treatment of scientific method during the 1950s and 1960s. The operations researcher is a model builder and thinks mathematically. He carries a bag of models with him to work: decision models, game models, queuing models, line balancing models, and so on. If one of them fits his assigned problem, the problem is solved immediately. More likely he will see the problem as a variant of some model, and will make the necessary adjustments. Or he may model the problem from the ground up, using pieces of other models as appropriate. His model will tell him what additional information he needs and what possible solutions he can explore; these actions will suggest corrections in the model, and so on.

When an OR person turns explicitly to scientific method, he will treat it as another model-building problem. For example, Russell Ackoff, a close associate of Churchman's and director of OR at Case Institute, collaborated with two Churchman students in publishing *Scientific Method: Optimizing Applied Research Decisions* (Ackoff et al., 1962). This work argues that the criteria of optimization are more highly developed in applied science (OR) than in pure science, so we should carry over what we have learned in the former to the latter. When we do this, we treat scientific method as a branch of decision theory, which deals with how to optimize two or more objectives given two or more possible alternative actions.

For instance, suppose we are doing a sample survey by mail questionnaire. Our primary objective is to find the relation between a dependent variable such as nonvoting and several hypothesized independent variables. In order to do this, we have the secondary objectives of maximizing the validity of our measurement of these variables and controlling the maximum number of possible interfering variables. We also want to maximize the honesty of the responses. All three objectives can be approached by lengthening the questionnaire. To maximize honesty and to control for yea-saying, we can repeat the same question in several different forms and state it both positively and negatively. To increase the number of control variables, we add questions that tap each variable. To increase validity, we add more indicators, more questions directed to some dimension or aspect of the dependent variable.

But as the questionnaire lengthens the rate of return goes down, since respondents will not bother to fill out too long a questionnaire. This biases the data, since only certain types of people will return it; so we have a conflicting objective of maximizing the representativeness of the sample.

The research problem is to optimize all these conflicting objectives. Survey researchers have devised many techniques over the years to increase their efficiency at this task. One can interview some of the nonrespondents and compare them with the respondents to see how far the questionnaire data are biased. However, interviewing is more expensive than sending out questionnaires, so this brings in another optimization problem. One can increase validity more cheaply by finding just a few questions that tap a depth variable most directly. One can find questions that control more than one contaminating variable. One can increase honesty by putting sensitive questions near the end where appropriate. "Where appropriate" points to another objective or constraint: proper sequencing of questions.

But in the end it is still necessary to balance conflicting objectives: measurement accuracy versus representativeness, lengthening versus shortening the questionnaire; validity versus reliability; cheapness (mail questionnaire) versus better response rate and flexibility (interview). We are back to McGrath's three-horned dilemma, except that here the dilemmas appear within a method.

In the above example, the objectives are known and the optimization problem is obvious. Ackoff observes that more commonly in OR not all objectives or constraints are known initially, and part of the problem is to discover them and make them explicit. Also it is never the case that all alternative techniques and procedures are known; a large part of problem solving consists in finding better procedures. Nor do we ever know all the situational constraints or interfering variables to be controlled. Thus scientific problem solving is mainly controlled search: search for interfering variables, for techniques, for implicit objectives. A "problem" in which everything is known and only the estimation and trade-off decisions remain is the limiting case of a well-defined scientific problem.

This approach to method places cost-benefit calculations at the heart of science. One can always achieve more precise measurement, more validity, more reliability, more representativeness, but at a cost. One can interview instead of mailing a questionnaire; interview more people, more times, with different interviewers, in several different countries; develop more precise indices; pretest more extensively; check interviews against depth observation and aggregate data such as voting data—but all these procedures cost time and money. In deciding whether to accept or reject a hypothesis for further study, one can always reduce Type I errors, but a cost of increasing Type II errors, and vice versa. Similar cost-benefit trade-offs occur in experimentation, participant observation, and all methods. Thus in science we can have as much warrant for our assertions, as much truth, as we are willing to pay for, at an exponentially increasing cost.

In the 1960s Churchman moved out of industrial OR to set up a part of the Space Sciences Lab at Berkeley, where he taught systems analysis for NASA. Systems analysis is a generalization of OR to apply to any kind of practical problem. At this time, his thinking also took on loftier, more speculative dimensions; one of his papers from 1963 is titled "The X of X" (in 1968a). He wrote about the application of systems thinking to human problems (Churchman, 1968b; see also Hoos, 1972, for criticism from within the Space Sciences Lab). He came to see science, not as an OR-type series of small optimizing problems, but as an inquiring system to be studied by systems analysis. Instead of tinkering with the details of existing practice he proposed to design a better science (*The Design of Inquiring Systems*, 1971). The result, the Hegelian inquirer, is Churchman's own major contribution to the philosophy of the social sciences. (See also Mitroff, 1974a, pp. 220–50.)

Churchman's procedure is to design several inquiring systems to fit the epistemology of several classical philosophers, and examine the strengths and weaknesses of each. Among others, he designs a Leibnizian inquirer, a Lockean inquirer, and a Hegelian inquirer.

The Leibnizian inquirer is a model builder. It begins an inquiry by looking for the simplest, most basic assertion about some chosen topic. The assertion is not based on observation, since observation is notoriously unreliable. It is based on reason. The assertion is discovered in the definition or essence of the thing being studied. For instance, if we are studying rational choice, the simplest assertion is that it is the choice of the best alternative. "Alternative" is part of the definition of "choice," and "best" is included in "rational." In demography the simplest assertion is that anyone alive in year t is either dead or a year older in $t + 1$, and either a year younger or not born yet in $t-1$. This follows from the definition of life as a process over time, from birth to death. If we are studying the logic of metropolitan growth (Banfield, 1974, chap. 1), the simplest assertion is that with population increase the city must expand either upward or downward or outward in space. This follows from the definition of a city as a space occupied by nonoverlapping people. If we are studying monetary flows among n cities, the simplest assertion is that the total outflow from all cities must equal the total inflow, since each outflow from one city is an inflow from another (Kemeny and Snell, 1962, chap. 6).

Since the assertion follows from the definition of the thing studied, it is necessarily true of that thing. This is a logical, necessary truth, discovered by reason.

Alternatively, the Leibnizian inquirer can use empirical data heuristically to suggest some simple underlying mathematical structure, some matrix or space or Markov chain that constrains the surface empirical clutter (Sylvan and Glassner, 1985, pp. 5–6 and *passim*).

The next step is to deduce other propositions from the first one, or from the first one plus other definitions. For example in the money flow model we can define rates of flow Rij, which are either $\rangle$, $=$, or $\langle$ than Rjk. If the deductions are logically valid, the new propositions will derive their truth from the first one; thus the first assertion is the foundation of the whole model. The way to guarantee the validity of the deductions is to move one step at a time, so that reason can inspect the deduction for validity.

The end result is a family of models, each based on the same basic assertion and different secondary definitions. These models are necessarily true of anything that fits the various definitions and relations of the model.

The problem is to find what empirically fits the definitions, and here reason is a poor guide. Do all or some human beings choose rationally all or some of the time? What is to count as a unit of population or unit of money? What is to count as an alternative for choice, and how is its value measured? As Mitroff observes, if we have a well-structured problem with components that clearly fit the definitions and assumptions of some model, the model-building approach works well; otherwise not (1974a, p. 223). The clarity and precision of a model can easily blind one to the realities of a messy empirical situation. However, the Leibnizian rationalist is not interested in the flux of surface appearance or in predicting that flux; for him, science gets at the underlying constraints that eventually control what happens. Thus a monetarist need not worry about what money is empirically; whatever it is, it will control prices (suitably adjusted) sooner or later, somehow.

A Lockean inquirer begins with data, and preferably the simplest data. Observation and reason are both unreliable, but observation is least unreliable in dealing with simple, small facts. Consequently, we should not try to describe some complex empirical situation as a whole; we must break it into the smallest parts and describe one part at a time. That is, we should quantify. Instead of describing a large crowd, we count them; instead of saying "a wealthy family," we reduce its possessions to dollars and count the dollars. Thus any empirical situation can in principle be reduced to numbers and then described accurately.

However, every counting process depends on rules and definitions that specify what is to be counted and what is to be ignored. Thus in counting a crowd, the observer must know whether the speakers are to be counted; those waiting to speak but who may not get their turn; the observers themselves; undercover policemen; hot dog sellers; children older than some age; passers-by who stop to listen, and if they stop, how many minutes they must stay before they become part of the crowd; people who leave early.

Thus every quantitative observation involves applying rules and criteria to immediate experience. Applying rules involves judgment, since there are always ambiguous cases. The Lockean system deals with this problem by introducing multiple observers, each counting the same crowd or questionnaire responses or citations or costs or votes. We depend on the judgment of the observers to deal with the ambiguous units. Then we count the observers who agree and count the amount of disagreement. This is known as replication. If the disagreement is large, the observation has failed; if it is small, we have produced data.

Second, we can repeat the counts after specified time periods to get a rate of change. Third, we can count one or more other entities over the same time span to see how the counts covary. The result is correlations, simple and multiple.

The Lockean inquirer does not produce necessary truths, but only estimates. There is almost always a margin of error, since observers rarely agree completely. Experiments rarely replicate exactly, even with the same experimenter. Nor are correlations ever perfect. But we can estimate—that is, depend on observers' judgments—whether the margins of error are small enough and the correlations large enough for some practical purpose.

The weakness of a Lockean system is that even the smallest observation depends on theory; what is to count as a unit? To count a crowd, one must specify who is included; and similarly for counting unemployment, family consumption, the value of output per man-hour, matrilocal residence. The Lockean inquirer handles this problem by depending on the judgment of multiple observers and measuring their disagreement. But agreement among observers may merely express a shared theoretical background; and if the shared theory is a bad one their agreement will produce bad data. How can a Lockean inquirer estimate the appropriateness of theoretical background? Plainly observer agreement is a hindrance to inquiry here, since it hides the problem.

The Hegelian inquirer uses disagreement to uncover such problems. If one observer or group of observers counts the number of families in poverty and finds that the number has decreased and is very small, then there should be another group of observers who find that the number is large and increasing. Each group then criticizes the other group's count. The disagreement brings the theoretical presuppositions of each count into the open: the first group uses an absolute measure of poverty, x income per year, and includes food stamps, backyard garden vegetables, assumed gifts from relatives, assumed income in the underground economy, and assumed public charity, while the second group uses a relative measure of poverty, x distance from national median income, and counts only official money income. The conflict forces each group to defend its assumptions, and this involves making them explicit and relating them to some systematic theory. It may also induce empirical investigation of the assumptions: estimating the amount and distribution of income in the underground economy, estimating the number of backyard gardens, estimating the consumption permitted by the official poverty level, and evaluating the standard of living allowed by the poverty level. Each of these investigations must in turn be undertaken by two opposed groups. One group must define the underground economy broadly to include the imputed value of household labor such as cooking and home auto repairs, while the other group defines it narrowly, as work that is paid for with money. So also for evaluation: one group will evaluate the poverty-level standard of living in terms of calories and clothing, and the other will evaluate it in social terms including reference groups, self-esteem, and life-cycle concepts. The conflict of values in turn should induce the groups to make their values explicit, systematic, and defensible, and so on; the dialectical inquiring process has no necessary endpoint.

A dialectical inquirer produces several kinds of results. First, each group of observers becomes more aware of its own assumptions and methods. Group B must observe and describe group A's assumptions and methods in order to criticize them. Churchman argues that "one person may be far more sensitive to another's reactions than the other is to himself" (1971, p. 155; 1963, pp. 1–2). As a result, group A hears itself described from the outside and gets a new, surprising slant on its own practice. In order to reject this description it must produce a counterdescription, and the resulting conflict-saturated inquiry should produce a more thorough, explicit, and systematic account of its practice and assumptions. At least some of group A's new self-description should represent increased self-knowledge rather than more elaborate self-deception.

Second, in the process of defending itself against criticism, group A may discard indefensible assumptions, improve questionable techniques, revise egocentric values, clarify ambiguous concepts, and broaden narrow or one-sided theories. Third, a third observer of the conflict between A and B may be able to work out a middle position, or a combination of components from A and B, or a new position that avoids the perceived weak points of A and/or B.

One result that is forbidden is for A and B to reach agreement—for example, on a definition and measure of poverty. This would stop inquiry and transform the Hegelian into a Lockean inquirer, in this example.

The Hegelian or dialectical inquirer will take on different characteristics according to the kind of opposition and conflict needed for a specific problem. The most fundamental kind of dialectical inquirer is constructed by combining a Leibnizian and a Lockean inquirer—that is, by combining model builders and quantifying empiricists in a single research group. An example is provided by the 1980 U.S. census (Mitroff, Mason, and Barabba, 1983). Mitroff and Mason are Churchman students who set up the Hegelian inquirer; Barabba was the census director who hired them and collaborated with them.

The problem was to determine the exact U.S. population on April 1, 1980, and its distribution by states and cities. For the model builder, the problem is solved by a simple demographic model: $P(1980) = P(1970)$ minus deaths and emigration plus births and immigration. $P(1970)$ is known from the 1970 census; births and deaths have been reported by hospitals and coroners, and immigration-emigration is reported by the immigration service. There are inevitably errors in all these figures since observation is always unreliable, but we can estimate whether the errors are cumulative or counteracting and adjust our figure accordingly. For the Lockean empiricist, the problem is solved not by armchair speculation but by going out and counting those people.

There are deficiencies in both approaches, which adherents of the other approach can easily point out. The demographic model is no more reliable than its component numbers, all of which are unreliable unless they have actually been counted. In particular, the immigration figures omit illegal immigrants, some of whom have since become legal by marriage or naturalization. Thus the model will understate the actual population. Conversely, the counting process must inevitably overstate the actual legal population. Some of the empirical people in the United States are not part of the U.S. population: illegal immigrants, legal tourists, temporary residents, foreign students on expired visas. Some of these, especially the illegal ones, will tell the census taker that they are citizens. However, the census taker will also miss some people of no fixed address who may be sleeping in abandoned buildings or subway trains.

Mitroff and his associates set up preliminary workshops in which both model builders and counters criticized each other and defended their tactics. Presumably the criticisms made each aware of their weak points and led them to improve their tactics. Then each group made its census estimate. The two estimates agreed, which suggested that both were wrong, since one should have been an overestimate and the other an underestimate. After more discussion, they decided to let the matter rest there. Perhaps the workshops had enabled both modelers and counters to reduce their errors enough; at any rate, the unexpected agreement had pretty well put a stop to further inquiry.

Murray Levine (1974) has developed a more limited version of the Hegelian inquirer focused only on data, not theory. Levine's model derives from legal practice. In a law court, the attorney for one side calls a witness to present evidence; then the opposing attorney cross-examines the witness to try to find weaknesses in the evidence. Evidence is valid only if it can withstand cross-examination and attempted rebuttal.

In social research, all known methods have weaknesses that can produce invalid data. Experimental data can reflect the role playing of the S, or the hostile "screw you" effect (Masling); survey responses can be part of the respondent's self-presentation; clinical responses can be selected or shaped by the clinician; aggregate data are sorted and counted by the categories of the reporting organization and the collecting agency to serve various tax and bureaucratic purposes (Cicourel, 1964); field experiments are influenced by unknown historical or contextual factors; and so on. Researchers know this, and try to reduce errors. But they tend to be less critical or uncritical of data that support their expectations and theories, reserving their full critical attention for disconfirming and puzzling data. To counteract this normal bias, Levine suggests that the PI (principal investigator) hire a reviewer to cross-examine all data, and especially confirming data. The reviewer-adversary should know the characteristic weakness of each type of datum, so s/he can look for that weakness in the data. Only data that can withstand adversarial review should be accepted as valid.

In clinical and field methods, the reviewer will be acting as a clinical supervisor of the researcher. In these methods the researcher is the main research instrument, so his or her biases and weaknesses will produce corresponding data weaknesses. A reviewer who knows the researcher well will know what sort of errors to expect and can focus the cross-examination on them. And, as with the Hegelian inquirer, selective cross-examination should gradually make researchers more aware of their own biases and more cautious about accepting even confirming data. Other methods will require other adversarial or reviewing tactics.

It will usually not be easy to design an adversarial or Hegelian inquirer. Levine calls for a mature adversary, one who is knowledgeable about the topic being studied. The clinical supervisor will need sensitivity and much patience to watch the field worker produce data. Churchman's research designer will have to find researchers who are strongly opposed to one another but who can yet communicate and tolerate one another. Or more likely the PI will have to assume personal responsibility for communication, interpreting the ideas of one side to the other side. The PI will have to act as referee in debate, rejecting tricky rhetoric and demanding an honest, clear presentation of each side's ideas and criticisms.

But these difficulties show that the designs are an improvement over Popper's rules. Popper's rule, Try to falsify your hypothesis, recognized the tendency to perceive and to look for confirming data, and the unwillingness to face disconfirming data. But he naively supposed that a rule, Try to falsify, would overcome this tendency. Since human beings are free and rational, they will recognize the logical importance of falsifiability;

and if they try, they can overcome their bias for confirming data. They are presumably free from their own personality.

Later Popper recognized that trying would not be enough, and he added the rule, Try to falsify others' hypotheses. But this rule brings us to the problems of communication and of toleration of adversaries. The same egocentrism that appears as a bias toward confirming data can be expressed as intolerance and misunderstanding of criticism. The Hegelian inquirer focuses on the communication and tolerance problem, assigning these tasks to the PI or "synthesis" function. To be sure, the design, even if successful, arranges communication and tolerance only within a research project and within a single theory. The larger problem of communication across different theories, Kuhn's problem of incommensurability, remains unsolved. Kuhn points to this problem when he asserts that communication normally occurs within a community sharing a disciplinary matrix.

Levine's adversary model points to an additional problem, the problem that we tend to produce or encourage confirming data, not just find them. This problem requires the adversary-reviewer to watch or participate in the data-forming process, or at least to retrace the steps afterward, to replicate the process.

Randall Collins has induced a somewhat different Hegelian inquirer from studies of the history of philosophy, both East and West (1989). Collins finds that intellectual history is a conflict process (p. 112; he would, of course). A school of philosophy defines its doctrines *in opposition* to another school, and develops by systematically negating the other school's ideas. Examples are Heraclitus and Parmenides, Epicurus and Zeno's Stoicism, the Vienna Circle and phenomenologists like Heidegger. There are exceptions.

Conflict leads each school to clarify its position in opposition, to make distinctions, to produce formal arguments and proofs, to develop logic and epistemology, and to strengthen weak points in its theory. That is, conflict leads to creativity. Historical periods in which there is only one school are periods of scholasticism, in which there are compilations of the basic texts, commentaries on them, classifications of the theory's categories and doctrines, and historical studies of the sequence of commentaries. Even in a conflict period there can be scholastics who ignore the opposite school and produce commentaries and catechisms.

In such a dialectical process, the two schools must have some underlying agreement that allows them to negate each other intelligibly; and a third school can arise by negating this area of agreement. Thus the minimum number of schools needed for creative growth seems to be two or three, as Collins observes (1989, p. 124). However, the maximum seems to be about six, he adds. After that, things start getting confused; there isn't much left to negate. Also, for a school to last more than a generation it has to have substantial political and social support, attract new adherents and allies, and maintain the attention and communication with a continuing opponent. Otherwise it shrinks, stagnates, and dies out. Thus there is limited social and intellectual space for philosophical schools, and conflict is in part a competition to hold on to a sufficient part of this space. "Conflict is limited by itself" (1989, p. 124).

Those who have noticed a bit of conflict in the social sciences may suspect that Collins's argument might apply there as well.

Collins obviously agrees with Feyerabend that a plurality of conflicting theories stimulates the creativity needed for science. But where Feyerabend, following Mill, calls for maximum pluralism, an ever increasing ocean of conflicting theories, Collins finds a more dialectical process in which three-plus is about the right number. In a dialectical inquirer the problem of communication is partly solved by the area of agreement between two opposite theories, which allows them to understand each other somewhat. Also three-plus theories can have enough political-social support and intellectual space to survive, while an ocean of alternatives do not. The National Science Foundation is not likely to follow Feyerabend's advice to fund research in voodoo, witchcraft, rain dancing, and demonology.

Randall Collins, like Feyerabend, disagrees with Kuhn's original account of revolutions (Collins, 1989, pp. 128–29). The accumulation of anomalies by itself will not produce a revolution; what is needed is a shift of political support that opens space for a new theory. The new theory develops by negating the old theory or by producing a synthesis of previously conflicting positions, not by explaining the anomalies. Finally, the old theory dies out (if it does) not because of its anomalies but because the available intellectual space is now occupied by other theories. And if anomalies do not produce a revolution, the "normal science" that Kuhn defends because it uncovers the anomalies is also irrelevant. It becomes Collins's scholasticism. For Collins and Feyerabend, and also for Churchman, conflict and creativity are what science needs.

5

Hermeneutics: The Interpretation of Texts

HERMENEUTIC PHILOSOPHIES and traditions have existed for centuries, flourishing especially in the nineteenth and twentieth centuries in Germany and other parts of continental Europe. They were concerned originally with understanding the Bible and other sacred texts, and with the interpretation of Roman law, which ruled parts of the Continent as late as the nineteenth century. But by extension all sorts of other texts could be subjected to hermeneutic techniques: the works of Plato and Aristotle, commentaries on the Bible and the Talmud, poetry and drama, myths and legends.

Since different texts require different interpretive techniques, the variety of texts studied contributed to the wide disagreement among hermeneutic philosophers as to the goals, techniques, and ultimate value of hermeneutics. For example, the basic problem of biblical interpretation was to find and correct the errors in the text, since medieval scribes had miscopied, left out words, and made imaginative corrections of passages garbled by earlier scribes. The purpose was not only to reconstruct the original text but to recover the exact original message of the author, God. The problem in interpreting Roman law was the continuous change produced by successive judicial interpretations in varying circumstances. The interpretations had narrowed or expanded the original meaning by adapting it to new circumstances. The problem was not to recover the original legislative intention but to adapt the relevant interpretations to current circumstances and sense of justice and thereby produce a new interpretation. In the case of a drama, the conscious intentions of the writer were unimportant, and the problem was to find the meanings embedded in the text itself so they could be expressed by the actors on the stage.

This chapter deals with only one current hermeneutic school, represented by Gadamer (1975, 1984, 1989), Apel (1970, 1977, 1981), Habermas (1967, 1970, 1971, 1977), and Ricoeur (1970, 1977). (See also

Radnitzky, 1970, sec. IV-F-3 for a brief presentation.) This school has focused on techniques and characteristics of interpretation in the social sciences. It derives most directly from Heidegger, Gadamer's teacher, but also draws on concepts and logic from the whole German philosophical tradition back to Schleiermacher, Hegel, Kant, and beyond.

Hermeneutics deals with clarifying the meaning of a text, and by extension the meaning of any human action, product, or expression that can be treated as a text. *Texts* include Supreme Court decisions, the legislative history of a bill, government archives, memoirs, speeches, interviews, Rorschach protocols, lab notes, working papers, Keynes's *General Theory*, a colloquium discussion or political debate, a dream report, an organization chart, a union contract, a myth, a World Bank report on a loan application by Nicaragua, a political demonstration with speeches, a small group session in an interaction process laboratory. By extension, a ceremony is a kind of spoken and acted text, a drama; a culture is in part a set of rules and examples for how to live, and its acting out is a larger drama; a building or a city means (symbolizes) the life that is and has been lived in it. Thus the discipline of architecture deals with the construction of meanings (L. Schneekloth, colloquium, Feb. 10, 1984). People experience the meanings, the ongoing shared life, when they use the buildings or walk down the street. David Harvey refers to "the semiotic of the city" and comments, "We have to learn to read the social and physical signs and codes of the urban milieu—to understand the signals of status and power as written into physical landscapes, for example—in order to survive" (1985a, pp. 265–66).

Some texts are current or recent productions; others come to us from the past. Current texts are accompanied by nonverbal communication—actions, gestures, and facial expressions—that supplement and help us understand the verbal message (Habermas, 1971, chap. 8). Remember Nixon's nervous, anxious hands and big smile in his 1960 debates with Kennedy, and his big fixed grin with Pat Nixon crying in the background in his 1962 concession speech; consider how the placement of leaders in a protest march or speakers at a demonstration tell us what organizations are supporting the demonstration and what compromises on policy produced their support. Texts from the recent past can be supplemented by interviews with survivors—that is, additional new texts. Texts from the distant past depend mainly on other past texts for their clarification. Consequently, the hermeneutic techniques of the historian differ somewhat from those of the current events researcher.

Nontexts—ceremonies, cultures, cities, dreams—require still different techniques. These actions and buildings have not been constructed with the deliberate intention of communicating a message. Yet they have been constructed, unlike tracks in cloud chambers; and like nonverbal communication they do express something to us and to participants. A cathedral or a ritual—a bridegroom breaking a wineglass with his foot—expresses some attitude toward something. The attitude and its object are symbolized, not verbalized, and the meanings of the symbols are more or less understood by participants. The outsider who wants to understand the "message"—there is no message—can study the incidental, accompanying texts and the cultural context, but must also participate to experience the meaning of the symbolism.

Both texts and nontexts are particular human expressions, and the hermeneutic task is to understand them in their particularity. According to Gadamer, hermeneutics is based on a feeling for the individuality and uniqueness of persons; it is a way to understand the inwardness of the other (1984, p. 57).

INTERPRETING A TEXT

Let us examine several typical texts to see what problems they present to the researcher and how the problems can be solved. Consider cabinet minutes from the British archives for 1937–38 (Colvin, 1971; Middlemas, 1973), or Caro's (1974) biographical interviews of Robert Moses, or a dream reported to a psychoanalyst (Erikson, 1964, chap. 2), or Schreber's memoirs (Chabot, 1982).

The British cabinet minutes tell the story of how British foreign policy toward Germany, France, and Italy developed in the period leading up to the Munich agreement. This history, as interpreted by Colvin and Middlemas, is of interest to students of foreign policy and crisis decision making. Robert Moses was the most powerful person in New York City politics from the late 1940s to the late 1960s; he headed up to twelve agencies, including the Triborough Bridge Authority, Long Island Parks Commission, New York State Parks Commission, and New York City Planning Commission. Consequently, his activities are of interest to students of New York City politics. Schreber was a paranoid psychotic, so his memoirs show us the phenomenology of paranoia—that is, how a psychotic experiences the world.

In all four cases, there is an overt message and a concealed message or subtext. In the interview and the dream, part of the overt message deliberately disguises or distorts the concealed message; in the cabinet minutes and the memoirs, the concealed message is simply omitted except for a few clues in the text. That is, Robert Moses would be expected to describe his own activities as entirely honorable and honest; dishonorable activities would be either omitted from his replies or reported in an honorable, official version. Cabinet minutes give an official summary of what was said "for the record," but not everything that was said or left unsaid. Schreber certainly did not think he was psychotic; he merely reported his experiences, the highly unusual experiences of a normal, respectable gentleman.

The researcher's problem is to find the concealed message, but also to interpret the denials and omissions in the overt message. Sometimes the overt message is also important, as in the interview; sometimes not, as in the dream report. One can call the interest in the overt message *surface hermeneutics* and the interest in the concealed message *depth hermeneutics*.

Interpretation begins with a general, vague hypothesis about the topic of the concealed message (Gadamer, 1975, pp. 236ff.). This hypothesis comes from:

1. *General knowledge about the type of text*—minutes, memoirs, interviews, or dream reports. For instance, we know that minutes report the official actions of a committee and the topics discussed, but say little about the disagreements and unofficial interplay and bargaining preceding the votes.
2. *Specific knowledge about this person or committee.* For instance, we know that unlike U.S. cabinet meetings of the 1950s British meetings of the 1930s involved serious discussion, open factionalism, and at times a check on the power of the foreign secretary. Consequently, we would expect to find a concealed message of factional interplay in British minutes, but expect Eisenhower's televised cabinet meeting to be pure propaganda for a Dulles policy proposal, as indeed it turned out to be. After Dulles's initial speech, there were questions from cabinet members and answers by Dulles. Then there was a short, awkward pause, whereupon Dulles fixed his attention on Agriculture Secretary Benson and said, "You may be wondering . . . ." Benson, startled, immediately responded, "Why, yes, I was wondering just that," and Dulles answered the question. Benson had missed his cue.
3. *Contextual knowledge of the situation reported in the text.* We know the British cabinet factions in 1937–38; Caro knew the participants and

issues in a situation before he questioned Moses about it; an analyst knows an analysand's general problems and methods of coping with them, as well as (usually) the events of the previous day, before he hears the associations to the dream report.

The hermeneutic maxim here is: No knowledge without foreknowledge. That is, we form an expectation about the unknown from what we "know." Our foreknowledge may be mistaken, or partial and misleading, or inapplicable to this text; but in that case the interpretation will run into trouble. If our foreknowledge is weak, we may begin with two or more contrary expectations and see which one works out better, or more likely we will simply fail to see what is going on. Our initial hypothesis, based on foreknowledge, directs our attention to certain passages in the text as the important ones. Thus our foreknowledge of the British cabinet factions, and especially Eden's shift in policy against appeasement of Hitler and his subsequent resignation, directs our attention to Eden's and Halifax's statements and to changes in Eden's line. Chabot begins his interpretation of the Schreber memoirs (Chabot, 1982, chap. 5) with a search for expressions of anger, because he had read that paranoid people are angry.

These passages in turn direct us to other, connected passages. We ask, why and how did Eden change his mind? Did Halifax have doubts too? How did the other participants take sides between Eden and Chamberlain? What were the two lineups and what issues were involved? Or, what was Schreber angry about? Did a common theme link the objects of his anger? Why did he deny or deflect his anger? The passages that answer these questions point in turn to other passages. Or in the Robert Moses interviews the references to particular powerbrokers, McLaughlin or David Rockefeller or Shanahan, lead us on to other people and organizations—the banks, the Democratic machine.

The interpreter eventually fits the particular passages into a connected, coherent story or interpretation. The meaning of each passage comes from its place in the whole story. For instance, Moses had a working relation with the Democratic machine; these were the exchanges and Shanahan was the middleman. This explains why the Triborough Bridge Authority hired certain people as lawyers or consultants; they were part of the Democratic machine, and Moses was paying off the machine. Moses had a working relation with the banks, which bought his bonds at a high interest rate and a fat closing fee, and provided political influence in return. Thus when David Rockefeller, head of Chase Manhattan Bank, gave a speech or made a phone call, we know what that meant. When Triborough money was deposited in Shanahan's bank, we know what that meant.

Some passages in the text do not fit into the story, or raise questions that the interpretation does not answer. Thus Chabot's story says nothing about Schreber's report that God was gradually turning Schreber into a woman, a woman whom He found irresistibly attractive. These passages in the memoirs disconfirm Chabot's interpretation and suggest a revision. A revised hypothesis will suggest other details that need to be found or clarified in the text; or some detail that fits the first hypothesis may not fit the second. Or the two hypotheses may suggest different interpretations of the same phrase. In all such cases of conflict, the interpreter tries to find or produce additional contextual details. The analyst will ask for more free associations to some passage in a dream report; the diplomatic historian will reread the relevant Chamberlain letters to his sister or search for additional texts by other cabinet members; the interviewer will ask Moses or Shapiro or some other participant more questions. The search continues until the available details and the revised general hypothesis fit each other.

This back-and-forth process (Radnitzky calls it "tacking" in the sailboat sense, and Stegmüller calls it "feedback," 1977, chap. 1) is called the *hermeneutic circle*. The initial hypothesis guides the search for and interpretation of details, which in turn revise the hypothesis, which leads to reinterpretation and further search, and so on. In case of conflict, the circle tends to widen farther and farther into the context on the one side and our foreknowledge on the other side.

The widening circle calls into question both hypothesis and details. Textual or contextual details can disconfirm an interpretation of a whole text, but a general interpretation can reject the reading of a particular passage, or can reject a word as a misprint or a careless error by the author. Thus in a dream report "I dislike" could be a misprint for "I like." In this case, the misprint is an intentional disguise of the message; Edelson calls it a "transformation" (1988, pp. 15–16). Similarly, a cabinet minister may quietly alter some damaging word or phrase in an archival document, and the historian has to detect the transformation and restore the original text.

An accumulation of details and of context that rejects successive interpretations calls into question our "foreknowledge," first of this case and then in a more general sense. If we are continually misreading the text, something more basic must be wrong in our approach. Perhaps this analysand only projects certain specific impulses and uses other defenses for others; perhaps Moses had more complex intentions or even quite different motivations in his dealings with Mayor Wagner. But conversely a revised general interpretation may call a whole new context into focus or project a whole new hidden meaning to be filled in with new or revised details.

The goal of interpretation is to produce a reading of the text that fits all important details into a consistent, coherent message, one that fits coherently into the context—the evolution of British foreign policy in 1938, Robert Moses's and New York City's biography, the analysand's life history—and one that is confirmed or consistently enriched by all later facts of this case. (Cf. Rubovits-Seitz, 1986, pp. 21ff.) In one variant hermeneutic theory, there is an additional requirement that the interpretation should reveal the producer of the text to be rational in some sense, since human beings are rational. This rule would not apply to the Chamberlain cabinet, but it would presumably apply to individual cabinet members. Would it apply to Schreber?

Is such a reading of a text true? There is danger of misunderstanding here. The interpreter is not looking for a universal law that is true forever; s/he is looking for the correct interpretation of this text, including both the surface meaning and the deeper meanings. One should therefore ask, is such a reading of this text correct or valid?

If there is a question about the validity of an interpretation, its validity can be checked on both the fact and the hypothesis side. Any particular fact can be checked by seeing whether it appears in other documents about that occasion or other free associations to the same theme by the analysand. The interpretation of a word or phrase can be checked by seeing whether it is consistent with other parts of the hidden meaning. Conversely, we can call our foreknowledge into question if it sometimes produces an expected interpretation that cannot make a coherent message out of the text, in context. To question our own foreknowledge, we must first focus on it and become aware of what we are assuming; then we must devise a different assumption, perhaps one suggested by this case, and see whether it produces better hypotheses. This process does not produce absolute truth, but a validity that can be improved within limits (Schafer, 1976, p. 50).

There are two limits: our ability to find or produce additional texts or nonverbal communications for further testing, and our ability to question our own assumptions and conceive of alternatives. It can happen that new documentary discoveries or new interviewing techniques produce facts that overthrow an accepted interpretation of the Munich agreement or the building of the World Trade Center. Also it can happen that a new theoretical perspective suggests interpretations that open a new range of possible meanings in old texts.

Indeed, the successive overthrow of accepted interpretations is a common experience of historians. The explanations of how World War I started have gone through successive changes in the 1920s, in 1930, in 1942, and the 1960s. The interpretations of the 1920s, such as Bethmann-Hollweg's memoirs, were from a national perspective, and they fixed blame on some other country, portraying one's own decisions as helpless reactions to the pressures of enemies and allies. Schmitt (1930) put these interpretations in a broader context of the events of decades preceding 1914, and tried to interpret each government's response to incoming messages as rational without fixing blame. New archival materials and memoirs enabled Albertini (1942) to produce a somewhat more accurate and detailed account. L.C.F. Turner (1973) added some important corrections, and Fritz Fischer (1967) reopened the old issue of blame by blaming German foreign policy before 1914 for a deliberate move toward war.

Some hermeneutic philosophers such as Apel and Habermas argue that the successive correction of historical interpretations enable us to understand our own past better and better, and by extension to understand our present society as it derives from the past. The maxim is: Each successive understanding is a better understanding. This argument seems too optimistic. Clearly, in 1930 we could understand the intentions and situation facing each of the participants in August 1914 better than any one of them could at the time; and it is fairly clear that our understanding had improved by 1942. But it is not clear how much farther this improvement can go in seventy years, because of the limits that our culture, society, and class impose on possible perspectives, and because of the increasing difficulty of finding new 1914 texts. But Gadamer's maxim, Each successive understanding is different, seems too pessimistic.

The improvement of interpretations is blocked when the historian is unable to imagine a different theoretical perspective. In this case, the historian's foreknowledge is immune to improvement, the range of possible hypotheses is very limited, and only facts can be tested. Interpretation moves only from theory to fact: the hermeneutic circle is broken. The general interpretation of the documents is given, and only the relevant facts are searched out and fitted into the given interpretation. Facts that do not fit are treated as puzzles that "pose the most intriguing questions of interpretation" or as simply unintelligible. Examples are the two monetary histories by Milton Friedman and Anna Schwartz (1963, 1982; cf. Diesing, 1985). In these works, the texts are tables of monetary statistics, minutes of Federal Reserve meetings, letters, and speeches by members of the Fed. The theory is Friedman's version of the quantity theory of money. Since Friedman and Schwartz can imagine no other theory, they impose it on the facts, proudly citing those that fit, adjusting others that do not quite fit, and expressing puzzlement or ignoring others that do not fit at all.

Let us pursue the issue of better understanding with a different example. Consider a text whose meaning is at least as difficult to capture as the meaning of the messages of August 1914: Keynes's *General Theory of Employment, Interest, and Money* (1936). The main problem here is not one of finding a concealed meaning, as in dreams, minutes, diplomatic messages, or memoirs. We can assume, *as a start*, that Keynes tried to express his whole meaning as clearly as he could. Later we may want to assume that he did not know all that he meant or was coming to believe, and we can shift from surface to depth hermeneutics. For instance, we can treat the awkward passages as evidence of an unresolved conflict between old and new in his thinking, a conflict that showed he had not yet worked out the implications of what he was saying.

The first published interpretations were the book reviews (Leontief, 1936; Pigou, 1936; Röpke, 1937; Viner, 1937; etc.) The reviewers ignored Keynes's warning in the preface referring to his long struggle to escape from old ways of thinking; that was Keynes's problem, not theirs. They relied on their understanding of the ordinary short-term equilibrium language Keynes was using. Their preunderstanding of the text was that it was an ordinary essay in economic theory, perhaps an extension of Keynes's 1930 *Treatise on Money*. The argument, however, was puzzling, not ordinary at all, and the conclusion contradicted established economic doctrine and values. The standard language and paradoxical conclusion suggested two general hypotheses about the text: either Keynes was tacitly rejecting some standard assumption such as the flexibility of wages, or he had committed errors of reasoning. The reviewers looked for details fitting these two hypotheses and found support for both. Accordingly, their reviews brought out the tacit unorthodox assumptions and the errors of reasoning as explanations for Keynes's unorthodox conclusion, the possibility of a short-term underemployment equilibrium.

These reviews were worthless as a basis for understanding Keynes's text. As Samuelson later commented (in S. Harris, 1947, p. 146), no one understood Keynes at first. This was an exaggeration, though.

The next published interpretation was Keynes's "General Theory of Employment" (1937), a retrospective understanding of what Keynes's main new ideas had been. He mentioned two: the indirect economic consequences of pervasive uncertainty about the future, and the implications of studying determinants of total demand in a closed system. At least one unpublished interpretation, that of Shackle (1968, xviii), had also focused on the uncertainty theme; Shackle had approached Keynes with the foreknowledge that uncertainty was a crucial unexplored characteristic of a modern economy, and that only works that dealt with uncertainty were really new and important. This foreknowledge sensitized him to the uncertainty theme in Keynes's work; he found it and realized how central it was. However, neither of Keynes's two themes had appeared in the reviews, nor did the reviewers' list of unorthodox assumptions appear in Keynes's self-interpretation.

Joan Robinson's interpretation (1965, pp. 92–94; 1973, pp. 1–8; 1978, pp. ix–xvi) was that of a participant observer. She had participated in the weekly discussions from 1930 to 1935 that produced the *General Theory*, and she traces the gradual change in the group's thinking as a way of leading us to the position Keynes occupied in late 1935. She mentions total demand and uncertainty (Eichner, 1978, p. xi), as Keynes does, but also Kahn's development of the multiplier in 1931; this enabled Keynes to deduce the equilibrium consequences of a change in fiscal policy in a situation where total demand is deficient due to investor uncertainty. Klein (1947) goes over the same ground as an outside observer, a recent convert, and reaches an interpretation similar to Robinson's.

What made these two interpretations superior to the 1936–37 reviews? They came from inside the Keynesian tradition. Robinson's and Klein's foreknowledge was Keynesian theory as of the 1940s, rather than the neoclassical theory of the reviewers. They understood terms like "animal spirits" and "investment multiplier"; they habitually assumed uncertainty and a closed national economy. They could look back and see their own ideas in the text, expressed rather archaically and laboriously. In going over the 1930–35 discussions, they could see their own thinking developing, and thereby come to see more clearly why they thought that way. They were reflecting on and interpreting their own thinking as well as the 1936 text.

They could also interpret the text in its historical context because they were participating in that history. That is, they could differentiate among ideas that were central, new ideas not clearly developed yet in 1936, incidental points and side issues, and ideas or modes of expression carelessly carried over from the past. They could interpret the text as part of a living process rather than as a static, isolated statement.

The same tradition produced a different interpretation in 1936–37 (Young, 1987). The weekly discussion group that Robinson and Kahn attended also at times included Roy Harrod and James Meade, who in 1936 interpreted Keynes's thought in a series of simultaneous short-term equations (Harrod, 1937; Meade, 1937). J. R. Hicks simplified these equations into a single IS-LM model (Hicks, 1937). These writers, however, read Keynes in the context of neoclassical theory. Harrod observed that all the old pieces reappear in Keynes, but in different places. Keynes had made some corrections of the old theory, such as dropping the assumption of short-run flexibility of wages. Meade listed eight conditions for a short-term equilibrium. Both writers missed Keynes's dynamic conception of how money and goods circulate irregularly in a closed economy. They heard Keynes describing conditions for a short-term equilibrium in a static economy; Keynes needed a theory of economic growth, which Harrod supplied in 1939.

Plainly these writers were still in process of moving into the Keynesian tradition in 1936, and were not yet quite familiar with their new surroundings. One cannot criticize them; the tradition did not yet exist, and even Keynes was not yet clear on the implications of what he had done. Remember how unclear Kuhn was in 1962 on what he meant by *paradigm*. A tradition takes time to develop. Later all three writers grew with the growing Keynesian tradition; consider for example Meade's magnificent 1972 summation, *The Controlled Economy*.

In the 1937–67 period, there were many other interpretations from within the growing Keynesian tradition. Each of these brought out one aspect of the book's message as central and expanded on it. Hansen and the "stagnationists" asserted that Keynes's main message was that mature capitalist economies (national economies) tend to stagnate. Kalecki (1939), Samuelson (1947), Tobin (1971) and others brought out the implicit mathematical structure of Keynes's thought, and deduced that a

Keynesian circular-flow system model under uncertainty necessarily fluc-
tuates around a moving equilibrium point. Harrod (1939) and later
Domar asked how these fluctuations that concerned Keynes could be
minimized, and developed the concept of an equilibrium rate of growth,
a rate that would avoid both overheating and subsequent stagnation.
Robinson later saw Keynes's main implicit message as the assertion that a
national capitalist economy can maintain a near-equilibrium rate of
growth only through a continual political redistribution of wealth from
the haves to the have-nots (1951, pp. 108ff.).

In the 1960s many Keynesians such as Modigliani (1984, p. 122),
Tobin (1971), and W. Heller (1967) saw Keynes's central message as the
instability of the British or U.S. economy, and their tendency to adjust
too slowly to disturbances. This implied the need for a government
stabilization policy, both fiscal and monetary. For Heller at his most
optimistic, it also implied the need for continuous monitoring of economic indicators by the Council of Economic Advisors, and rapid, small
countercyclical fiscal or monetary shifts. Finally, Davidson (1978), and
Hyman Minsky (1986) focus on Keynes's treatment of money and banking as his central message. Minsky argues (1986, pp. 100ff., chap. 8, p.
183) that Keynes's essential idea was the interaction of money-creating
financial institutions with investment, production, and consumption to
produce inherent instability. Davidson finds this idea of financial instability foreshadowed in the 1930 *Treatise on Money* and thus finds a continuity between 1930 and 1936, contrary to Robinson, Klein, and Keynes,
who saw a change.

All of these messages, and more, are implicit in the 1936 text. The text
has many meanings, closely related to each other. The development of the
Keynesian tradition consisted of bringing out and expanding these meanings one after the other. The original densely packed text has expanded
into a panorama of meaning. The meanings are not always consistent with
each other; the conflicts among left, right, and center Keynesians bring
out the implicit ambiguities or latent contradictions or different potentialities in Keynes's thought. In this respect, the Keynesian tradition is typical.
"What constitutes a tradition is a conflict of interpretations of that tradition, a conflict which itself has a history susceptible of rival interpretations" (MacIntyre, 1977, p. 460).

The mathematical Keynesians like Kalecki, Klein, and Tobin also
corrected errors in Keynes's text. Keynes, like Marshall before him and
Robinson after him, had little regard for mathematical language in eco-

nomics, and used it mainly as a gesture toward more mathematically inclined readers. He used the mathematical expressions familiar to him, not fully realizing that these static partial equilibrium equations were unsuited for expressing his more dynamic conception of the economy (Leijonhufvud, 1976, pp. 94–96). As Robinson comments (1979, p. xiv): "It was precisely from the concept of equilibrium that Keynes was struggling to escape." These careless partial equilibrium equations probably helped to mislead the reviewers of 1936–37, as well as Harrod and Meade.

About 1967 the interpretation of Keynes's *General Theory* entered a new phase (Leijonhufvud, 1968; Robinson, 1978, chap. 1; Minsky, 1975; Coddington, 1976; Morgan, 1978). These critics felt that some of their fellow Keynesians had strayed too far from Keynes's own thought and had lost central parts of Keynes's message. They were referring to the exponents of the "neoclassical synthesis" such as Samuelson. Joan Robinson calls them "bastard Keynesians." The neoclassical synthesis people were trying to reach an understanding with the monetarists. They hoped to clarify the exact disagreements between Keynesians and monetarists, reduce these to empirical terms, and resolve them by empirical evidence. In order to do this, they used the empirical IS-LM language devised by Hicks in 1937 to explain Keynesian ideas to neoclassicists. IS-LM looked familiar to the neoclassicists: two curves cross, and where they cross, the two factors are in equilibrium. But the variables are Keynesian: one curve deals with total investment and savings, and the other with liquidity preference and money. The IS curve represents those combinations of interest rate and national income at which total investment and savings are in equilibrium, and the LM curve represents those combinations of interest rate and income at which L (money demand) equals M (money supply). IS-LM could deal with such issues as the following: To what extent do interest rate changes effect changes in total investment? What is the distributed lag in the effect of budget changes?

Critics such as Morgan objected that Hicks's IS-LM language was unsuitable for expressing Keynes's own ideas. They observed that Hicks was a neoclassicist when he devised it and repudiated it later after becoming a true Keynesian (Hicks, 1974). The language describes relations in static equilibrium, and thus cannot easily describe the dynamics, the fluctuations and feedback loops, that concerned Keynes. Also the IS curve combines C (consumption) and I (investment), which Keynes distinguished, so that influences from M (money) to I to C cannot be expressed easily. Also the LM curve assumes that the monetary authority determines the quantity of money, while Keynes argued that the quantity varied according to bankers' and borrowers' expectations of profitability (H. Minsky, 1986, pp. 116–19, 131, chap. 10). However, Keynes himself had expressed his agreement with Hicks's 1937 IS-LM article (Blaug, 1976, pp. 161–62, but cf. Robinson, 1979, p. xiv; 1981, p. 79). Consequently, the return-to-Keynes people have to reject Keynes's assent as a polite error that obscures his real meaning. Freudians similarly have to reject some of Freud's tentative, poorly thought out speculations in order to recover his real ideas.

We see here a conflict between two opposed tendencies in a tradition. One tendency is to work out the implications of some central message in the original text: clarify it, correct errors of expression, expand it, enrich it, apply it to new cases and thereby bring it up to date as the legal scholars did with Roman law, and systematize it. The other tendency is to reject all these changes and return to the founder's original message. Both tendencies appear in psychoanalytic theory and recent Marxism. Marxism has expanded into a variety of traditions, each emphasizing some concepts and themes and rejecting or playing down others. We even have "bastard Marxists" now, the analytic Marxists who are trying to clarify and modernize Marx by putting Marxist equations on a foundation of individual rational choice.

For a hermeneutic philosopher, both tendencies are useful. Even after decades of interpretation and theory development there may well be additional neglected meanings in the original message, meanings that can be brought out by careful reconstruction of the founder's thoughts. But the tradition itself has brought out and developed many implicit meanings of the text in all directions, and thus understands it far more thoroughly than the original writer could have. Thus the return to the founder might enrich or even correct the tradition but cannot replace it. In addition, not everyone who says, "Return to the original text!" actually understands the whole original message; I remain skeptical of Leijonhufvud's interpretation.

Conversely, either tendency by itself can easily lead to distortion and loss of meaning. Accommodating a theory to alien ideas, as with the bastard Keynesians (according to Robinson), can lose central concepts and produce a weak hybrid. But staying entirely with the original texts, as with orthodox Marxism, can produce a rigid, sterile dogma and scholastic quarrels over details.

The above paragraphs on Keynes illustrate mainly ideas from Gadamer; the next paragraphs take ideas from Habermas and Apel.

Consider now the successive interpretations of Keynes's *General Theory* by non-Keynesians, and specifically Keynes's opponents the neoclassicists. There has been some improvement in forty years, from the complete misunderstanding of the 1936–37 reviews to a partial understanding of some specific doctrine in the 1940s and 1950s, to a fuller understanding by a few neoclassicists in the 1970s. However, others like Pigou (1952) never did achieve any understanding of the text. Hicks (1939) and Fellner (1946) understood that Keynes's argument dealt with the short run under uncertainty, where many standard neoclassical assumptions were invalid. They decided that Keynes had repeated some unorthodox observations of the neoclassicists Wicksell and Robertson, and added new twists to them (Fellner, 1957). Indeed, Keynes showed that the interrelation of these puzzling short-run phenomena was such as to postpone the arrival of long-run equilibrium for a long time (Patinkin, 1956, chap. 14), though not indefinitely, as Keynes seemed to claim (Viner, 1964). Specifically, in the short run the quantity produced tends to change faster than prices, just the reverse of what occurs in the long run (Leijonhufvud, 1968). Viner (1964) comments that after a long struggle to understand Keynes he thinks he understands and appreciates the work more, and that he recognizes the communication problems that prevented his 1936 review from being adequate. Like Hicks, Fellner, and Patinkin (1956), Viner understands Keynes's theory as a theory of short-run fluctuations that supplements neoclassical theory.

Patinkin similarly comments (1976, p. 83) that after much effort he thinks he finally understands Keynes better, and sees the errors in a 1949 article of his criticizing Keynes: "I . . . can still remember how strange and even difficult it was for me during my later graduate studies to have to learn to think in terms of demand for aggregate output as a whole; . . . it had been thoroughly ingrained into us that the demand function for a good could be defined only under the assumption of ceteris paribus; . . . economists . . . were only willing to speak of the demand function for an unimportant good. . . . How then could one validly speak of a demand function for the aggregate of all goods taken together?" (Patinkin, 1976, p. 83). He also argues that Keynes did not assume wage rigidity, money illusion, or absolute liquidity preference, contrary to earlier neoclassical interpretations. Unlike Viner (1964), he asserts that Keynes's work really was revolutionary.

Thus some neoclassicists could finally, after decades of effort, achieve an understanding comparable to that possessed by Klein, Samuelson, Tobin, Robinson, and the like from the start. Why the difference?

The hermeneutic problem for neoclassicists is different. It is the problem of understanding a text written in a different language, the problem of translation (Habermas, 1967, chap. 8). The 1936 reviewers did not realize this; they thought they were reading a particularly garbled, poorly written text in partial equilibrium equations, the only economic language they knew. (Their experience must have been similar to mine when I once tried to read Husserl's *Cartesian Meditations*. I was utterly baffled.) Later, some neoclassicists like Viner came to realize in some degree that there was a problem of translation, and proceeded more carefully.

Translation is possible because two languages are similar, and necessary because they are different. One begins by moving from the similarities to the differences. Many words in two related languages, say, Danish and Norwegian, are the same. Some will seem the same but actually have different connotations; here the naive translator will err unknowingly. Some are different and will pose an immediate problem. The careful neoclassical reader of Keynes will come up against these different concepts one at a time, and will search for their meaning one at a time, in the context. Then he will translate the word into his own language. But he is still reading Keynes in neoclassical Walrasian or Marshallian terms. As a result, part of the text will be familiar, part will seem familiar but be misunderstood, and individual parts will seem new. Thus the translators of Keynes discovered specific new ideas in him: a model of short-run fluctuations with positive feedback, a claim that the demand for money is unstable, an argument that return to full employment equilibrium is delayed, absolute liquidity preference. These bits and pieces became Keynes's contributions to (neoclassical) economic thought. They missed other specific ideas that translated poorly: "uncertainty" appears in both languages but has very different meanings (compare Keynes with Knight, 1921).[3] "Transactions demand for money" seems pointless to *some* neoclassicists; "multiplier" translates poorly—see Friedman and Meiselman's 1963 attempt—and "animal spirits" does not translate at all. They also missed the meaning as a whole, because the whole meaning into which they fitted these pieces was a neoclassical theory.

There is a similar problem of translating empirical meanings, operational definitions, because of the language difference. Thus Brunner complains, "The meaning of traditional Keynesian theory, on an empirical level beyond formal classroom exercises, remains obscure" (in Hafer, 1986, p. 109). Brunner's language is St. Louis-type reduced-form equations, which he has stoutly defended as essential to any sound scientific method.[4] So he means that it is hard to express Keynesian ideas such as positive feedbacks among fiscal policy, investment, and consumption in a reduced-form equation. But Keynesians have argued that the large structural models, or at least a quite expanded four-quadrant IS-LM diagram, are essential to express the empirical meaning of their theories.

The advanced translator learns to think in the new language and translates the text by whole meanings rather than a word at a time. This is still difficult and will require paraphrases and rearrangement of concepts, but at least the translator will be aware of the problem.

The problem with naive translation is that the hermeneutic circle does not work. The translator's foreknowledge is in his own language, and this is the wrong context for the puzzling individual concepts he has to translate. His preliminary expectations about the text will not fit the text, as in the case of the 1936 reviewers who thought Keynes was trying to clarify some puzzle in neoclassical theory. Hence the expectations will produce mistranslations and a strange, garbled text. Only the advanced translator who can think in Keynesian concepts has the linguistic foreknowledge that will produce adequate hypotheses about the text's meaning.

What is the point of translation? Why should neoclassicists bother to read Keynes (1936), since they will inevitably fail in the attempt to some degree? For example, Robert Lucas sees no point in reading Keynes: "I *don't* like that book. . . . I find it carelessly written . . . sometimes dishonestly written. I don't like the bullying tone. . . . He's got this great idea for solving index number problems. . . . It's a ridiculous idea. What the hell was he thinking about? . . . There's so much arbitrariness in the book" (in Klamer, 1984, pp. 50–51). Obviously, Lucas has missed the message entirely. He has focused on issues of interest to him like index number problems, issues that did not concern Keynes. Also he is the first reader to claim that the book has a bullying tone.

There are three reasons for trying to read Keynes, which however are not conclusive. One is to enrich one's own thinking with Keynes's occasional insights. Languages, Habermas observes, are not sealed off but are porous. They grow by absorbing concepts from other languages. Thus neoclassical theory can grow by adding an occasional Keynesian idea, and vice versa. This has indeed happened in past decades, as Samuelson among others has insisted. A second is to make possible mutually intelligible communication as a basis for discussion and criticism. The two schools of economists can criticize each other's theories and data adjustments and interpretations only insofar as they understand each other. According to Blaug (1980), much progress in mutual understanding has occurred in recent decades. A third possible reason is to move into the Keynesian theoretical tradition and live there, permanently or temporarily. Some may even want to live in both communities, though this is difficult. Understanding, says Gadamer, is knowing your way around a tradition—being able to interpret a text easily, seeing connections to other texts, knowing how to use the ideas found there (1975, p. 231). The person who understands Keynes from inside the tradition no longer has to translate the text.

To sum up the argument this far: an interpretation of a text begins with foreknowledge of the historical situation or context of the text, plus general knowledge of this type of situation, person, committee. This foreknowledge plus a preliminary reading —the table of contents, chapter 1—produces a preunderstanding or hypothesis about the general message of the text. The hypothesis guides the search for the important passages and their construction into a connected argument. The details that do not fit force a revision of the hypothesis, renewed search, and rearrangement of the message. Facts from the context can be called in to test alternate hypotheses, and the revised preunderstandings call for correction of the foreknowledge.

Adequate foreknowledge is important though not indispensable for a valid interpretation. Foreknowledge is more likely to be adequate if the interpreter comes from the same tradition, school, culture, language community as the text author. In this case the interpreter shares the author's way of thinking, perspective, tacit assumptions, problems, and goals. Because this preunderstanding is likely to be not too far off, the interpreter will be sensitive to the small signals that point to tacit assumptions and that make references to context.

The tradition that the author and interpreter share develops through successive interpretations of basic texts that bring out, perhaps exaggerate, implicit or hidden meanings and work out implications. The tradition grows by making ideas and assumptions explicit, working out implications and puzzling over contradictory implications, drawing in parts of other traditions, and adapting ideas to new circumstances. Thus the interpreter, located later in the tradition, can understand an early work better than the author, and better than early interpreters who focus on the new explicit meanings and a few implications. Thus Robinson claims that "Keynes . . . did not see quite clearly what he had been doing till after the book was published" (1979, p. xv).

Interpreters from a different tradition have inadequate or misleading foreknowledge and require great sensitivity and adaptiveness to produce a valid interpretation. Their problem is to translate, or ideally to allow themselves to be socialized into the author's tradition or language community. Socialization involves living through the community from its start by reading the main texts, or interacting patiently with current carriers of the tradition, or both. Unsocialized translators will fit pieces of the text's meaning into a new text they write in their own language by filling in their own tacit assumptions, problems, and ways of drawing implications. An example is my present interpretation of the hermeneutic tradition.

If an interpreter does not recognize a problem of translation, or if his mode of interaction is more projective than internalizing (explained in chapter 10, below), he will project his own way of thinking and assumptions onto the text and produce a misinterpretation.

THE ACTIVE INTERPRETER

The hermeneutic approach does not require detachment or neutrality of the scientist. It requires involvement, even participation in the culture of the author. Indeed, it denies that neutrality is possible. Interpretation is an active process that begins with foreknowledge and is limited to the ideas interpreters can think and the contextual material they can find. Interpreters necessarily bring their own way of thinking to the text, and their interpretations express their experience as well as the meanings implicit in the text. Valid interpretations require an experience that somewhat matches the author's, or else a mode of experiencing that draws in and internalizes others' ideas.

The activity of the interpreter is more visible if we shift from historical to current texts, such as the biographical interview and the dream. To interpret a dream properly, the analyst needs foreknowledge not just of this type of analysand but of this particular person. He gets this particular foreknowledge through long continued interaction in which he allows himself to be drawn into the analysand's world through transference; that is, he learns to play a role the analysand offers him. But the analyst also brings his world to the analysand through countertransference and through teaching the analysand his language (Schafer, 1968, pp. 34–37).

The two construct a common culture in place of a shared tradition, and thereby learn to understand each other. Gadamer calls this process a melting-together (*Verschmelzung*) or fusion of separating horizons—a rather mixed metaphor.

The dream-text is constructed within this common culture, so the analyst's foreknowledge is adequate insofar as he has learned to participate in the culture. However, the language of the dream is in part language he has contributed, so to some extent he gets back his own thoughts in the dream. The meaning of the dream is partly his meaning, and to recognize that part as his contribution he must know himself.

Similarly, in order to prepare for his interviews of Robert Moses, Caro had to immerse himself in New York City politics by living there, reading the political texts of those decades, and interviewing many participants (Caro, 1974, pp. 1167–69). To write his biography of Lyndon Johnson, he moved to Johnson's West Texas boyhood neighborhood, where his wife socialized with the women and they relived the life style of the 1920s. This enabled him to understand Johnson's early political agenda, such as rural electrification (*Michigan Country Lines*, Jan.–Feb. 1984, p. 12). But his socialization into New York City politics was inevitably shaped by his preconception (foreknowledge) of politics, so it opened up some aspects more than others. This slanted socialization reappeared in the questions he asked Moses, Shapiro, and others, so the resulting texts were in part a product of Caro himself. A Marxist would have asked somewhat different questions and filled in a somewhat different politicoeconomic context (see, for example, Lichten, 1986).

The same thing happens in the interpretation of historical texts, though much less noticeably because the texts seem to be located in the fixed past, rather than in the living tradition that includes and fulfills the past (*aufhebung*). The development of the Keynesian tradition was not simply a logical deduction from a model provided by Keynes; each major participant-interpreter contributed creatively to the tradition. For instance, James Tobin's mathematical bent, quite different from Robinson's antimathematical approach and Keynes's haphazard equations, expressed itself in families of Keynesian system models that generalized the implicit logic of the *General Theory*, explored the consequences of alternative postulates, and provided a broader, more flexible Keynesian way of thinking about particular economic conjunctures. Had Tobin's "Yale School" and Klein's Pennsylvania Wharton School never come into existence, the Keynesian tradition and therefore the meaning-for-us, the *significance* in Hirsch's sense (1976, chaps. 1, 5), of Keynes's *General Theory* would have been different.

The active engagement of the interpreter contrasts sharply with the scientific detachment or neutrality postulated by logical empiricists or IL analysts, and this contrast is one source of misunderstanding and disagreement between the two traditions.

THE INTERPRETATION OF CULTURE

Up to here we have been dealing with the interpretation of spoken or written texts. We now extend the argument to the interpretation of actions and expressions (*Objektivationen*) that can be treated as texts. This topic takes us to the practice of the cultural anthropologist or sociologist doing field work, the ethnographer. The main references here are Paul Ricoeur, "The Model of the Text: Meaningful Action Considered as a Text" (1977); Clifford Geertz, *The Interpretation of Cultures* (1973, chap. 1); Jack Douglas, *Investigative Social Research* (1976); and Michael Agar, *Speaking of Ethnography* (1986).

A culturally prescribed action is like a text in that it expresses or means something to or about those who move through it. Like a text, the steps in the sequence contribute to the meaning and to the movement toward completion. Also, as with a text, the actors can provide verbal interpretations of their actions during the process or afterward; that is, they can explain what they are intending to do or what they mean to express. These running interpretations can also serve to patch up breakdowns of coordination among the actors and can supplement the nonverbal cues that normally coordinate the action.

The ethnographer who wishes to study a foreign culture or social milieu must first make contact with the people, then move into the milieu and live there. Like the neoclassicist wishing to understand Keynes, one must be socialized into the milieu or practice to understand it as its members do. This takes time, months and years. During the time of moving in, one is assigned and takes a sequence of roles: stranger or spy, novice or meddler, contact and messenger to the outside world, and eventually friend, member, or even expert. Each of these roles, moving from the outside to the inside of the culture, affords a different view of it; each new role opens a deeper level of meaning.

The cultural practice or "text" first appears to the ethnographer as a more or less puzzling sequence of actions and statements, verbal and nonverbal: a Yucatán farmer beginning spring planting by collecting field stones, piling them up somehow in the middle of the field, laying or spilling some grains of corn on the pile, and kneeling near it—to tie his shoelace perhaps? Or a large manure pile carefully maintained year round in front of the Alpine house—why in front? The sequences contain smaller statements, some of them directed to the ethnographer: a smile, a stare, a stern "That's credit, not money!"—a hurried "I'm going to the bathroom, be right back" (Peter Blau).[5]

Each of the actions and statements means or intends something, and calls for some response, implicitly or explicitly. The larger actions intend some overall result that fits into a larger practice. The small statements mentioned above assign a role to the ethnographer, and the ethnographer's response serves to accept or to shift that role, and therefore affects the future sequence of statements directed to him or her.

One way to discover the meaning of an action or statement is to place it in a context and see how it moves that context toward its completion. Clearing stones from a field or aging manure are part of a technological cycle, a farming practice. But praying at the stone altar also is part of a religious cycle, an act of submission to the deity or nature who makes the crops grow; and the prominent manure pile also is a ceremonial expression of who one is, symbolizing membership in a farming community and asking for recognition.

The ethnographer's preunderstanding of types of contexts—ceremonial, religious, technological, sexual, status-asserting, political—appropriate for this type of culture, suggests contexts to be tried on to understand a puzzling action or statement. Once a context is set up, other actions can be collected to fill in the structure of the context and to correct mistaken preunderstandings of what that context should be like. These corrections in turn improve our understanding of the original action or statement—the hermeneutic circle again.

Another way to discover meanings is to ask informants. "Asking" can range from casual remarks designed to keep someone talking, through comments or questions about events as they come up, to elaborate focused interviews with senior people about how things ought to be done. Still another way is to participate in a practice, making sure someone will correct one's mistakes.

In both these techniques one is eliciting the natives' interpretation of their practice. Thus the ethnographer's account is an interpretation of an interpretation, as Geertz has emphasized (1973, p. 9). These techniques are analogous to asking Keynesians to explain why Keynes used the wage unit as a unit of measurement, and then trying to use it oneself in an argument.

But the natives' interpretation cannot be taken as *the* meaning of an action or statement, for four reasons. First, the informant is never conscious of the full meaning of a practice. Culture is largely carried on as unconscious statements and responses that maintain a shared practice. Consider, for example, nonverbal expressions of class or ethnicity or religion or occupation or homosexuality in our culture. We are aware of some of the signals we constantly send and receive, but not all of them.

Second, the informants' interpretation of their own practice will normally pretty it up: assert honorable intentions, describe an idealized practice, give atypical examples while keeping silent about goof-ups or dishonorable episodes, in order to maintain self-esteem and the esteem of others (cf. Douglas, 1976, pp. 93–103). Similarly, a prime minister's memoirs will give an idealized account of what he or she intended, said, and did.

Third, the informant, treating the ethnographer as novice, may give a superficial, simplified account. Fourth, the informant, treating the ethnographer as outsider or spy, may intentionally give a bland, official version of a dishonorable or illegal practice. For example, an ethnographer studying a massage parlor was told, unanimously by massagers, customers, and the boss, that no sex acts of any kind occurred or were permitted in the parlor (Douglas, 1976, pp. 143–46). In this case the ethnographer was in part being treated as a boyfriend by the massagers; they wanted to maintain a respectable appearance.

For all these reasons the ethnographer must treat informants' statements to a *hermeneutics of suspicion* (Ricoeur's term), that is, to depth hermeneutics. This consists of searching for a covert message that is concealed but also hinted at by the overt message. The overt message is not false; it is the appearance or idealized interpretation of the practice, its outward or public aspect. The hidden message or messages are not the whole message, but only the deeper layers of it. The whole message includes its outward appearance or public face. Thus the evidence for an interpretation includes not only showing how the parts of a message or practice cohere as an intelligible sequence; it also includes showing how the outward layers of meaning conceal but also express the deeper layers. The hermeneutics of suspicion will be discussed more fully in the next section.

Expressed differently, each message, practice, or interpretation is directed to a particular ethnographer's role. If the ethnographer is seen as a spy or boyfriend, he will get one message or practice. The ethnographer as novice or student will get a deeper message or practice; as externalized superego, a still different one; as trusted member of the culture, a still different one; and so on. All messages are part of the cultural practice. Similarly, all participation is participation in a role, so the participant experiences only one aspect of the culture.

This in turn implies that an adequate ethnography usually requires multiple ethnographic roles, either sequential or simultaneous. Male and female ethnographers will experience different aspects of a practice, as will younger and older ones, outsiders and insiders. Nor is one of these roles privileged; the skeptical outsider may see hidden aspects of a practice that the well-socialized insider, trained to share the natives' self-interpretation and self-deception, may miss.

Does the culture have to be a foreign one? No, ethnographers can study their own culture in the same way. In 1930 Lloyd Warner came back from field work in Australia and applied his techniques to the culture and social structure of Newburyport, Massachusetts ("Yankee City"). Soon other ethnographers were studying "Elmtown," "Plainville," "Middletown," "Lakeport." Schneider and Homans (1955) studied American kinship terminology for what it revealed about American family structure.

Here is a new kind of hermeneutics. It produces not knowledge but self-knowledge. When we read Warner's account of the five social strata in "Yankee City" and the practices that maintain the dividing lines between strata, we are sensitized to our own class-typed life style and our treatment of others according to their class. Similarly, when we read the institutional economists' interpretation of our own political economy, we can see the connection between changes in our own work and broader systemic changes; we understand our place in the system better. We understand both the causes of our behavior, the institutional forces that make our work, our life style, our beliefs and values what they are, and the meaning of our behavior, how it unconsciously presents what we are to ourselves and others.

These case studies are suitable for producing self-knowledge because they look at our society or culture from the outside. The foreknowledge of the ethnographer consists of a theory and typology of cultures, based on extensive cross-cultural research. He comes to "Elmtown" with the attitude, "This place is supposed to be one of those. Let's see what that kind looks like up close." Then he lets himself be socialized into the society as though he were a stranger. By forcing himself to be taught again the things he formerly did habitually or unconsciously, he gets a fresh look at them and transmits this in his report. The hermeneutic maxim here is: All self-knowledge is mediated (Radnitzky, 1970, 2:47–48).

Apel and Habermas call this kind of case study "critical social science" or "science with an emancipatory interest." Learning about the causes of our behavior is supposed to give us a certain psychic detachment from those influences, a certain measure of freedom to reject them, or at least a knowledge of what social changes might free us from them—or maintain them. When we read in Galbraith (1973) of how advertising produces wants, our wants, and why advertising is inevitable in our society, or when Edelman (1962) shows us how the symbolism of politics shapes public opinion, our opinion, the awareness of these influences is supposed to partly immunize us against them. Human beings do not yet make their own history, Apel observes (1977), because they are determined by causal processes that evade conscious control. But an emancipatory social science, by bringing the causes into consciousness, can contribute to their eventual control, at least sometimes or in some circumstances.

The present work is an attempt at an emancipatory social science, directed however only at social scientists. (Habermas and Apel would surely disapprove such a narrow aim; they want a broader emancipation. To this I would reply, "The educators must first be educated.") This work assumes that when we read of research by sociologists or psychologists of science (discussed in chapters 6–10, below) we will be able to see ourselves in the reports. When a sociologist shows how socialization expresses itself in a scientist's concepts and loyalties, we should be able to recognize our own socialization into science expressing itself in our thought. Or when a psychologist describes cognitive styles, their strengths and weaknesses, we might be able to recognize our own cognitive style. Then, having somewhat recognized what we are doing, we can try to correct the weaknesses and build on the strengths. That is emancipation.

Habermas's concept of emancipatory science assumes that social causal processes operate differently from causes in physics, sometimes at least (Stockman, 1983, pp. 148, 150). Presumably forces like gravity and radioactive decay are inexorable; we can use them but we cannot change them. But some social forces or at least social regularities might be changed once we become aware of how they constrain our thought and action. Consider for example cognitive processes (see chapter 9). When we read about availability bias or matching bias, we get to recognize ourselves doing that. Then, if we judge that the bias makes us overconfident about our insights and interpretations, we can suspect and discount the hypotheses produced by it, we can deliberately counteract it, we can ask a friendly critic to watch for it in our first drafts.

Or consider science policy (see chapter 8). When we see how current policies of the funding agencies produce a certain kind of research and theory, certain "in" issues for current discussion, certain "generally accepted" knowledge, we get to see how we have been taken in. Science policy works through our "free" choices of what to read, think about, research. Those choices weren't so free, after all. Then we can decide whether to go along, criticize or "bore from within," ignore those topics and try to read and write for a different audience, or possibly get involved in political action to change the policy. That is emancipation, a slow and very limited process.

An emancipatory work such as the present book does not proceed by argument but by description. It does not attack errors of reasoning or interpretation—hidden assumptions, non sequiturs, conflations, contradictions, ambiguities, or conceptual muddles. Such attacks merely bring out a defensive response, and the battle is on. Nor does an emancipatory science argue for a conception of what science ought to be. Rather, it describes scientific episodes or developments or processes in such a way that readers may be able to see something of themselves there. Or, if not themselves, they may be able to recognize others. What they do after that is up to them.

DEPTH HERMENEUTICS AND PSYCHOANALYSIS

We return finally to one of our original examples, the dream report (Erikson, 1964, chap. 2), to consider depth hermeneutics in more detail. The main texts for this section are Paul Ricoeur, *Freud and Philosophy* (1970); Jürgen Habermas, *Knowledge and Human Interests* (1971, chaps. 10, 11) and "Die Universalitätsanspruch der Hermeneutik" (1970); and Gerard Radnitzky, *Contemporary Schools of Metascience* (1970, sec. IV-F-4. See also Winson (1985), who approaches dreams from a neurological information-processing perspective, and who asserts, "Dreams tell things as they are in the unconscious mind" (p. 228); Haskell (1986) surveys current dream research both hermeneutic and nonhermeneutic.

Depth hermeneutics assumes that the surface meaning of the "text" hides, but also expresses, a deeper meaning. It assumes a continuing contradiction between the author's conscious and unconscious mind, a false consciousness, which appears in the text. The author wants to say one thing but also somehow says a different or opposite thing without knowing it; if questioned, the author would deny sending the hidden message or would reject it. Yet the message appears in the text in more or less distorted fashion.

Ricoeur (1970, pp. 32–35) observes that there have been three major theorists of false consciousness and distorted communication: Marx, Nietzsche, and Freud. All three advocated a "hermeneutics of suspicion," a search for the hidden message from the speaker's unconscious. For Marx, a ruling class must deny that it rules; that is, it must propagate and believe a doctrine that asserts our society to be one of universal freedom, while yet justifying institutions that in fact maintain its rule. Thus the Soviet ruling class declares that it represents the idealized vanguard workers in an emerging classless society, to justify its jailing and repressing of actual Polish and Czech workers. For Nietzsche a person's selfish will to power must hide itself behind professions of love, service, impartiality, in order to dominate people without arousing their suspicion. For Freud a person's infantile desires and fears must be hidden behind a front of adult rationality to maintain one's respect and self-esteem, and to avoid punishment.

Two previously cited works provide brief examples of Marx- and Nietzsche-type interpretations of a text before we turn to psychoanalytic interpretation. Keynes's *General Theory* presents a facade of impartial scientific objectivity; yet upon analysis of certain passages, we find that he is actually writing from the perspective of the British Treasury, where he worked as an advisor. The treasury is implicitly presented as rational and farsighted, in contrast to the rather short-sighted, emotional businessman, and as serving the welfare of the whole society impartially. The problems of the British economy are implicitly described as short-run, temporary, and solvable by a rational monetary and fiscal policy—a policy that the British government can institute because it, too, is rational and impartially concerned for the general welfare. This hidden message about government comes along with the overt message about the economy. The contradiction is between the professional social scientist's conscious impartiality and an unconscious identification with the ruling class.

Caro's biography of Robert Moses presents a Nietzschean interpretation of Moses's texts and actions. Moses's official image was that of a selfless public servant who modestly accepted the responsibility of twelve official positions repeatedly pressed on him by successive mayors and governors but who scarcely bothered to pick up his meager paychecks; a master builder and visionary planner who modernized a whole metropolis; a friend of the masses who provided public housing, parks, playgrounds, and roads to get to them. By contrast, Caro's interpretation shows us a man who loved power and was corrupted by it; whose youthful idealism had already expressed his drive for power and who gradually dropped the idealist mask as his power grew; who lived like an emperor at public expense; who forced successive mayors and governors to reappoint him; whose contempt for the masses was expressed again and again—for instance, by ruining a whole neighborhood for no discernible reason; whose planning consisted of going where the money was, so that his constructions and financial planning served the highway lobby and its associated corporations and ruined public transit. (For a Marxist critique of Caro's interpretation, see Alcaly and Mermelstein, 1976, chap. 16.)

Freud's depth hermeneutics differs from the above two examples in that his interpretations are given back to the author of the text. This would of course be pointless in the case of Robert Moses. It is essential to psychoanalysis. If a dream is a "message" from the unconscious, and if the analyst can decode the hidden message, then when he transmits the message back to the analysand the latter learns about himself. He appropriates the meaning that was foreign to him; the unconscious becomes conscious. The purpose of this mediated self-knowledge is gradual self-mastery, control and transformation of the infantile wishes and fears so that the analysand can free himself from their compulsion. "Where *It* was, there shall *I* be" expresses Freud's conception of the aim of his technique.

Psychoanalysis is thus a science with an emancipatory interest. Indeed, according to Habermas (1971), it is the most developed example of such a science, and therefore the most valuable and advanced of all the social sciences, the one others should imitate where possible. However, Gadamer would disagree.

The emancipatory interest and the circumstances associated with it make psychoanalytic interpretation different from other forms of interpretation. As with ethnography and interviewing, the author or participants in the text are present, so it is possible to check the interpretation with them in some fashion. Unlike ethnography and interviewing, one cannot simply ask, "Is that how you do it?" or "Is that what you meant?" because the dreamer does not know what he (it) meant to say. Indeed, the same resistance that forced the dream-message to come out in disguised form would presumably operate to reject the message when the analyst presents it. The author does not want to know about the "it" that is making him miserable, though he does want to be "cured" of his misery.

However, the author can be asked to produce more texts, in the form of free associations to the dream, that serve as context. In addition, the analytic session and the events of the preceding days serve as context. Insofar as the analyst knows the author's recent life history, and insofar as he knows what sort of turmoil was going on that day, he can interpret the characters and events of the dream as an expression of that turmoil.

For another thing, interpretation must be subordinated to the therapeutic aim of analysis (Ricoeur, 1970, pp. 406–10). Therapy consists in dissolving the patient's resistance to self-knowledge. The resistance to interpretation is a continuation of the repression that produced the neurosis in the first place, and the repression occurred because the conflicting demands, prohibitions, desires, and fears were too much for the young child to handle all at once. Consequently, a complete interpretation of all those forces, supposing that the analyst knew what they were, would still be too much to handle. That is why the patient does not want to know about that part of himself; he can't face "it." Therapy consists in working through the fears, prohibitions, etcetera, one by one, cutting them down to size, and accepting them into consciousness. Interpretation should be piecemeal, bringing up just enough unconscious material for the patient to handle but not enough to overwhelm him.

Ricoeur's account of psychoanalytic interpretation has been criticized by Roy Schafer (1983, pp. 240, 234) as out of date. Ricoeur depended heavily on Freud's texts from about 1895 to 1910 and ignored later developments in the psychoanalytic tradition. At that time Freud did believe that therapy consisted in dissolving the resistance and making the unconscious conscious through interpretation. The messages from the unconscious, such as dreams and jokes, were the texts to be interpreted. However, later experience suggested that interpretation and dissolving resistance were not enough (Meissner, 1981, pp. 88–91). The unconscious that persisted into the present was expressed in the patient's infantile ways of relating to other people. To grow up he had to realize how he was relating, but he also had to work out more adult ways to relate. Therapy consisted of the analysand recognizing his past in his present actions and feelings, and also learning more appropriate interpersonal relations. This stage of psychoanalytic theory was called the *object relations theory*, for no good reason (Keller, 1985, pp. 72–73).

The purpose of interpretation in object relations theory is to show the analysand how he is repeating infantile relations in adult life. He is treating someone like a father, mother, older or younger brother; he is transferring infantile dependence, rage, fear, desire, on to some unsuspecting adult. We all transfer relations and feelings learned in childhood on to adult relations all the time (Holland, 1982), but the neurotic does so compulsively, helplessly, and inappropriately. The purpose of interpretation is to help the analysand recognize this unconscious transference so he can correct it. "Rather than bringing the analysand back to his past, the transference allows him to see more clearly the patterns of the past in the present" (Roth, 1987, p. 123).

The most readily available transference is the transference to the analyst. The analysand regularly treats the analyst as though s/he were a father, mother, or even a despised younger brother (Peterfreund, 1983, p. 8). The transference is right there being played out live, so it can be interpreted as it occurs. And since any complex basic relationship contains many contradictory feelings and roles, built up layer on layer over time like the archeologist's prehistoric garbage dumps, these layers can be interpreted as they come up in the analytic context.

The analyst does not even need to speculate about the infantile origin of the present transference, but can wait until the analysand brings up the past by association. Then he can ask questions and make connections. Nor does he look for a particular past event that started the whole trouble, as Freud did in his early therapeutic explorations. The various layers of past relations are all embedded in the present relation—the garbage is still here—so different periods of the past will appear at different stages in the analysis of the transference.

The subject matter of interpretation is now the analytic relation itself, plus the analysand's other current relations. Dreams are incidental. The analysand provides a running narrative telling of the day's events, reactions to them, memories, feelings, and so on. The narrative has a nonverbal context of body language, tone of voice, forgetting. The analyst interprets the narrative in context by bringing out the repeated but not explicitly verbalized themes, the not quite expressed feelings, the omissions that indicate repression. The analysand can agree, or make corrections, or reinterpret the original narrative. Thus analyst and analysand together constitute a community of interpretation (Schafer, 1984).

Over time, the narratives and interpretations construct a history of the analysand's childhood relations, but they also construct a history of the analysis. Each history clarifies the other: the interpreted transferences clarify what is happening in the analysand's current relationships, but the developing analysis brings out new aspects and deeper layers of the childhood history (Schafer, 1983, chap. 13). Here is a new kind of hermeneutic circle.

The object relations theory simplifies the problems of interpretation without giving up the emancipatory aim. For Ricoeur and early Freud, the analyst has to decode the dream all by himself, then withhold the message until the patient is able to handle it bit by bit. This puts the burden of checking the validity of his interpretation entirely on the analyst; if the patient disagrees with the interpretation, that is simply resistance, not disconfirmation. Few analysts can bear this burden; the tendency would rather be to apply preexisting theory to the case, a one-directional interpretation. Peterfreund condemns such interpretations as "stereotyped" and provides several examples (1983, pt. I).

But in the object relations approach, the analyst interprets the ongoing transferred relationship as it is played out. He tries to verbalize the feelings and attitudes that the analysand is expressing right there. The unconscious appears as those feelings and attitudes that the analysand is not quite able to recognize or accept, though they are being expressed or hinted at. Thus the analysand, not the analyst, can check the correctness of an interpretation by attending more carefully to what he is feeling or wanting just then. Of course, he might be wrong, too; he might want to be agreeable or disagreeable just then. A correct interpretation is one that enables the analysand to recognize deeper feelings at the edge of experience—it makes the unconscious conscious—but also enables the analysand to go beyond the interpretation to understand other experiences and remember other buried feelings and desires (Peterfreund, 1983, pp. 205ff.).

This approach to interpretation is similar to the client-centered therapy of Carl Rogers (1961), for whom the ideal interpretation went just a bit beyond the experiences that the patient could already recognize. Rogers's theory is different, however. Also the emphasis on current relations, including the transference relation to the analyst, is similar to the approach of the Chicago psychoanalytic school (Alexander and French, 1946).

If the analysand has to check the validity of an interpretation against his own experience, and if the analysand can use an interpretation to discover and understand new things about himself, then he is a partner in the interpretive process. This is the *therapeutic alliance* (Meissner, 1981, chap. 4; Peterfreund, 1983, chap. 15), which Freud also emphasized in later works.

Each partner brings essential resources to the alliance. The analysand brings the texts to be interpreted and a past to be reconstructed; the analyst brings his interpretive skills. Since the past and the texts belong to the analysand, he has a counterweight to the analyst's prestige (Chabot, 1982, pp. 57–62), and he does not have to accept the analyst's every suggestion.

Ideally, the alliance goes through several stages. First the analysand provides data (texts) by letting his thoughts and feelings come out freely and by learning to verbalize and express his inner life. If there is a dream, he reports that too. Then he learns to test the analyst's interpretations for correctness, to correct the errors, and to use the new self-understanding to explore his own experience and memory further. Finally, he learns to interpret his own actions and his own past as it is repeated in present relationships. At this point, the analyst is no longer necessary; interpretation has become self-interpretation.

Schafer has a second criticism of Ricoeur and of Freud. According to Ricoeur (1970, bk. II, pt. I), Freud correctly vacillated between an energetics and a hermeneutics. The energetics treats man as a *thing*, an animal or even a machine that needs energy to run. The dream apparatus "is man insofar as he *has been* and *remains* a Thing" (Ricoeur, 1970, p. 114). The energy that runs the thing is the drives or libido that pushes toward pleasure, gets diverted into the ego's tasks of resisting danger, gets tied up in relations to people, gets dammed up and breaks loose, gets sublimated or secondary-reinforced into art and work. The hermeneutics treats man as a social being who acts purposefully, communicates meanings, understands and misunderstands. The energetics treats man as determined by physiological forces; the hermeneutics treats man as free and rational. Both views are correct, though they contradict each other; therefore, Freud correctly vacillated between them.

The two sides of man join in dreams. "Dreams, inasmuch as they are the expression of wishes, lie at the intersection of meaning and force" (Ricoeur, 1970, p. 91). That is, the dream appears as a text, as words with meanings; but the meanings have been put there by a primary mental process which converts energy into a symbol. The dream speaks of desire; but desire is a psychic expression of hormones and brain chemicals like phenylethylamine. Dreams are messages from the unconscious; but the unconscious is a thing, the body, energy. In the dream "it speaks" (Ricoeur, 1970, p. 433).

Schafer rejects this interpretation of the It (1983, p. 234; 1976, chap. 5). He agrees rather with Habermas (1971, chap. 11), who argues that Freud's whole metapsychology of energy discharge, stimulation, damming up, and running out was simply a self-misunderstanding. Freud thought he was doing natural science and that neuroses would eventually be explained by laws of physiology and chemistry, but in his actual clinical practice he was doing hermeneutics. Similarly, Schafer argues that if we stick to actual clinical practice all we encounter are texts, narratives with meanings, and the texts tell us of actions conscious and unconscious, not forces and energies. The language of forces and determinism is the analysand's way of disclaiming responsibility for his own actions (Schafer, 1976, chap. 7). For instance, "a slip of the tongue" or a "Freudian slip" suggests that my tongue is making trouble; but actually I spoke, not It. "It escaped my mind" suggests that the embarrassing memory slipped out the window and got away despite my efforts to keep it locked up; but actually I forgot. "Conflicted," "inhibited," "overwhelming urge to" suggest forces that push me around; but actually *I* want, *I* fear, *I* want to, though I think I shouldn't.

From this perspective, the Id is something I create to shove off responsibility for my actions. (See Habermas, 1971, chap. 10, esp. p. 258: "the ego objectivates itself in the id.") I create my "instincts" by repression, by excommunication from conscious social life. They are "intentions that have turned from motives into causes." Thus instincts and the id are a kind of deformed language, not psychic forces. One goal of analysis is to enable the analysand to recognize himself, his childish self, in his actions and transferences. "Interpretation brings home to the analysand the extent to which and the terms in which the analysand has been the author of his or her own life, unconscious and preconscious and conscious; and how the analysand has been disclaiming this activity" (Schafer, 1976, p. 8). Freud's epigram, "What was *it* shall become *I*," really means that we learn to use *I*-language instead of the *it*-language of forces and urges as we come to take responsibility for our actions. Once we recognize that these infantile fears and rages and prohibitions and desire and jealousies are our own inappropriate actions, we can learn painfully to give them up, adapt them to the adult world, or at least live with them.

Gilligan provides an example of the shift from *it*-language to *I*-language (1982, pp. 116–23): "As Sarah describes her feeling of being in control, her pronouns shift from *it* to *I*, marking the end of the time of just drifting along" (p. 122). Previously, she says, her decisions "were based elsewhere . . . it was coming from somewhere else." "The reality that this is a baby just sort of dumped me out on my head." "Wow, there it is, panorama, you cannot hide from it anymore." Gradually, she takes responsibility for her own pregnancy: "I think it was very nearly a conscious decision to get pregnant. I was thinking about kids a lot. . . . It was something I really wanted to do. . . . I had done a pretty good job [of fooling myself] for a couple of years. . . . I really did want to get pregnant." "I see the way I am and watch the way I make choices."

(The reader may by now have noticed a typical hermeneutic problem of translation: what is the proper translation of Freud's "*das Es*"? Technically, as "the id"? Literally, as "the it"? Or simply "it"? These three translations and their associated differences of meaning come from three variant developments in the psychoanalytic tradition. Similarly for translation of Freud's "*Was Es war soll Ich werden.*")

Kovel (1978) disagrees with Habermas and with Schafer's second criticism and agrees with Ricoeur. Mankind is a unity of contradictory opposites, a unity of nature and culture. We begin as nature, as cells, as organisms with needs. The needs for food, family, symbolization, sex, contact are our nature that stays with us and determines our actions. Out of nature comes personhood. Our self or personality is socially constituted and maintained, beginning with the mother-child relationship and constituted by language and by culture, but it also expresses our nature, the needs that must somehow be satisfied.

Our unconscious, the nature that continues in us, is taken into the self, made conscious and known, through symbolization and self-reflection; but it can never be entirely known. Our needs are socialized, transformed, sublimated; but they must still be satisfied somehow. In analytic discourse, in dreams, in self-reflection, we transform energy into meaning; but the energy remains biological.

Nature is what comes before and is overcome, humanized, by human activity. Nature is the past, our infancy and before, that continues in our *seemingly* rational, purposive actions. Through work we transform nature, the ecosystem, to adapt it to our cultural goals and ideals; but the laws of the ecosystem limit our efforts. Insofar as we destroy the ecosystem, we destroy ourselves.

Freud's genius, according to Kovel, lay in recognizing the man-nature tension and maintaining it in his ambivalent theorizing.

Similarly, Spiro (1979) argues that Schafer's existentialist emphasis on taking responsibility for our own acts exaggerates our freedom. Schafer expresses the worthy ideal of self-determination, but in fact not all our mental functionings are under conscious control. We are in part physiologically determined. The id is only in part an evaded responsibility; in part it is the nature that continues in us.

Both interpretations agree that psychoanalysis is an emancipatory science, though they disagree on the meaning of *unconscious mind*. For people like Schafer, the unconscious is what has been excommunicated from social life, repressed, and therefore it can be brought back into communication by depth hermeneutics. For people like Kovel and Ricoeur, the unconscious is in part nature, the human being as a thing, it. Depth hermeneutics can make us aware of the nature in us, give it names and therefore meaning, but it continues in us as our nature. We are both person and organism, indivisibly.

RELATION TO OTHER
PHILOSOPHIES OF SCIENCE

Hermeneutics and Logical Empiricism

The hermeneutic philosophers see themselves as the polar opposite of the logical empiricists, and use that contrast to clarify their own position. One general attitude is that logical empiricism is the correct philosophy for natural science while hermeneutics is appropriate to the cultural sciences. Logical empiricism deals with the science of things, while hermeneutics deals with the sciences of human beings, including communication, symbolization, action, culture.

The OL (ordinary language) analysts have made a very similar distinction between natural and social science. Natural science deals with causes; social science deals with reasons. Natural objects move or change in a lawlike manner; human beings, being rational, act according to reasons. The result was an IL-OL debate over whether causes and reasons are the same or different, and whether natural and social science are the same or different.

Alas! The hermeneutic philosophers have been conned (and many social scientists as well). The logical empiricists knew no more about natural science than they did about social science. They were not

Kuhnians or pragmatists, studying actual scientific history or practice; they were logicians, whose aim was to specify what any study must necessarily be like to be science at all. When they referred to selected scientific episodes, they used the episodes as illustrations of their logic, and as rhetoric to persuade the reader that their logic was indeed the logic of science. Some frequently cited episodes—the Copenhagen interpretation and Azande witchcraft—served as stereotyped bones of contention in disputes. The bones had been stripped of all scientific context.

But we can look at other scientific episodes that give a different picture. If an ethologist goes to live with a tribe of chimpanzees, learns their ways, learns their gestures and signals, and joins in their games, or if a psychologist teaches a gorilla sign language and holds conversations with it (her?), is that natural science or social science? The subjects are not human but the methods are hermeneutic. Conversely, a Wolpe-type behavior modifier can apply electric shocks or other stimuli according to schedule with the aim of producing a statistically observable change in the output of the organism; what kind of science is that?

Or consider the theory of plate tectonics in geology. The theory is not a set of laws, because it deals with one object, the earth. It is a history which explains the present configuration of the earth's surface and predicts earthquakes and volcanic eruptions. Or consider medicine, the natural science background of both Ludwik Fleck and Freud (Fleck, 1983, intro.). In medicine, unlike chemistry, the interest is in the unique, complex, and abnormal. Consequently, the medical practicioner works with types, not laws; there are types of diseases and variations within each type. The medical scientist is necessarily historicist, since a disease has a time path, and recognizing it includes locating its present point on a partly typical, partly unique time path. In these respects psychoanalytic therapy, as described for example by Peterfreund (1986) is medical and therefore natural science.

Let us therefore set aside the old argument of whether the natural and social sciences are the same or different; there is too much variation in both natural and social sciences to make any meaningful answer possible. We can then reformulate the opposition between IL analytic philosophers and hermeneutic philosophers in more fruitful ways. Apel and Habermas have produced one such reformulation since 1965. Logical empiricism, they assert, is appropriate to any science or method whose implicit goal is to find causal or statistical laws that enable us to control something. Prediction and deductive explanation are corollaries of control. Hermeneutics is appropriate in any science whose implicit goal is to improve communication and mutual understanding; a corollary goal is to facilitate joint action, or in general living together. Then there is a third kind of science typified by psychoanalysis; its goal is emancipatory. Emancipation is achieved through self-knowledge of the causes that determine one's consciousness and behavior. This science includes both causal or statistical laws and interpretive techniques that reveal the hidden operation of the causes (Habermas, 1971, appendix).

Since the classification is abstract, actual disciplines like psychology can fall into two or three of the classes, and in general the social sciences exemplify all three kinds of science. The classification is an example of the Kantian dialectic. That is, it is a static classification that avoids any contradiction or conflict between thesis and antithesis; they are just opposite. This means that logical empiricism can be correct in its domain and hermeneutics can be equally correct in its domain. However, Apel observes, the domain of logical empiricism cannot simply be the natural sciences plus parts of the social sciences. Natural science is practiced by a community of scientists who must understand each other to continue their work; but their understanding is continually broken by scientific advance, with its new concepts and even revolutions. Consequently, hermeneutic techniques are essential even in the natural sciences, in the interpretation of scientific texts (Apel, 1970, 1977, 1980, chap. 5).

Another reformulation is provided by the old nomothetic-idiographic distinction. IL analytic philosophers think of science as general laws, and treat explanations as deductions from those laws. Hermeneutic techniques produce an understanding of particulars: particular texts, persons, histories, cultures; and treat explanation as laying out the structure of the particular and its context. For example, Harré (1978) argues that the proper use of statistics is to select the typical member of a set of people, towns, organizations, groups, etcetera, for intensive hermeneutic study. Then, having found the detailed structure of the case, one can try to generalize to other instances of that type.

Still another position is to reject logical empiricism for any kind of science (Gadamer, 1989). Scientists always approach their subject matter with some kind of foreknowledge or preunderstanding, which they use to interpret the experienced world. There are no given facts, no protocol sentences; our data result from an interpretation (pp. 29–30). Thus even in natural science there is a sort of hermeneutic circle, though no texts or meanings are involved and though *understanding* would have a quite different connotation. Gadamer's suggestion is strongly supported by recent developments in cognitive psychology (see chapter 9, below).

Logical Empiricism and Hermeneutics

The treatment of hermeneutics by logical empiricists falls into two categories: ignorance and misunderstanding. For several decades hermeneutics was known as the doctrine of *Verstehen*, which said that a researcher could by empathy get direct access and direct knowledge of someone else's motives. The invalidity of *Verstehen* was conclusively exposed by Abel in a 1946 article that was regularly cited by logical empiricists and IL analysts for decades thereafter. Abel observed that the direct access to another mind was a delusion; the empathy stayed in one's own mind. Therefore all one could get by empathy was a hunch, not knowledge. Such hunches could be generalized into hypotheses and then tested experimentally or statistically against observable events, to get confirmed knowledge. Murray Wax (1967) argues that that's not what Weber meant by *Verstehen*. He asserts that Weber's *Verstehen* was a form of pattern explanation and interpretation, and cites his *Protestant Ethic and the Spirit of Capitalism* as an example. Abel in his reply to Wax expresses regret that his article was misread as a criticism of *Verstehen*, but repeats his assertion that the technique can be used only as a source of hypotheses to be tested by quantitative methods.

More seriously, Abel's caricature of *Verstehen* has no similarity to hermeneutics, as Stockman (1983, p. 147) and others have pointed out. Abel remained confined within the positivist categories as of 1946: sense data or observable data come from the external world, hypotheses come from us, and scientific method consists of comparing the two. Thus empathy must be either an illegitimate source of weird sense data, or a legitimate source of hypotheses. But hermeneutics depends essentially on communication, verbal and nonverbal, made possible by a shared language, shared tradition, shared cultural practices, and translation. Our foreknowledge and preunderstanding which we bring to the text or practice, our empathy, also comes from shared traditions and practices, not from a personal intuition. Thus the distinction between a private self and an external world is completely foreign to hermeneutics (cf. also Apel, 1977, p. 305).

More recently a few surviving IL analysts seem to have actually read some hermeneutic texts and misunderstood them, much as the 1936 reviewers misunderstood Keynes's text by reading it within their theoretical framework. Thus Rubinstein (1983, p. 117) asserts that for hermeneutics in its extreme form confirmation is not necessary; all interpretations are equally good if they fit the text. Hermeneutic truth is a function of perspective, and since there are many perspectives there can be many true interpretations. An interpretation is "merely a way of organizing the data, perhaps only one of several possible ways, a hermeneutic exercise without necessary existential implications" (Rubinstein, 1980, p. 11). Eagle (1983, n. 5) similarly asserts that in hermeneutics truth is irrelevant, and all interpretations are equally valid.

This misreading brings out the contrast between the IL-influenced psychologist's conception of an impersonal hypothesis-testing process and the hermeneuticist emphasis on the interpreter's personal involvement in the hermeneutic circle. For the analytic psychologist or philosopher, the ideal truth is impersonal, and the mundane scientist's inevitable personal involvement in his research is a defect that should be reduced as far as possible. For the hermeneuticist the clinician's personal involvement is a resource to be used to discover the hidden meanings of the "text" before him. The analytic philosopher has an ideal of a single best truth that is the same for all; everything that falls short of this truth is false. The hermeneutic philosopher has a conception of multiple complementary truths about a complex practice or text. Each role in a practice, each location in a textual tradition affords a somewhat different interpretation, some deeper than others but none irrelevant (cf. Rorty, 1979, pp. 373–74).

Both approaches suggest rules for discovery, testing, and revision, but the two sets of rules are different. The validity of an interpretation can be increased (1) through the many checks occurring in the hermeneutic circle, and (2) through the correction of perspectives during the development of a tradition; but we never arrive at the one absolute truth.

Hermeneutics and OL Analysis

Many OL analysts, such as those represented by Harré and Secord (1972), are in broad general agreement with the variant of hermeneutics presented in this chapter (Apel, 1981). As Apel observes, the two traditions have come together from different starting points. The hermeneutics people have moved from how to interpret texts to an emphasis on shared tradition as the basis of interpretation to a focus on ordinary language as the shared basis of communication. Some OL people have moved from semantic puzzles, represented in the 1950s by articles on the meaning of "the," "=," and "that sounds odd"—the Austin-type analysts—to an interest in forms of life, cultures, and a philosophy of communication. Therefore, both groups are now focusing on ordinary language as the primary basis of communication, and both groups treat the social sciences as properly the study of intentional, rule-governed communication rather than the search for transhistorical laws of human behavior.

Hermeneutics and Karl Popper

The relation to Popper is more complex. Popper's grand system building has extended to the field of interpretation, and he has developed his own hermeneutic theory (1972, chap. 4). According to Popper, we understand an action by assuming it is rational and then reconstructing the situation to which it is a rational response. He calls this *situational analysis*. This is a narrow formula because it applies only to deliberate individual action. It does not apply to texts or to social constructions like ceremonies and cultures. The reason for this narrowness is Popper's methodological individualism, his insistence that all social action must be reduced to individual action. Radnitzky (1970, pp. 140–41) incorporates a Habermas-Apel hermeneutic theory into a generally Popperian philosophy of science, and criticizes Popper's own hermeneutics as too narrow. Blight (1981) criticizes Popper's ignorant diatribes against psychoanalysis and argues that Popper and Freud actually had much in common. He argues that Popper's evolutionary epistemology and hermeneutics is the proper framework for psychoanalytic theory. On the hermeneuticist side several people have incorporated Popperian ideas. Bauman (1978, chap. 10) proposes that Popper's philosophy is the proper one for natural science and the natural-science kind of social science, since logical empiricism is dead. E. D. Hirsch (1976, chap. 2) argues that the hermeneutic circle is really a version of Popper's conjecture-and-refutation sequence.

These various amalgamations suggest that Popperian and hermeneutic philosophies of science are compatible in various ways, especially if Popper's dogmatic assertions about psychoanalysis, historicism, and methodological individualism are discarded.

Hermeneutics and Pragmatism

Habermas (1967, pt. III) asserts that Kaplan's pragmatic approach is so liberal and tolerant that it can recognize the hermeneutic practice that actually occurs in the social sciences. Pragmatism is thus the gate that can open up the study of hermeneutics for Americans, after positivism had walled it off as irrelevant to science. However, the same close involvement in scientific practice that enables pragmatists to study actual interpretive techniques prevents them from understanding the full hermeneutic program, which goes well beyond practice. Thus Kaplan recognizes that social scientists study both meanings and causes, but does not make a fuss over the distinction; they study all sorts of things in all sorts of ways and get into all sorts of troubles.

I believe this judgment is correct. I was surprised to learn in 1970 that I had been practicing hermeneutics all along in interpreting scientific texts and cultures (Diesing, 1971, p. 318); I thought I was doing a loose kind of participant observation (ibid., chap. 21). A good ethnographer of science studies everything available: texts, lab apparatus, game theory, computer modeling in Fortran, chance remarks about values, socialization techniques, expressions of deference and condescension, citation networks, data quality control, the process of organizing a research project, questionnaire construction, whatever. When meanings show up, one studies them too, along with the ways others study them—content analysis, semantic differential, hermeneutic circle. . . . In writing this chapter, I have probably confused hermeneutic techniques with my experience of writing a historical case study or with anthropological reports of experiences in the field, despite my attempt to keep them distinct. As for the larger hermeneutic project, I have not once in this chapter managed to use the word *transcendental*, as in *transcendental hermeneutics*, *transcendentalpragmatic*, *transcendentalphilosophical*, *speech transcendental rules*. I have not yet managed to sort out the many meanings and connotations of this term and others like it, which the true hermeneuticist finds essential for expressing his deeper thoughts. Those seeking to understand the full hermeneutic theory will have to go to the originals, where they will for instance learn to distinguish among *Verdinglichung*, *Vergegenständlichung*, *Objektivierung*, and *Objektivation*, all loosely translatable as "objectification."

Another partial disagreement between hermeneutics and pragmatism is about method. Hermeneutic philosophers tend to favor participant observation and clinical interaction in the study of contemporary cultures, societies, groups, and individuals (see, for example Bleicher, 1982, chap. 8). In participant observation and related methods, the observer becomes part of his subject matter and experiences it from the inside as well as from the outside. This is analogous to the textual interpretation process in which the interpreter should become or be part of the tradition in which his text is located. In both cases participation in the tradition or the culture or group provides the proper foreknowledge and preunderstanding of a text or practice. This preunderstanding enables the ethnographer or clinician to construct an adequate interpretation of a subject and to test the interpretation in practice. "Sociological theories are interpretations of social reality developed in the successive clarifications of pre-understood meanings in contact with an object that can answer back and endorse or reject proffered accounts" (Bleicher, 1982, p. 141).

I welcome this appreciation of participant observation, since the latter is, after all, my own favorite method. But I have failed to find an appreciation of the serious weaknesses and shortcomings of case study methods. The involvement of the ethnographer or clinician in a case makes it too easy to project one's own preunderstandings into the case and find "objective" justification for them. In clinical interviews especially, the authority of the analyst is sometimes difficult to withstand, allowing him to project his ideas into the patient's thinking and get them back as supporting evidence. In political case studies and monetary histories, a selective search for data can easily produce propaganda disguised as historical interpretation. Methodologists are aware of these weaknesses and recommend supplementary use of quantitative statistical and experimental techniques to check details of an interpretation where possible. More fundamentally, hermeneutic techniques work best when the researcher has no power over the people he is studying. Their power over him allows the hermeneutic circle to work—that is, it prevents him from imposing his preunderstanding on the case.

The hermeneutic sociologist is rightly very skeptical of aggregate data; he observes that quantitative measurement is based on a preunderstanding of shared meanings or on the preunderstanding of agencies interested in social control, and quantification converts these meanings to numbers, thereby hiding the bureaucratic bias (Cicourel, 1964). Pragmatists have made the same point, showing how U.S. census data are produced to fit various theoretical and bureaucratic specifications (Mitroff et al., 1983). But aggregate data, while defective and misleading for the unwary, are no worse than clinical or interview data. Control is also possible in a clinical context, and participant observation of a society's underdogs can also be used by those in power for control purposes, as Gouldner has observed. No method is foolproof, and all can be misused by those in power.

SOCIAL SCIENCE
STUDIES ITSELF

6

Macrosociology of Social Science

Science is an activity of human beings acting and interacting, thus a social activity. Its knowledge, its statements, its techniques have been created by human beings and developed, nurtured, and shared among groups of human beings. Scientific knowledge is therefore fundamentally social knowledge. As a social activity, science is clearly a product of a history and of processes which occurred in time and in place and involved human actors. These actors had lives not only in science, but in the wider societies of which they were members.

—*Everett Mendelsohn (1977, pp. 3–4)*

THE MERTONIAN PARADIGM

THE MODERN macrosociology of science begins with the work of Robert Merton in the 1930s. The evidence for the above statement consists of citation counts of journal articles (Cole and Zuckerman, 1975), reports of informants (Storer, 1973, esp. p. xi), and acknowledgments and tracing of ideas in leading works such as Hagstrom (1965). Many sociologists of science since 1960 were Merton's students or students of students (Cole and Zuckerman, 1975, p. 155), and others took up and developed some of his ideas, for instance, Blissett (1972) and Mitroff (1974a). When the Society for Social Studies of Science (4S) was founded in 1975, Merton was invited to be its first president.

Merton's first work, his Ph.D. thesis, was a study of the institutionalization of science in seventeenth-century England. This was an "externalist" history of science; that is, it argued for the interdependence of science and extrascientific factors, both ideal and material: Puritan values and economic and military needs and resources. His later sociological work was internalist, ignoring the effects of society on science; Karl Mannheim's 1929 work, *Ideology and Utopia*, was externalist, tracing the effects of class membership on the ideas and thought patterns of scientists, and reflecting on the implications for the nature of knowledge.

149

Thus Merton's work contributed to a shift from the pre-1940 externalist sociology of science to later internalism.

The Mertonian paradigm for sociology of science was developed between 1938 and 1957 (Storer, 1973), and thereafter Merton and his disciples used it in their empirical studies. *Paradigm* is used here not in Kuhn's sense of an exemplary empirical study that is imitated in later empirical work. It is used in Merton's sense of a set of systematically related ideas, categories, and propositions that is used to suggest empirical research topics and to interpret data.

Merton's paradigm is a theory of the social characteristics of Kuhn's *normal science*. The ideas of the two theorists are very similar. Merton called Kuhn's book "merely brilliant" (Cole and Zuckerman, 1975, p. 159; Merton, 1977, p. 105), and devoted thirty-eight pages of his 1977 memoir to Kuhn, compared to three pages for Popper. There are numerous positive references to Kuhn in the writings of Merton's followers, far more than the references to the next most frequently cited authors: Imre Lakatos and Abraham Kaplan.

Merton's paradigm is functionalist; it is a theory of the structural characteristics that are needed for a scientific community to maintain itself, and what happens when these characteristics are not adequately present. For a Parsonian functionalist these are naturally among the fundamental facts to be known about any social institution. One conceives of society as an interaction among a small set of institutions, each with its own proper goal: the goal of the economy is to mediate between society and natural resources to produce goods and services, the goal of families is to socialize new members, the goal of the polity is to maintain the system, and the goal of science is truth. Each goal derives from the various things a society needs to maintain itself. Each institution has its own proper values that direct it to its own goal and that maintain its autonomy from other institutions. Also each institution has its own structure of relations that hopefully operates to produce the needed results. A structural deficiency, or interference by other institutions, weakens the productive process and leads to deficient results, and this deficiency puts a strain on other institutions as well. All existing societies undoubtedly have deficiencies and strains, but they must also be doing something right or they would disappear.

Mertonian functionalism differs from that of Parsons on a few points. For one thing, Merton elsewhere (1949, chap. 1) emphasizes the possibility of functional alternatives, that is, the possibility that a society or institution can maintain itself in more than one way. In other words, a particular characteristic may be sufficient but not necessary for self-maintenance. For example, Merton asserts that though Puritan values in fact contributed to the development of science in seventeenth-century England, other values may have had the same effect had there been no Puritanism (1973, p. 192). However, Merton's later paradigm does not specify possible functional alternatives for contemporary science. Second, Merton emphasizes functional and structural conflict somewhat more than Parsons does (Merton, 1976, pp. 126-32). A process may be functional for one institution and simultaneously dysfunctional for another, and a process that solves one functional problem will normally make another functional problem worse. Structural conflict normally exists within roles, between norms and counternorms of a role, between roles within a status, between statuses of a status set, between normatively permitted goals and means (Merton, 1976, chap. 1). Merton asserted that his functionalism combines Marx and Durkheim, while his teacher Parsons's functionalism is straight Durkheim (pp. 126–29). In Merton's first book (1949) Durkheim is cited most frequently and Marx second.

The difference, however, is not that Merton recognized social conflict and Parsons did not. It is rather that Parsons transformed empirical conflict into analytical conflict between categories in his theory. Where Merton posited conflicting norms within a role, conflicts that could deeply disturb and disorient a person, Parsons described conflicts between the proper values of two different institutions. Thus the values of a family should be particularist-ascriptive while the values of an economy should be universalist-achievement, and mediating processes were functionally necessary to manage this conflict. However, by *family* Parsons meant *L-subsystem*, which included all activities that helped perform the L-function, and not a concrete family. A concrete family participated in all four subsystems, though mainly the L-subsystem. Similarly, *the economy* did not mean a particular tavern, which could be performing primarily L and I functions, plus a little A and G, but rather anything that contributed to the A-function. Consequently, a paralyzing conflict between ascriptive and achievement values in an individual becomes a conflict between A and L subsystems. Also when Parsons discussed particular groupings he focused on the mediating processes that buffered conflict: phase movement and dual leadership in families and small groups, and hierarchical levels in formal organizations. For Merton, however, *society* meant particular communities, and the conflicts were empirically in those communities.

Third, while Parsons, rhetorically at least, hailed the growth of a single sociological paradigm—his own—Merton called for a plurality of paradigms in sociology (1976, pp. 129–43).

For both Merton and Parsons a scientific community (that is, contemporary science) maintains itself insofar as it solves two functional problems: an internal one and an external one. Internally, any community is a unity of differences or of opposites, an organic unity, as Durkheim called it. Differences are needed for the division of labor involved in carrying out the community's actions; unity is needed to coordinate the actions. Externally, the scientific community is an interdependent part of society that yet must maintain some autonomy. It must be interdependent because the larger society provides the resources and uses the products of scientific activity; but it must be autonomous because its goal, truth, is different from the goals of other institutions. Too much autonomy would lead to stagnation because of declining resources, and perhaps aimlessness because the product would not be used by anybody; too little autonomy would turn scientists into propagandists, politicians, businessmen, industrial engineers, or thrust them into some other extrascientific role.

The scientific community solves its internal problem, unity in difference, by its shared values. Presumably all communities are united in part by shared values, but the values of the scientific community must be those that direct scientists to their proper goal. Merton asserted in 1942 that scientists in fact share four basic values: universalism, communism, disinterestedness, and organized skepticism (1973, chap. 13). Merton claimed to find these values in statements by leading scientists, in expressions of approval and disapproval, and especially in expressions of moral indignation.

Universalism is the norm that truth claims ought to be judged according to pre-established impersonal criteria, not by the personal or social attributes of the claimer. The opposite value, particularism, asserts that people of a particular race, or class, or gender, or at a particular university or research group, have special access to the truth or to some truth, so that personal characteristics of the claimer are relevant to judging a truth claim. Universalism rejects distinctions among scientists and thus includes them all within the same community, while particularism divides them by nationality, school, age cohort, or some other category.

Communism is the norm affirming that the products of science belong to the whole community since they have been socially produced. A corollary is that scientists ought to publish their findings and share them in other ways. The opposite value, private property in ideas, is also accepted to the extent that scientists are given recognition and esteem for their achievements. But when scientists keep their research secret, as with classified research, that retards scientific work by preventing others from building on the secret achievements.

Disinterestedness means that scientists ought not promote their own ideas ahead of others' ideas, but should promote and use all relevant ideas impartially. This value follows from the first two, which assert that all truth claims should be treated equally and impartially. The opposite value, interestedness, would enjoin journal editors to publish certain ideas and authors and reject others, enjoin teachers to glorify their own ideas and ridicule and distort others' ideas, encourage advertising and rhetoric. Merton does not assert that scientists never push their own ideas; he is asserting that it is wrong to do so, and if everyone did it there would be no collaboration, no scientific community.

Organized skepticism means that nothing—no beliefs, facts, values, techniques, practices—should be immune to questioning and doubt. Nothing is sacred. This value, however, should apply only within science; the scientist as citizen may be emotionally committed to religious, political, or economic values (1973, pp. 264–65).

A fifth norm, added later, was ethical neutrality toward one's subject matter (Elkana, 1976). Approval or disapproval of the people or behavior one is studying would bias the scientist toward finding characteristics that fit a personal ethical attitude. As a result, scientists with different attitudes would produce different interpretations of a topic, all of them biased, and science would be fragmented along ethical lines.

Examination of these values reveals immediately that any science founded on them will inevitably come into conflict with society. All societies cherish some sacred elements, religious or otherwise, and there is always the danger or suspicion that the scientist's habitual skepticism will spill over into social iconoclasm. Consequently, Merton observes, there has been hostility to science from the seventeenth century on because of its apparent questioning of received religion or the political or economic system. Universalism conflicts with national patriotism, and Merton reminds us of the nationalistic fervor even of scientists during the two world wars; indeed, Merton himself expressed some of this wartime fervor in his 1942 article (1973, chap. 13). Thus insofar as these values solve the internal problem of unity they worsen the external problem of maintaining interdependence with the society. The two functional problems conflict.

The conflict is manageable insofar as the values of society are not too different from those of science. There will always be some differences—for instance, on patriotism and religion—but some conflict between science and society is desirable to maintain scientific autonomy. Merton argues that in seventeenth-century England the conflict was manageable because certain Puritan values agreed with the values of science: the equality of all men before God was a form of universalism; the belief in reason and experience rather than revelation was a form of disinterestedness and even limited skepticism. He also argued in 1942 that democracy, vaguely defined, embraces values hospitable to science: it affirms universalism, the equality of all people before the law, and rejects discrimination on grounds of race, creed, class, or sex. However, a capitalist democracy, which values private ownership of property, clashes with the value of communism, which forbids private property, and Merton gives examples of this conflict. Scientists are sometimes tempted to patent a discovery and make money on it, or to charge a consultant's fee for using their expertise to discuss someone else's research, or even to "pick someone's brains" and then rush to publish the ideas under their own name. Thus ideas become private property, and free discussion is inhibited by fear of theft.

By 1957 Merton had turned his attention to a third functional problem, that of motivating scientists to produce new knowledge. The original list of norms was negative and procedural, but a growing science needs positive goals, and rewards for achieving them, to keep scientists moving. The motivation function is met by two new norms. One is the achievement of originality, a value directly connected to the goal of producing new knowledge. Scientists ought to produce new ideas, experiments, and techniques, and should be honored and esteemed when they do so. Achievement motivation is encouraged during the training of scientists, but is also carried over from early socialization in an achievement-oriented society. The opposite value, ascription, or being loved for who you are rather than what you have done, is appropriate for families but not for science. Science thus flourishes most easily in an achievement-oriented society.

A conflicting norm is humility, which combines the basic norms of disinterestedness and of skepticism toward one's own achievements. The requirement of humility serves to moderate the divisive effects of achievement motivation, since without humility scientists would get absorbed in glorifying their own achievements and belittling others', and the scientific community would break up into conflicting schools and egotistical individuals. However, the conflict between the achievement and humility norms produces a great deal of ambivalence, as scientists try to be humble and disinterested but still somehow claim the recognition due them.

Indeed, despite the humility norm a great deal of conflict does exist in American sociology, resulting partly from the drive for individual and group achievement and partly from the diffusion of social conflicts into science (Merton, 1973, chap. 3, originally 1961). The conflicts are intense enough to produce stereotyped distortions of opposing views, a breakdown of communication, hostility and name calling, rhetoric and contempt. Yet this conflict is functional for science, up to a point. It increases the solidarity of deviant schools, and thus strengthens them in their resistance to the dominant orthodoxy. The excitement of conflict attracts recruits to the dissenting schools and enables them to maintain the essential skepticism toward orthodoxy. Here Merton takes over the ideas of his student Lewis Coser (1956) about the positive functions of social conflict. Conflict is essential to the maintenance of community in a variety of ways.

In 1963 Merton generalized his 1957 observation that two norms can conflict: he provided a whole list of conflicting pairs (1976, chap. 2). Included in the list are versions of his four original norms: universalism, communism, disinterestedness, and skepticism. Apparently every scientific norm coexists with its own opposite, and scientists must ambivalently obey now one and now the other, according to circumstances. Here is another source of scientific conflict, as scientists urge opposite norms of a pair on each other.

The norms of science are in part maintained by socialization in the larger society, in family, school, and church. But in part they must be maintained by scientists. This responsibility falls mainly on leading scientists, the ones whose achievements have already been recognized and honored. These people already embody the norms of science, one hopes, so they set an example. They can also distribute recognition or censure to others, and especially can encourage dissent, skepticism, and humility. Insofar as they fail to do this or set a bad example themselves, they weaken the scientific community.

It is important to remember that for Merton the health of the scientific community is not guaranteed. The functional requirements of science are not easily met, especially since they conflict; the norms need not be maintained, the necessary autonomy from society may weaken, dissent and skepticism may be stifled, leading scientists may set bad examples, and so on. For example, Merton himself was not always humble (Lang, 1981, p. 92; Merton, 1976, pp. 59–61). Indeed, the values of science themselves are self-destructive to some extent: "The culture of science is . . . pathogenic" (Merton, 1973, p. 323). Rose Coser (1975) has argued that Merton's primary focus is on conflict and contradiction, on the deviance and disorder produced by social institutions even at their best, and this focus is also apparent in his treatment of science. Similarly, Lewis Coser asserts, "Merton's world is composed of multiple ambiguities, of conflicting and contradictory demands and requirements" (1975, p. 5).

Merton's treatment of the pathology of science is based on his famous 1938 article, "Social Structure and Anomie," reprinted twenty-eight times from 1949 to 1975. The general idea is that culturally approved means may not be adequate to achieve culturally-prescribed ends, so that individuals must either use illegitimate means or fail to achieve ends, or both. They can't win.

He describes four forms of pathology. (1) Plagiarism, and data massaging and selection to fit one's theory. Here the original achievement goal is met by illegitimate means. (2) Repeated publication of trivial work and academic recognition for sheer quantity of publication; here the means of research and publication are used, but the goal of originality given up. (3) Withdrawal from research into teaching and academic administration; here both goal and means are given up. (4) Withdrawal into fantasies of future glory when one's masterpiece is finally published and acclaimed. An extreme example once occurred at the University of Chicago, where a French professor labored for decades on a definitive study of some writer, dropping occasional hints about its profundity; but at his death his will was revealed to contain a directive to burn the manuscript. Since the profession had not sufficiently recognized his genius during his lifetime, he explained, it was unworthy of receiving the fruits of that genius. Merton provides other examples (1973, p. 436).

Nevertheless, Merton affirms his belief that the values of science effectively minimize deviance, and science is basically sound. Hagstrom (1965) similarly asserts that anomy is rare in current science. The signs of anomy would include abundant publication of trivial papers that no one reads, little communication, and no agreement on the prestige ranking of scientists. Hagstrom ignores the first form of pathology: use of illegitimate means such as data massaging. However, various studies such as Sahner (1979) suggest that massaging is not uncommon. Another technique that Sahner mentions is to use a computer to search for correlations in multivariate data, then invent a hypothesis that fits the discovered correlations and write a paper that begins by deriving that hypothesis from some existing theory and then claims to test it. Sahner cites studies of published articles that find the null hypothesis falsified in 80 percent, 97 percent, and 100 percent of the articles.

We turn now to an examination of Merton's own values, through content analysis, in order to locate his paradigm, and of the Mertonian school, in science and in society. That is, we shift to externalist sociology.

In his early articles up to 1942, Merton expressed a rejection of Nazism for its racism and its totalitarian control of science. Against Nazism he asserted democratic values of respect for individual dignity and equal treatment of all without regard to race or creed. After 1942 the "defense of democracy" theme dropped out, and Merton concentrated on the self-maintenance needs of an autonomous science (cf. Hollinger, 1983). He did not participate in cold war anticommunism; for instance, he did not participate in the CIA-sponsored Congress for Cultural Freedom, unlike Daniel Bell or Ed Shils, among others. His chief cold war concern in the early 1950s, and Talcott Parsons's as well, was the McCarthy witch-hunting in the universities; this interfered with the autonomy of science. Marx for him was a sociologist, and Marxists had contributed many valuable ideas and also some bad theorizing to sociology.

From 1949 on, Merton expressed concern over the problems of policy-oriented sociology, and the conflict between science and politics. The political or industrial policy maker is a client who needs sociological research and advice to devise effective policies—for instance, a policy to curb anti-Semitism or to promote racial integration. But policy makers are likely to be shortsighted or have too narrow a grasp of the problem, and in any case they have no appreciation for the policy scientist's more general theoretical concerns. The scientist ought not do poor research to suit a client's narrow needs, and should not oversell science, raise exaggerated hopes, to get research grants. However, since practical problems are many-faceted, the policy sociologist ought to collaborate peacefully and tolerantly with people from other disciplines.

Merton's community was sociology, sharply defined, unlike Parsons, who combined psychological and sociological theory and knew some economics. But within sociology he welcomed diversity and conflict, arguing that multiple cross-cutting conflicts avoid polarization and maintain the unity of the discipline. He welcomed dissenting movements, arguing that orthodoxy was deadening to science. He even welcomed the microsociological dissenters against his own orthodox paradigm, while criticizing them gently (1973, pp. 373–75). Merton was a cosmopolitan, but his cosmos was sociology. In the late 1970s, however, he welcomed the convergence of disciplines as a development for the future (1977, p. 113).

Merton believed in the social responsibility of the corporation (1976, pp. 85–89). The increasing moral sensibility of our society calls on corporation leaders to improve employment opportunities for minorities, train the hard-core unemployed, clean up industrial pollution, and provide better public transportation.

From the above we can see that Merton, like Parsons, was a liberal New Deal Democrat committed to government and business action to solve social problems. He was neither a leftist critic of American society like Galbraith (Merton, 1973, p. 125) nor a glorifier of our great American democracy like the anticommunists. In science he and the Mertonians are professionals, committed to their own discipline and its skills and expertise. The discipline is policy-oriented: the professional sociologist's partner-and-opponent is government. Government provides the financial support that makes large-scale research possible, and applies research findings to social problems. This implies a fundamental conflict between the professional's commitment to systematic objective truth and the policy maker's concern with specific, immediate problems. Each shares the other's concerns, but the partnership prospers insofar as each preserves his own autonomy. Merton's "professional" location in society determines the particular meaning of *autonomy* for him: autonomy from one's patron, government. Similarly, Hagstrom's worst nightmare is the possibility of political control of research by government funding agencies (1965, chap. 3).

Merton's social location also determines the particular meaning of *ethical neutrality* for him. He is not at all neutral about the desirability of solving social problems—unemployment, poverty, race prejudice, pollution. Nor is he neutral about government and corporations; they are benevolent, responsible problem solvers. The norm of neutrality applies only during research into a problem. The researcher ought not to sympathize with parts of the problem, like the unemployed, since that would

bias research: he would tend to overlook the contributions of the unemployed to the problem, and would assign more blame elsewhere. Nor
ought the researcher favor one solution over another, for the same reason. The responsibility of selecting a solution belongs to government and
corporations, since they are paying for it. The researcher can however
evaluate and criticize their solution if he has been neutral in diagnosing
the problem.

A 1972 article, "Insiders and Outsiders" (in 1973, chap. 5), provides a
view of further complexities in Merton's position in society. The shifts of
position in this article suggest either an unstable coexistence of contradictory values or changes in successive drafts. The topic is the black pride
movement and the women's movement, two dissenters against Mertonian
orthodoxy. Their specific claim is that blacks have a special insight and
understanding of black culture, and that women have a special understanding of women's world. Merton first associates this claim of "black
science" with Nazi "Aryan science," and pulls out the old 1930s epithets
of racism, ethnocentrism, and chauvinism. Against the claim of knowledge by ascription—that is, that women can understand women better
than men can just because they are women—he asserts the professional's
claim of knowledge by achieved skills. But then he reverses himself and
agrees that downtrodden groups like blacks do have a special perspective
on society; because they have been oppressed, they can see things that
whites cannot see. They can see oppression, from the inside. Indeed, the
very concepts and words of white sociologists hide the social suffering and
humiliation of other groups. They objectivize and depersonalize these
experiences with concepts like *social disorganization* that point to an abstract structural problem out there. (Objectification, of course, expresses
the researcher's ethical neutrality). As examples of such "sociological
euphemism" Merton cites *his own* concepts: "Analytically useful concepts
such as social stratification, social exchange, reward system, dysfunction,
symbolic interaction are altogether bland in the fairly precise sense of
being unperturbing, suave, and soothing in effect" (1973, p. 131).

Not many social scientists are able to take the perspective of a critic and
see their own shortcomings. Merton's achievement is rare and impressive.

MERTON'S FOLLOWERS AND CRITICS

Unlike the Popper people, Merton's followers and his critics are two
different sets, and the critics are more in agreement with his post-1961

ideas than the followers are, sometimes. Perhaps Merton has outdis-
tanced his followers. The followers, nearly all students and students of
students, have produced quantitative empirical studies that illustrate Merton's earlier ideas. Like good professionals, they have used citation
counts, causal modeling, and network analysis because these were the
latest scientific techniques, whether or not they especially fit Mertonian
functionalism (Ben-David, 1978; Hargens, 1978). With regard to the
norms of science, Hagstrom (1965), Crane (1965), Gaston (1970), and
Cole and Cole (1967, 1973) have found that for certain samples and
fields, the norms of universalism and communism are mostly followed.
Deviation is rare (Cole and Cole, 1973, pp. 256–58). Critics found
much deviation in other samples. Mulkay (1969) cites the Velikovsky
case, in which scientists broke all sorts of Mertonian rules. (But cf.
Bauer, 1984, who argues that it was Velikovsky who broke the rules, so
thoroughly that scientists were justified in rejecting his claim to be scientific.) The issue, however, is not whether scientists act according to
Merton's norms; Merton himself asserted that they often do not, but
pointed to expressions of disapproval as evidence that the norms were
accepted and enforced as obligations. But they may have been ignoring
one norm, and getting disapproval for it, in order to follow an opposite
norm, as with Merton's original achievement-versus-humility pair.

Thus the issue is what norms scientists do accept in practice, or
believe they accept. Statistical studies of conformity to Merton's 1942
norms do not address this issue, because they fail to inquire about counternorms. Instead, it is necessary to interview or observe scientists closely
and individually to see what norms they accept. As Mitroff points out
(1974a, pp. 15–18), the problem is that Merton got his 1942 norms from
public statements by great scientists from Newton to Freud; but these
geniuses may have been providing an idealized or simplified public image
of science. Merton's norms and others like them may well exist as ideals,
but very different norms-in-use in Kaplan's sense (as discussed in chapter
4) may govern practice. Or a Mertonian norm may coexist uneasily with
its opposite, as in Merton's 1961 list.

Blissett (1972), using depth interviews and a mail questionnaire to
two samples of physical scientists, found both kinds of normative ambivalence, ideal-practice and norm-counternorm. His respondents accepted
universalism in the abstract but particularism in practice; they affirmed
that truth claims ought to be judged impersonally, but agreed that the
prestige and institutional affiliation of a scientist does affect the accep-

tance of his work. The statistical studies of Crane (1965) and Cole and Cole (1967) are consistent with Blissett; they found that young scientists at prestigious universities get more publications accepted and other forms of recognition than similar scientists elsewhere. With regard to skepticism and emotional neutrality, Blissett's respondents split about fifty-fifty. Half asserted that scientists ought to be skeptical and detached from their own theories, and half urged commitment and emotional involvement while a theory is being worked out and communicated. Mitroff (1974a) found a great deal of normative ambivalence in his interviews with moon scientists. Some of his questions asked their opinions about Merton-type norms, especially communism, disinterestedness, and skepticism (p. 43). He found other norms asserted in their replies, including counternorms to the original set. In nearly all cases, his respondents asserted the validity of both norm and counternorm. Specifically, many of them, like Blissett's respondents, argued that scientists ought to be emotionally committed to their own theories. They ought to look for supporting evidence, push their ideas in public, repeat them in different forms, sell them. Yet they ought also to respect negative evidence and change or drop a refuted theory. The argument is that true theories and facts are more likely to emerge from a continuing clash of strongly committed partisans than from disinterested observers. The latter may make good judges, but since they don't care which theory is true, they are unlikely to make the sustained effort needed to dig out relevant facts, adapt and develop their theory when it encounters trouble, and get the attention of their busy colleagues. Yet even the partisans ought in principle to be able to accept a strong opposing case. Thus Mitroff's data support Merton's 1963 assertions about the importance of normative ambivalence.

There was much ambivalence about Merton's norm of communism. Many of Mitroff's respondents urged the importance of secrecy to prevent theft; they were obsessed with stealing, both intentional and unintentional. Their rule was, keep your research secret until you are ready to publish, but be sure to publish before the opposition does. The same picture of secrecy, spying, and a frantic race to publish appears in James Watson's *Double Helix*. Hagstrom (1965) also emphasizes the value of secrecy in a competitive field.

One of Merton's norms is missing: humility. A Newton or a Freud can afford to strike a humble pose in public, because he knows he will get the recognition due him, or if necessary his disciples will get it for him. But

Mitroff's moon scientists, like Watson and Crick, had to scratch and fight to get their little bit of fame. "The single result that stands out is the intense masculinity of these scientists. And indeed masculinity may be too kind or dignified a word. It is closer to the truth to say that it is their intense, raw, and even brutal aggressiveness that stands out" (Mitroff, 1974a, p. 144). Merton could reply: moon geology and DNA research are both "hot" fields where discoveries are coming in pell-mell. Such fields have always been highly competitive and have attracted the most competitive people. They are not typical (Merton, 1973, chap. 15). Merton's actual reply (1976, pp. 59–61) so thoroughly misrepresents Mitroff's statements (1974a, pp. 11–17, 73, 276) that it had best be passed over as a misunderstanding.

But if opposite norms coexist in a community, as Merton proposes, which norm applies in a given situation, or do both apply? Mulkay argues that with opposite norms available, any action could be justified by one norm and criticized by another, and even the same norm could be interpreted differently (1980, pp. 59ff.). Thus norms can be used as arguments in disputes; they divide rather than unite scientists. Mulkay (1979) found just such a situation in Mulkay and Edge's case study of radio astronomers (Mulkey and Edge, 1973; Mulkay, 1976a); the Cambridge group he studied urged secrecy for themselves, and their competitors urged communism. The competitors called for earlier publication of Cambridge results to allow for wider discussion, replication, and the advance of science; the Cambridge people defended their secrecy as affording them time to check their results, give student researchers recognition, and avoid distortion in the press. The communism-secrecy pair operated just as the competition-protection pair operates in foreign trade policy: competition for others, protection for me. Mulkay cites Gouldner, a Merton student, who observes that "what one conceives to be moral, tends to vary with one's interests" (Mulkay, 1979, p. 70).

This is just the sort of conflict that Merton called attention to in his discussion of normative ambivalence.

Mulkay and Edge's case study suggests that institutionalized norms and counternorms do not necessarily unite the scientific community, but provide material for disputes in the race for recognition. If their case is typical, there is no unified scientific community, but only small quarreling networks that form around a theory or problem, put out a series of publications, and then dissolve or merge into other networks. The proper way to study these small networks is microsociological: watch individuals negotiate agreement on their facts and findings, watch them construct evidence, watch them beat down adversaries with the norms of science. The macrosociology of science is pointless because its subject matter is chaos.

According to Mulkay (1975), Merton's 1942 norms are a prettified picture of science put out by scientists for public consumption. Scientists have indeed announced such norms in public, but they don't act on them. Merton has made up a "storybook image of science" (Mulkay, 1976b). Randall Collins (1975, pp. 473–79) calls functionalist sociology of science "neosaintly science"—idealized statements of norms that no one follows and empirical research that defends the fairness of scientific organizations. Actually, he says, scientists are very argumentative people. The career goal of a scientist is to get others to read his publications and discuss them. They read others' publications solely to find ways to get others to pay attention to them. What passes for truth is those ideas that get picked up and repeated, probably those with flashy labels like "Matthew effect." The proper way to study this endless cacophony is microsociological. Mitroff (1974b) provides a possible resolution of this disagreement. He suggest that the norms of communism, emotional neutrality, and disinterestedness apply in a well-established, well-unified community doing "normal" science, while the counternorms of secrecy, emotional involvement, and interestedness apply in new fields or during crisis times. During normal times the problems are well defined, the techniques are established, and the criteria of solution agreed on. In crises or new fields, the problems are ill defined and there is no agreement on facts, concepts, techniques, and solution criteria. Mitroff observes that in his case the arrival of new evidence, moon rocks, permitted the solution of some well-defined problems but not the ill-defined ones. The Mulkay-type microsociologists have studied new fields where there is much confusion, and perhaps here Merton's macrosociology does not apply. Merton's own community, the functionalists, was the dominant sociological community from about 1950 to 1970 and was also prominent in political science (later) and anthropology (earlier). Mullins (1973) calls functionalism Standard American Sociology, "faith of our fathers, with us yet." Consequently, Merton's experience was in a large community with shared norms. In such a community, people are sure to read each other's papers, agree with them, praise them, and cite them, so they can afford to be disinterested, humble, communistic, and so on.

If you like this resolution, feel free to believe it. Mitroff no longer does (personal communication).

EXTERNALIST SOCIOLOGY:
THE SOCIAL LOCATION OF SOCIAL SCIENTISTS

A maximally objective science . . . will be one that includes a self-conscious and critical examination of the relationship between the social experience of its creators and the kinds of cognitive structures favored in its inquiry.   —*Sandra Harding (1986, p. 250)*

Externalist sociology of science begins with the observation that scientists are also members of society. *Members* means that they locate themselves somewhere, in some social class, status, and roles. Their experience in this location, direct or empathetically shared, inevitably affects their thinking; as Sztompka observes in his eulogistic profile of Merton (1986, p. 38): "The social relations in which a man is involved will somehow be reflected in his ideas." That is, social scientists are more aware of some problems and developments than others, and they perceive or experience these problems from the perspective of where they are. They empathize with certain people in the problem, or with certain problem solvers, and therefore bring certain interests or values to their diagnoses. Consequently, scientists who locate themselves in different classes or social relations will produce different descriptions, evaluations, and theories. Conversely, one should be able to read back from a theory or disciplinary matrix to the social location that made such a theory possible. The influence of the different social locations on science tends to fragment social science along class, ethnic, or gender lines and thereby weaken the community that Merton regarded as essential to science. His norm of ethical neutrality had the function of weakening external influences and thereby preserving community. However, the counternorm of ethical involvement has the opposite effect of justifying fragmentation along social lines.

The most convenient place to begin examining the social location of social scientists is with the earlier observation of the social location of the Mertonians. The question here is, if the Mertonians are professional sociologists in partnership with government, what kind of science is appropriate to this social location? For the Mertonians, government has overall responsibility for system maintenance and the well-being of society, perhaps assisted by some far-sighted, socially responsible corporations. Sociologists can study some undesirable situation like race prejudice, but it is government's job to manage the situation (Parsons, 1967, chap. 13). Sociologists research and advise, governments act. In other words, Mertonian science is a system- or problem- or policy-oriented science.

A policy-oriented science must look for causes of social or industrial problems, where *cause* means "some frequently contributing factor which can be affected by policy, and whose change affects the problem." The politician wants a handle or lever on the problem so he can do something about it, and the scientist's job is to find a lever. The conflict of interest is that the politician wants a handle on this problem, and quick, while the scientist wants to find the variety of possible handles on this sort of problem, and perhaps its connection to other problems. More generally, scientists need not even be studying problems; they can study the causal interrelation of factors that could become involved in some type of problem. In order to understand labeling as a cause of juvenile delinquency, it is necessary to understand the labeling process in its various conditions and circumstances. Nor do scientists have to conclude that this sort of problem has a solution, though scientists who find solutions are more likely to get new research grants, other things being equal.

The problem, or more generally the network of probabilistic causes, must be located out there, not here. The scientist and the politician are not part of the problem, they are part of the solution. Also the problem, or the topic of study, must be limited in time and space, in relation to possible resources for solution. Thus in both the Keynesian and the Parsonian functionalist tradition, the social system or economic system is a national system with a boundary around it, and attention is focused inside the boundary. The Almond-Apter developmental functionalists similarly treat each developing country as a separate unit of study. Studies of international trade will limit themselves to the international economic system and usually focus on one country's trade.

In short, this kind of science is objective, detached, causal and/or functional, and specialized. The result is the sort of theory that Merton calls "euphemistic"—unemotional, impersonal, preferably quantitative. Also, to express and protect the scientist's professional skill and professional status, some of the concepts and techniques must be technical, just as a doctor's handwriting on a prescription must be illegible except to the pharmacist. For example:

We can write the mathematical expectation of the covariance of consumption and income as:

$$
E\left[\frac{1}{n-1}\sum_{g=1}^{G}\sum_{i=1}^{n_g} c_{ig}y_{ig}\right]
$$

$$
= E\left[\frac{1}{n-1}\left(\sum_{g=1}^{G}\sum_{i=1}^{n_g}(c_{i,g}^p + c_{i,g}^t)(y_{i,g}^p + y_{i,g}^t)\right.\right.
$$

$$
\left.\left. + \sum_{g=1}^{G}n_g(c_g^p + c_g^t)(y_g^p + y_g^t)\right)\right]
$$

$$
= E\left[\frac{1}{n-1}\left(\sum_{g=1}^{G}\sum_{i=1}^{n_g}(c_{i,g}^p y_{i,g}^p + c_{i,g}^t y_{i,g}^p + c_{i,g}^p y_{i,g}^t + c_{i,g}^t y_{i,g}^t)\right.\right.
$$

$$
\left.\left. + \sum_{g=1}^{G} n_g(c_g^p y_g^p + c_g^t y_g^p + c_g^p y_g^t + c_g^t y_g^t)\right)\right].
$$

(Eisner, 1958, p. 987)

In English, the expectation is the same as the expected covariance of
permanent and transitory consumption and income in all combinations.

The professional's treatment of the policy maker is quite different. It
is not causal, impersonal, quantitative. The policy maker is assumed to
be rational, have free will, make decisions on the basis of advice, have
political courage in the sense of being willing to take risks that might
mean losing the next election, make mistakes he will later regret, even
goof up completely and make the problem worse. He is a partner in a
dialogue, not an object of quantitative study, prediction, and control.

For example, Gusfield (1976) notes that in drinking driver research the
driver is objectivized as a neutral object, the problem. He is neither blamed
nor pitied. "The drinking driver stands as an object outside the emotional
ambit of the writer and the reader . . . in constructing him as a neutral
object, control is enhanced" (p. 30). Emotional and moral language is
reserved for the partner-and-opponent, the politician. Phrases like "patent
failure," "pathetic," "look with utter amazement" appear in reference to
the politician (pp. 27–30). Here is another function of Merton's norm of
value neutrality: it serves to objectivize the problem.

In policy studies, which focus on the policy maker, we get a very
different kind of science. It is not objective, detached, and euphemistic.
A policy study interprets the policy-making process sympathetically, as

the process looks to the policy maker. It describes the policy maker's line of thinking, explains the diagnosis and intended solution, traces the intended and actual implementation, and evaluates the result in terms of the policy maker's goals. It may also evaluate the goals and suggest changes.

We can name these two phases of professional science the Object and the Subject. The Object is out there carrying on. We study its regularities and the probabilistic causes by which those regularities can be influenced; we devise indicators to measure its state or rate of change: unemployment rate, MMPI score, IQ, Gini coefficient. The Subject is here with us, a partner in dialogue. The partner consults, plans, acts; we advise, explain, evaluate, request more money. The two categories are similar to Habermas's "science with an interest in control" and "science with an interest in communication," or hermeneutic science. However, in contrast to Habermas's much more abstract Kantian scheme, here each of the two phases presupposes the other; neither makes any sense without the other. Professional social science is simultaneously controlling for society and hermeneutic for policy making.

What happens if we reverse our location and our line of vision? The Mertonian sociologist looks at a social problem from outside it, detached from it, and indirectly from the perspective of a government agency. What happens if we locate ourselves inside the problem looking out? This is the social location of black or female sociologists, who speak for the downtrodden and oppressed, according to Merton. Many of the symbolic interactionist and structuralist studies of the Chicago school fall into the same category. These include Alfred Lindesmith's study of drug addicts, Erving Goffman's study of mental patients and gamblers, Becker and Geer's study of medical students (1960), Suttles's study of slum dwellers (1970), Bruce Jackson's study of prisoners, Rasmussen's study of massage parlors (in J. Douglas, 1976), Ned Polsky's study of hustlers, beats, and others (1967). Anthropological studies of dependent and colonialized peoples are also similar, as well as works like Piven and Cloward's *Regulating the Poor* (1971).

In this sort of science, the scientist becomes part of the "underdog" group through participant observation and tries to understand how these people manage amid deprivation, disrepute, or dependency. He treats them as Subject, constructing a livable world for themselves, or failing and going under in despair. This sort of science is not at all causal, quantitative, detached, objective; it presents people to us as they see themselves, vividly and directly. Medical students see themselves as "boys in white," in Becker and Geer's phrase (1960), not as Merton's euphemistic *The Student-Physician* (1957), which objectively locates them out there in the role structure. (Howard Becker pointed out this contrast to me.) Its purpose is not to find causal regularities that can be used to predict and control, but to help us understand and sympathize with these people as human beings, and thereby understand better the human in all of us. It is a hermeneutic science.

Another group at the periphery of Merton's vision is represented by John Kenneth Galbraith the "leftist critic of American society." This group includes mainly economists—the institutionalists—and political scientists—the bureaucratic politics theorists of the 1970s. For these people, government is part of the Object. They describe the dynamics of this Object in technical, objective terms: bureaucratic symbiosis, standard operating procedures (or SOPs), in-and-outer, action channels. They show how all people in government including the president are constrained by their position to take certain predictable stands, either partisan or uncommitted, and show how the policy-making process is determined by these organization dynamics. Individuals have a range of freedom or maneuver space, just as they do in functionalist theory, but their basic line of thought and action is determined by their organizational position.

From this perspective, it is naive to think of government as a rational problem solver concerned with keeping the society running. Its "concern" is rather to keep itself running, to keep doing what it does. Kharasch's Third Axiom is: Whatever the internal machinery does is perceived within the institution as the real purpose of the institution (1973, p. 13). "Internal machinery" is defined as whatever the employees do, such as filing documents.

The people at the top levels of government may well see themselves as rational problem solvers, bravely trying to manage one crisis after another in this very complex world, and this self-presentation is accepted by the Mertonians. But the bureaucratic politics people reject this subjective account in favor of detached observation of actual bureaucratic routines. Instead of treating government as a policy initiator, they treat it as the dependent variable, responding to organizational and social pressures in predictable ways. Most of the pressure comes from business— that is, other large organizations in bureaucratic symbiosis with some government agency. The military budget, for example, is a product of organizational dynamics of the weapons firms, who provide employment and campaign contributions to the districts of key congressmen, who in turn vote the funds for the Pentagon, whose bureaucratic need for expansion makes it receptive to the new weapons suggested by the weapons firms. Sometimes the initiative comes from the Pentagon agency and moves around the cycle from there (Melman, 1970).

The institutionalists do a similar analysis of the corporate sector.

The Subject for the bureaucratic-institutionalists is the people—the consumers and voters and citizens. The scientist is writing for them, not for government. His or her purpose is to show them how they have been fooled by advertising and political propaganda and the symbols of government. And once they realize this he can show them how to influence government and even to counteract corporate influences. The scientists in the consumer-environmental movement are further prepared to act as advisors and spokespersons for the consumers. They can do the technical research on nuclear power safety regulations or waste disposal or food additives, then testify at hearings induced by a consumer organization, then sue the government if necessary to get a regulation enforced. Thus government agencies, like EPA or FTC or OSHA or NRC, become arenas of combat between the people and the corporations, each represented by their own professional scientists (Nelkin, 1984).

For the Merton-type professionals, one of the norms of science forbids carrying scientific controversy outside of science to the people; this is condemned as a low blow, since ordinary people don't understand professional science and can easily be stirred up by simplified and biased stories. Indeed, these "scientists" who go to the people with biased stories must be ideologically motivated and therefore poor scientists. Also, they argue, airing controversies in public weakens the prestige of science. The only proper nonscientific audience is the government agency responsible for dealing with the relevant social problem. But for the environmentalists it is pointless to communicate with government agencies or Merton's enlightened corporations in any language other than lawsuits and threats of lawsuits, since they don't care about problems in society. All they care about is their SOPs. Ordinary people are concerned, since they are the ones affected by the problems; and they are intelligent enough to understand a scientific analysis of pollution or poverty if it is explained in nontechnical language. Indeed, these citizens who can throw off the illusions of political symbolism and corporate advertising (unlike the Mertonian professionals, who get taken in), these Davids, or Lois

Gibbses, who can take a stand against the government and corporations, are pretty brave and even heroic.

The issue here is not whether any of these perspectives on society is the correct one. It is simply that the different locations that scientists take in society give them different angles of vision and therefore produce different kinds of science. Looking at poverty from the outside as a social problem calling for government action produces one kind of theory; looking at poor people from within their midst, as one of them, produces a different kind. Looking at government from the inside as a rational, responsible policy maker produces one kind of political theory; looking at it with detachment as a large organization interacting with other large organizations produces a different kind. Looking at an election campaign from the perspective of individual voters making a public choice produces one kind of theory; looking at it from the perspective of a candidate's advisers deciding on what image to present produces a different kind. (See Diesing, 1982, for a discussion of different perspectives in social science.)

What induces social scientists to take a particular location in society? Presumably personality factors and education affect individual choices. But the perspectives themselves come into prominence as a result of dramatic changes in society. The 1945 bipolar world that defined the United States and the Soviet Union as permanent opponents brought to prominence the perspective on the USSR as the enemy to be contained and defeated. The sudden appearance of a large number of new world states in the 1950s produced a concern for how these states could be helped to develop politically and economically—a concern that naturally treated the "modernizing elite" in power as the Subject to be advised and helped, while the peoples and institutions were the Object to be managed and modernized.

The liberal professional science of Merton, Keynes, or Almond flourishes in periods of liberal government committed to expanded welfare services, full employment, and foreign aid to modernize the ex-colonial countries. In the United States, this period was about 1933–75 and in Britain 1945–79. It was the period when the economic advisers were established in U.S. councils, when antipoverty and economic development and urban development and foreign aid programs flourished, when research funds and aid to education expanded accordingly. This period, 1933–75 or so, was also the period of a relatively closed U.S. economy, or at least when the internal effects of international competition were not yet manifest, so that problems could be defined within a national or municipal boundary. At such times the liberal idealization of government is plausible, the need for objective problem-oriented research evident, and the research funds available. But when agencies administer on and on, expanding as their associated problems expand, when countercyclical policy gets tangled in stagflation, devaluation, and the political business cycle, when the developing countries are overwhelmed in debt, dictatorship, and dysentery, or when the agencies and research funds are eliminated by a conservative government, liberal science loses some of its aura of practicality and immediacy.

The "underdog" movement grows out of liberal social science as its internal opposite. In the 1950s and 1960s, and also thirty years earlier, liberal science focused its statistical-survey attention on the social problems—the slum dwellers, delinquents, immigrants, criminals, mental patients, addicts, the unemployed. But some sociologists came to see these Objects as Subject, bravely trying to survive in a very difficult world; these scientists reversed their identity and joined their Subject through participant observation. The list includes Saul Alinsky, Clifford Shaw, and William Whyte in the 1930s; Richard Cloward, Herbert Gans, S. M. Miller, and many others in the 1960s. With this reversal also came a reversal of the solution: the underdogs should organize against their oppressor, government, with its slum clearance and highway projects and regulations that produce permanent welfare dependency.

The impetus for the bureaucratic politics movement was the Vietnam War, a grotesque caricature of liberal foreign aid to a developing country. What kind of policy-making process continued this war year after year to no discernible purpose? Schurmann (1974) calls it "a bureaucratic war from start to finish," and Ellsberg writes of the "stalemate machine" (1972). The bureaucratic politics theorists argued that the liberal slogans of responsible government developing and protecting democracy in Vietnam were symbolic politics, a disguise of reality; the reality was bureaucratic routines and presidential image making.

Thus the various perspectives that come to prominence and flourish for two or three decades are reflections of dramatic developments in the world system—to some extent. The 1945 bipolar world that defined the United States and the Soviet Union as permanent opponents; U.S. economic hegemony after 1945 that produced a permanent flow of surplus capital, some of which went into social welfare and research; the dependency of Latin America and South Asia on U.S. capital, with ensuing revolt and military repression; the necessary export of U.S. capital to strengthen its own competitors in core countries; the resulting opening of the U.S. economy to international competition and the resulting decline in the rate of profit after 1965; the resulting shift away from corporate liberalism by the corporate policy planning groups like the Business Roundtable and the resulting decline in the welfare state and the rise of conservative social scientists; the vastly increased mobility of capital resulting from the postwar need to export surplus U.S. capital, and the resulting decisive weakening of labor; the attack on unions and the defeat of labor in the early 1980s—all were stages in the continuing evolution of the world system which were reflected in social science.

But if the distribution and the changing vitality of social scientific movements reflect changes in society in part, then knowledge also reflects those changes. Knowledge can be lost as well as discovered with changes of perspective, and the growth of knowledge becomes problematic. The pragmatists' belief that science can advance through a reflection on its own methods and a correction of persistent errors assumes scientific autonomy; but if science is socially constrained, the constraints can prevent self-correction.

SCIENCE AND VISION/FANTASY

> In heaven, I replied, there is laid up a pattern of it, methinks, which he who desires may behold, and beholding, may take up his abode there. . . . He will live after the manner of that city, having nothing to do with any other.   —*Plato, Republic IX*

> You don't trust economists. They deal in a make-believe world.
> —*Don Sheahan, bond trader, Nikko Securities*
> *(reported Jan. 16, 1988)*

This section deals with what Schumpeter called *vision* and Mannheim called *utopia*. When a scientist locates himself somewhere in society, this location gives him a perspective on society; he looks at society from where he is (Subject) to where he is not (Object). Each perspective brings with it a vision, both of self and of not-self. According to Schumpeter (1949), a vision is a conception of a set of phenomena as related and as important, and therefore worth analyzing. A vision sets the task for a research program, the task of analyzing the phenomena, finding their interrelations, and finding the factors that produce or maintain or change them. In addition to this cognitive aspect, a vision also has a valuational aspect: the phenomena ought to be either maintained or changed. The valuational aspect is approximately what the Edinburgh sociologists call *interests* or *concerns* (Barnes, 1977, chap. 2, esp. p. 28).

The two contemporary visions that Schumpeter describes are both negative. First, he describes a Keynesian vision of a society stagnating because of chronic underconsumption. The failure to buy enough produces chronic overproduction, which produces unemployment and low capital investment, which produces more unemployment, which produces underconsumption. Economists ought to analyze each of these factors and their causes: the causes of underconsumption, unemployment, low investment. When one has found the causes and the interconnections, one will be in a position to prevent or reduce or counteract underconsumption and stagnation.

The second vision is the neoclassical vision of monopoly as evil. In this case, the cause of monopoly is thought to be obvious: it is caused by the failure to enforce the antitrust laws. Government bungling is the cause of monopoly. (That's what they taught me at Chicago). Research focuses not on the cause, but on the presumed bad effects of monopoly: perhaps higher prices, or lower quantity, or poorer quality, or lack of innovation. Demonstrating one or another of these bad effects will provide justification for enforcing the antitrust laws.

Each of these negative visions has a positive side, and the positive side is what Mannheim called *utopia*. Keynes's positive vision was of a benevolent, responsible government supplied with good economic advice and accurate economic data, a government that could counteract underconsumption and low investment so as to maintain the economy on a full-employment growth path. The neoclassical positive vision was of a monopoly-free competitive market that could distribute its rewards optimally and fairly.

A positive vision idealizes, and its negative side demonizes. Keynes's benevolent, well-informed, and well-advised government was an aspiration to work toward and a standard for evaluating actual government performance, not a reality. The perfect self-cleansing market devoid of all market failures and market power and externalities was an ideal and a standard, not a reality. Its negative side, government interference and monopoly, describes government as always bungling and monopoly as always inefficient.

Similarly, the anticommunist vision of totalitarianism shows us Stalin's crimes, an ever present thought police, outside agitators stirring up trouble worldwide, and a military continually planning aggression and testing our resolve. Its positive side shows us our democracy, in which all can participate equally by voting in elections and all thought is free of interference. The Marxist vision of a classless society in which people can control their own work is an idealization, and its negative side of a capitalism continually in crisis and continually producing misery somewhere is a demonization.[6]

A positive vision, the idealization, seems to relate to the scientist's own location, the Subject, and a negative vision is located in the Object somewhere. Thus Keynes located himself in the British Exchequer as an adviser, and his vision of a benevolent, responsible, wise government describes his patron and advisee. Conversely, the rather dumpy, erratic, bumbling economy that he envisioned out there was the Object. The antimonopoly neoclassicists empathized with the small businessman who lives by estimating market trends and adjusting his buying and selling to them. He projects his disappointments onto the Other, government and the monopolists, who interfere with the Market. Government is always messing things up with taxes, new regulations, paperwork, minimum wage laws; and the monopolists always seem to win. Hence, antimonopoly. For the anticommunists, democracy is us, U.S., and totalitarianism is out there, its tentacles spreading through Cuba and El Salvador to get us. Marxists empathize with workers, so their utopia consists of unselfish, skilled workers who find personal fulfillment in their work and who long to manage their own production process collectively. The demonized Other is the Boss, with the whole weight of capitalism behind him, who ignorantly interferes with work, gets rich off of our work, and finally fires us.

Each vision/fantasy brings with it one or more *interests* or *concerns*. If the vision is positive, the interest is in maintaining and protecting the idealized social phenomena. If the vision is negative, the interest is in counteracting and neutralizing the demonized phenomena, or perhaps in managing them and improving their working by reference to some goal. Thus for the anticommunists we ought to study the Soviets' aggressive foreign policy and also their worldwide subversive machinations, so that our government can counteract them and defend the Free World. We ought also to study the workings of our democracy in order to display them publicly and thereby inoculate people against communist propaganda. For the liberal government advisers, we ought to study social problems so that we can advise our government how to manage them. The free market vision brings an interest in displaying how the Market works, and also a concern for the various interferences such as the welfare program (Murray, 1984) that ought to be removed. The vision of a self-managing society brings a concern for the dynamics of the world capitalist system, including a search for possible changes that might move us toward socialism and an ecologically sound society.

Schumpeter regarded all four of the above visions as false, except the democracy vision, but he argued that such visions are essential to science. He had his own vision too, of course: the brilliant, creative big businessman, the Henry Ford, who could break through dead routines and galvanize a whole society to new heights of productivity. He asserted that the Keynesian "stagnation" vision and the neoclassical "monopoly" vision had both petered out by 1949, but they had in the meantime been valuable for science. A vision focuses the attention of a school of scientists on a set of phenomena and motivates them to study, search out, analyze. It sensitizes them to empirical traces of the vision, suggests interpretations of seemingly random events, and points to a deeper reality or structure behind appearance.

Thus the stagnation-full employment vision sensitizes one to economic indicators: employment levels and changes, investment, consumption, saving, interest rates, wage rates, price levels and changes. Indicators need to be improved, leads and lags studied, comparative data gathered. The vision suggests connections among the indicators, and these hypotheses can be tested and revised. It suggests new data to be gathered: how investment decisions are made, the effects of temporary unemployment on consumption levels, the actual size of various investment multipliers. Finally, a vision that has been filled out by empirical research can suggest a policy-relevant interpretation of complex phenomena.

A vision is falsified or wears out over time, according to Schumpeter, when the empirical researches it suggests continually run into unexpected and puzzling results, and when its policy-relevant interpretations don't work either. Thus he asserts that the antimonopoly people consistently failed to get solid evidence for the various evils that their models attributed to monopoly. However, in the meantime we have learned a great deal from their research and from Keynesian research, and the few persistent diehards who keep trying may even bring out additional data and correlations.

Perhaps Schumpeter was too optimistic about the possibility of falsifying visions. Both the Keynesian and the neoclassical vision have lived on, with changes, for several decades since 1949. A vision is not a description; it is a desired, or rejected, state of affairs. It is an idealization, so empirical factors that do not fit it can be dismissed as temporary obstacles, or blamed on some envisioned demon. Thus scientists with an anticommunist concern can dismiss apparent political changes in Moscow as superficial, temporary, or even as a scheme to lull the Free World into relaxing its vigilance. And they may be right.

Put differently, actual current events are either obstacles or facilitating conditions for the fuller realization or elimination of a vision. The scientist's interest is in *possibility* as well as actuality. The Keynesian or Parsonian is interested in imagining possible government policies to reduce unemployment or poverty or racial conflict, and the antimonopolist is interested in possible monopoly side effects of some antipollution regulation or civil rights law. But different and even opposite possibilities can coexist in an actual situation. Thus scientists with different visions can describe the same situation differently and both be correct. What is an obstacle for one can be an encouraging development for another.

For example, Studdert-Kennedy cites two studies of Third World agriculture based on two different visions, each probably correct in its own way (1975, chap. 8). One study by Hamza Alavi is of rural Pakistan and is based on a Marxist vision of workers and peasants rebelling and taking control of their own work. The other, by Clifford Geertz, is a study of rural Indonesia, based on an ecological vision of rural catastrophe through overpopulation, plus a vision of possible technocratic-rational exploitation of scarce resources. Studdert-Kennedy observes that a Marxist like Alavi would interpret Geertz's overcrowded, passive village as a case of massive alienation, and would look for possibilities of awakening the people through a radical political movement (pp. 193–94). He continues: "But Geertz does not respond to that possibility as a real one; . . . he expects a disaffiliated peasantry to become . . . the victim and accomplice of some form of totalitarian regime" because of the need for comprehensive rational planning to avoid mass starvation (p. 194). For good measure, Studdert-Kennedy mentions two more conflicting treatments of Indonesian agriculture based on different visions: Mary Douglas's vision of Indonesia's possible integration into the emerging world free market, and Balandier's vision of symbolic protest against exploitation. Studdert-Kennedy concludes, "Though an empirical analysis under either of the two perspectives might share a good deal of common ground, at the most crucial level the two interpretations cannot be reconciled, and at this stage the appeal must be to assumptions which cannot be subjected to empirical verification or disproof" (p. 192). In other words, class-based perspectives and their associated visions of possibilities cannot be easily proved or disproved.

Up to here we have considered what a vision contributes to science. Now reverse the picture. Every focusing of attention on something draws attention away from or hides something else. Every sensitization to traces of hidden phenomena can also produce an illusion of nonexistent phenomena. Every interpretation that systematizes a mass of seemingly arbitrary events can also project an imaginary order into them. Or, in general, our own vision sensitizes and guides us to an underlying reality, while other visions produce fantasies and blindness.

For example, the vision of a free market has pushed aside the problem of externalities, has neglected or denied validity to the study of how tastes are formed and changed (as in Homans's statement, "People like the damndest things"), has ignored advertising and addiction, has rejected the empirical study of investment and consumption decisions as irrelevant, has treated market power (except monopoly) as a temporary aberration of no theoretical significance. The concept *natural rate of unemployment* has brushed aside nonmonetary causes of unemployment as unchangeable and probably unknowable, and the other "natural" rates do the same thing.

Some fantasies are simply exposed in time, leaving the original vision untouched. Steven Possony's 1967 fantasy of a tricontinental people's war that Mao was about to unleash, until U.S. firmness in Vietnam dissuaded him, is now forgotten. Cheryl Payer's 1974 praise of the North Korean development strategy, which avoided the clutches of the IMF and the World Bank, is now exposed as fantasy. Jeane Kirkpatrick's 1987 hallucination of Soviet scheming underlying the January 1987 South Yemen coup was easily exposed by journalists, and Lyndon Larouche's 1976 warning of an imminent World War III was another paranoid fantasy.

Collective fantasies, shared by a whole school or community, are more difficult to give up. Perhaps the persistent negative evidence can still be explained away, or perhaps someone can devise a foolproof version of the theory. Keep trying! Examples are the law of comparative advantage in international trade, still taken seriously despite many fruitless attempts to overcome the Leontief paradox, and the related law of one price.[7] Some Shaikh-type Marxists still take the falling rate of profit seriously, long after other Marxists have cited the negative evidence (Hodgson, 1974), have pronounced an obituary on the law (Parijs, 1980), and have pointed out the erroneous assumptions in the mathematics (Roemer, 1981, chaps. 4–6). And these examples are merely derivatives from central visions—the self-regulating market and the perpetual crisis of capitalism. The visions are affected even less by persistent negative evidence.

The worst development is the loss of the distinction between vision/fantasy and reality. When scientists come to believe that their vision is not merely an idealized future goal but the actual deep structure of society right now, further empirical research is unnecessary. Their task is rather to expose this reality for all to see. At this point, science has passed over into propaganda. To assert that the Soviet Union is as of 1983 a classless society, and not merely an approximation or tendency toward, is propaganda. Conversely, to assert that as of 1983 the Soviet Union is a totally Stalinist totalitarian evil empire is propaganda. To assert that the free market works solely by information and persuasion, not power, and to imply that this ideal Market actually exists (Lavoie, 1985) is propaganda. Propagandists believe that they are simply revealing the essence of things, abstracted from accidental impurities and embellishments; but this fixed essence has become impervious to empirical research, because any deviations from it can be dismissed as ephemeral accidents. Truly, Lavoie lives in a make-believe world. In his world the Market conveys all needed information flawlessly and all planning fails; in the real world there are many different kinds of (imperfect) markets, each calling for, and maintained by, a different kind of planning (Chandler, 1990, and earlier works).

The problem for science is to get the good without the bad, to use a vision as a heuristic guide or framework for research without coming to believe in it as unquestionable reality. The difficulty lies in the valuational component of the vision. The value component is useful insofar as it energizes researchers to search for the empirical workings of the phenomenon, to clarify or revise parts, and to fill in details. But when the interest in the good or the bad is so strong that it demands unquestioning loyalty and action, then science has passed over into propaganda.

So we return by a different route to Merton's (and Mannheim's) requirement of scientific autonomy. Scientists always locate themselves somewhere in society, and use their direct or vicarious experience in that location to guide their research. The experience, idealized as vision, suggests the social concerns, the phenomena and problems that should be studied, and the goals appropriate to those phenomena.

However, effective empirical research requires some detachment from the visions and interests that drive one on, and even some skepticism. Detachment enables one to accept data and results that do not come out as expected, and enables one to follow leads that point toward different explanations and theories. Detachment enables one to remember that the vision is an idealization/demonization, that reality is more complex, that other visions also can capture important possibilities and aspects of reality. Too strong an attachment to one's class position turns one into a propagandist, unable to distinguish between vision/fantasy and deep reality, unable to concede the validity of other visions.

Merton was right.

NOTE

Those social scientists who recognize no vision at all in their research might try a different approach. I suggest that they think about the method they use in their research. Perhaps they locate themselves in science as a practicioner of a method, and their experience with this method might help them understand the visions of other scientists.

Every method has problems, pitfalls, weaknesses. In one's own method, these are experienced as challenges to be overcome. A *good* experimenter is aware of experimenter effects, biased samples, subjects' interpretations of the experiment, the problem of ecological validity, robustness, construct validity, and so on. During a long schedule of experiments one hopes to solve these problems one by one with proper care, and one looks forward to a time when most of the problems will have been managed and a definitive result achieved. That is vision, though not Schumpeter's version.

In present research, one is always dealing with difficulties; but underlying this process is the ideal method, practiced by a good experimenter, that will eventually produce truth decades from now.

Other methods, however, are regarded from the outside with a more skeptical eye. Those researchers too are dealing with problems, perhaps too routinely or clumsily, but they are not really aware of the more basic weaknesses of their method. A *good* researcher can probably achieve results with any method, but these are ordinary, competent researchers. Experimenter effects and subjects' personality effects, for instance, can never be fully managed, and the attempt to do so produces even worse distortions. Realistically, it's hopeless; definitive results are not possible. That is lack of vision, which we save for others' methods.

7

Microsociology of Social Science

IT IS TIME once again to give chaos its due, and as always bring some order to it. The Mertonian scientific community was unified by shared norms and counternorms which enabled scientists to work together and achieve a shared truth. But Merton's critics such as Michael Mulkay and Randall Collins have maintained that these norms are fictions that scientists have invented as part of their struggle for professional prestige and foundation grants. Scientists are not disinterested, not self-skeptical, and certainly not humble, the critics assert; they push their own ideas dogmatically and persistently. They do not judge others' ideas on universalistic criteria, but accept ideas that are similar to their own or useful to them, and criticize, misrepresent, or ignore the rest. In short, they act like Mitroff's brutal egotists, the moon scientists.

What then prevents scientists' communication from degenerating into Agassi's criticism of all against all? How can shared truth emerge out of egotistic strife? Ravetz has raised the issue most directly: How does it happen "that out of a personal endeavour which is fallible, subjective, and strictly limited by its context, there emerges knowledge which is certain, objective, and universal"? (1971, p. 71). He devotes part II of his book to this issue. Or, if "certain, objective, and universal" knowledge is too much to hope for in the social sciences, how can we get even plausible, temporary, partial understanding out of egotistic self-display?

The microsociologists find an answer in close-up detailed studies of particular scientific episodes. These studies reveal how the disorder that is always present in scientific work is continuously transformed into order. The order and unity that the Mertonians attributed to an ideal community of all scientists is now found in the minute-by-minute activities of one, two, or three researchers. The techniques these researchers use are not unique to science. Scientists are social beings like the rest of us; they maintain order in their social relations and activities in the same ways that other people do.

Thus the microsociological approach requires us to begin with individual research and move step by step toward actual, not idealized communities and eventually to public knowledge. Perhaps if we move carefully forward a step at a time in this fashion we will get a more secure result than if we try to solve the whole problem at once.

The microsociological researchers divide themselves into a number of groups who differ slightly on method, theoretical background, and theoretical focus of interest. There are the ethnomethodologists—Garfinkel, Lynch, Livingston, Sacks, Woolgar, et al.—deriving from Schutz, Merleau-Ponty, and Heidegger; the constructivists—Knorr, Latour, Sutton, influenced by Bourdieu; the Edinburgh school—Barnes, Bloor, Law, Shapin, MacKenzie, Edge, Dean; the empirical relativist or Bath School—H. M. Collins, Pinch, Travis, Pickering, W. Harvey; and many others not easily classifiable—Mulkay, Restivo, Chubin, Potter, Yearley, Krohn, Whitley, Weingart, Gilbert, et al. Knorr-Cetina and Mulkay (1983), a good survey of the whole field, distinguishes eight research programs including the weak program, the mild program, and discourse analysis in addition to the above. Apparently they are as divided as the science that they study. As for predecessors, Ravetz, who is often cited, asserts that Kuhn "has, as it were, created the new paradigm which we all follow" (1971, p. 73).

There is disagreement here between the Mertonians and the anti-Mertonians; both claim Kuhn as their own. The Mertonians focus on Kuhn's scientific communities, since these communities are the real source of knowledge; the anti-Mertonians argue that Kuhn provided a scheme by which social factors could influence the content of science, while for Merton the content of science should be independent of social influences (Mulkay, 1980; Barnes, 1982). The macrosociological issue of social influences on science, which Edinburgh people such as Barnes and Bloor have emphasized, has been discussed in the previous chapter. Restivo (1983) argues convincingly that the real Kuhn was a Mertonian, while the microsociologists are all anti-Mertonian. (See also Law and French, 1974.)

The microsociologists are unified by a journal, *Social Studies of Science*, coming out of Edinburgh. They all use variants of the ethnographic or participant-observer method; they watch and listen inside a laboratory or observatory, try their hand at staining slides and mixing chemicals, tape-record and analyze lab discussions, informally interview the researchers afterwards. In textual analysis, they compare successive versions of an article with what they have observed and with interview material. The purpose is to find out what actually happens inside one lab and then watch the results get transformed into journal articles, controversies, and finally public knowledge.

Nearly all these case studies deal with experiments in a laboratory, so their conclusions should apply most directly to experimental psychology and especially to animal experiments. We can also consult our own experience to see how relevant they are to other social science methods.

THE RESEARCH PROCESS

We begin with the ethnomethodologists, the most meticulous and detailed of all the laboratory observers. The stated aim of the ethnomethodologists is to rediscover the problem of social order in the details of scientific practice (Lynch et al., 1983, p. 205). Disorder breaks out constantly; as Knorr-Cetina observes, "A day in the laboratory will usually suffice to impress upon the observer a sense of the disorder within which scientists operate, and a month in the lab will confirm that most laboratory work is concerned with counteracting and remedying this disorder (Knorr-Cetina and Mulkay, 1983, p. 123). Lab rats get rambunctious and refuse to let themselves be operated on properly; or one will emerge from its box at the start of a trial, yawn, scratch itself, and amble back in again when it is supposed to be running a maze in record time. A human subject will request time off to light a cigarette. Materials are not uniform in quality; some equipment is not the most appropriate, but it will have to do; the tissue slide is not cut or stained properly to show the relevant cells clearly, the telescope must be properly adjusted to get the signal (Garfinkel et al., 1981). The researcher must constantly clear a path through these circumstances. "Actual scientific practice entails the confrontation and negation of utter confusion" (Latour and Woolgar, 1979, p. 36). Norms and counternorms are irrelevant to this problem (Lynch, 1985, p. xiv). One technique is to make on-the-spot decisions: will this count as a trial, will this botched slide count as one instance, would it be fair to give that lazy rat a little nudge? (Notice the norm there.) Another technique is to negotiate agreement; if one researcher sees something and the other doesn't, the first can offer the compromise statement that he might have seen something resembling it. Thus he saw the resemblance and the other saw the contrast. Or one can negotiate the loan of better equipment, by rearranging the research so as to interest the possessor of the equipment.

The order that the researcher produces is mainly a temporal order (Lynch, 1985, chap. 3). This is Heidegger's "temporalization" (pp. 53, 76). The parts of a process must go in a certain sequence: the tissue section must be cut first, then stained, then mounted. Several sequences can be fit together, so a waiting time in sequence 1 can be filled with a step from sequence 2. Or a sequence can be interrupted to deal with a malfunctioning apparatus. This temporal order reappears as a spatial order on the lab table: pieces of equipment are arranged in groups according to their place in the sequence, and often used tools are set up where they will be handy. These sequences and locations are then repaired and adjusted when disorder breaks in. For example, Schrecker reports that when a sequence moved too fast for him he almost knocked over a flask and then set it in the wrong location, thus producing disorder; as a result, his hands "were engaged in a territory whose spatial arrangements did not adequately exhibit the sequential organization any longer" and he KNOCKED OVER THE FLASK. Then he reestablished order by picking up the flask again (Lynch et al., 1983, pp. 228–29). As Lynch et al. comment, "Much of what evidently makes up the orderliness of scientific activities "*is not worth talking about*" (p. 208).

We can divide this ethnomethodological order into two parts. One is the sequences and spatial arrangements as they should properly or ideally be, apart from accidents. The other is the actual constructed order that corrects accidents and breakdowns so as to reestablish some approximation to the ideal order. The second order derives from the first (Bourdieu, 1977, p. 3). Thus the two kinds of (negative) disorder that Lynch distinguishes—which he calls "oops!" and "what went wrong" (1985, pp. 115–18)—exist only as negations of the ideal or proper order.

The ethnomethodologist observes the production of the second order, the constructed order, but the first is not observable by his method. Short sequences can be understood internally; the slide must be stained and mounted before it can be photographed. But the photographed slide is a step in a larger sequence; where does this order come from? Lynch notes that there seems to be some overall research design, though he could not find it himself. He vaguely speculates that the lab director might know what is going on, but the researchers themselves are only carrying out orders (1985, pp. 63–64). The first order, the overall research sequence, thus comes from outside in the form of orders. As Knorr-Cetina concludes, "The scientists' laboratory selections constantly refer us to a contextuality beyond the immediate site of the action" (1981, p. 81).

The first order, the research design, can also be discovered by participant observation. However, one does not discover it by watching; that yields the second or constructed order. One discovers the research design by listening and asking questions—of the research director, not the assistants who carry out orders. This was in fact my objective (Diesing, 1971); I was looking for actual research designs. I listened, asked questions, read field diaries and published accounts of "first days in the field." After listening, one can watch, but what one sees is different from what the ethnomethodologist sees. The latter, looking into a cage in the lab, sees a bit of water and perhaps spilled water; I see a reinforcer.

The actual research design is different from the official research design published in a later article or book, and also different from the actual research sequence, the second order.

From several research designs we can induce rules of method by noticing what works and what doesn't work. These rules are heuristics, advice on how to proceed to get results. They belong to Kaplan's "logic in use" and Simon's "logic of discovery" (1977). For instance, in mathematical modeling one rule is: to model a complex situation, locate the fundamental relation in it, model the simplest version of that, and then add the complications one by one. This does not always work; so there is a second rule: take a few standard models off your shelf and try to see the situation as one of these models. Next focus on the difference between model and situation and try to fit it into a variant of the model. If this does not work, then, as a third rule, try to break the situation into parts and model one part . . . .

Experienced researchers have learned a number of such rules or heuristics and include them in their research design. The problem of order is to apply these rules to particular research situations to produce actual research. This is what the constructivists study (among other things). For example, the researchers in Latour's lab accidentally discovered a brain hormone, which they nicknamed "somatostatin" (Latour, 1981a). The problem then was to construct analogs to this hormone that would be more effective. An analog is a chemical with the same structure as somatostatin except that one or more components are different.

The first step in the research design was necessarily to determine the structure of somatostatin. Since different researchers normally interpret lab happenings differently (and since variants of the hormone may have had different structures), this was a matter of negotiating agreement (Latour, 1981a, p. 54). The structure they compromised on had 2.6×10^{22} possible analogs. Search rules, heuristics, were needed to guide the search through this enormous space to find the few best analogs. Latour studied the search process after it had gone on for five years and produced 286 analogs. How were these 286 selected for manufacture and testing?

Latour induced at least four rules: (1) Delete each of the fourteen original components, one at a time. (2) Replace each component, one at a time, with alanine, a promising amino acid. (3) Ditto for tyrosine. (4) Replace each component with a right-handed version. These rules were parts of the first order, the ideal search process. But they could not be applied systematically because of the disorder that had to be accommodated. "When you get closer to the research process, the multiplicity and the chaos increase" (p. 58).

One accident was the attempt of some researchers to try this brain hormone on the pancreas. A new diabetes drug would be worth millions, so the pharmaceutical industry moved in on the research, and the criterion of effectiveness was revised. The main researcher happened to receive a supply of an amino acid and tried it because it was handy. Another researcher suggested that the agreed-on structure of somatostatin was wrong and was missing one part. Still another researcher found that results with one analog suggested new possibilities. Here we are not dealing with "oops!" disorder, but with sudden opportunities, insights, and intuitions that ought to be incorporated into the search process. The outcome, the second order or actual research process, combines these emergents with the rules in an unpredictable though fairly rational sequence. "To understand the research process one has to look exactly in the *middle* of order and disorder" (p. 61).

Latour calls the research process "bricolage." Knorr, in a similar case study, writes of "tinkering" and "making things work" (Knorr, 1977; Knorr-Cetina, 1981, chaps. 1–2). Latour also cites Heidegger's saying "*Gedanke ist Handwerk*"—scientific thinking is a handicraft (Latour and Woolgar, 1979, p. 171). It is a form of practical reasoning, not of pure logic. Bourdieu calls it "regulated improvisation" (1977, chap. 2).

I believe a similar process occurs in social science research. For example, in our crisis bargaining research, part of Glenn Snyder's ideal research design was to make it interdisciplinary. (See Snyder and Diesing,

1977.) So he set up a seminar in 1964 and invited about fifteen people from all sorts of disciplines. After two years, four senior faculty from four fields remained, so he "made it work" with us. Later, two junior researchers quit because they refused to accept a military research grant (Project Themis); we managed, sadly, without them. One later returned; he found National Science Foundation money acceptable. A basic rule of historical method is to study the first-hand reports of all major participants in a conflict, to get a well-rounded view, and this requires facility in several languages. For instance, one cannot understand the 1958 Lebanon crisis adequately without reading Camille Chamoun's memoirs, in French. I read some atrociously one-sided case histories that were based on only English-language sources. But Snyder had to make do with the available language skills, and assigned the cases accordingly.

Where do the rules of scientific method come from? When a researcher is constructing an ideal research design, where does one get the parts? Some of the rules, such as: Try alanine at each location, or Try a game model on a conflict situation, come from experienced success. One could say they are deduced from a general rule: If it works, use it again. Other rules, such as the historian's rule: In studying a crisis read everyone's memoirs but don't believe any of them, come from experienced failures, like the atrocious propaganda pervading the international politics literature. Ravetz (1971, pt. II) focuses on the latter kind of rule, the kind based on past failures. He argues that the craft of scientific research consists chiefly of knowing the pitfalls that await a research project and designing the research to avoid them. In other words, the first or ideal order is constructed out of a foreknowledge of the disorder that lies in wait. Instead of puzzling over "what went wrong" accidents, as the ethnomethodologists' subjects do, one builds devices to forestall them. But since no one can foresee all the pitfalls and opportunities that come up, tinkering is still necessary. The second-order or actual research process accommodates the planned research design to whatever comes up.

So far we have moved two steps from the immediate, phenomenologically constructed second order of the ethnomethodologists—adjusting telescopes, picking up flasks—toward the goal of objective knowledge. (1) We have moved from the second, constructed order to the first order of a research design which incorporates heuristic rules of method, and a craft or *Handwerk* which adjusts these rules to the circumstances of the research situation. The rules tell how to work effectively with certain types of materials or problems, and how to avoid common pitfalls (for example, T. Barber, 1976). The craft is a practice of diagnosing specific pitfalls and opportunities. (2) Both rules and craft are derived from previous research experience and transmitted by apprenticeship, informal conversation, and the writings of methodologists. Thus they transcend the immediate research situation and draw in a collective experience, a social practice.

The product of research is still private, located in the lab or the research group. The next step therefore must be to make the private results public by publishing them. (The following account is based mainly on Knorr-Cetina, 1981, chap. 5; Gilbert and Mulkay, 1981; and Latour and Woolgar, 1979.)

The constructivists and discourse analysts emphasize that there is always a difference between the actual, private research process and the published account. The goal of the private process is to reach agreement in the research group; the goal of the public process is to persuade some selected scientific community. Consequently, the research results must be *recontextualized*, taken out of the private context and transformed to fit the public context.

The published paper must begin where the intended readers presumably are, that is, with the existing theory and data that they accept. It can then either build on what is accepted, or criticize and undermine it. In either case, the research problem must be located in existing theory, not in the actual research. Since the results, the solution, are already available, a problem can be selected or manufactured from the literature to fit the available results. There must be abundant citations from the literature to connect the paper to what is already accepted, and to show solid scholarship.

The style of the paper must be persuasive. It must use impersonal language and proceed methodically step by step, as though anyone could easily replicate the results. The method is idealized as standard procedures and automatic results. In other words, the actual process is reversed in the paper: actually the results are constructed, crafted, by tinkering with available materials, but in the paper the results inexorably come straight from Nature as the researcher clears a path and then passively stands aside.

Here as elsewhere the constructions of the constructivist laboratory observers come closest to the practice in experimental psychology. In anthropology, for instance in Latour's lab ethnography, an impersonal-replicability style would make no sense. Instead, the accounts are necessarily personal but matter-of-fact, listing step by step what "I" did, as though things actually happened in that inexorable, purposeful, methodical order. The clinical paper has a different style again; it omits the analyst's misinterpretations and fumbling and mentions mainly the key interpretations that led to a flood of insight.

In the theoretical section, the rhetoric guides the reader into the proper attitude toward a theoretical assertion."A long held assumption" or "People have believed" signals that a theory is about to be demolished; "Experimental results show" announces the Voice of Nature revealing the truth. "A few sociologists have come to see" or "There has been a growing recognition" (Gilbert and Mulkay, 1981, p. 269) announces a new truth that the article will build on.

To illustrate the results persuasively, the writer selects the best slides or the best quantitative tables. Or, if people are involved, one selects especially apt quotations, as in the present work, the lab ethnographers' reports, or the clinical case history. Here as elsewhere the ethno-methodologists' quotations are the most meticulous phonetically and temporally, with silences measured to 0.1 sec.; but also selected for persuasiveness. If the best tables and charts are not so good, one can explain away the difference from one's conclusions, citing interfering factors and the crudeness of the instruments. Or one can tinker, trying various leads and lags or correcting for presumed sampling error. In short, as Latour and Woolgar (1979) assert, the purpose of the research paper is to persuade the readers that no persuasion is occurring.

Finally, the writer must anticipate possible objections and answer or deflect them. The writer imagines specific critics reading the paper, locates points they could attack, and supports the argument at these points with a data table, quotation from some authority, or at least a citation that will deflect the critic's attention.

Do these tactics work? No. They serve rather as an entrance ticket to the public arena; a paper that did not use them would be rejected by editors and referees as poorly written. Once the paper is published and enters the public arena, different mechanisms come into operation to determine the fate of the researchers' constructions.

THE PUBLIC ARENA

The rationality of the public arena is midway between the unreflective order of everyday research—arranging things on a lab table, scheduling interview appointments—and the objective, public knowledge we seek. Consequently, we should expect to find a complex, many-sided process, subjective in some ways and more objective in others. The micro-sociologists have focused on one aspect of this process, the interpersonal or social exchange aspect. But this focus does not deny the existence of others: the political aspect (discussed in chapter 8), the cognitive aspect (chapter 9), and the personal aspect (chapter 10). One must understand all of these aspects to understand its complex rationality. A quick and simple characterization, perhaps in terms of information theory or cyber-netics, such as a mathematical modeler or a mathematical thinker would want to make, is bound to be one-sided and inadequate. Nor is it enough to list a series of factors, social, cognitive, political, that influence public discussion, as though one or two of these factors produces a rational outcome and the others interfere. Rather, it is necessary to *see the process as* social, to *see it as* cognitive, as political, and so forth, to understand it. It is all of them simultaneously.

The first step in dealing with a publication that enters the public arena ought to be hermeneutic. In order to deal with a new work of science, the reader must first understand it. This involves interpreting it within the author's tradition, not the reader's tradition. One discovers the author's tradition by studying positive citations, references to ac-cepted theory (accepted in a tradition), references to erroneous or out-moded theories (other traditions), and biographical data. If the tradition is different from one's own, one must move into it by reading all the major works from the beginning on, and if possible by talking to members of the tradition to see how they think. Then one has a context for interpretation. In some cases it may also be helpful to locate a personal context, the author's personality, so that some passages or the whole structure can be interpreted as moves in a personal process. Consider, for example, the stiff supercautious writing style, full of distinctions and qualifications and classifications and boundaries, of Talcott Parsons's writ-ings around 1950 or so, which loosened up in his later works. That's part of his personal kind of functionalism, a part that produced many remark-able boundary and classification-type insights when he got it under con-trol. In practice, social scientists normally omit the hermeneutic process. If the work is written in their own tradition, they understand it and relate it to their own thinking and research. If it is written in a different tradition, they impose their categories and beliefs on it, and misunder-stand it. Then they evaluate it as false.

In the case of literature reviews, reviewers will sometimes select experimental reports to fit their own categories, and then simplify and interpret them to fit their theories (Berkowitz, 1971).

The following account of the public arena is based on Bourdieu's fundamental article "The Social Conditions of the Progress of Reason" (1975). See also Bourdieu (1977); Latour and Woolgar (1979), which builds on Bourdieu; and writings of the Edinburgh School such as Pickering (1981).

In Mertonian sociology, the main social process in the public arena is the exchange of recognition for original achievement. Scientists who build on and extend accepted knowledge, or who correct an error or resolve some puzzle, ought to be recognized for their contribution to knowledge. Those who provide more evidence for what is already known ought to be recognized for achievement but not originality. Original error ought to receive no recognition.

Who would most readily evaluate an article as an original achievement? Someone who understands it and who shares its assumptions and categories (accepted knowledge)—that is, someone working in the same tradition. In a Mertonian context, the primary obligation to recognize falls on the elite of the community, since they have the responsibility to maintain the community in working order. But the elite are precisely the people whose theorizing constitutes the accepted knowledge of the community. Consequently, the article they recognize recognizes *them* by building on their work and extending its applicability. It is an exchange of recognition, a gift exchange. When the elite say, "Well done, thou good and faithful servant" (Matthew 25:14–29), they do so because the servant has brought back a good profit for them on the capital they have provided.

If we aggregate these gift exchanges within a community, we see that since the elite are always one partner in the exchange, they get the most recognition. Their ideas are being used, extended, applied, supported, and their works are cited. This is the *Matthew effect*—"Unto him who hath shall be given"—though not Merton's version of it.

Other members of the community are also likely to recognize the work, in part because they understand it and agree with its "accepted knowledge." Their public recognition is also part of a gift exchange. They give recognition and receive ideas they can work with and data they can cite in support of their work. But insofar as ordinary members of a community are competitors for group recognition, they can be expected to be more qualified in their recognition, accepting part and criticizing part (for example, Knorr-Cetina, 1981, chap. 4; Latour, 1982). Their recognition says to the community, "recognize her (and thereby my work which she builds on), but recognize me too."

The simplest form of recognition is the citation, which says, "This publication exists." A positive citation says, in addition, "and is worth reading." A few words of praise are better, and building on the work is still better. The recipient of such a gift incurs an obligation, unless the recipient is a member of the elite. In that case, it is normal homage, and can be acknowledged with a plain citation. However, the elite can also bestow recommendations for jobs, research grants, and editorial acceptance. Rejection of a work as false is most likely to occur when the reader misunderstands it because it is in a different tradition. This concept is the hermeneutic version of Kuhn's "incommensurability." Misunderstanding consists of forcing one's own categories and problems onto the work, and then finding that (1) its reasoning is confused, (2) it evades the important problems, and (3) it repeats old errors. For example, analytic philosophers normally misinterpret the microsociologists as relativists (for instance, Freudenthal, 1984). *Relativism* in their categories is an absurd position, illogical, an ancient error; it means that no knowledge is possible at all. This is not what relativism means for the Bath School (see, for example, H. Collins, in Knorr-Cetina and Mulkay, 1983). Next, one of the nagging problems of the analytic philosophers is that since some facts are more or less theory-laden, how are the conclusive empirical tests essential to a real science possible? The microsociologists do not answer this question because it is not a problem for them; hence their work evades the real issues for the analytic philosophers. Another such problem is: How can rationality, the domain of philosophers, be separated out from irrational factors, the domain of mere sociologists? Again, the sociological works evade this important issue because their concept *social* is different from that of the philosophers. I mean to pick on the analytic philosophers, but I could cite much of the literature of the social sciences as well.

Next, a reader who has worked through the hermeneutic process and come to understand a work in a different tradition may still reject it. Consider the previous example of the relation between rational and social processes. Analytic philosophers such as Laudan (1981) argue that social factors can properly be cited in explaining errors of reasoning or research, but are irrelevant for explaining correct reasoning and research design. If a writer adds 2 and 2 and gets 4, we do not need a social explanation; we merely observe that the writer knows how to add, knows how to reason. The sociologist who understands this distinction will reject it because it assigns the lower realm of error and irrationality, the realm of bad science, to sociology and reserves the realm of good science for philosophers. Thus Knorr-Cetina (1988) argues that social factors are not interferences, but instruments of knowledge. The experimenter's sensitivity to indicators is learned; the ethnographer's use of talk to probe and interpret overt, visible happenings is learned; and so on. Conversely, the rare analytic philosopher who understood the microsociologists' argument that reasoning in the public arena is a social process would still reject it, because it leaves little or nothing for analytic philosophers to do. This argument *in its sociological aspect* is a struggle over turf, analogous to the Berber families' struggle for control of agricultural land (Bourdieu, 1977). In addition, it is a struggle over social status, since people who study the logic of good or real science are of a higher status than those who study the bad stuff.

However, not all problem formulations, distinctions, and definitions within a tradition can be understood as a claim for exclusive jurisdiction. Some scientists call for joint jurisdiction by several disciplines or traditions, and these formulations would be accepted by members of the included traditions. For example, the Katona-type empirical studies of consumer behavior stake a claim for survey researchers in this area, without disputing the legitimacy of economists' theoretical work on the consumption function. The two disciplines can collaborate.

Finally, competitors within a community might reject part of a publication while citing and agreeing with most of it, for reasons given above.

Rejection tactics vary according to whether the publication has been understood or not. If it is misunderstood, the simplest form of rejection is to mistranslate the argument into one's own categories and thus make it absurd. Or one can omit the argument and call names—for instance, calling the hermeneutic philosophers "hermeneuts." Or one can exaggerate or simplify the argument, driving it to an extreme, to "show where it logically leads" or "make it more interesting" (Newton-Smith, 1981) before refuting it. Or one can pick out a weak spot, a careless detail, and exaggerate its importance as evidence that the whole work ought to be rejected. Or one can point to questions it does not answer, questions that are important in one's own theory but not in the publication.

If one understands the publication, one can reject it by "deconstructing" it, revealing the private research process, the decisions and assumptions, behind it. Some traces of the private process can be dug out of the publication: the footnotes listing the assumptions behind particular numbers in the table, the selection of the sample, the construction of an index, the reasoning justifying the use of some indicator to measure a depth variable, the use of one definition of probability rather than another, the absence of reference to some French or German memoir or history and the use instead of a secondary source, the list of interviewees and evidence of gullibility toward one interviewee, the degree of aggregation of the data which obscures some effects and brings out others, reasons for discarding certain data which, coincidentally, would have eliminated the discovered correlation (Landsberger, 1970), a laconic "For reasons unnecessary to relate, the selection was limited to . . . " (West, 1945, p. vii). Then in each case one can suggest an alternative process of tinkering that would yield a different result. A different indicator, a different interview, a different measure of consumer income, different questionnaire items, a different lead or lag, will always give a somewhat different result. Indeed, one can carry out the alternative process in one's own experiment or mathematical model. Other traces of the private process can be found by interviews with participants, or decades later in memoirs and letters. For example the letters of Freud and of Keynes have recently been used to deconstruct publications by these scientists.

This is the process that is systematized in Murray Levine's "adversary model" (1974). The rational function of deconstruction is to test the published data for external validity. Only data that survive cross-examination in the public arena ought to be accepted as valid.

The point that the constructivists emphasize is that *all* scientific results are constructed, not just the false ones. Consequently, all can be deconstructed. Some decisions and selections and assumptions and adjustments must always be made. This does not mean that deconstructions are always *valid* when they move a publication from the "objective" to the "subjective" category, merely that they are always *possible*.

Scientists tend to use a double standard in the public arena. They describe their own work in terms of an idealized method to hide their construction; but they deconstruct opponents' work. The elite in a community maintain agreement by accepting insiders' work as instances of idealized method, but they deconstruct dissenting works, pointing to the difference between actual and ideal methods and calling for conclusive evidence and complete controls (Blissett, 1972, p. 117).

The worst fate a publication can suffer is to be ignored. This happens when there is no community that can use or build on its ideas and data, and also no community whose turf is threatened by it. Such a work exists in an empty space; it neither comes out of a current research tradition nor leads into an enrichment of some tradition. Who now has heard of Scudder Klyce's *Universe*? This was a large, scholarly systematization of existing knowledge, as of the 1930s, but it did not relate to the research interests of any active group of scientists, so no one paid any attention to it. Similarly Ludwik Fleck's 1935 book, *Genesis and Development of a Scientific Fact*, remained unread and unknown until the late 1970s, when the constructivists suddenly developed similar ideas and started citing Fleck as supporting evidence (1979, intro.).

Given these characteristics of the public arena, or in Bourdieu's terms the scientific field (1975), what strategies are available to the young scientist starting a career? Bourdieu distinguishes two, a succession strategy and a subversion strategy.

A succession strategy consists of being a "good and faithful servant" in some existing community. The simplest way is to become a student of some community leader; or one can join by paying homage to a leader, using his theories, and building on them. This strategy guarantees readers for one's writings. It also is likely to get recognition and recommendations from the leader and qualified recognition from other followers. The main payoff goes to the leader, whose theory is being developed; but the follower accumulates citations, gets included in conferences and edited volumes, gets recommended for research grants or included in research projects, gets invited onto convention programs. That way one can quickly make a name for oneself within the community, or in Bourdieu's terms accumulate symbolic capital. Soon other people will discuss and build on one's ideas, and if one can compete effectively with other followers, one gets promoted to the position of close associate of the leader, part of the community elite. Ideally, as the leadership ages, one can succeed the old leadership, if the community still exists.

A subversion strategy consists of criticizing the paradigm of some community and setting up a new paradigm (in Merton's sense of paradigm). This strategy is risky because it almost guarantees rejection at best and the limbo of noncitation at worst. Consequently, most young scientists will avoid it. For example, Bill Harvey (1981, pp. 148ff.) describes how a student, Holt, accidentally got an experimental result that flatly contradicted some laws of quantum mechanics. He could have declared that he had disproved those laws, but he would promptly have been buried under an avalanche of rejection, insult, and misrepresentations and then forgotten. So Holt took the safer tactic of declaring publicly that his experimental result was erroneous. He then tried for two years to find the error, hopefully following up all the critical objections his teachers could invent. He failed; the result was consistently replicated. However, his efforts earned him the forgiveness of the community leaders. Holt had had bad luck, they concluded; his experimental results were consistently wrong, but it wasn't his fault. He was a good experimenter.

That one didn't work according to Levine's model.

A subversion strategy, Kuhn's "revolution," is more promising if there is a small group willing to pursue it together. Then they can announce a new paradigm, cite each other's writings, set up conferences published as edited volumes, and (they hope) make a big enough splash to attract disciples. If they succeed, they immediately become the community elite, accumulating symbolic capital rapidly in a stream of publications and citations and appointments and research grants. The microsociologists are an example of a group pursuing a successful subversion strategy. Their early articles are full of bold pronouncements that something new is happening, something important is being studied for the first time, a start is being made, science is now advancing.

Two circumstances, external and internal, provide the social conditions for a successful subversion strategy. Externally, political circumstances may suddenly produce an age cohort of disaffected young social scientists. Consider New Left Marxism, for example. The few American Marxists of the 1950s—Sweezy, Baran, Marcuse, Aptheker, Genovese—were ignored or scolded; Sweezy and Aptheker had no university appointment. After 1965 the civil rights movement, the student movement, and the vicious, evil, lying, murderous U.S. foreign policy produced a large number of graduate students who rejected existing conceptual frameworks and looked for a theory that would explain U.S. foreign policy; hence, Marxism.

Internally, an existing community may get so large and successful that there is little recognition left for newcomers. Nor is there prospect of long-run rewards. The succession is already decided, and indeed the successors have already established several variants with their own subcommunities, as in the many varieties of functionalism in the 1960s. A few of the new age cohort may establish close relations with one of these successors. The rest face a bleak future in the functionalist or symbolic interactionist community; hence, microsociology.

Bourdieu (1977) mentions a third strategy, an insult strategy. An insult is a challenge to a duel, and the winner exhibits prowess and gains recognition. If the challenge is thrown down to a powerful leader, even a draw or small loss exhibits one's prowess and gains one recognition. Examples are all the criticisms of Talcott Parsons and Herbert Blumer in the 1970s, beginning with Gouldner (1970) and his "Parsonsian" epithet. A book criticizing one of these two was certain to get journal reviews, whether the reviews were critical or not is irrelevant. Nor were Herbert Blumer's complaints that he had been thoroughly misrepresented relevant; truth was not at issue here, but recognition of critical ability.

An insult strategy is most effective if it comes from within one community and criticizes a leader of a different community. The critic gets recognition both for critical ability and for upholding the accepted truths of the community. Thus it is a variant of the succession strategy. A safer but lower payoff tactic is to criticize an ordinary member of a different community. Such challenges must be accepted, and the result is a dispute. Disputes are normally inconclusive; they begin and end in disagreement.

These three strategies are the ones open to new entrants, though established scientists such as Gouldner can also adopt an occasional insult tactic. The elite are in a different strategic position. They already have all the symbolic capital they need: anything they write will get published, read, discussed, cited, used; they can have research grants almost for the asking; a hint will bring them offers of university appointments. Their task is rather to maintain harmony among their followers, arrange for an orderly succession, and promote alliances with other communities; that way their works will continue to be influential in ever widening circles. All of Merton's system-maintenance tasks become rational self-promotion strategies for Bourdieu (1975).

In particular, established leaders do not have to respond to challenges, or can turn them aside with a nod of friendly recognition. They have no need to demonstrate prowess, and it might even be undignified to respond to an unknown challenger. Their followers can take care of him. It is also rational to welcome a bold new paradigm and offer an alliance with it. Consider for example Bernard Barber's 1982 review of Barnes's *T. S. Kuhn and Social Science*. Barber is a student and longtime close associate of Merton; Barnes of the Edinburgh School is one of Merton's earliest critics. His book continues Barnes's attempt, begun in 1970, to appropriate Kuhn's enormous prestige for the anti-Merton forces. Barber's review is most friendly and generous. He heaps praise on Barnes from all sides, then chides him gently for misrepresenting functionalism, and asserts that functionalists mainly agree with Barnes. He then asserts that functionalists have always been constructivists, but have been unable to do lab ethnography and the like because of ignorance and a lack of expertise; he welcomes the Edinburgh studies. After two very subdued criticisms of Barnes, he concludes with a call to "give up prejudice, stereotypes, hostility, and defensiveness." This call for an alliance with the microsociologists, a call Merton also has issued, is rational; but the microsociologists' prejudice, stereotypes, and hostility was also rational in 1975–82. They had to get established, accumulate symbolic capital, before they could make peace. In political science, David Easton issued a similar welcome to the New Left political scientists in his 1968 presidential address before the American Political Science Association.

Do social scientists really have to follow one of these rather sordid strategies? Can't they just quietly search for truth? Bourdieu's answer would be that a few fortunately placed individuals may have different strategies available, but most new social scientists are compelled by market forces to pick a succession or subversion strategy.

First, to be able to search for truth one must at least have a university or research appointment, since searching for truth takes time. But to get tenure one must publish, and to publish one must do research—experiments or surveys or field work or case studies. But such research usually requires a research grant, and the bigger the grant the bigger the project and the subsequent publications. But to get a grant one needs previous publications, that is, previous research . . . .

Latour and Woolgar call this cycle the investment cycle; publication requires research, which requires a research grant, which requires publication (1979, chap. 5, esp. p. 201).

The new social scientist cannot break into this cycle immediately; one must first borrow some working capital. One can do this either by getting recommendations from a teacher who is a community leader or subleader (succession strategy) or by attracting attention with proclamations of a new paradigm (subversion strategy). The working capital must rapidly be transformed into publications. These in turn can be the basis for a small individual grant leading to a few more articles. Such articles can be the basis for a bigger grant involving hired researchers or his own graduate students and leading to a book or two, and perhaps a successor grant. At each step one's symbolic capital, one's recognition, is larger, and at each step one must invest this capital in new research, and so on endlessly.

Latour and Woolgar contrast their investment cycle with the Mertonian gift exchange, recognition for original achievement, or actually recognition for recognition. The gift exchange, a precapitalist process, is external to research. It provides a presumed external motivation to publish, but does not affect the research process itself. Latour and Woolgar's scientists don't need gifts; they need jobs and research grants. They are caught in the investment cycle, which forces them to publish and publish, and which determines the direction of their research: their research is directed to getting more grants.

Why should new social scientists let themselves get caught in this rat race? They are forced to do so by the market, that is, pressure from competitors. There are always others who could get included in a research project or who could get hired. There are always others applying for the research grants, and most do get turned down. Nor are the competitors equal; some are well-established, well-known scientists who, by the Matthew effect, are more likely to get the available grants. Those who get turned down for grants and tenure will not have much time or resources to search for truth.

In short, the searcher for truth must accumulate ever more symbolic capital and reinvest it, or fail and disappear. Accumulate! Accumulate! That is Moses and the prophets!

The pressure to accumulate has actually inceased since 1945, first because of the increasing number of social science researchers competing for recognition and research funds, and second because of the increase in available research funds. According to Ravetz (1971), the increasing competitive pressure has gradually transformed science into what he calls "industrialized science." Ravetz was describing the natural sciences, but some of his observations may apply also to the social sciences, in lesser degree.

1. The rate of scientific discovery and of obsolescence has been speeded up. With several competitors working in the same area, the first to submit a good research proposal or journal article will get the recognition, and the others will have to supply the recognition by citing and building on the winner's work. A good research proposal, in turn, must

be up to date in its citations; and if it can cite unpublished reports of others' work in progress, that is even better. The tempo is fastest in experimental psychology, according to a citation study reported at a 1976 meeting of the 4S (Society for Social Studies of Science). I am told that you are out of it if you stop scanning the experimental psychology journals for about three years.

2. In order to maintain a winning tempo of research, experimenters have to organize their research more efficiently by increasing the division of labor and tightening research schedules. A big winner like Raymond Cattell has to have several research projects running at all times. He himself, the PI (principal investigator), has to concentrate on designing the projects, hiring researchers, writing grant applications and expenditure and progress reports, in a steady stream. His assistants, the co-I, supervise the research and help him write the final reports, journal articles, and convention papers. Graduate students do the actual research and earn coauthorships. These experimenters are disciples of the mythical Dr. Grant Swinger, interviewed by D. S. Greenberg in 1966, head of the National Animal Speech Agency (NASA), which had its origins in the president's challenge to the nation to teach an animal to speak by 1970 (Greenberg, 1967).

3. A by-product of grantsmanship is the information crisis. Each PI writes an initial report of the theoretical or social problem with which the proposed research will deal, as a way of alerting colleagues in the field. The article is a rewrite of the grant proposal. The researcher reports the research design and current progress in a conference or convention paper, which is published in the convention proceedings, a nonbook. The final report to the funding agency, which concludes with a statement of the urgent need for more research, must of course also be published. Sometimes revised versions are later published in an edited volume or festschrift, and an expanded version with later results may be published as a book.

The purpose of these publications, except for the book, is first to claim proprietorship in the research design and data for citation purposes, and second to advertise the results in a variety of public forums aimed at different readers or listeners. But because of the flood of publications, few people read these reports, in the natural sciences at least. Ravetz cites a paper by Urquhart which reports that, of the journals in the Science Library in London, about half were not used at all and another quarter were used once in the year of his survey (1971, p. 49). Researchers scan the abstracts to find references they can cite in their arguments, but citation does not require reading the whole article, to say nothing of replicating it or checking its citations.

In summary, as graduate students begin to move into the public arena they are faced with the imperative of building up and reinvesting their symbolic capital in continuous research. The successful ones, the ones you have heard about, manage to move into an existing or new community that can use their publications as material for its own productive efforts. They in turn find in the community the materials they need for the manufacture of knowledge—ideas, data, research techniques, discussants, and critics. Community members help each other get a wider audience by citing each other's works, but they also compete for the approval of this audience. The most efficient producers and advertisers gradually (or suddenly in new communities) move into a leadership position in which their ideas are used and cited by newcomers. As their leadership and their symbolic capital becomes more secure, they become spokespersons for the movement, editing surveys of latest developments (Knorr-Cetina and Mulkay, 1983) or writing a definitive account of its achievements. They also move into foreign relations, deploring the bickering and misunderstanding that goes on among different communities, calling for a start at interdisciplinary collaboration, and developing a broader theoretical synthesis that includes other communities as parts or allies of their own community. If their fame is great enough they can even build an empire (Talcott Parsons), assigning various research communities their proper places in a great collaborative scientific advance.

We have now progressed far enough to be able to catch a glimpse of our ultimate goal, truth or knowledge. Knowledge is a manufactured commodity that has both use value and exchange value. The researcher "buys" the ingredients for his product by citing the earlier producers whose ideas he is using. Then he puts together his own product and tries to get it published. The payoff to the earlier producers is the citations and the use of their idea; these provide recognition—that is, symbolic capital. If the new product is not published, it fails, of course; but if it is published and not cited, it also fails. After a few years have passed, it probably will not be cited; other, more recent works by competitors will be cited and used instead.

The successful producer avoids such failure by producing for a definite market, some active research community. Then, having accumulated symbolic capital, one has to use it within a few years to get the next product published, read, and cited. One cannot put capital into a bank for fifteen years while raising children and studying others' works. By that time, one's name and products will have been forgotten; one's capital will have lost its value and one must start over.

We see that knowledge or truth is a very perishable commodity, less perishable than grapefruit, but more perishable than even American-made cars. It has to be used within five to ten years, before it spoils. A very few products last for several decades, but most products have little or no value from the start (Fuller, 1988, pp. 29–30).

SCIENTIFIC COMMUNITIES

If the fate of a publication in the public arena depends on how it fits into the current interests of some research community, then the growth of scientific knowledge depends *in its social aspect* on how those communities develop over time.

Bourdieu, with his theory of symbolic capital, and Mulkay (1980, pp. 19–21), suggest that a successful community goes through a typical cycle that should last a bit longer than a generation. It should begin explosively as a small group which attracts attention by bold pronouncements of a new paradigm, a new subject matter, a new foundation, a new start. These statements are actually announcements of an opportunity for original achievement. The statements attract entrepreneurs eager for recognition, who rapidly produce original achievements in the new subject matter. Their payoff is recognition by founders and newcomers, and they in turn pay tribute to the community founders whose ideas they cite and develop. The members of the community recognize one another and thereby accumulate symbolic capital; but the real payoff, the surplus value, comes from recognition by newcomers. As the community expands, the level of competition increases and the opportunity for recognition decreases, so the attractiveness of the community to newcomers declines. Thus the rate of expansion and of surplus value production declines.

The main disciples dominate the research projects, conferences, and graduate students. The followers become junior researchers in projects run by subleaders, and their work is cited under the subleader's name.

Newcomers with almost no symbolic capital, small entrepreneurs in an oligopolistic market, find it very difficult to get recognition and an independent research grant; and, having published, they find that few will cite or use or even read their work. A few newcomers manage to develop some small unique product that other researchers can use, some statistical technique or concept.

At this stage, it no longer pays to join the community, except as a student of some main disciple or subleader, and the prospect of founding a new community becomes more attractive. One or possibly two of the founding attempts succeed, and a new community appears and rapidly reaches critical mass.

Meanwhile the main disciples in the old community differentiate their theories in order to retain recognition or even expand their following. If they merely repeat the original formulation, the credit goes to the founder or founding group, and they are forgotten. As a result, the community disperses into subcommunities with variant theories. However, at this stage the community stops growing and may decline in numbers, as followers and newcomers rush to join some new movement. The leaders' peace proposal to the new movement is rudely ignored and the old theory is attacked, simplified, and distorted—for instance, the microsociologists' distortions of Merton. Some of the variant subcommunities no longer attract followers, and they stop growing and are forgotten. One or two subcommunities may expand for a while and become independent movements with their own main disciples and subcommunities.

As the original founding group dies off, the original community has disappeared. In its place are two or three aging former subcommunities whose elite were subleaders in the original community. New scientists move into the still expanding new communities and ignore the old theory. They are taught a distorted version of it and regard it as obviously false. Its failure shows off the success and promise of the new theory by contrast.

The above is a simplified sketch of American sociology in the last forty or fifty years. (The main source is Mullins, 1973, updated in 1983.) Mullins uses citation counts to trace the trajectory of seven main theory groups during the 1960s. Functionalism and symbolic interactionism, which had their explosive growth in the 1950s, had stabilized and had a settled heirarchy with subcommunities. Five new theory groups appeared in the 1960s: exchange theory, causal models, ethnomethodology, radical-critical sociology, and Mullins's own network analysis. In his 1983 update he reports that two of the new groups, ethnomethodology and the radical-critical theorists, continued to expand successfully in the 1970s, while network analysis and causal models seem to have declined and become special techniques. Another small group, the forecasters or futurologists, have collapsed. Functionalism has essentially disappeared, while a variant of symbolic interactionism has been unexpectedly revived in the 1970s. However, its final disappearance cannot be long postponed. Mullins writes of the United States; but functionalism came later to Germany and is still very much alive there (J. Berger, 1982). Berger (p. 353) quotes Habermas (1981, p. 297): "Keine Gesellschaftstheorie kann mehr ernstgenommen werden, die sich nicht zu der von Parsons wenigstens in Beziehung stellt." That is, you have to study Parsons.

One sign of the passing of functionalism is its reduction at the hands of critics to a single concept: functional explanation. This counterfeit concept was invented by nonfunctionalists who were trying to fit the theory into their own categories and thereby "clarify" it. Then it was used by other social scientists as an example of an error that their theory avoided. Their theory consequently was superior to functionalism; social science had progressed.

An early critic was Nagel (1961). Nagel was a logical empiricist; he conceived of scientific explanations as deductive-nomological: A causes B; A, therefore B. The occurrence of B, the effect, is explained by the previous occurrence of A, the cause, plus the causal law connecting A and B. But functional explanations did not look like that, after Nagel had "clarified" some of them. They seemed to be backwards: the function of A is to cause B; B is needed, therefore A. Illogical, even teleological, Nagel comments.

Another source was Stinchcombe's 1968 book on causal modeling. Stinchcombe discusses a variety of ways in which causes can be interconnected. One way is by feedback: A causes B; part of B feeds back on A and shifts it. He called that model "functional," a very loose, imaginative metaphor. Stinchcombe in the 1960s and after was eclectic in his thinking; he used ideas from various sources without being exclusively committed to any one theory. His 1978 work, *Theoretical Methods in Social History*, criticizes Parsonian functionalism and emphasizes individual rational choice rather than generalized functional problems. "A functional strain . . . creates troubles for the people in it" (p. 120). His 1983 work on the forces of production looks vaguely Marxist. His 1985 article on social insurance illustrates his "functionalist" feedback model: rising levels of social tension activate a mechanism which selects a social insurance policy. Feedback from changes in tension levels sustains or changes the policy, until a lowering of tension stops the mechanism. In all cases, Stinchcombe suggests, the final policy is a contributory transfer payment scheme in which workers pay for their own insurance (1985, p. 419).

The main recent sources of the concept of functional explanation seem to be G. A. Cohen (1978), and Elster (1979). (For later discussions by these two writers, see the chapters and references in Roemer, 1986.) These two in turn refer to Stinchcombe and Nagel. Elster as of 1979 is a rational choice theorist, as are the critics who cite him (such as Hechter, 1983, p. 10; 1987, p. 24; and Heijdra et al., 1988). For Elster, one must explain an event by showing how it resulted from the rational choice of one or more people. But neither the Stinchcombe model nor the Nagel model refers to anyone's rational choice, so they are not explanations. Functionalism is unscientific. Cohen's plea that a "functional explanation," while unsound, is at least the start of an explanation, an explanation sketch, is rejected. Game theory will provide the explanations. As an enthusiastic game theorist, I cannot disagree; but such a development would supplement functionalism, not invalidate it.[8]

A decade from now some eager innovator can write "Who now reads Talcott Parsons?" and treat this as a sign of scientific advance. (See also Bryant, 1983, though Bryant's question is factual, not rhetorical.) Several decades later some enterprising Lou Schneider-type sociologist[9] can resurrect Parsons and declare to an incredulous discipline that there were some good ideas way back there. Or in psychology, a Jerry Fodor can assert that Gall, the nineteenth-century founder of phrenology, "appears to have had an unfairly rotten press" (1982, p. 14) and that Gall actually had a pretty sound basic approach. Faculty psychology, misrepresented and dismissed in one paragraph in Baldwin's 1911 *Dictionary of Philosophy*, is an approach well worth pursuing today (pp. 23–24).

Pickering (1985) reports a similar development in British high-energy physics of the 1970s. Research and publication in this field depends crucially on access to the one British atom smasher, and access is controlled by a peer review committee. By 1970 the old high-energy community had fragmented into several subcommunities, each represented on the peer review committee. Suddenly a new community appeared with a new research program. The new program had less explanatory power than the old, according to Pickering, but it was new. Its members gained access to the committee and, since they were unified, they outvoted the scattered old groups. Within two years the old groups were almost shut out of research. Thereafter graduate students were trained only in the new program, and a continental group of physicists designed a new machine to the specifications of the new theory. Here was a revolution without crisis or anomalies or, indeed, without progress.

In summary, if we look at scientific communities through the concepts of the microsociologists we find an intellectually random coexistence and succession of communities. The rapid growth of a new community draws members from older ones, and the diminishing opportunities for original achievement in mature communities induces entrepreneurs to try founding new research programs. A few ideas from an old theory are translated into the new frameworks; the rest are caricatured, ridiculed, and forgotten. Some communities become very large, with complex theories and extensive empirical work, and last for decades; others flare up and decline in a few years.

The rate of appearance of new research programs depends on the amount of investment capital available for new research. Thus Mullins (1983) notes that the 1960s were a time of rapid expansion both of sociology departments and of research funds. The result was the appearance of several new research programs. In the 1970s and even more in the 1980s both funding and jobs stopped expanding and then declined; hence, no new theories and the decline of some old ones.

We will give Latour the last word on the work of the microsociologists (1981b, p. 212): "Knowing what a science is made of, we should not want to develop one. . . . We do not want and do not intend to be scientists."

Perhaps Merton was right. Perhaps humility is essential to science after all.

We seem to have lost our way, and need to pick up a different thread to follow. Bourdieu (1975) suggests that the course of social science is politically determined; so also does H. M. Collins (in Knorr-Cetina and Mulkay, 1983, p. 96). Randall Collins (1989) presents historical evidence that philosophical schools have flourished and expanded when they had strong political support, and have shrunk without such support; perhaps the same is true of social science. Let us explore this possibility next.

8

Science Politics

FOR THE MERTONIANS, social science is an autonomous subsystem of society unified by its own institutionalized values. The values have to be maintained by socialization and by rewards handed out by elite scientists for conformity. However, Mertonian empirical investigations have complicated this scheme by suggesting that all or nearly all norms are accompanied by equally valid counternorms. The resulting normative ambivalence produces conflict as well as unity, since scientists can urge norms on others while they themselves follow counternorms. Shared values thus can serve as rhetorical devices in disputes, rather than as unifying forces. Consequently, the unity-disunity balance must be determined by something other than the norms-counternorms themselves.

Similarly, the norm of value neutrality, which maintains autonomy, is opposed by the counternorm of value commitment or involvement, which reduces autonomy. Value neutrality and value commitment each require or presuppose the other, as with the other norm-counternorm pairs. For instance, the Mertonian-functionalist commitment to social self-maintenance through government requires detachment, value neutrality, in the study of social problems, and vice versa. Consequently, the degree of scientific autonomy also depends on the nature and strength of social and political influences on science.

But the microprocesses of negotiation, construction, and accumulation of symbolic capital (discussed in chapter 7) provide neither unity nor autonomy; they produce a kaleidoscope of shifting theories, research networks, and presumed facts. What, then, maintains the unity and autonomy of the social sciences—or are these qualities illusions?

In this chapter we take up the issue of autonomy by looking at some political influences on social science. Mendelsohn et al. (1977, pp. 17–20) and van den Daele (1977, pp. 40–48) argue that Merton neglected the political control of natural science in England after 1660. They assert that scientists researched topics of interest to the political authorities and shunned topics and methods that might have offended the authorities or made them suspicious. They were not "disinterested" and "skeptical" in areas that touched political and religious authority. "The boundaries chosen for the new knowledge and the social forms adopted for its practice were boundaries socially imposed and self-consciously accepted" (Mendelsohn et al., 1977, p. 20). "The virtuosi of the Royal Society . . . were seeking a niche within society, not the reform of that society" (van den Daele, 1977, p. 41).

Similarly, Weingart (1983) argues that the many political, social, and legal uses of social science have politicized it, too, in that various political groups have an interest in pushing for certain areas of research and denigrating other areas. The natural sciences are highly politicized; think of research on the causes of acid rain, the effects of cigarette smoking on health, chemical and biological warfare, global warming effects, genetic engineering, the causes of cancer, evolution. Political influences do not determine the conclusions reached, but they constrain research by determining the definition of the problem, the amount of funding available for various topics, the amount of evidence needed to establish some finding, the use and publicizing of some conclusions and the suppression and ignoring of others. How much of this has been going on in the social sciences?

For the Mertonian functionalists, such political influence on scientific practice interferes with the autonomy that is necessary for the achievement of knowledge. Some influence is unavoidable, but continuous influence would subvert the disinterested, skeptical, ethically neutral search for truth. The source of political influence is the necessary interdependence of science and government: science needs the funds that government and the economy can provide, and government and the economy need the knowledge and techniques that science can provide. The funding agencies will inevitably have some influence on research topics, methods, and personnel, but the Mertonians hope and believe that the influence will not be great enough to subvert scientific autonomy. Merton and Lazarsfeld, at the Columbia Bureau of Applied Social Research, were keenly aware of the importance of funding and of its threat to scientific autonomy (Converse, 1987, pp. 248ff.).

For *externalist sociology of knowledge*, a second source of political influence comes from within science; it comes from the fact that social scientists locate themselves somewhere in society. They are necessarily receptive to political influences coming from that location. Thus the

Mertonians are sensitive to and suspicious of government influence; other social scientists ignore government influence but are receptive to other influences. The location of social scientists also sensitizes them to certain social problems and concerns, and it desensitizes them, in varying degree, to other problems and concerns. Thus Talcott Parsons, a New Deal Democrat, was in the 1960s concerned with promoting equal opportunity for blacks and maintaining the stability of the two-party system (1967, chaps. 13, 8). Bluestone and Harrison (1982) are sensitive to class conflict and are concerned with the well-being of workers.

Note that for *internalist sociology of science*, political influences come from outside science and can be managed by proper boundary maintenance. For externalist sociology, the influences are internal to scientists; society is in science. Internal political influences can be managed by self-awareness—that is, by looking at oneself from another's perspective.

A third kind of political influence comes from the internal power structure of scientific communities. The elite of a community, such as Merton, do not merely promote the norms of science; they also use their power to promote certain theories and promising lines of research. They can do this in their capacity as advisers to the funding agencies and by their recommendations for hiring and promotion.

The specific topic of this chapter is the first kind of influence, that of the funding agencies on social science research. How, and to what degree, do funding agencies affect the selection of research topics, the definition of the problems, the methods used, the researchers employed, the knowledge that is produced, and the eventual scientific consensus on what is true? Perhaps political influence merely focuses research efforts and makes the resulting knowledge more relevant to our society. That would be real interdependence and sufficient autonomy: the funding agencies point to the problems, and the researchers define them and find the answers.

The influence of funding on research is so pervasive that we tend to take it for granted. We have probably all experienced the gentle hints that funding is available for certain types of research, the memos listing application deadlines, the proudly displayed example of professors who provide a good research start for their students. These devices persistently nudge us to commit government-sponsored research: not for ourselves, but for our students. The benevolence and impartiality of government and private foundations are continually presented to us, and we are resocialized into the liberal-professional identity of the Mertonians.

Let us not prejudge the issue of political influence. According to Shonfeld (1972), who for a time headed the main U.K. funding agency, British social scientists tended to plan a research project first, then look for funds to support it. But John Ziman disagrees; he believes that British social scientists tend to select research topics to fit available funding (personal communication, 1985). According to Useem (1976a), the prospect of government support has a significant impact on the substantive and methodological plans of U.S. social scientists, especially among those who have had prior funding and have gotten used to funded research. His citation-count evidence, however, is indirect, while Shonfeld's and Ziman's is impressionistic, so the question remains open.

PERSPECTIVES ON SCIENCE POLITICS

The issue of political influence on the natural sciences since 1945 has been discussed vigorously and often—without agreement, of course. Indeed, the casual reader can easily experience bewilderment at the very different historical accounts of the government-private foundation-science relation. We will use two of the various perspectives on the government-foundation-science relation as our "pair of lenses" or "Hegelian inquirer" through which to look at the historical record. Both perspectives were developed mainly by observers of the natural sciences, and it is an open question as to how well they apply to the social sciences. As we look at the historical data, we can ask: How would this history be interpreted from each of the two perspectives? What comes out clearly and strongly from each perspective, and how does the same material look from the other perspective? What is omitted or distorted by each perspective, and does the other perspective reveal, correct, or just compound the distortion? Which interpretation seems more plausible, or are both together more plausible than either one?

Readers may find one of these two perspectives obviously correct and the other one perverse and ideologically biased; that is the reader's problem.

The first and most common perspective defines the political funding situation as a "partnership" or "uneasy partnership" between government and science. Writers using this perspective include Don Price (1967), Harvey Brooks (1968), Gene Lyons (1969), Lyons and Morton (1965), Michael Reagan (1969), Gilpin and Wright (1964), Penick et al. (1972), D. S. Greenberg (1967) less explicitly, and others. The Mertonians also have the "uneasy partnership" concept. These writings come out of the 1960s; they reflect on the government-science experience since 1940 or 1945, and many see trouble ahead as of the late 1960s. Nielsen (1972, 1985) exemplifies this perspective from his location in the private foundations; he emphasizes the uneasy government-foundation partnership. For the foundations, the troubles came in 1969 and again in the late 1970s and the 1980s.

In this view, both government and science knew by 1945 that they needed each other, and they gradually groped their way into an unstable and suspicious collaboration that was damaged by some unfortunate incidents from 1965 on, but still continues. The collaboration was helped along by the mutual recognition that we were in "a period of national peril" from the Soviet Union (Lyons and Morton, 1965, p. 4) and had to stick together despite our differences. The atomic bomb showed the military what magic those scientists could perform, and they wanted more of that magic without quite knowing how to get it. Scientists were sometimes queer people and had to be handled carefully. In the 1950s the expanded responsibility of the military overseas, defending the Free World, made them want information about these far-off areas, and they turned to the social scientists. Other government agencies realized later that they could use help in understanding the various domestic problems that they were supposed to manage, problems like poverty and illiteracy.

Scientists in turn badly needed funding, and the war showed them what a bottomless well the government was. Physics and astronomy needed bigger and bigger research instruments, atom smashers, and 200-inch telescopes, at unbelievable cost; sociologists were developing large-scale survey techniques; and in the 1950s political scientists were eager to study all those new states in Africa and Asia, a whole new subject matter that had suddenly appeared. Wartime collaboration showed them that the money could be had: the Manhattan Project and, in sociology, the extensive surveys of military and civilian opinions and attitudes, effects of bombing on enemy morale, and so forth (Converse, 1987, chaps. 5–7). Some of the military surveys were published in The American Soldier (Stouffer et al., 1949, 1950). The postwar problem was to get that money without the military strings attached. In short, scientists wanted research funds to spend as they pleased, and government wanted technical help and information, new weapons, policy advice and evaluation.

The "uneasy partnership" authors report that the developing collaboration was retarded at first by mutual suspicion. Some physicists, including Einstein and Norbert Wiener, reverted to the traditional civilian suspicion of the military after 1945, and argued that any acceptance of military money would ultimately compromise scientific integrity. Others became wary of government involvement during the McCarthy years 1950–54, fearful that a government connection might expose them to witch-hunting and character assassination, as in the Oppenheimer case. On the government side, some congressmen such as Carroll Reece of Tennessee shared McCarthy's suspicion of scientists, and especially of sociologists, who might be socialists or even secret Marxists. And if Oppenheimer had consorted with Communists, other physicists might have too. Reece and other congressmen apparently had trouble distinguishing *social science* and *socialism*. Reece suspected that socialists and Communists had infiltrated the foundations, especially the Ford Foundation, and were using that money to finance revolution (Whitaker, 1974, pp. 106–07).

However, such suspicions were mostly held by extremists on both sides, and subsided after 1954, these authors assert. The Cox Committee and Reece Committee hearings uncovered no scheming secret Marxists or socialists among the recipients of foundation funds (Lyons, 1969, p. 278), and the military succeeded in persuading most scientists that they did not intend to subvert science (Greenberg, 1967, p. 135). To further allay congressional suspicions, the category *behavioral science* came into use in the early 1950s to emphasize that nothing socialistic was intended in funded research (Lyons, 1969, pp. 279, 282–83; Handy, 1964, p. 10).

The real and permanent problem in the partnership was the conflicting goals of the two partners, as Merton had already pointed out in 1949. The goal of science is truth, and this requires long-term, secure, unrestricted support that allows scientists to follow the evidence wherever it leads. It also requires complete freedom to publish results and to discuss them with the international scientific community (Penick et al., 1972, chap. 1). The goal of government agencies is the management of immediate problems, and this requires problem-focused and practice-oriented research. In some cases it also requires secrecy from other countries or other agencies. Budgetary rules require annual budgets and at least post-auditing accountability, which requires endless paperwork from busy principal investigators to justify the need for some machine or international travel.

As a result the uneasy partnership inevitably involves compromises at best and fraud at worst. Scientists must adapt their research projects to fit the categories of the funding agencies, and perhaps disguise their real interests to make the project appear useful to government. Funding agencies must offer complete freedom of research and publication, with restrictions in implementation to come later, or can hope to "pick the brains" of the researchers afterward to get the information and advice they really want, or can hope that some of the projects at least will suit their needs somehow. In practice, according to Greenberg at least (1967, chap. 12), the scientists got the better of the bargain. They had almost complete autonomy to pursue the truth, and they did get away with much chiseling on equipment that duplicated what they already had, travel funds, fake consultantships, and so on. Research grants financed much extraneous activity in those days, and many departments and individuals equipped their labs with slightly used tape recorders and other machines.

However, with goodwill on both sides, and with the few extremists unobtrusively kept out of the action, both sides benefited. In 1952 Speaker Rayburn had quietly appointed a moderate committee staff that could tone down the Cox-Reece investigation hysteria, and conversely the foundations carefully checked funding applicants' names against the official list of known Communists (Whitaker, 1974, pp. 106–07). As a result, the pursuit of truth has not been significantly diverted by politics, and ever increasing federal funding advanced science greatly—until the Project Camelot flap in 1965.

The opposing perspective, which appeared in the 1970s, is exemplified in D. Dickson (1984), Boehme et al. (1983), Salomon (1977), Schuon (1972), and Rose and Rose (1976). Arnove (1980), and Berman (1983) focus on the private foundations. Science politics for these writers is concerned first with who controls research—who defines the problem, who sponsors and participates in research, who evaluates and uses the results. Second, it is concerned with who benefits from science, directly and in the first instance. Different kinds of beneficiaries require different kinds of research and different methods, so the choice of topic, assumptions, and method is also a choice of beneficiary. There are two kinds of science, technocratic and democratic. Technocratic science is controlled from the top, from corporate boards of directors, the Pentagon, elite organizations. Democratic science is controlled more from the bottom, by the people involved or affected by a problem. There are two classes of beneficiary corresponding to the two kinds of science: technocratic science benefits the corporations, the government, the military, and the scientists, while democratic (critical) science benefits the people. Actual funded science has been mainly technocratic, with some democratic science in the late 1960s and 1970s.

In this perspective, the petty differences between technocratic scientists and their patrons should not obscure their fundamental community of interest. The corporations fund high-tech research because high-tech means profit. More generally, ready access to current research enables corporation planners to anticipate the direction of research and plan products that will incorporate that research as it occurs. Scientists profit from consultantships with the users of their research, and some of them set up their own companies and profit even more from their discoveries. Universities profit from patented successes: Crest toothpaste, Gatorade, warfarin (rat poison), and genetic engineering. (I am told that Gatorade wasn't actually that profitable.) Government benefits from high-tech because it strengthens the competitive position of U.S. industry, and because advanced technology can be doled out to Third World countries as rewards for political obedience and as ways of controlling their industry. The military like to support research of all sorts because it gives them a bigger political and economic role in the ever expanding permanent war economy. Scientists like military funding because it is lavish and relatively unsupervised, thus giving them more research and budgetary freedom. All three types of patron use the prestige of science to legitimate their policies and their power: "Confidence in science has often been used . . . to help suppress challenges to the concentration of power in the hands of political elites" (D. Dickson, 1984, p. 323). For example, the nuclear power industry assures us that nuclear power is safe and cheap; nuclear scientists have said so, and they know. The nuclear power industry never breathes a word about all the "democratic" nuclear scientists who warn that nuclear power is dangerous and ultimately expensive, considering the problem of storing nuclear wastes and decommissioning old power plants.

A democratic politics of science develops in several stages, according to David Dickson. First, there is a popular demand for research on the "side effects" of new technologies (Ravetz's "reckless science"), that is, their effects on people and on the environment rather than on profit. What are the long-term effects of DDT, acid rain, asbestos, PCB, urea formaldehyde, mirex, kepone, video display terminals, ultra low-frequency submarine communications? Second, the utilization and sometimes the funding of this new research requires new agencies—EPA, OSHA—and new laws—the Clean Air Act, the Toxic Substance Control Act, the Nuclear

Waste Policy Act. But public interest groups must participate in these new agencies so they do not become servants of the corporations they are supposed to control, as the Nuclear Regulatory Commission did. There was some popular participation in the 1970s, but the Reagan administration ended that.

Third, according to David Dickson et al. we need a new science that invents techniques that are socially useful, rather than techniques that produce profit and centralized power. For example the workers at Lucas Aerospace Industries in Britain in 1975 worked out a program of conversion from aerospace products to vehicles for the handicapped, low-pollution gas-electric cars, prosthetic devices, and solar and wind power for small communities, among other projects (Carnoy and Shearer, 1980, pp. 221–30). Management rejected their proposal. Fourth, the new scientific expertise should be directly available to communities so they can deal with their own technical problems, just as corporations and military hire scientists to address their problems. Such expertise has been available in "science shops" in Holland since 1973. There is also a science shop in California, partly funded by a grant from the Science for Citizens program of the National Science Foundation (D. Dickson, 1984, pp. 328–29).

The Dutch science shops consist of a location where a citizen can explain a problem to a professor or assistant, who then diagnoses the kind of machinery or engineering needed and looks for a graduate student willing to design and perhaps construct the desired equipment. However, Boelie Elzen told me that they are rarely used.

Boehme et al. (1983) observe that a democratic politics of science involves controls over science and thus inevitably arouses scientific opposition. Scientists want to develop a new technique and then cash in on it, in profits, publications, and new grants. But a proper policy would require them first to study the long-term "side effects" that can interact with many other "side effects" to produce biological and ecological damage. Indeed, a proper science policy might reduce or close down some research areas like nuclear power and oil shale extraction and expand others like solar power. Both research areas, nuclear and solar, can be equally scientific, so the choice of topic does not subvert science but only directs it to a different part of the truth.

But a technocratic politics of science also involves controls over science, according to Boehme et al. It provides funding for research that promises short-term corporate profit, such as nuclear power and military equipment, and refuses to fund research on ecologically sound but unprofitable technology. These controls also arouse some scientific opposition, and in fact the theory of democratic-technocratic science grew out of opposition to such controls. The theory was developed by the Science for the People group in the United States; by the environmental, ecological, and public interest scientists; by the Radical Science movement in Britain, Holland, and other countries; by the Intermediate Technology Development Group in North America, and by similar scientists elsewhere. Consequently, when leading science spokesmen like Don K. Price, Harvey Brooks, and Alvin Weinberg discuss a science-government partnership, they are not speaking for science but only for technocratic science. Partnership is possible only because these spokesmen have already accepted the point of view and goals of the military, the corporations, and imperialist governments. They really are concerned about Soviet aggression or Japanese competition or some crime wave, though they may easily disagree with their patrons about the most effective solution. They can also desire more freedom and flexibility in their research; they want to be relatively equal partners, not employees.

SCIENCE POLITICS, 1945–1985

The historical works on science politics suggest that the postwar period can be divided into three phases according to the rise to prominence of one type of funding agency. Each type of agency existed throughout the period, but each successively went through a rapid rise in total funding, then a stabilization or gradual decline. As one type declined, another type was rising rapidly.

The first phase or wave was dominated by military funding. We will examine chiefly the Office of Naval Research (ONR) and RAND, the main military agencies. This wave crested in 1965 with Project Camelot, and subsided somewhat in 1968 when the Mansfield Amendment transferred Project Themis funds to NSF in order to reduce the funding influence of the military. The second phase was dominated by government funding—NSF, NIMH, HEW, HUD, LEAA, the Labor Department—plus some private liberal foundations like Ford, Rockefeller, and Carnegie. The concerns here were domestic social problems, including poverty, mental health, political apathy, racial conflict, civil rights, crime, and urban decay; and internationally the economic and political development of the developing nations and their protection against communist subversion.

The phase began in 1950 with Ford Foundation support for behavioral political science, reached dominance in the late 1960s with the poverty and civil rights programs, slowed down and crested in the mid-1970s, and declined somewhat during the 1980s. (See tables 1–3.) For example, total HUD research funds declined from $51.3 million in 1981 to $17 million in 1986 (Quarles, 1986, p. 228). Even RAND got into urban problems in this phase. Its 1969 budget was 20 percent civilian work; in 1970, with the military in disfavor due to the Vietnam War, 35 percent went for civilian work, mainly urban problems (P. Dickson, 1971, chap. 6).

The third phase, beginning in the 1970s, saw an upsurge of conservative private foundations and research institutes: the greatly expanded Hoover Institution, the Heritage Foundation (founded 1973), American Enterprise Institute (founded 1943, greatly expanded in the 1970s), Cato Institute (founded 1977), Pacific Foundation, and smaller industry-financed agencies like Coors, Manhattan, Institute for Contemporary Studies (M. Boskin, director), and Liberty. In the 1980s their combined annual budget of something like $60 million was larger than the NSF budget but was dwarfed by the combined government civilian budget (excluding NSF) of about $300 million (Quarles, 1986). The conservative concerns are mixed, but generally include reinterpretation of history— Roosevelt tricked us into World War II, the Federal Reserve started the Depression, the civil rights movement has hurt blacks, the poverty program has increased poverty—plus being anti-government regulation, anti-communism, antiunionism, and pro–free market. This is the phase in which high-tech research became dominant in the physical and biological sciences; the high-tech Office of Science Policy was established in 1976.

Phase 1: 1945–1965

The end of the war left the military with high prestige and with the problem of adapting their organization to peacetime conditions. They

TABLE 1

NATIONAL SCIENCE FOUNDATION FUNDING
FOR SOCIAL SCIENCES EXCLUDING PSYCHOLOGY
(in thousands of current dollars)

1952	1954	1956	1958	1960	1962
—	—	—	554	2,996	9,183

SOURCE: Controller's Office, National Science Foundation.

TABLE 2
NATIONAL SCIENCE FOUNDATION FUNDING FOR SOCIAL SCIENCES AND PSYCHOLOGY
(in thousands of current dollars)

	1967	1969	1971	1973	1975	1977	1979	1981	1983	1985	1986
Total	24,100	26,117	31,882	43,317	49,431	65,397	64,058	51,673	42,440	52,840	—
Psychology	8,040	6,334	5,429	6,441	9,112	11,381	12,453	11,332	8,513	11,513	—
Social science	16,060	19,783	26,453	36,876	40,319	54,016	51,605	40,341	33,937	41,327	34,800[a]

SOURCE: Division of Science Resource Studies, National Science Foundation.

a. Estimated.

TABLE 3
HEW Funding for Research and Program
Development, Excluding NIH
(in millions of current dollars)

1960	1963	1965	1966
46	90	154	313

SOURCE: Murray, 1984, p. 35, from HEW data.

were very impressed with the atomic bomb, radar, sonar, and other devices scientists had invented during the war, and wanted more of those weapons. The recipe seemed to be to hire scientists and then leave them alone, mostly, and somehow new weapons would appear. However, it was not clear that the scientists wanted to continue their wartime collaboration. A few cold war fanatics like Edward Teller were enthusiastically staying on, but others were leaving and would have to be persuaded.

Some social scientists like Stuart Chase and Talcott Parsons were campaigning to get some of that science funding for the social sciences, but they had no weapons to offer the military. Other scientists were busily lobbying Congress for research funds, arguing shamelessly that all the applied research during the war had "depleted the stockpile of basic knowledge" (Nisbett and Ross, 1980, p. 40).

The situation was complicated by rivalry among the three military branches. To get those physicists and chemists and engineers signed up, each branch had to offer better working conditions than the others, and sooner. The navy came in first with ONR (1946), sold with an extensive public relations campaign around the universities (Greenberg, 1967, p. 135). They assured the scientists that ONR grants were for pure research, were unsupervised, results publishable, and grantees would be chosen by a scientific advisory committee on purely scientific grounds. That was just what the social scientists wanted, but there was only $100,000 in the initial budget for psychologists, and nothing for other social scientists.

The psychology grants were administered by the Human Resources Division, presumably on the theory that psychology could help the navy manage its personnel better. The five areas of study in 1945–50 were: comparative studies of different cultures (one grant); structure and functions of groups (five grants); communication of ideas, policies, and values (two grants); leadership (five grants); individual development (five grants) (Lyons, 1969, p. 137; Guetzkow, 1951, chap. 1).

The last four of these are plainly related to manpower management: how to organize effective groups with effective leaders, how to communicate with them and maintain morale. As such, they are of interest not only to the navy but also to any large organization and are central topics in social psychology. Most of the grants funded ongoing research programs by established researchers including Festinger, Cattell, J.R.P. French, M. Mead, Asch, McClelland, and the Michigan Survey Research Center. The research dealt with perception, concept formation, memory, learning, decision making, opinion change, labor-management mediation, and group leadership. One article, by Fred Fiedler, dealt with leadership in relation to combat crew effectiveness; the others had no direct military applicability (Guetzkow, 1951, chap. 1). This would seem to be a case of successful partnership, with social psychologists getting unrestricted funding and the navy getting some intangible prestige.

Meanwhile, the Veterans' Administration and the National Institute of Mental Health were responsible for the human debris left from the last war. They therefore provided research money for clinical psychology (Graham et al., 1983, p. 159). By 1955, ONR, NIMH, and the air force provided a substantial part of the research funds in social and experimental psychology.

The air force entered the competition next, in 1947. They set up a research arm similar to ONR, which had a psychology section (table 4). However, their main entry was RAND, a semi-independent research organization which could design its own projects and refuse or reformulate air force projects. The social science unit soon began to concentrate on systems analysis using mathematical techniques. They applied their analytic tools to problems that the Air Force set them (Quade, 1964). The most famous of these problems was the 1951–53 Wohlstetter study of strategic bomber bases (ibid., chap. 2). Given the strategic mission of being capable of bombing Soviet industrial areas, the assigned problem was where in Europe to locate the bomber bases. The RAND group decided that the bases should not be located in Europe at all because the Soviet air force could destroy the bombers on the ground. They should be located in North America behind the U.S. radar shield, and refueled at a variety of forward bases; ground refueling was cheaper than in-flight refueling. This redefinition of the problem led to changed specifications

TABLE 4
FUNDING FOR JOURNAL ARTICLES, 1950–1970

Funding Source	No. of Articles			
	1950	1955	1960	1970
ONR	13	24	25	15
Army	0	1	4	3
Air Force	0	50	18	21
NASA	0	0	0	9
Total military	13	75	47	48
NSF	0	5	31	69
NIMH-NIH	2	18	60	202
Other HEW: Education	0	0	0	19
Total civilian govt.	2	23	91	290
Carnegie-Ford- Rockefeller-SSRC	1	10	20	2
Other (mostly Canadian)	9	7	11	45
University	13	21	26	54
None	146	210	134	241
Total funding credits	38	136	195	439

SOURCES: *Journal of Social Psychology*, *Journal of Experimental Psychology*, *Journal of Abnormal and Social Psychology*.

NOTE: Short comments and funding for computer use were not counted. Some articles credit two or more funding agencies.

for the design of new bombers, and also to changes in the defense of North American bases against surprise attack.

This case has been cited to show that the funding agency can benefit from allowing the scientist freedom to redefine the given problem; the air force estimated over $1 billion savings from this project.

RAND, along with other agencies and private foundations, also promoted the study of the Soviet Union. The other agencies include ONR, Carnegie, Ford, and Russell Sage (Lyons and Morton, 1965, pp. 4ff.). The basic assumptions of these studies come out clearly in the report of the 1947 RAND planning session on Soviet studies (Lyons, 1969, p. 171). Given the Truman-Kennan containment policy, two fields of investigation were recommended: (1) "clarifying the motivations of the decisions and policies followed by the Russian political and military elite";

(2) "analyzing internal weaknesses in the social structure of the USSR
. . . which can be exploited for American aims."

Here, at the very start of the cold war, the Soviet Union is defined as
the enemy to be contained, and the problem that social scientists are to
solve is how to neutralize that enemy by finding and exploiting its weaknesses. The Soviet Union does not have to contain us; we are not
aggressive. The Soviet Union is the problem and the U.S. military are
the solution.

The Harvard Russian Research Center, funded by the U.S. Air Force
and the Carnegie Fund, had the similar aim of assessing the strengths and
weaknesses of the Soviet system (Lyons, 1969, p. 172). Their method
was to interview refugees and defectors. The interpretive context for the
interviews was provided by the goal of containment. One can hardly
imagine a more biased sample for interviewing; but the refugees must
have told the anti-Soviet researchers what they wanted to hear, so their
accounts sounded plausible (Field, 1955). Fainsod's book on Smolensk
(1958) was based on municipal documents captured by the Nazis—a
more reliable data source than refugee interviews, and an interesting
study.

The Russian Research Center was subject to more direct control by
the funding agencies and the FBI (O'Connell, 1988). The FBI used
information from the center to alert academic administrators to the presence of suspected dissidents suitable for purging on their staffs. The U.S.
State Department intelligence service used unpublished data from the
center. An uncooperative associate director was dismissed by Harvard
under pressure from the funding agencies. What kind of science is this?

The RAND point 1, clarifying the motivations of the political and
military elite, was the origin of the 1950s "science" of Kremlinology. The
assumption of inherent aggressiveness, derived from the military assignment to contain Soviet power, was simply extended to internal politics.
Each Soviet leader was assumed to be in a continual struggle for power
with every other, apart from tactical coalitions. Policy proposals were
nothing more than tactics in this struggle. Then the Moscow newspapers
were studied for evidence of the daily ups and downs—the location of
leaders on a reviewing stand, someone's inspection trip to Khabarovsk
(away from the center of power), an article criticizing or supporting some
power station manager who was a client of some leader. (The assumptions
of Kremlinology are explicitly stated as fact in Horelick and Rush, 1966;

see also Slusser, 1973, for an example of well-documented, ingenious Kremlinology.)

By the 1960s, a massive body of pure theory and confirmed fact had been erected on these military foundations, funded by a variety of agencies. The 1947 RAND origin had long since vanished from sight. The new scholar (myself) was confronted with a formidable body of evidence and a well-developed interpretive scheme that simply had to be taken most seriously.

Among the facts were the Penkovsky papers. Penkovsky, a spy for the CIA, had written a book of observations and reports on daily life in the Soviet government, which was somehow smuggled out two years after he was caught and executed by the KGB. The papers confirm the assumptions of Kremlinology and the aggressive bases of Soviet foreign policy. The original papers, however, were top secret. The CIA released a translation, and upon requests for the Russian version released a translation back into Russian after some delay, claiming it was the original. (These papers are cited as fact in Payne, 1970, pp. 16–17, 56, for example.) Recently we have been offered the Shevchenko papers by the CIA (Associated Press, June 27, 1985). The first version was rejected by the publishers as dull, with no spying and no conversations with Soviet leaders. The second version, three years later, is full of thrilling spy chases, plus intimate verbatim conversations with Soviet leaders all the way back to Khrushchev, when Shevchenko was in his twenties.

On the other hand, Kremlinologists have expressed suspicion of the Khrushchev memoirs, supposedly smuggled out by a British journalist, which give a very different version of Kremlin policy making. What is fact and what is propaganda here?

RAND researchers were also among the first—perhaps *the* first—to produce studies in the tradition of containment and deterrence theory (see, for example, Ellsberg, 1956). Here the problem was defined as how to contain the inherently expansionist Soviet Union. The Soviets, of course, cannot practice deterrence, since we have no aggressive intentions. They practice counterdeterrence, a response to our deterrent moves. Research and seminars on this theoretical foundation took place at Harvard, MIT, Penn, National War College, Georgetown, Johns Hopkins, Institute for Defense Analysis (a consortium of nine universities), and UCLA. They were supported by grants and scholars from RAND, Ford, Carnegie, Hoover, AEI, and others (Lyons and Morton, 1965, chaps. 7–8). Here was another solidly entrenched "research program" whose truth could hardly even be questioned by the impudent new scholar.

But Rand and the foundations could not have developed Soviet studies, Kremlinology, and deterrence theory (up to 1971) all by themselves. They had willing partners in the universities, who shared the military cold war outlook on the Soviet Union. Some of them at Pennsylvania— Strausz-Hupe, Kintner, Possony—even outdid the RAND theorists— Speier, Ellsberg, Wohlstetter—in their fervent anticommunist patriotism. Here our second perspective points to the harmony of beliefs and values between the scientists and the military that underlies their partnership; but it misrepresents their shared fervent patriotism as somehow selfish or "technocratic."

Not all foreign policy theorists shared the military assumptions—for instance, Anatol Rapoport and Boulding, the Quaker, at the Michigan Center for Conflict Resolution—and these researches too were supported by foundation grants from Bendix, Carnegie, and ONR. ONR, remember, is also a military funding agency; the second perspective misses these differences among the military services. Military funding policy is by no means uniform.

We return finally to the first of the ONR categories: cultural studies. Here was some money for the anthropologists, and especially the Human Relations Area Files (Lyons, 1969, pp. 174ff.). The main area of interest was Micronesia, where the U.S. Navy was administering the islands. But with turmoil in the Middle East and the communist victory in China, these two areas also came under study, funded by ONR, ARPA (military), and some foundations. "Finally, the success and machinations of Fidel Castro in Cuba reawakened the historic but sporadic interest of Americans in the problems of Latin America" (Lyons, 1969, p. 176). Among the Americans whose sporadic interest was reawakened was the army, which "was involved in a number of military assistance programs in Latin America [and] supported military civic action programs" (p. 178)— such as the Brazilian military's voluntary assumption of the burdens of government in 1964—and "was engaged in joint training ventures with Latin American military units" in the Panama Canal Zone. The CIA also was interested in these areas; it exchanged information with the anthropologists, and also quietly loaned some personnel to the anthropologists working in the field (Orlans, 1973, pp. 44ff.).

The CIA also collaborated informally in Morris Janowitz's researches on the military role in Third World politics, funded from 1959 to 1968 by the U.S. military. The SSRC had been trying for over ten years to sell some sociology to the military, and struck gold with Janowitz (Schulman et al., 1972).

Top officials at the Ford Foundation were quite annoyed to discover quiet CIA collaboration with their Third World researchers in the 1950s. Three times officials went to CIA headquarters and "raised hell," apparently without success (Berman, 1983, p. 61). However, they had no objection to CIA collaboration in the Congress for Cultural Freedom, which was devoted to spreading anticommunist propaganda in the Third World (pp. 143–45). According to Whitaker (1974, pp. 157–66), the CIA unobtrusively collaborated with thirty-nine private foundations in research and funding from 1952 to 1967.

The military-CIA research topics on Latin America were fundamental scientific ones: sources of social change and instability, causes of violence. One of the projects, Camelot, was funded by the army counterinsurgency program. The army had been assigned the task of controlling Communist insurgency by President Kennedy, so they named the project "Camelot." Unfortunately, they failed to notify the U.S. embassy in Chile of the project; some anti-Americans heard of the project and used it to embarrass the United States by accusing the anthropologists and their informal collaborators of spying; there was quite a flap; and the project was quickly canceled (Lyons, 1969, pp. 167–69).

How did the anthropologists and sociologists involved feel about the project? Irving Horowitz, a left sociologist (as of 1965), provides an account based on interviews (1965). First, they were very impressed with the $4–6 million grant, which was peanuts for the army. Second, they had heard of the freedom allowed social scientists at RAND, and hoped to have or arrange similar freedom to do "fundamental" research. Third, many did not like working for the army, but thought they could pacify or educate the army. They thought of themselves as reformers, boring from within. Others hoped to prevent another Cuban revolution; they agreed with the army assumptions. Most resented their subordinate employee role and wanted the science-military relation to be more equal.

Here is the "uneasy partnership" theme in full display—as an instrument of self-deception.

Horowitz scathingly points out the scientific inadequacies of the project (1965, pp 260). The research design was plagued by ambiguities. It assumed that a stable military-governed country, Paraguay, is the ideal and that all instability and change is bad and probably communist-inspired. The U.S. Army's role in these countries is assumed to be good, because the army is presumed to be a stabilizing agency. Similarly, U.S. influence in general is assumed to be good. "The problem should have been phrased to include the study of 'us' as well as 'them' " (p. 262). Revolution is assumed to be bad. Horowitz also criticizes the army for defining the problem and hiring intellectual manpower to solve it, rather than "submitting a problem to the higher professional and scientific authority of social science" (p. 263). That is, he wants an equal partnership.

Finally, he complains that the army canceled this scientifically unsound project on political rather than on scientific grounds, and concludes (p. 266):

> We must be careful not to allow social science projects with which we may vociferously disagree on political and ideological grounds to be decimated or dismantled by government fiat. Across the ideological divide is a common social science understanding that the contemporary expression of reason in politics today is applied social science, and that the cancellation of Camelot . . . represents a decisive setback for social science research.

Try our two perspectives on that one.

Military funding increased again briefly in the 1980s (D. Dickson, 1984, pp. 109–15). Star Wars, pushed by President Reagan's science adviser, is mainly research money. The Mansfield Amendment was essentially nullified in 1979. Military control over publication of military-funded research has tightened since 1977 or so (pp. 147–56). Charles Iklé, former head of social science research at RAND, was an undersecretary in the Reagan administration Defense Department, where he provided funding for research and conferences on low-intensity warfare (anticommunist guerrilla campaigns). However, this wave seems to have crested about 1988.

Phase 2: 1950–1975

Funded research on social problems goes back to the 1920s and before. However, we will begin with the Ford Foundation, the largest private foundation, whose first funding program was adopted in 1950 (Nielsen, 1985, pp. 4–6). The funding patterns of the Carnegie and Rockefeller foundations are fairly similar. The Ford program committee was concerned with problems of widespread political alienation among the U.S. electorate, nonparticipation in politics, racial discrimination, unequal educational opportunity, and the danger of another depression. These were liberal concerns, and the result was a liberal funding program. Its goals included:

1. Promoting world peace through the United Nations.

2. Promoting U.S. democracy, including civil rights, control of concentrated power, and improved electoral and policy-making processes.

3. Improving the U.S. economy, including raising employment levels, granting more equal economic opportunity, and improving labor-management relations.

4. Improving education, including the educational use of the mass media.

5. Social research to be applied to the promotion of democracy and management of social problems (Seybold, 1987, p. 188; Nielsen, 1972, chap. 5; Magat, 1979, pp. 18–19).

In retrospect, says Magat, "These objectives were so broad and comprehensive that virtually everything the Foundation has done in the ensuing years can be rationalized as flowing from the original blueprint" (1979, p. 19).

Since the Ford Foundation had so much money (hundreds of millions) and so little organizational structure and expertise at first, it chose to operate mainly through large block grants to existing organizations (Magat, 1979, pp. 42–61). The foundation wanted social reform, but it wanted existing community or national organizations, plus new ones it set up, to do the reforming. This sometimes resulted in tacit bargaining in which the Ford Foundation would notify an organization of its interest, and the organization would have to devise a program that would be acceptable both to Ford and to the conservative political structure in which the organization was embedded (Marris and Rein, 1967, pp. 15ff., 93–104); Moynihan, 1969, pp. 40–43). Even so, the foundation's liberal activism stirred the wrath of conservatives in Congress and elsewhere, such as the Reece Committee (Nielsen, 1972, pp. 82–85, 97–98; Magat, 1979, p. 31).

Under point 1, promoting world peace, Ford gave $22.4 million to the United Nations. The Ford, Rockefeller, and Carnegie foundations also gave various grants to the Council on Foreign Relations, Institute for Strategic Studies, Brookings, and international affairs centers at Harvard, MIT, Georgetown, Berkeley, Stanford, Princeton, Geneva, Oxford, and London (Berman, 1983, pp. 102, 153). Thus their funding overlapped that of RAND. Brookings got funding under several headings totaling $36 million by 1979, and Ford grants supported books on foreign policy by Kissinger, Schelling, early Halperin, and others (Magat, 1979, pp. 56–57, 111–13).

Under point 4, education, large sums were given to colleges, hospitals, and medical schools, plus several newly created Funds for the Advancement of Education (Nielsen, 1972, pp. 84–88). Rockefeller and Carnegie funding supported higher education in the "developing" countries (Berman, 1983, pp. 115, 131–36).

To promote point 5, social research, Ford set up the Institute for Advanced Study in the Behavioral Sciences in 1954. It also provided funds to the National Opinion Research Center at Chicago, the Bureau of Applied Social Research at Columbia, the SSRC committees on political behavior and on comparative politics, the Russell Sage Foundation, and political behavior programs at Michigan, Chicago, North Carolina, and Columbia. There was also a program of fellowships in comparative politics and in political behavior.

I analyze the point 5 funding under two headings: domestic research and developing countries research. The goal of funding for domestic research was to promote the empirical study of political and social behavior (Seybold, 1987; Seybold, in Arnove, 1980). This included the study of how public opinion is formed, what the distribution of opinion is, how opinion is brought to bear on policy formation, the causes and consequences of political participation and apathy, voting behavior, the beliefs of political leaders, governmental processes at federal, state, and local levels. The favored method was survey research, plus case studies of governmental processes. The foundation wanted empirical research because of its goal 2, promotion of democracy, including popular participation and improved electoral and policy-making processes. To improve in these areas, one needed to know how they were operating and what the causes of the deficiencies were.

The foundation also wanted a political theory that would celebrate the virtues of American democracy, to combat political alienation. They found pluralism, and decided to support it. Thus the ideal research proposal was a study of political behavior that revealed the plurality of groups participating in politics, and the possibility of any group winning once in a while.

Similarly, the Russell Sage Foundation used Ford money and its own money to fund research on adoption, mental rehabilitation, family counseling, children's hospitals, social indicators, drug use, and social welfare programs (Schulman et al., 1972). Here the goal was to understand social problems, to facilitate their management by social agencies.

Research on developing countries, area studies, was funded through the Social Science Research Council and later through individual research fellowships. SSRC was established by the Rockefeller Foundation in the 1920s; between 1956 and 1969 Ford, Rockefeller, and Carnegie provided over three-fourths of SSRC funding (Berman, 1983, pp. 105, 107). The goal of area studies was to understand political processes in the developing nations, so as to provide enlightenment to U.S. foreign policy (p. 100), and so as to facilitate the development of U.S.-type democracy in them.

The director of the SSRC area studies program was Gabriel Almond from its beginning in 1954 until 1963 (Almond, 1970, pp. 11–21). Under Almond's direction, the researchers adapted the newly emerging functionalism (such as Marion Levy, 1952) into a theory of political development. The seven functional categories (Almond, 1970, p. 96), derived from U.S. politics, provided neutral categories for comparing different political systems, and also specified Ford's goal of political development, a pluralist multiparty democracy.

The consequence of Ford funding was to strengthen and expand behavioralism, pluralism, and quantitative survey research in American politics and functionalism in comparative politics (according to Seybold, 1987). Both of these approaches came to dominate the discipline by the early 1960s. In a 1967 survey, 70 percent of behavioralists in political science were thirty-seven years old or younger, which means that they had picked up their behavioralism as graduate students since the early 1950s, the period of Ford funding (Seybold, in Arnove, 1980). Dahl (1961) credits Ford for promoting the successful behavioral revolution. Incidentally, this "revolution" did not fit Kuhn's pattern in the slightest degree.

However, the above externalist account needs to be supplemented by internal considerations. Behavioralism and pluralism were already prominent in political science in the early 1950s, in David Truman's *Governmental Process* (1951), and in earlier works by SSRC director Pendleton Herring, by V. O. Key, SSRC director Charles Merriam, and back to Bentley's *The Process of Government* (1908). Thus Ford-SSRC could easily buy the research efforts of prominent political scientists. In addition, the logical empiricist philosophy of science that was dominant in the

1950s instructed scientists to depend on observable, quantifiable behavior. Consequently, any move to make political studies more scientific in the 1950s would have emphasized the quantitative study of political behavior, except in international politics where game theory was coming in via Morton Kaplan (1954), and RAND. Ford funding strongly promoted this development but did not originate it; the partnership between researcher and funding agency was quite harmonious in this case.

The main alternative political theory in the 1950s was elitism, especially the works of Floyd Hunter and C. Wright Mills. Mills's *White Collar* (1951) and *The Power Elite* (1956) were both funded by SSRC plus two smaller foundations. Hunter's *Top Leadership, USA* (1959), based on field interviews and not behavior, was funded by the University of North Carolina Political Behavior Committee, the committee Ford had set up. However, once the *The Power Elite* appeared, Mills's next funding request was turned down by Ford. He got no more Ford-SSRC money. Hunter financed his 1959 study with leftover funds from his initial grant of about $10,000 to study Atlanta—*Community Power Structure* (1953). He was told about 1956 that he would get no further funding (Seybold, personal communication, based on an interview with Hunter and comments by informants at Ford).

Twenty years later, Magat (1979, p. 161) expressed regret over the Ford Foundation's "blind faith in modern social science techniques, especially the quantitative, and in the possibilities of social engineering."

We turn now to government funding for research on social problems, which got under way in the 1960s with the poverty program. Funding began with a 1961 NIMH grant to a Manhattan settlement house (Marris and Rein, 1967; Moynihan, 1969, pp. 43, 51), plus grants from the Ford Gray Areas project (Magat, 1979, pp. 119–23; Moynihan, 1969, pp. 35–36). The settlement house became the prototype of the national Mobilization for Youth program, and Ford ideas became the basis for Kennedy's 1961 juvenile delinquency program (Magat, 1979, p. 121; Moynihan, 1969, chap. 3, p. 64).

The thinking behind both programs was at first that of Cloward and Ohlin, *Delinquency and Opportunity* (1960) (Marris and Rein, 1967, pp. 19, 24; Moynihan, 1969, pp. 45ff.). Richard Cloward and Lloyd Ohlin, at the Columbia School of Social Work, were advisers to the Manhattan settlement house and embodied their ideas in its program. Ford thinking was quite similar. Based on Merton's 1938 article "Social Structure and Anomie," it asserted that delinquency was a deliberate response to the lack of opportunity to achieve socially approved goals. Social reform therefore would consist of providing opportunities: jobs, employment information and counseling, relevant education, vocational training, legal aid, and community services. Accordingly, Mobilization for Youth provided community services, Gray Areas money provided educational experiments and services, and the 1961 Area Redevelopment Act tried to promote employment (Donovan, 1967, pp. 24–25).

However, when the various poverty agencies were established after 1965 and began funding their own research, the emphasis shifted. These agencies were responsible for reducing poverty, and therefore sponsored research on the causes of poverty (Aaron, 1978, chap. 2). The first poverty agency, the Office of Economic Opportunity (OEO) was staffed by RAND-type systems analysts trained in cost-benefit analysis. They asked: (1) How do we define poverty? How many poor people are there, given this definition? (2) What are the causes of poverty? (3) What are the possible options for reducing poverty, and what are the costs and benefits of each? (Haveman, 1986).

Question 1 called for a quantitative definition, income level, and then for research to measure the extent of poverty. Question 2 got three answers: not enough jobs; low earning power; and racial discrimination by employers (Haveman, 1987, p. 14). However, the jobs were supposed to be produced by general economic expansion, which would trickle down to the poor (p. 15), and discrimination was a Civil Rights Commission issue. That left earning power, work skills, as the main OEO task.

There were various theories as to why the poor had inadequate work skills. One theory pointed to broken homes where the father was absent, thus damaging the young boys' role model, identification, and self-esteem, and making it difficult for them to work steadily. Or it might be an inadequate sense of time, which made them late for work too often. Or perhaps their diet was deficient, making them sickly and weak (Haveman, 1987, p. 16). More generally, it might be a complex of characteristics in their upbringing, a "culture of poverty," which was transmitted from generation to poor generation. (On the "culture of poverty," see Ryan, 1976, chap. 5.)

The result of this causal reasoning was quantitative, multivariate research, since there were many poor people and probably several causes of their poverty. Of the poverty researches reported in *Psychological Abstracts* for 1970, 82 percent were estimated to be quantitative-statistical, and 16 percent situation-oriented (Goldstein and Sachs, 1983, p. 30).

Situation-oriented research continued the original Cloward and Ohlin thinking that saw poverty life styles as a response to lack of opportunity. It focused on the antecedent situation—jobs, housing—rather than on poor people themselves. In other words, the OEO researchers looked at poverty from the outside, from the perspective of a government agency responsible for dealing with this social problem: poor people. They had objectified the poor into a cost-benefit problem. The Cloward minority looked at poverty from the inside, from the perspective of the people living there.

Once a variety of "causes" had been statistically located, federal poverty programs were set in motion. Head Start was supposed to correct culture-of-poverty deficiencies, a school lunch program with plenty of catsup would improve diet, various manpower training programs would provide work skills, job interview training would correct bad self-presentation habits (Wellman, 1969), loan guarantees would provide the working capital for starting a business (Orren, 1974), and so on.

The next step was evaluation research, to enable the agency to report to Congress on how the program was working. The administrative needs of the agencies determined the design of these studies. The agency's program was the independent variable, and one or more poverty indicators measured the dependent variable. If the two did not correlate to the .05 level, the program had no effect; if they did, it did. Ray Rist (in Goldstein and Sachs, 1983) points out what was omitted: (1) The independent variable was the agency's *official* program, not what it actually did. The agency's actual program was not studied, for instance, by participant-observation; it was the solution, not the problem. In other words, there was no investigation of possible agency inefficiency or poor performance. (2) Other changes in the situation were ignored; they were not part of the agency's assigned objective, or the agency was not responsible for them. Thus the evaluation studies were prevented from concluding that a program was effective in unexpected ways.

Evaluation research also created a need for secondary foundation-supported research. To evaluate, one needs indicators, so indicators were developed for poverty and other social problems—crime, alienation, deficient education, poor health, pollution, lack of social mobility (Penick, 1972). Also, one needs methodological studies of evaluation research, and eventually evaluation of evaluation research. Goldstein and Sachs (1983), funded by a now deceased poverty agency, Community Services Administration (CSA), is an example of the latter.

The same pattern appears in the research on crime funded by the Law Enforcement Assistance Administration, later renamed the National Institute of Justice. The 1986 program of the Institute of Justice is listed as "crime, its causes and control," with a budget of $9.3 million (Quarles, 1986). Since the objective is crime control, funded research focuses on career criminals to find indicators for locating them so they can be caught. Or it examines the consequences of various types and lengths of sentencing in relation to the probability of recidivism (Casper, 1984).

Similarly, the U.S. Labor Department funds studies of labor markets and job training programs; Health and Human Services funds studies of drug prevention, causes and treatment of addiction, and epidemiology, and also supports studies of child day care, health care, geriatric care, health promotion programs, employment agencies; the Department of Education funds research on how to improve education; and so on (Quarles, 1986).

This sort of research produces a Mertonian type of social science. It deals with small, isolated problems out there that will fester away unless something is done. Problems are objective and quantifiable; they are assumed to be limited, immediate, short-term, and each can be dealt with in isolation by a single government agency. Thus OEO was concerned with the characteristics of poor people, but not with employment levels; that was the province of the Council of Economic Advisers, and they didn't care about poverty, only about the economic indicators. Racial discrimination was the turf of the Civil Rights Commission. The minimum wage was the concern of the Labor Department; foreign trade and investment, that of the Commerce Department. The scientists, advisers of the agencies, were similarly specialized. Similarly, the Civil Rights Commission's sponsored research dealt with the effects of school segregation and desegregation on racial attitudes (Weiss, 1977, chap. 5). It was not concerned with poverty, family life, or other influences on racial attitudes; that belonged to HUD or OEO or some other agency. Its concern was to produce scientific evidence to support legal requirements to desegregate.

In one case two government agencies, the Economic Development Administration (EDA) and the Appalachian Commission, were accidentally assigned the same problem in the same region, Appalachia. So they ran side by side, each in its own way, each ignoring the other (Zysman, in OECD, 1980, chap. 4).

From the "uneasy partnership" perspective, this is typical professional

social science. The professional social scientist believes in doing objective, value-neutral, specialized, quantitative, limited studies using
middle-range theories; the government agencies need exactly such studies. They are partners.

From the "democratic" perspective, it is typical technocratic science.
The poor, old people, students, drug addicts, the unemployed, Third
World peoples did not request or help to design the research, are not
consulted during the research, and are not informed of its results. Indeed,
some government agencies are reluctant to allow publication; or they
insist on prior clearance (Fainstein and Fainstein, 1983, p. v, ex-HUD).
Fainstein and Fainstein rejected a HUD grant because of the clearance
problem. Its effect is to increase administrative power (Schuon, 1972, p.
151), power to reform and pacify from above. Goldstein summarizes
critics as saying that social scientists, who are ambitious, do what the
powerful want, let the powerful formulate the questions, and study the
weak (Goldstein and Sachs, 1983, p. 32). "They become intelligence
agents for those in power," comment Schulman et al. (1972, p. 26; see
also Orlans, 1973, p. 38). The private foundation support for education,
running into the hundreds of millions, has gone almost entirely to elite
universities and institutes in the United States and abroad. The effect has
been to train elite leaders to manage Free World affairs or to advise those
in power (Berman, 1983, pp. 99–105).

However, there have also been "democratic" studies. As with deterrence and Soviet studies, funded perspectives dominated but did not
monopolize the field. In education research, the Ford Foundation funded
Bowles and Gintis (1976), a Marxist critique of U.S. education (Berman,
1983, p. 104). In poverty research, there were studies, like Piven and
Cloward (1971), that located the poverty problem mainly in government
and the economy; studies that focused on the self-organizing efforts of the
poor, like Kramer (1969); and studies that focused on dual or segmented
labor markets in the Doeringer and Piore (1969) tradition. None of the
above studies was funded, but Orren (1974), a highly critical study of
government policy, was funded by the National Institute for Mental
Health. Also, the National Science Foundation has funded a considerable number of studies of segmented labor markets in the later 1970s
(personal communication). NSF does not fit the pattern of the other
government agencies at all; it seems to fund a great variety of research.

Ford has since 1969 also given money for "democratic" political action: $38,750 to the Congress for Racial Equality (CORE) for a black

voter registration drive in Cleveland, which then elected Carl Stokes mayor (Whitaker, 1974, p. 114); and in the 1970s gave money to community groups, street gangs, minority businesses, inner-city schools, public interest law, women's rights groups, child care, and black colleges. In the 1980s it provided money to help the homeless, refugees, and pregnant teenagers (Nielsen, 1985, chap. 4).

Phase 3: 1975—

The liberal social problems studies continued at a fairly steady rate in the early 1970s. Meanwhile, the climate of opinion among business leaders was changing. Silk and Vogel (1976) noticed the changed mood in a 1973 series of meetings of business leaders; the businessmen spoke of being vulnerable, on the defensive, fighting for their lives, as the country moved toward socialism. They fought back after 1973 on a variety of fronts, including making larger gifts to conservative foundations. As a result, these foundations expanded both in budget size and in numbers. New institutes like Heritage and Cato rapidly expanded to the $10-million-a-year level (Nielsen, 1985, chap. 3). For example, Richard Scaife, a Mellon Foundation trustee, has put $10 million a year into those institutes since 1973. Conservative fundraisers like Richard Viguerie, with a mailing list of 20 million people, have also contributed. In 1979 William Simon and Irving Kristol set up the Institute for Educational Affairs to channel conservative money into research. The result has been an outpouring of conservative publications.

The conservative foundations fund policy-oriented research, conferences, policy studies, background papers, news analyses, syndicated articles, propaganda films, radio programs including anticommunist broadcasts to sixteen Latin American countries, Radio Free Europe, and a Talent Bank of conservatives available for government appointments (Whitaker, 1974, pp. 152–55; *Manchester Guardian*, Dec. 1, 1985; Peschek, 1987, chap. 1). The policy studies are disseminated throughout government, including the White House, and the other materials are widely broadcast through the mass media. The conservative foundations seem to be more interested in influencing public opinion than the liberal agency-sponsored studies, whose primary intended audience is the government sponsor and other specialists.

For purposes of comparison with the second phase, consider Martin Anderson's study of poverty (1978, Hoover funding). Anderson argues that there is practically no poverty in the United States; the illusion that poor people exist is the result of misleading liberal statistics. The statistics counted money income but neglected in-kind or nonmonetary income: home-grown food, food stamps, Medicaid, free shelter provided by relatives, charity, soup kitchens, and so on. When monetary estimates of these consumption goods are added to estimated aggregate money income and divided by the number of poor, their average income is above the official poverty line. A poverty agency would never fund such research.

Liberals, of course, can dispute these statistics with government funded research: if in-kind income is imputed to the poor, it should be imputed to everybody, and then the official poverty level would be quite a bit higher. More than two-thirds of Anderson's in-kind income was medical insurance, so his argument is really that poverty was eliminated by the enormous increase in health care costs. In-kind income is not evenly distributed (Smeeding, in Goldstein and Sachs, 1983, CSA funding). There is also the issue of whether poverty should be defined in absolute terms, a fixed level of purchasing power (conservative), or in relative terms, a certain percent or number of standard deviations from the median income (radical, liberal). These disputes are inconclusive (Aaron, 1978, chap. 2; Haveman, 1987, pp. 66–69).

Charles Murray (1984, Manhattan Institute funding) observes that the latent poverty rates correlate positively with the rate of federal anti-poverty funding after 1967. Latent poverty is calculated by subtracting welfare assistance from total money income, and comparing the nonwelfare total with the official poverty level. Up to 1967, the amount of latent poverty decreased; after 1967, as the poverty program expanded, latent poverty stopped decreasing and in the 1970s, increased somewhat (p. 65). Murray's interpretation is that for teenagers the available poverty funds—CETA, AFDC, and so forth—were comparable to or greater than the pay from entry-level jobs. Thus it was rational, though shortsighted, to go on welfare. The result was that many teenagers did not learn skills and work habits and became dependent on handouts. Thus the poverty program to some extent fostered dependency and permanent poverty. However, Murray accepts liberal objections that other factors are involved to some extent. He does not mention the other factors.

The general conclusion of conservative-funded research is that the liberals' social problems do not exist (as with Anderson, 1978); or, if they exist, they were created or made worse by government (as with Murray, 1984); or at least they could be solved by eliminating some government action and letting the market work. What little involuntary unemployment exists can be eliminated by eliminating the minimum wage, so the labor market can balance itself. Inflation can be eliminated by a fixed monetary growth rate, eliminating Federal Reserve discretion. Depressions can be eliminated by 100 percent reserve requirements for banks. Education could be improved by establishing an education market through government vouchers. Advertising is pure information, which helps consumers and lowers all prices by improving the efficiency of marketing. Deindustrialization, if it actually exists, can be eliminated by allowing capital to move freely and ending government protectionism and loan guarantees (McKenzie, 1984, Pacific Institute, Heritage funding). That way incompetent managers would be eliminated by bankruptcy, merger, or leveraged buy-outs, industries would move to the best locations for labor, resources, and tax breaks, and the American people would get exactly as much industry as they were prepared to pay for.

Underlying such research is the assumption that a system of free markets in all aspects of the economy would produce a long-term general equilibrium in which all resources would be distributed optimally and there would be consequently no social problems. Researchers dealing with a specific problem then look for the interference with market forces that produced or sustains it. Or they look for short-term circumstances—incompetent or routinized management, demand or supply rigidities, kinky curves, an oil cartel, labor immobility—that produce temporary dislocations and temporary problems. The proper role of government then is to manage the money supply and contain the communists. The primary method of conservative science is the application of mathematical models to aggregate data, sometimes enlivened with illustrative case studies. There might be a rational-choice model, a public goods model (n-person Prisoner's Dilemma), a perfect competition model, a general equilibrium model, an oligopoly model, and so on. Empirical discrepancies point to the interfering factors or short-term circumstances that cause the problem; or they suggest a modification of the model.

One cannot claim that the conservative foundations by themselves produced this expansion of conservative research. There had to be conservative social scientists for them to hire. The Hoover Institution, for example, funds established conservatives like Milton Friedman, Sidney Hook, Seymour Lipset, as well as younger scholars. Rather, the foundations smoothed the path of research for conservatives, speeded up and multiplied their publications, encouraged communication by funding conferences. Without the foundations there would have been conservative research, but not nearly as much. For example, Murray (1984, p. x) credits the Manhattan Institute with pushing his research on the welfare program: "Without them, the book would not have been written." Indeed, the institute made sure the book was also well publicized: it arranged publicity meetings between Murray and editors, journalists, academics, and television interviewers (Peschek, 1987, p. 63).

Clarify the picture by contrasting it with the situation for radical social science. There has been a great deal of radical research since 1970, but most of it is unfunded. The NSF has funded some; the poverty agencies have funded a little, such as the work of Bluestone and Harrison (1980, 1982). The one fairly radical institute, the Institute for Policy Studies, has to scratch for its meager funding. In West Germany the small Max Planck Institute at Starnberg, Bavaria, directed by Jürgen Habermas, produced radical government-funded research in the 1970s, but had no monopoly on such research.

Thus radical social science was not called into existence by funding opportunities, and by analogy conservative research was not either. Nor was the environmental and ecological research of "democratic science" called into existence by funding. Funding came afterward: from public interest groups and community organizations, and a little from NSF. Funding has affected the quantity of each kind of science but not its existence.

In retrospect, the Starnberg institute in West Germany can be seen as an appendage to the West German Social Democratic governments of 1969–81. The institute became a Christian Democratic campaign issue in 1977 under the slogan, "Keep politics out of science." When the CDU got into power in 1981, they abolished the institute. The philosophical instigators of this move included Gerard Radnitzky, Hans Albert, and other Popperians, funded by the Thyssen Foundation; they were defending Popper's Open Society of toleration and free discussion by helping eliminate a nest of totalitarians (Hübner et al., 1976; Boehme et al., 1983, Max Planck funding; Stockman, 1983, p. 233; Restivo, 1984). The "totalitarians" like Habermas got teaching positions at Frankfurt, Bielefeld, Darmstadt, and elsewhere, but without government research funds.

CONCLUSION

The history of science policy in the United States, even a superficial history like this one, does not allow a simple generalization about the influence of the funding agencies on social science. And the more closely one looks at the lists of projects funded the more complex the picture gets. Nor have we touched on the topic of how governments use social research, which is even more complex (Weiss, 1977; Berger, 1980; F. Heller, 1986). It does appear that the broad historical sequence of funding emphases is not arbitrary, but reflects the successive concerns of the funding agencies. (But see McHoul's research on our perception of historical patterns, discussed in chapter 9, below. I may have projected the sequence into the data.) In the postwar period, the military concerns were the management of their expanded responsibilities, which included disturbed veterans and the containment of the Soviet threat. As Soviet aggression shifted from wartime military expansion to postwar subversion and agitation, counterinsurgency became a military and CIA concern. The Soviet space shot in 1957 focused attention on engineering education. Meanwhile, the corporate liberal foundations—Rockefeller, Ford, Carnegie—were concerned with promoting democratic capitalist development in the Third World and social tranquility and prosperity at home, for both selfish and humanitarian reasons. Worsening economic conditions in the 1970s focused the attention of funding agencies on the problem of improving U.S. economic performance and reducing the excessive 1960s goverment generosity to labor, the environment, the poor, and other social problems.

But these same interests were shared by a good number of social scientists. Liberal scientists shared the interest in solving social problems; conservative social scientists shared the interest in improving U.S. economic performance; and some of both groups shared the interest in containing the Soviet peril.

These shared interests are the empirical basis for the soundness of the "partnership" interpretation. The funded researchers were not just hired labor; they went along willingly and often initiated the projects themselves.

The "uneasy partnership" interpretation reflects the continuing and varied conflict within the partnership. In phase 1, in the period of some mutual suspicion, the ONR was the junior partner, funding projects of no immediate interest to itself in hopes of getting some indirect eventual return. By 1965, the "Camelot" year, the divergence of interest between military-CIA funding and social science researchers became painful to the researchers at least, with their resolve not to sell their souls to the military and their resentment at having the problems defined for them.

By the late 1970s, the military clearly were making the research and publication decisions, and researchers were the hired brains. However, in the 1970s the NSF was continuing the earlier ONR pattern (Useem, 1976b). Shonfeld's British experience of the late 1960s (Shonfeld, 1972), if his report is correct, fits the early ONR-RAND-NSF stage in which researchers were devising their own projects. Useem's U.S. study (1976a) fits the later stage when social scientists had become dependent on continued funding and had to fit their plans to what funding was available.

The "uneasy partnership" interpretation is a self-definition. As such it expresses the social scientist's desire for more status and more independence from the funding agency. The "pure searcher for truth" is another self-concept that justifies these desires and resentments. It also hides the reality: funded researchers do not seek truth in general, but are expressing their social concerns whether liberal, conservative, or (rarely) radical. The liberal social scientist would not join a Hoover-funded project to prove that the civil rights movement has been bad for colored folk, and might even regard the project as ideologically biased; the peace researcher would be unhappy working on a RAND project on the siting of aircraft refueling bases or on how to minimize the effects of nuclear winter. Conversely, the conservative researcher, who could see the aircraft bases project or Herman Kahn's 1965 study of nuclear escalation in a U.S.-Soviet confrontation as neutral applications of systems analysis, would object to the ideological bias in a study of how to apply Charles Osgood's Graduated Reduction of International Tension model, a Richardson Process model. Osgood was a communist dupe, apparently.

The second perspective interprets technocratic science politics from the outside. Consequently, it misses the internal variations and conflicts and ambivalences among those in power and focuses on the power relations themselves. It asserts that the funding agencies are mostly, usually, in the main, instruments of power, and they hire scientists to clarify problems of current concern to the powerful. Funded social scientists are mostly willing servants of power, either out of a professional concern to sell their research skills or because they identify with the powerful and share their concerns. Those who do not wish to serve power, the various radical scientists, the "critical" or "democratic" scientists, and the peace researchers, will find fewer funding opportunities. There are few Stewart Motts among the corporate elite.

Nielsen (1972) provides a view from inside the foundations that supplements or corrects the outside view of the second perspective. Nielsen begins by condemning "the ill-informed creeds of the Old Right on the one extreme, [and] the New Left on the other" (preface). He rejects David Horowitz's simplistic Marxist view (as of 1972) that the foundations, dominated by the financial and corporate elite, must necessarily support the status quo against those advocating revolutionary change or indeed any change (pp. 7, 406–07). He stresses the foundations' independence from government and corporations, which allows them to provide challenges and criticisms of the status quo. But in the end he laments the foundations' near absence of creativity and social challenge (p. 426). Their political stance ranges from liberal-conservative to ultraconservative; they are "overwhelmingly passive, conservative, and anchored to the status quo" (p. 406). When they occasionally support some dissident ideas, it is out of fear of instability if social tensions are not reduced (p. 410). The most liberal foundation, Ford, has balanced its very small contributions to leftist groups and research, about 4 percent of the total, with much larger contributions to conservative research centers (pp. 414–16) such as Hoover, Georgetown, and the American Enterprise Institute (Whitaker, 1974, p. 152; Magat, 1979, p. 66). Nielsen (1985, chap. 15) repeats his 1972 evaluation.

Note, however, that Nielsen is criticizing the foundations. He is urging them to give more support to bold, creative new ideas for dealing with the problems of our time (1972, chap. 22). He wants them to seize the opportunity that their independent position gives them to criticize and change an unsatisfactory status quo. They haven't done that.

In summary, the politics of science 1945–85 has institutionalized the dominance of conservative and liberal social scientists by supporting and multiplying their research. This has reduced somewhat the diversity of perspectives within social science without actually eliminating any perspective. Substantial funding for "democratic science" will not occur until there is a secure Social Democratic government farther left than that of the German Social Democrats of the 1970s.

9

Cognitive Processes in Social Science

"ANYONE ATTEMPTING to come to grips with the booming [sic], buzzing confusion that is contemporary cognitive psychology is likely to be left with an actual or metaphorical headache. . . . Cognitive psychology often seems to resemble the messenger in *Alice in Wonderland* who went in all directions at once" (Eysenck, 1984, p. 1). "We are like the inhabitants of thousands of little islands, all in the same part of the ocean, yet totally out of touch with each other. Each has evolved a different culture, different ways of doing things, different languages to talk about what they do. Occasionally inhabitants of one island may spot their neighbors jumping up and down and issuing strange cries; but it makes no sense, so they ignore it" (Claxton et al., 1980, p. 15). After these startling beginnings, both Eysenck and Claxton go on to give totally different histories of cognitive psychology (Eysenck, 1984, chap. 1; Claxton et al., 1980, chap. 2). Howard Gardner gives a still different history, though he agrees that the field is splintered (1985, chap. 5, p. 130). Robert Rubinstein (1984) gives a still different history.

Alan Allport's history (Claxton et al., 1980, chap. 2) has cognitive psychology beginning in the late 1940s with information theory and the invention of computers. Eysenck's history begins in the late 1940s with perception experiments (Bruner and Goodman, 1947; Bruner and Postman, 1949) that reacted against behaviorism. Bruner's own history (Bruner, Goodnow, and Austin, 1956, pp. vii–ix) refers especially to psychoanalytic ego psychology as a source, but also mentions his reaction against both behaviorism and information theory. Let us follow up Eysenck's history first.

Bruner et al.'s reaction against behaviorism was not total, since both behaviorists and cognitivists used the same method: experimentation. Consequently, that part of the behaviorist conceptual scheme that adapted it to experimental treatment was preserved by the cognitivists.

In addition, anyone who broke totally with behaviorism in the 1940s would have been ignored (Bruner, 1983, pp. 107ff.).

The Hull-Spence-Woodworth conceptual scheme was stimulus—intervening variables—response. Of these three components, stimulus and response were the observable, experimental components, the independent and dependent variables. (This was pre-1950 behaviorism, when S and R were still observable.) The intervening variables were the theoretical components, for example, *habit* and *drive* for Hull. Since habits and the like were unobservable, they were *hypothetical constructs* (McCorquodale and Meehl, 1948), whose validity could be tested by using them to predict the observable response. The cognitivists retained the experimenter's stimulus-response categories and substituted hypothetical cognitive constructs for Hull's habits. Thus in the Bruner and Goodman study (1947), the stimulus was a coin, the construct was the relative valuation of money by rich and poor children, and the predicted response was the variable reports of the size of the coin.

The cognitive variables proliferated, but the basic conceptual scheme persisted into the 1970s: stimulus—perception—selective transfer to short-term memory—cognitive operations—response (Eysenck, 1984, p. 3; Evans, 1982, p. 35). The stimulus was a cognitive task, and various verbal responses and elapsed time gave clues to the intervening cognitive processes.

By the 1970s this scheme had collapsed, according to Eysenck (though some psychologists would disagree) and had been replaced by various dichotomies—stimulus-driven versus expectation-driven, serial versus parallel processing, hierarchical control versus heterarchy or fluctuating control—and the answer always seemed to be: both, more or less (Eysenck, 1984, p. 360). Processes proliferated, each related to its own experimental setup or paradigm, whose results were often not replicable with a slightly different experimental paradigm (Evans, 1982, p. 111). Or if a process did appear again, its scope would be limited. Low-level theories to explain these processes proliferated, and often several theories could interpret the same data with slightly different concepts. For instance, *memory* concepts include "iconic, echoic, active, working, acoustic, articulatory, primary, secondary, episodic, semantic, short-term, intermediate-term, and long-term" (Eysenck, 1984, p. 361). Actually Eysenck left off a few: precategorial, sensory register, and response buffer (Claxton et al., 1980, p. 14); also event, generalized event, situational, and intentional (Schank, 1980). Serious criticisms of the whole field appeared in the 1970s (Eysenck, 1984, pp. 360–61, 362–64; Claxton et al., 1980, chaps. 1, 5; Neisser, 1976, chaps. 1, 3). Critics observed that the experimental tasks were highly artificial, so that the cognitive strategies of the S need not resemble any real-life cognitive process. The connection between hypothetical cognitive construct and predicted response was often tenuous, leaving much room for varied interpretation of the data. Small samples and constantly varying tasks made for unreliable data. Bruner himself has expressed serious misgivings about the whole experimental enterprise (Bruner, 1979, epilogue), but cannot conceive of a good alternative; he muses vaguely about turning to poetry, art, Freudian theory, even philosophy for fresh insight.

Alan Allport's history (Claxton et al., 1980, chap. 2) focuses on computer modeling of cognitive processes or artificial intelligence (AI), which has coexisted uneasily with cognitive psychology since the 1960s. The most important early work was Ashby's *Design for a Brain* (1952); but the work that is now cited as the *Urwerk* is George A. Miller's "The Magic Number 7 ± 2" (1956) which called attention to a curious regularity, perhaps a coincidence, but thereby helped to found a new field. Miller, Galanter, and Pribram (1960) was another fundamental early work, along with Newell and Simon's work on IPL, an early modeling language.

The thinking of the AI people is computer-mathematical and holistic—neural networks, subroutines, debugging, terminals, rules; it is very different from the atomistic linear-causal-variable-controls thinking of the experimenters. Consequently, the coexistence was uneasy indeed in the 1960s. I remember a sarcastic, derisive joke about G. Miller et al., 1960, told by experimenters;[10] and from the AI side, Eysenck reports the comment, "The relationship of AI to traditional cognitive psychology is the same as that of astronomy to astrology" (1984, p. 372, citing Minsky and Papert, 1972, p. 34).

Apparently in the 1970s the relationship became friendlier, with some psychologists picking up some AI ideas and vice versa. Experimenters like Wason and Michael Eysenck have welcomed AI models for their theoretical clarity and fruitfulness, and apparently Eysenck hopes that AI will bring some order to the cognitivist chaos (1984, pp. 365–73). Experimenting and model building have even been combined (Kosslyn and Pomerantz, 1977; Kosslyn, 1983). According to Schank (1980), the two methods, plus the new cognitive interests of linguists, came together as a new field, cognitive science, about 1976. However, Schank ends his article with a plea to experimenters, AI modelers, and linguistic field workers to take each other seriously; so apparently some distinctions remain. Similarly, according to Kintsch et al. it is not clear whether cognitive science is one field or eleven borderline specialties (1984, pp. 16, 77).

The present chapter cannot claim to do more than sample a few prominent ideas and "findings" from the above field or fields. We begin with some contributions the experimental cognitive psychologists have made to understanding social science, and then shift to AI.

COGNITIVE PROCESSES

The most general finding is the extremely limited reasoning power of the experimental subjects tested. Subjects persistently scored very low on reasoning tasks, fell into several typical errors, and often were unable to correct their mistakes even when these were pointed out. Some writers have expressed alarm over this finding and argued that scientific method should be changed, or even assigned to computer programs, to accommodate the unexpectedly low reasoning power of human beings (Mahoney, 1976; Faust, 1984). In addition to this negative finding, experimenters have uncovered and studied a number of quasi-rational or semirational techniques that subjects use to carry out cognitive tasks. These techniques are called "heuristics" (Kahneman and Tversky) or "practical reasoning" (Wason) to distinguish them from the pure reasoning that appears so infrequently and erratically. I shall take up these two findings in sequence.

Negative: Low Reasoning Power

I shall exemplify the many experiments on deductive inference with one well-known example, the Wason selection task or paradigm (Evans, 1982, chap. 9). The subjects are told that a set of cards has been constructed, each of which has a letter on one side and a number on the other. Then they are shown four cards lying on a table, for example: *R*, *J*, *2*, *8*. They are instructed to test the following hypothesis: if there is an *R* on one side of the card, then there is a *2* on the other side. To test the hypothesis, they are to turn over *only* those cards that are necessary for the test. They are also often asked to give their reason for each selection, or to verbalize their thinking during selection.

The student of logic will recognize the logic of this paradigm. The hypothesis is $p \supset q$ (if p then q), and the cards are p, $-p$, q, $-q$. The two cards that test the hypothesis are p, $-q$. A p tests the hypothesis by modus ponens: $p \supset q$ A q on the reverse side confirms; a $-q$ falsifies. A $-q$

$$p$$
$$q$$

tests the hypothesis by modus tollens: $p \supset q$ A p on the reverse side

$$-q$$
$$-p$$

falsifies; $-p$ fails to falsify. Other experiments use sentences like "Some p is q, p or q, $-p \supset -q$."

The subjects in one set of experiments got the correct answer 4 percent of the time (Evans, 1982, p. 159). This result was typical. Most subjects turned over p (modus ponens) or tried both p and q but not $-q$. The general interpretation from this and many other experiments is that subjects do not use modus tollens, attempted falsification, to test a hypothesis; they look for confirmatory evidence (Wason and Johnson-Laird, 1972, chaps. 13–14). In experiments presenting both positive and negative data they selected the positive data and ignored or reinterpreted the negative data. In experiments that required subjects to call for additional data to test a hypothesis, they called for possible confirming data. In extreme cases they persisted in trying to confirm their hypothesis even after the experimenter had declared it false. For example, one experimenter, Mark Snyder, searched for experimental conditions that would induce subjects to use a strategy of falsification and failed (Higgins et al., 1981, chap. 8).

Scientists are no different, according to one experiment which ran the Wason task on a group of scientists. The results matched results for nonscientists (Griggs and Ransdell, 1986).

Another, less surprising, finding from these experiments is that negative propositions, $-p \supset -q$, are especially difficult to handle. They take longer and there are more errors. The interpretation is that a negation, $-p$, is understood by reference to an implied positive statement, p, which makes the reasoning circuitous and difficult (Wason and Johnson-Laird, 1972, chaps. 2–5).

Faust (1984) focuses on judgment tasks, which involve probabilistic reasoning from statistical data. For example, subjects are given various suicide statistics and asked to judge the likelihood that a particular suicide victim was unmarried. Or they are given diagnostic test results (MMPI) and asked to give a clinical diagnosis. This topic goes back to Meehl's *Clinical vs. Statistical Prediction* (1954).

Performance was consistently poor, worse than a mechanical repetition of base rate probabilities. Subjects showed all sorts of bad habits: they reached a quick judgment from some initial bits of information and did not correct it from later information; they focused on some striking instance (availability bias, as discussed in Tversky and Kahneman, 1973, 1974; Jervis, 1976, pp. 239ff.) that may have been marginal or irrelevant; they did not realize the unreliability of small samples; they forgot about regression to the mean; and so on. Faust concludes that scientific practice would be improved by minimizing the need for human judgment, by substituting machine judgment or at least machine-assisted judgment. Mahoney (1976, chap. 7) proposes that scientists should adopt Bartley's and Agassi's "comprehensive critical rationalism" (see chapter 2 above)—everybody should criticize everything—as a corrective to the illogicality of scientists. Why criticism would be any less illogical he does not explain.

Faust also suggests that the real point of a Kuhnian paradigm is to serve as a nonrational aid to scientific judgment. Given the complex and contradictory data available in any scientific field, scientists are likely to nonreason every which way and produce a great variety of incompatible theories almost at random. But a striking paradigm channels their thinking (availability bias) and produces nonrational agreement. The result is a scientific community sharing a single (arbitrary) theory. This is precisely what Lakatos called "mob psychology" in his (mis)interpretation of Kuhn, except that he didn't like the idea; he assumed that scientists are rational.

Similarly, Nisbett and Ross observe that the effect of scientific evidence is to polarize opinion, since supporters of each theory interpret the evidence to fit their theory and become convinced that they are right and everyone else wrong (1980, pp. 169–72).

Another finding is that subjects are apparently not aware of their own cognitive processes. The processes seem to be "nonverbal," unconscious, and only the conclusions appear in consciousness. Then, when asked to explain what they did, subjects produce a rationalization (Nisbett and Ross, 1980, chap. 9; Evans, 1980, pp. 291–92; Evans, 1982, chap. 12). This finding explains why scientists and other people believe they are rational; their introspection produces a rationalization of the products they find in consciousness.

Discussion

Let us interpret the cognitive psychologists' negative finding in the light of one of their own positive findings. The negative finding is that human reasoning power is extremely limited and weak. The positive finding is that subjects interpret a negative statement as a denial of a tacit assumed positive statement. What then is the tacit positive statement about human reasoning that is being denied by the psychologists? We find that for the British and some U.S. psychologists the positive statement is Popper, and for the Minnesota people (Faust, Meehl) it is logical empiricism. Scientific reasoning consists of trying to falsify hypotheses, or at least of formally deducing statistical probabilistic predictions and testing them against sense data. For example, the Wason paradigm is so set up that the "correct" solution involves falsification.

But the psychologists do not themselves use Popper's method, any more than Popper himself did. Consider Evans's *Psychology of Deductive Reasoning* (1982). Evans proposes that since there are so many different experimental paradigms we should induce general cognitive principles by a survey of the many results (p. 253). This directly opposes Popper's rejection of induction. Evans suggests that the proper procedure is to map a new field in outline first, and then gradually fill in details: "I must say that construction of precise models is premature, when we do not have a clear, general picture of the organization and function of cognitive systems" (p. 256). This directly contradicts Popper's rule that we should first propose precise and therefore easily falsifiable hypotheses. Evans prizes supporting evidence, not the falsifying evidence that Popper says he should cherish: "This is the best evidence reviewed in this section to support the idea . . . " (p. 251). According to Popper and the Wason paradigm, he should have said, "This evidence is worthless, because it supports the idea." When negative evidence appears, he suggests auxiliary hypotheses to explain it (p. 228) or reinterprets the negative evidence: "We cannot dismiss the theory on the basis of this evidence, however. It may be that . . . " (p. 248), or describes the negative evidence as suggestive but not conclusive (p. 255). Only when negative evidence and puzzling findings persistently accumulate does one conclude that the whole approach is somehow mistaken: "When a field of research becomes dominated by false assumptions, then it is important that this be demonstrated" (p. 255). This sounds like Lakatos or Kuhn, not Popper.

Does this mean that Evans is irrational, or does it mean that Popper's account of scientific method is wrong? If we study the problem facing the cognitive psychologists, we can see that their method, the method of practical reasoning, is appropriate and Popper's method is not. Popper's problem is how to determine the falsity of a hypothesis. Discovery of a hypothesis is not a problem for him; discovery is a psychological process and his logic has nothing to say about it. Consequently, hypotheses come to Popper's scientist free of charge from an unknown source, and discarding one as false is no loss at all.

But for the psychologists the problem is to explore and map a largely unknown field, cognitive processes. It is a discovery or search problem. Given this problem, it is appropriate to begin by analogy with some known territory, experimental behaviorism or formal logic, with appropriate differences noted as they occur. It is appropriate to try to establish some outpost, say, perceptual defense (Postman, 1953) or availability bias, as a base for further search. Having established the existence of some process, it is appropriate to explore its boundaries, its robustness in different experimental designs, its parts or variants, and then go onto a neighboring or a more inclusive phenomenon. Negative data are to be expected in the early stages of exploration and should not be taken too seriously; they merely remind us that we are still groping in the unknown. But the positive data signal that we are on to something. At a later stage, negative data are useful for redirecting inquiry and for mapping boundaries, but not for discarding the process one has discovered. Only when troubles and puzzles and theories proliferate does one suspect that something went wrong at the start of the enterprise and that perhaps a different approach is necessary. Even then one does not abandon the carefully built up theoretical edifice; one suspects rather that it is skewed or wrinkled in unknown ways and hopes to straighten it out eventually, or rescue the good parts at least. Thus the cognitive psychologists confirm their own account of practical reasoning by their practice.

For example, one could say that Mark Snyder's search for ways to get people to falsify was a long irrational search for confirming evidence, evidence that people are Popper-rational. However, it would be more appropriate to see him as exploring the robustness of the Wason phenomenon.

Hold it! Don't sit there smugly thinking, "I knew it! We are rational after all. Hurrah!" To say that practical reasoning satisfices is not to say that it is perfect. It may be very poor in some respects. However, we should evaluate it by the needs of actual research methods, not by the ideal standards of the logical empiricists and formal logicians. The needs of research are not known conclusively, so caution is appropriate (Nisbett and Ross, 1980, p. 276 and *passim*).

However, Cherniak argues that heuristic, practical reasoning is probably more effective than formal deductive logic (1986, chap. 4, esp. p. 89). Some formal deductions are extremely complex, and the limited space in working memory would make such deductions cognitively impossible. Problems of access and cross-access to long-term memory locations prevent other deductions and can prevent the discovery of inconsistencies. Heuristics provide a rapid though not foolproof way of working within these cognitive limits.

Positive Findings: Heuristics, Practical Reasoning

The following account is drawn mainly from the work of the Kahneman-Tversky school, as summarized in Nisbett and Ross (1980), and also from Bruner and others.

Bruner provides a general scheme of practical reasoning that can include many particular processes and individual variations (Bruner, 1973, p. xxii and chap. 13; cf. also Simon, 1977, p. 45; Langley et al., 1987, pp. 58–59; Klahr and Dunbar, 1988). Anglin, the editor, asserts that this scheme applies equally to perception, concept attainment, problem solving, discovery of a scientific theory, and learning a skill. There are three steps: (1) The subject makes an inferential leap from given data to a hypothesis, based on stored background knowledge. (2) The hypothesis is checked against new data to see whether it fits. (3) If it matches the new data, it is retained; if it does not, it is modified to fit the new data. Notice that this is a confirmation strategy in that there is no search for falsifying data.

1. The subject begins with the initially given data (matching bias) and does not ask how representative or reliable they are. That comes later if at all. If many data are available, the subject might focus on a striking or vivid instance (availability bias) that is probably atypical. The data are coded or interpreted in the context of background "knowledge," and the hypothesis will adapt the data to fit the background (Nisbett and Ross, 1980, chap. 4). For instance, if the data seem to contradict the background, the hypothesis might be "some hidden process is operating to

skew these odd data." (Warning: the example is mine, not Bruner's.) The initial hypothesis might be a complex statement that relates many features of the data to background knowledge (wholist strategy) or might pick out some small, limited feature of the data for attention (partist strategy). Subjects seem consistently to prefer one or the other strategy (Bruner, 1973, chap. 9; Bruner, Goodnow and Austin, 1956, chap. 5).

2. The initial hypothesis is usually protected against disconfirmation by new data, *up to a point* (Nisbett and Ross, 1980, chap. 8; Wason and Johnson-Laird, 1972, chap. 16). If new data do not seem to fit the hypothesis, several protective tactics are available. One tactic is to interpret or adjust the data to fit the hypothesis. Another is to exaggerate the importance of the old data in retrospect. Another is to search for additional confirming evidence (Jervis, 1976, pp. 294ff.). Still another is to check a variant or variants of the initial hypothesis against the new data (Wason and Johnson-Laird, 1972, pp. 206–08). That is, one searches the hypothesis space for the one version that best fits incoming data. Nisbett and Ross correctly observe that these tactics are not necessarily irrational, since they may be protecting a sound hypothesis against misleading or mistaken evidence (1980, p. 168). However, if the new evidence continues to be negative, the initial hypothesis is eventually abandoned. Only in extreme cases does a hypothesis mold all new data to fit itself, and thereby rigidify itself by positive feedback.

3. Once an initial hypothesis set is abandoned, the new hypothesis either picks out some feature common to new and old data (partist strategy), or tries to include many common features in a more complex statement (wholist). The search for common features tends to start with the original data (matching bias), and later data that do not agree at all are set aside as puzzling (McHoul, 1982, tactics 1, 6). In extreme, "pathological" cases, the old disconfirmed hypothesis will reappear in disguise and the later disconfirming data tacitly rejected (Wason and Johnson-Laird, 1972, chaps. 16, 18). But, conversely, at times the data might be reorganized around some new vivid instance (availability bias), and the initial data reinterpreted (McHoul, 1982, tactic 2), or even rejected as unrepresentative or of poor quality.

All hypotheses relate data to background "knowledge" about the specific subject. Thus they exist in a taken-for-granted context that determines their latent meanings and possible implications (Wason and Johnson-Laird, 1972, chap. 7). They are not isolated propositions to be manipulated by the rules of formal logic, and their implications do not take on the truth-table values of T and F, but the content-specific values of plausible-implausible and relevant-irrelevant. They deal with meaningful connections and processes—causes, intentions, structures, plans—not with the abstract intersects and disjunctions of Venn diagrams. For example, if a wholist hypothesis about some complex data set takes the form "All A are B"—all the rutabagas here are large, yellow turnip-shaped root vegetables—a plausible inference would be "All B are A," though by Venn diagrams the inference is invalid (Evans, 1982, p. 111; Kelley, 1973).

If background knowledge is so important in data interpretation and hypothesis formation, what happens if the cognitive task is set in unfamiliar territory? In that case the subject supplies a background model by analogy. The unfamiliar territory is connected to known territory at a few points (representativeness heuristic) and the known is then mapped onto the unknown as a hypothesis. If the initial hypothesis is disconfirmed and modified, the differences between the two fields are gradually noted and the initial analogy given a more limited scope.

The contrast between formal logic and practical reasoning also appears, by analogy, in the area of decision making. Here the classical model is that of maximizing rationality: a rational individual is one who lists all his or her goals, lists all available alternative actions, predicts the consequences of each action for each of the goals, and selects that alternative that maximizes expected utility. Defenders of this model of course allow shortcuts and approximations: discounting future consequences beyond a certain time, allowing fuzziness based on uncertainty, neglecting some unpromising alternatives to economize on calculation time. But the evidence shows that people still do not reason that way, at least in business and in international politics. Cognitive psychologists have constructed an alternative theory of practical reasoning that includes Herbert Simon's bounded rationality, Tversky's "elimination by aspects," and cognitive dissonance or cognitive balance theory (Jervis, 1976, chap. 11). This alternative theory allows for absolute and noncomparable goals, unknown or vaguely known goals, changes of goals through dissonance reduction, feedback, and new opportunities, and heuristics for dealing with uncertainty (Snyder and Diesing, 1977, chap. 5).

These experimental accounts suggest that practical reasoning (and decision making) is a fairly flexible, varied process that can be effective in some cognitive tasks and can be adapted to others, but can also produce error and absurdity. The proper policy then is to focus on its weak points and find ways to prevent or correct the worst errors. Weak points include willingness to rely on small, biased samples; over-reliance on initial data or vivid instances; too much protection of a theory against disconfirming data; failure to recognize and question background assumptions; too much exploration near an initial disconfirmed hypothesis and not enough exploration of more distant hypothesis space (anchoring bias); too much reliance on an analogy and failure to recognize disanalogies.

Nisbett and Ross suggest a few comments that one can use to jolt an experimenter out of such errors (1980, chap. 12). They include: "What hat did you get that sample out of?" "What do the other three cells look like?" "Now look at the data from the vantage point of . . . " "You're bolstering your theory with processed information." They also suggest that vivid examples can be countered by different vivid examples, and statistical errors can be countered by training in statistics.

Minsky (1983), following Freud's argument, suggests that humor is often a product of practical reasoning gone astray into absurdity. In particular, analogy and metaphor are essential heuristics for exploration, but can easily produce error and even nonsense. So we laugh. Minsky also suggests that humor is a socially evolved tactic for pointing out others' errors in reasoning and perhaps preventing their recurrence.

However, Minsky, Nisbett, and Ross all doubt that much improvement in scientific reasoning is possible. The basic barrier is lack of self-awareness. If cognitive processes are largely unconscious, therapy will produce more elaborate rationalizations and self-deceptions rather than improved cognition. We can think that we have avoided some standard error this time, but we are only tracing a more circuitous route into the swamp.

In particular, Nisbett and Ross regard the Fundamental Attribution Error as hopeless. This is the error of explaining our own behavior as an intentional response to the situation we are in, but explaining the behavior of others as caused by their personality, social background, and cognitive processes. The problem is not that we know ourselves any better than we know other people, or any worse either; it is rather that different data are available in the two cases (availability bias). We see the situation around us, so the situation is available for explaining (rationalizing) what we do. But the behavior of others is always attached to their body, so by availability its causes must be somewhere inside there.

The fundamental attribution error is at the root of the differences of perspective in the social sciences (see chapter 6). Social scientists always locate themselves somewhere in society, or outside looking in, and wherever they locate themselves, the Subject, they see the situation around them as the context and occasion for their rational action. But when they study the Object out there, they see it as moved by some complex of causes, dispositions, and urges. So if we classify welfare clients from the outside as a class of people, we naturally ask what the distinguishing characteristic of this class is. Is it their family structure, upbringing, IQ, time sense, low self-respect, inability to defer gratification, poor education . . . ? But if we look at welfare as something *we* are getting, we see forces coming at us: labeling, the phone bill, an unresponsive landlord, dead-end work, the pink slip. The forces are out there, and we do not see our role in shaping or encouraging them. A Keynesian or survey researcher can understand businessmen from the outside as moved by an expected standard of living, a marginal propensity to consume, animal spirits, bullish and bearish moods; a neoclassicist can understand businessmen from the inside as planning to utilize available resources to meet expected demand, and planning future consumption to maximize enjoyment with due regard for risks and contingencies. The psychoanalyst tries to fathom the patient's unconscious, but the analysand feels the analyst's personality surrounding him and does not recognize his own role in shaping the interaction. If the fundamental attribution error is incurable, differences of perspective are a permanent feature of the social sciences. A few of us can have our perspectives shifted, but the locations and their perspectives remain.

On the other hand, the errors of the various perspectives cancel or at least supplement each other (Diesing, 1982, chap. 14). It is possible to develop limited collaboration between different or opposed perspectives such that social scientists at least are made aware of the partiality and bias of their theories.

Nisbett and Ross suggest that overconfidence is a second hopeless error. It occurs to me that the probable source is scientists' rationalizations, which fool them into believing that they are pretty smart fellows (notice the availability bias and fundamental attribution error in that intuition). Wason and Johnson-Laird (1972, chap. 16) cite the subject who said, "The machine isn't working. I have the right answer, but it keeps printing out 'error.' It must be stuck somehow." (There! See how we use vivid examples?) If overconfidence is an incurable characteristic of social scientists, what becomes of Merton's norm of humility? Is that rationalization too?

ARTIFICIAL INTELLIGENCE

We turn now from experimental "findings" to the mathematical constructions of AI. The experimenters relate observable output to the presented
information, and theorize about the unobservable cognitive processes
that transform one into the other. The AI people construct programs that
will transform information into output, and instruct the program to report its workings step by step. Consequently, they know what its cognitive processes are, because they have made the unconscious conscious.
But they do not know whether exactly the same processes occur in
human information processing; nor do the processes need to be the same.

Of course, there are many variations and intermediate methods here.
One medical diagnostic program was constructed to imitate the diagnostic processes of a medical school diagnostician; the M.D.'s processes were
discovered by extended participant observation (Clancy, in Kintsch et
al., 1984, chap. 3). This program continues a tradition of simulating
individual cases begun by Colby (in Tomkins and Messick, 1963, chap.
9). There is also the Newell and Simon tactic from the 1950s of having
subjects verbalize while performing a cognitive task, to give the model
builder suggestions for his construction.

Yet the experimenter's linear-causal thinking is very different from
the holistic and modular system thinking in AI, so communication and
collaboration are difficult (Kintsch et al., 1984, chaps. 2, 4, written by
Lehnert and Haugeland). The experimenter wants simple, highly controlled input, to facilitate correlation with output; the model builder
wants a program that can perform complex real tasks, like writing a story,
answering questions about an input essay, making a medical diagnosis,
playing chess. The experimenters give us names—availability bias, fig-
ural bias, anchoring bias—that point to presumed inner sources of observable output; but an AI model should produce the same outputs as incidental effects of its normal working. There is also a conflict over turf: "Most
of the heat underlying professional debates is a territorial reaction about
who owns what problems" (p. 23).

Consequently, the shift to AI focuses our attention on the detailed
structure of the unconscious mind, or active brain, as the neurologists
call it.

Within the AI community we can distinguish, among other actors,
one pair of partners-and-opponents: the computer modelers and the philosophers. The modelers try to embody more and more of human intelli-

gence in a computer program, helped by suggestions from the neurologists; the philosophers, such as Dreyfus (1979) and Weizenbaum (1976), keep pointing out shortcomings in the results. The modelers are always optimistic, always living in the near future when their new language or model will have been debugged; the philosophers are often pessimists, arguing that even the new model or language will still fall short. One result is occasional disagreement: "Fodor doesn't know the frame problem from a bunch of bananas. This is probably why he misunderstood what McDermott was saying" (Hayes, in Pylyshyn, 1987, p. 132).

The philosophers are descendants of the philosophers of the 1950s who reacted instinctively against the Turing test, against the very idea that a machine could have a mind. They were protecting their shrinking turf: mind. But as the AI programs got more complex, the philosophers had to get more explicit about the impossible barriers ahead, and this forced them to get immersed in the actual practice of AI modeling. Thus they made themselves useful as critics and interpreters.

Conversely, some modelers at least seem to welcome more and more difficult challenges, spurning their latest success as inadequate and looking forward to the next seemingly impossible task. Thus Schank (1986) rejects the Turing test as superficial; it has already been passed (p. 2) and must be made more difficult (p. 11). Then he belittles his own successes: "The claim of this book is that any person, or computer program, who would express his understanding of an article such as this by a summary statement such as [here he gives an example] would be rather inadequate. Or, to put this another way, we have built programs that could create such summaries" (pp. 72–73).

The following discussion draws mainly on the theory of Minsky (1975) and the MIT school (Winston, 1975, 1979; I. Goldstein and Papert, 1977; De Mey, 1982). Other schools such as the Stanford-Yale school are developing fairly similar models, so Minsky can be taken as typical (for example, Bobrow and Winograd, 1977; Schank and Abelson, 1977).

The structure of mind is apparently modular (Fodor, 1982). Mind or brain is composed of a large number of interconnected modules, each activated in a specific situation such as entering a restaurant, meeting a friend, taking out a chessboard, or reading data on the rate of inflation. Minsky calls these modules *frames*; others have called them *schemata, scripts, scenarios, world views, cell assemblies* (Hebb), or simply *models*. *Microworlds* are different; they belong to a previous stage in AI.

Frames are hierarchical networks with top, middle, and bottom sectors. At the top are general characteristics of the situation or thing or person. The middle sector consists of *subframes*, each representing a variant or a subtype, a particular friend or a type of restaurant or data source. At the bottom are *terminals*, or *slots*, sets of questions about details. Minsky suggests that these terminals usually have typical or standard answers filled in, which exemplify the kind of answer that is appropriate, and which can be printed out in default of more specific input.

For instance, suppose we are in a hall and see a door along the side wall. Door = knob, rectangular shape, hinges, swings open, open it. Unlock? Pull or push? Those are the standard parts and questions. But there are variants. All doors open, but some are revolving or sliding doors or oven doors that swing downward or trapdoors that swing upward. When we see a knob or rectangular shape or something swinging, the frame *door* is activated and we rapidly fill in the slots, or assume a standard door.

Next, the frame *door* passes control to *room*: rectangular shape, walls, ceiling, floor, walk in. That is, we expect a room behind the door. Subframes are types of room: classroom, broom closet, lounge, office. Questions are chairs, tables, light switches, windows, floor material. As we enter the room, we use cues—furniture, coat hooks—to switch to one subframe, then fill in the question slots for that frame. Immediately we have a particularized model of that room, including the large part that we cannot see yet.

Or if we are reading inflation data, there is an immediate choice point: *consumer price index, wholesale price index, implicit price deflator?* Each of the three paths has cross-connections to other frames, the connections varying according to whether one is a monetarist, Keynesian, or institutionalist. CPI might be connected to crop reports, market structure, mortgage rates, interest rates, M_1, M_2, foreign exchange rate, trade balance, tariffs; WPI might be connected to wage-price spiral, unions, oil prices, M_1, M_2; thence to fiscal and monetary policy, the next election, the opposition party. That is, the data activate a series of questions whose answers define the particular political-economic situation and explain the data. In the *room* frame the questions are answered by visual or tactile search (in a dark room); in the *inflation* frame the questions are answered by library or memory search for data, or by analogy with an already particularized inflation frame.

The slots in a frame are also usually connected to action subroutines:

chair means sit down, a *slippery floor* means walk carefully, M_2 means the Fed and the discount rate, M_3 means banks and reserve ratios.

A frame may be activated by a sensory cue, or internally by an activated goal as when one looks for a bathroom door along the hall, or by another frame. It may be activated in waking life, or in imagination, or in dreams. In other words, action and thought can be directed both by environmental cues and by plans and expectations. Either can also interfere with the other and take control of information processing.

Activation of a frame may occur at the top, or bottom, or middle, and move up or down as a successive series of questions. Thus the *door* routine connects to *room* at the top of the *room* frame; but the sight of a light brown surface through a window might cue *desk*, then *classroom*, moving up from the bottom. In the latter case we might immediately get a picture of a standard classroom without any more sensory input, as the standard answers in the slots get printed out.

A frame is a search routine, a series of questions about the situation one is in, a heuristic of discovery (Neisser, 1976, chaps. 4, 6, 7; DeMey, 1982, chap. 11; Langley et al., 1987). According to Dreyfus, following Heidegger, we are always situated in some sort of activity, always moving through a process or toward a goal. The frame or scenario constitutes the setting (classroom, restaurant) and the process (talking, eating) through which we move. In research the theory or the exemplar we are following tells us the steps to take, the data to uncover, where to find the data, the data processing needed. That is, the slots in the frame determine what questions to ask and what kinds of answers would be appropriate; the frame constitutes our expectations or preunderstanding.

The answers are a product of both input and expectation. Ambiguous or missing input can activate the standard answer in the slot—we see what we expect to see. Or we keep looking until we find something that "makes sense," fits the slot. Irrelevant, coincidental input can also be interpreted to fit into a slot in a currently active subframe, as when a noise or somatic input is incorporated into an ongoing dream, or a friend we were intending to call appears in the distance, only to turn into a stranger as he approaches. Clearer input can fill in the slots of the frame with new answers, thereby producing a more detailed model of the thing being studied. Sometimes clear but unexpected input can override expectations, by cueing some other subframe that breaks in on the active frame, the expectation.

The overriding of expectations by some other frame can produce learning, that is, change of frame. Change need not occur; the other frame can take control: "Oh! It was one of those! I see"; or, "Well! Attitudes must have changed on that topic!"—and both frames continue unchanged. But the connection can become established as another association; or new branches, alternatives, disanalogies, can be added to the frame. "Thinking begins first with suggestive but defective plans and images that are slowly, if ever, refined and replaced by better ones" (Minsky, 1981, p. 128).

Similarly, Winograd suggests that the hermeneutic circle is a good analogy for the refinement of frames in learning. The simple or defective frame is the preunderstanding that guides search and interpretation; the interpreted data enrich and sometimes revise the preunderstanding. The eventual result is a particularized interpretation and, sometimes, a more complex and effective preunderstanding (Winograd, 1980, pp. 223–24).

McHoul (1982), provides a good example of the interplay of expectation and input in the hermeneutic process. McHoul instructed subjects to interpret a poem that was presented to them line by line. The poem was meaningless; it consisted of randomly chosen lines from the work of a single poet. Thus each successive line was sure to conflict sharply with the pattern of meaning, or story, that the subject was constructing. There were several tactics: (1) interpret the line to fit the anticipated meaning, perhaps by adjusting expectation a bit. (2) Revise the poem's meaning to fit the new line and reinterpret some previous lines. (3) Postpone interpretation in bafflement until the next line. (4) As a last resort, declare the poem meaningless. McHoul stated that his major finding was the reciprocal influence of expected pattern on interpretation of a line (1), and of line on the expected pattern (2). This is the hermeneutic circle.

Memory too can change when its expectations are overridden (Lehnert, in Kintsch et al., 1984, pp. 40–41). *Memory* is another name for the network of frames. The particularized subframes are the things that have happened, and the general frames are the things we have learned to do and expect. And since frames have multiple connections at various levels, a memory can be activated in a variety of ways; it does not have just one address, as in earlier models.

Learning is one process that has not yet been adequately modeled, so we have to rely on the aspirations of the modelers and the criticisms of the philosophers here. The most obvious suggestion is that frames should grow continuously through experience; as we walk through many doors we develop subframes of door types, more subtle cues to whether the door opens in or out, right or left, more routines for locking or unlocking. As we learn more about inflation, we similarly develop more subtypes: the German hyperinflation, the Latin American debt inflation, the food subsidy-suppressed inflation, the wage-price spiral. We develop many more connections to other frames such as agricultural policy, and more subtle cues that activate the subframes.

However, most frames are also social, learned, and shared (Freyd, 1983), so they can be taught. Dreyfus (in Pylyshyn, 1987, pp. 98–103) lists several stages in the learning of a skill. The novice learns basic features or steps of a process; variations (subframes) in how to perform the main steps; situational cues that suggest which variation is appropriate; paradigm examples of how to adapt a technique to a situation by laying out a path through it; and how to recognize similarities and dissimilarities. Dreyfus stresses that mostly we learn *how*, not *that*: "When things are going well experts do not solve problems or make inferences or figure out anything at all; they simply do what normally works, and it normally works" (p. 102).

This argument suggests that problem solving may be another learned skill, another frame, perhaps along the lines of Newell and Simon's General Problem Solver. One type of problem could be how to fix a frame that doesn't work, as Dennett suggests (in Pylyshyn, 1987).

Another current problem is that of providing adequate context for interpreting input. The frame people have been very much aware of the importance of context; and indeed the development of frame theory was one step in the process of providing adequate context for cognitive processes.

The need for context became apparent through the failures of early models: the early programs that simply put a dictionary into the computer memory—for instance, in machine translation—didn't work. Thus *order* means different things in a restaurant scenario, a classroom scenario, a committee meeting scenario, and an Elks letterhead. The cognitive psychologists also discovered the importance of context in the practical reasoning process (pp. 250–52, above).

Frame theory itself was intended in part as a solution to the need for context. The frame provides the *limited, relevant* context that gives meaning to words like *order* and to perceptual bits like angles and colors. The proper frame is supposed to be activated by some input cue; thus the phrase "first order of business" cues in the *agenda* scenario which gives meaning to *order*, and salt and pepper shakers on a table cue in the *restaurant* or *dining room* scenario, which gives a different meaning to *order*. Or if we are in a hall, the *hall* frame provides a context for *door*, specifying what kind of door to expect. Or a wider context can be activated by multiple connections, associations, at lower levels of a frame. Some of the connections are to motor neurons or printout routines: *doorknob* means, in part, "Grab it and twist."

The manifold connections among frames are supposed to provide a broader secondary context for interpreting ambiguous input. A clause in a labor-management contract, or the latest foreign trade figures, activates a whole network of frames, on and on: the Fed, the Group of Seven, Korean labor unrest, U.K. investment in U.S. industries, Bridgestone, Brazil, OPEC, cartels, Texas bankruptcies, Continental bank, FDIC, H. Minsky, 1986. A contract clause activates a grievance scenario, management policy and motives, transportation to work, membership meetings, and so on.

We may distinguish several kinds of connections or transfers between frames (Haugeland, 1981, chap. 2). Normally control is *passed on* from one frame or subframe to another, as in *door, room*. A series of such transfers is a list or plan, and the plan routine maintains control of the transfers: *door, room, blackboard, write, talk*. Or the series can be uncontrolled, as in free association: white hair, grandfather, security, death, my evil eye (Erikson, 1964, chap. 2). Second, control can be *taken away* by interruption, cued by environmental or somatic input or by some parallel plan. Third, control may be *broadcast* without a clearly intended receiver.

But there may be a need for a still broader context of general background knowledge for interpreting input. Controlling the potential complexity of access and of updating of backround knowledge is one version of "the frame problem." Bobrow and Winograd (1977) suggest that background knowledge, along with basic search strategies and self-monitoring, may have to be programmed in as a generalized foundation for the frames. They mention concepts of time, events, plans, motives, actions, causes, possibility, as knowledge that is relevant to all frames and must always be accessible. Similarly, Minsky lists cause-effect, time, purpose, locality, process as basic common-sense concepts that will have to be worked in somehow (1981, p. 124). Dreyfus (a philosopher) agrees that background knowledge is essential, but doubts that the frame people will succeed in programming it in (in Haugeland, 1981, chap 6). He observes that Husserl made a similar attempt to understand human knowledge as frames, search routines, and found that more and more background knowledge was needed (p. 182). Heidegger argued against the project, asserting that the needed background is simply our whole shared everyday world. Dreyfus comments, "Programmers rush in where philosophers such as Heidegger fear to tread" (p. 183).

We are not concerned with whether the AI people will solve the background knowledge problem; maybe they won't. But the holistic emphasis on the importance of context does concern us. If the meaning of data depends on broad contexts, then the logical empiricist attempt to base knowledge on context-free sense data, red patches and pointer readings, was wholly misguided. Frame theory agrees rather with Dewey's fundamental 1931 article, "Context and Thought" (rpt. in Bernstein, 1960), which argues that experimental data, for example, get their meaning from the experimenter's theories, his research problem, his technical knowledge, the equipment, the subject's habits and dispositions and language ability. Data are a joint product and component of all these contexts. For Dewey, too, like Heidegger, there is an ultimate context for social science: experience, that is shared experience, the social process.

The interconnection of frames which provides some context also provides several interpretations of creativity, ranging from the mechanical to the deliberate. Routine, mechanical creativity is simply the unexpected routes that programs take through complex interconnected frames. Even the early geometry theorem–proving programs of about 1960 were mechanically creative, in that they could produce new and unexpected, but neat and valid proofs. Much routine creativity is defined as "bugs," errors in the program to be corrected by debugging. And so also in human beings.

At the level of insight, Bruner suggests that creativity may consist of unusual transfers in which the strange context changes some meaning or routine (1979, chap. 1). The transfer could be produced by an analogy-transform in which one initial transfer, A is like B, triggers a whole series of connections up and down the frames. Schank works out a more deliberate kind of creativity. He suggests that a creative explanation involves having a large stock of explanation patterns in memory; finding an unusual one for this case; and changing it to make it fit the case (1986, chap. 6). The changes involve searching through several kinds of analogies. Schank hopes to develop such a program soon.

Self-knowledge is simply a self-schema or frame (Nisbett and Ross, 1980, chap. 9). This is a cognitive science version of the old "self-concept," including body image. Our introspective self-knowledge is a product of this frame: if I feel fat, bloated, that is body image; if I appreciate the clarity and brilliance of my thought, that is self-concept. In other words, our self-knowledge is no more immediate and direct than our knowledge of others. In both cases, our organized expectations tell us what we are experiencing. As with other frames, the self-schema normally sorts incoming somatic and external data into its slots to provide an introspective description of how we feel. It also provides the context that gives meaning to our plans and actions and goals. And as with other frames, clear and dramatic input can override and even change its categories by cueing other frames that interrupt the self-display routine. The cognitive psychologists have made this same point about self-knowledge.

The sharing of frames in conversation has been studied a good deal since the mid-1960s (Winograd, 1980; De Mey, 1982, pp. 27ff.; Graesser and Black, 1985). According to Winograd, the failure of machine translations based on dictionaries set off an inquiry into meaning, communication, and conversation in ordinary language, an inquiry that is still under way.

It appears that communication requires an other-schema as well as a self-schema and a representation (frame) of the topic being discussed. To communicate with the other, the program must have a concept (frame, schema) of what the other already knows or believes about the topic, plus some of the other's background knowledge. The other will interpret statements in terms of what he already "knows" about a topic, so all effective communication will have to adapt to that context. For instance, the statement "We're invited to a shower" will cue in the other's *shower* scenario and thereby activate a set of expectations and rules. But for someone who does not know what a shower is, the phrase will have little meaning; and for someone whose *shower* frame includes slots for soap and hot water, or umbrellas and rubbers, the phrase will produce a misunderstanding. The phrase "the consumer price index for March" will cue in the other's *inflation* frame, with all its associations and expectations. To communicate effectively about inflation, the program must have a concept of the other's *inflation* frame—is it monetarist, Keynesian, institutionalist, or Marxist?

After a frame or frames for self and other have been activated, the program will begin to build a representation or story of the conversation itself, and use that representation as well to interpret the meaning of new statements (Winograd, 1980, p. 218). A new statement is expected to be a coherent part of the conversation story, as well as being intelligible in the context of background knowledge.

Breakdowns in communication indicate that one's other-schema and/or one's concept of the conversation differ from the other's own background knowledge and/or story of the conversation. The program can repair a breakdown by communicating parts of the other-schema, to see where they fail to match the other's activated frames. Communication is in part a noticing and repairing of breakdowns, as Heidegger had noted in his 1927 *Sein und Zeit* (Winograd, 1980, p. 235).

Denzin's account of conversation, based on symbolic interaction theory, agrees with the above account (Denzin, 1970, pp. 10, 24).

A successful, self-repairing conversation is not simply an exchange of information. It is a goal-directed performance whose goals are specified by speech acts (Graesser and Black, 1985, chap. 2; Winograd, 1980, p. 233, both referring to Searle, 1969). According to Searle, an OL (ordinary language) analyst and critic of AI, a speech act affirms a commitment or a goal and thereby gives pragmatic meaning to utterances. Questions are speech acts that activate a particular conversation frame. The goal of a conversation, as affirmed by initial questions, might be: Give me information; Show me how much you know; Testify to the truth in court; Admit that your position is absurd (rhetorical questions); Let's share complaints; or Let me show off how much I know.

Different speech acts will produce very different conversation stories. A "Give me information" story set up by the other's questions will consist of finding the gaps in the other's knowledge and filling them in; a "Show off how much I know" story will focus on what the other knows and will avoid or conceal the gaps. An effective conversation program should contain a variety of conversation frames and activate the correct one from initial questions.

McClelland and Elman (1986) suggest that a conversation program should provide for the simultaneous activation of many frames—that is, many hypotheses as to what is going on in the conversation. This program involves parallel processing, since each frame is simultaneously active in interpreting utterances. When an utterance fits the expectation of one frame, that frame becomes more active and simultaneously inhibits the activity of competing frames. Eventually one or several mutually consistent frames come to dominate interpretation and responses, and a conversation story fitting that frame is constructed.

Parallel distributed processing or PDP (Rumelhart and McClelland, 1986) is partly an outgrowth or successor to frame theory and partly an application of ideas from neurology. One essential characteristic of a frame is that it is supposed to be a network, not a list. That is, input is not supposed to run down one channel at a time, with everything else sitting there inactive. It is rather supposed to activate connections up and down the frame, and these connections should then activate other frames and subframes, and so on. Such a spreading activation would rapidly produce chaos, so inhibition of one channel by another is also necessary. "Taking control" is one form of inhibition.

PDP carries the idea of inhibition much farther, supported by neurological evidence that brains work mainly by inhibition. Input cues can activate a number of frames simultaneously, and continuing input stimulates some frames more than others. The more active frames inhibit conflicting parts of less active frames without turning off a frame completely. A shift in input shifts the pattern of activity and inhibition, and a plan (list) can simultaneously shift it in a different direction.

In this type of model, a concept is not a particular node in a network, taking its meaning from all the connections, direct and indirect, to other nodes. It is a pattern of activation over many frames, again including the connections which it activates and inhibits. Learning is not merely making new connections and adding subframes and branches, but adjusting the strength of activating and inhibiting connections.

The analogy in social science would be a researcher, or group project, or community, that maintains several conflicting and supplementary theories simultaneously. The research process produces continuing changes of each theory, and also fluctuating patterns of dominance among the theories. Each theory's meaning includes its relation to the other theories, including overlaps, contrasts, similarities, and supplements. However, the details of PDP remain to be worked out.

SUMMARY AND CONCLUSIONS

The AI and experimental psychology results are different but not really conflicting, as of 1975–85, because they approach cognitive processes from opposite directions. AI studies cognition from inside a cognitive program, while experimenters approach it from outside. In other words, AI synthesizes cognition while experimenters analyze it (A. Collins, 1977).

An AI modeler constructs a program, runs and debugs it, and sees what output it gives. He also tells the program to report its own process, so he can see how the process produced the output. An experimenter works from both input and output toward the unobservable intervening process. He postulates a regular inner cause of observed output regularities (that is, he uses availability and representativeness bias—Nisbett and Ross, 1980, chap. 6) and gives the hypothetical cause a name. Whether or not the supposed causes exist as such, the result is an accumulation of examples of cognitive outputs to be puzzled over.

Both approaches give us a highly tentative and incomplete knowledge of cognition. AI works through debugging and revision of models to produce better output, and gradually tries to produce more complex output. Marr comments that the first twenty or so AI theories were all too simple or wrong (in Haugeland, 1981, chap. 4, esp. p. 136). This includes the self-organizing systems approach (Yovits et al., 1962) which supposed that an empty, Lockean tabula rasa program could be taught to learn with proper input; the separation of memory banks from programs; the template-matching programs; and the context-free "microworld" models of abstract objects to be moved around on instructions. De Mey (1982, chap. 1) traces AI development from bits of information and pattern recognition to the construction of world models or frames. Winograd (1980) does the same for language. However, the frame theory is still programmatic—Minsky slyly describes it as a search routine, a series of questions for research (1975, p. 212). A few good working programs exist (Kintsch et al., 1984; Winston, 1975), but others are in process or in plan and may not work.

Experimentation works through devising hypotheses that suggest novel experimental paradigms and thence produce piles of cognitive outputs. The result is chaotic, to be sure, as Eysenck sadly reports (1984, p. 1), but one can always "find" regularities, persistent characteristics of human cognition, in the data. The experimental regularities—heuristics or biases, hypothesis formation strategies—are recognizable as outputs of the AI neural networks, so the results of the two approaches are not contradictory.

The most general finding, from both directions, is that reasoning is not a process of formal logical deduction. It is a heuristic process of search, or discovery, in which theories (frames) provide the questions and the expected answers and data provide material for actual answers. Inferences are content-specific and depend on a broad context of tacit knowledge. Formal deductive logic and also probability theory are special-ized mathematical models that have the same limited, qualified applica-bility to data as other mathematical models. They certainly do not consti-tute a foundation for science or scientific methods. Marvin Minsky, for one, is quite emphatic on this (1981, pp. 123ff.; see also Schoenfeld, 1983).

Practical reasoning is rational in the sense that it works in everyday life, and in the sense that it can reflect on itself and improve itself. The first sense is not relevant for social science reasoning, which goes beyond everyday experience. As soon as we go beyond the everyday-life world, we lose all but a tenuous contact with reality. The reason is that expecta-tions and the various biases normally control the interpretation of am-biguous data, which are rarely clear and complete enough in social sci-ence to override expectations and survive the selectiveness of the biases.

Consequently, the second sense is the important one for science. "Only a process that can reflect on what it has done—that can examine a record of what has happened—can have any consequences. [For in-stance,] our ability to debug a computer program depends on . . . traces and records" (M. Minsky, 1975, p. 273). This implies that any rationality in social science consists not in its having sound logical foundations but in its ability to find and correct past errors. The agreement is with the Popperians and the pragmatists rather than the analytic philosophers.

By self-reflection we cannot mean introspection, which has proved to be unreliable. Reasoning is apparently a largely unconscious process, and only its products and traces are conscious. Various cognitive psychologists credit Freud with the early exploration of unconscious mind, while reject-ing most or all of psychoanalytic theory (for example, Nisbett and Ross, 1980, chap. 10; Kosslyn, 1983, chaps. 3, 7); and indeed the Simon-Newell verbalization tactic is similar to Freudian free association. Verbal-ization and free association can evade the censor, or the rationalizer, enough to give the experimenter some clues to cognitive processes. Maybe (Schoenfeld, 1983, esp. p. 351).

But if self-reflection is not an introspective process, as the early phenomenologists supposed, what is it? Apparently the cognitive psy-chologists define self-reflection as their own experimentation and model building. They are the ones who have discovered the various biases, and have demonstrated the effects of expectation and background knowledge on information processing. They are the analysts of the unconscious who reflect our biased reasoning back to us and make us face what we are.

They are the ones who deflate our grandiose delusions of infallible logic and objective observation. They have even provided some suggestions for therapy—maxims, heuristics, training in statistical thinking, humor. This book attempts to contribute to the psychologists' project of self-reflection.

The two approaches, experimentation and model building, give us characteristically differing accounts of practical reasoning. The experimenters have necessarily focused on the outward, observable aspects of search, namely, the treatment of data and hypotheses during cognitive tasks. The AI people have focused inward, on the constructive and interpretive activity of mind.

The experimenters tell us how people rely on characteristics of data that could be revealing but can also be misleading; how they preserve their hypotheses and beliefs against ambiguous or seemingly negative evidence, up to a point; and how they modify hypotheses to more or less fit new evidence. They tell us of an inductive process that works well with clear, simple data but works unevenly with complex, ambiguous data. The inductive stance of the subjects may be an artifact of the experimental design, in which subjects are presented data and assigned a cognitive task. Nevertheless, insofar as social scientists use induction—for instance, in the various case study methods—the experimenters have pointed out characteristic biases that need to be guarded against and counteracted. They include anchoring bias, availability bias, matching bias, representativeness heuristic, analogy heuristic, and the fundamental attribution error.

In contrast with the artificial, enforced passivity of the experimental subjects, the AI models give us an active mind that searches for data with its lists of questions, that interprets data to fit expectations, up to a point, and that fills in details by analogy where data are not available. They tell us of an interpretive process that structures experience to fit theory, and that fills in or modifies the details of theory to fit experience.

This account too is relevant to social science methods. Much and perhaps most social science is data interpretation, the construction of stories (Ward, 1973) or histories in which human plans and causal strands are so interwoven as to produce the observed outcome. The AI people show us how theory (frames) produce these interpretations, and show us how to produce better, more objective interpretations.

Economists and political economists know how to fit masses of official data about GNP, CPI, M_2, or M_3, investment, unemployment, interest rates, debt, budgets, elections, into a story that explains why things have worked out this way and what is really happening now. They know how to adjust data that do not fit and to reject as coincidence regularities that do not fit. When their predictions do not work out they know how to find interfering influences. Each theory, whether monetarist, Keynesian, institutionalist, neoclassical, or Marxist, produces its own history. Thus we have a monetarist history of the 1929–33 Depression (Friedman and Schwartz, 1963, chap. 7); a business cycle history (Schumpeter, 1939); a Keynesian-institutionalist history (Galbraith, 1955); a Keynesian history (Kindelberger, 1973; Temin, 1976); an international trade approach (Fleisig, 1976); and a Marxist history (Block, 1977, chap. 2; M. Bernstein, 1987). Hirsch and de Marchi (1986) analogize the storytelling process to a trial, in which opposed attorneys try to construct a persuasive account that will leave their client (that is, their theory) victorious. Only, there are no judge and jurors, just attorneys talking past each other.

Similarly, clinicians know how to make a tentative diagnosis of a case from presented data, and know what additional data will confirm or disconfirm their diagnosis. This process has already been modeled (Clancy, in Kintsch et al., 1984, chap. 3). Each disease has a list or a pattern of symptoms that suggest its presence and a list of other symptoms that reject its presence. The expert apparently reasons directly from data to diagnosis (Patel and Groen, 1986). But when the positive symptoms suggest two or more possible diseases, the negative symptoms reject one or more of these; or a combination of positive symptoms points to one diagnosis as the most plausible. Experts have more cues, more symptom-disease connections than novices, including weak and unusual symptoms (Johnson et al., 1981).

The role of expectations, theory, in constructing stories is both positive and negative. Positively, theory guides the search for data and for the hidden connections that explain the surface phenomena; theory leads us to the reality behind appearance, the disease behind the symptoms. Negatively, theory ignores, overlooks, or rejects data that do not fit its categories, and shapes ambiguous data to fit its expectations.

A good theory, then, is one that is both detailed enough to guide search effectively and flexible enough to accept disconfirming evidence and to change accordingly. How is this possible? Frames do not have any slots that specify disconfirming evidence, so they simply cannot recognize such a thing (Higgins, 1981, chap. 3). At most they can register puzzlement and tell us what is unexpected and needs attention (Schank and Childers, 1984, p. 115). The exception is Clancy's medical diagnosis model (Kintsch et al., 1984, chap. 3). In frame theory, the only way a datum can override the expected answer in a slot is to cue in an item of some other frame, which then interrupts and takes control. Then the new data are transferred to the original frame and modify it. That is, we have to be able to recognize the unexpected data as something different, not just error or coincidence or interference; and that requires being able to interpret them in a different frame.

Thus learning, self-correction, depends on multiple connected but different frames, each responsive to different aspects or facets of data. This sounds like Feyerabend's pluralism, except that the AI researcher demands a pluralism of theories or perspectives within an individual. A social pluralism composed of one-perspective individuals would not be self-corrective, since each monad could interpret the "errors" of all the others within its own framework and learn nothing. Elsewhere I have argued that this is the problem with Milton Friedman's monetarism: his single theoretical framework is so closed off against alternative frames that it can assign almost all the data to existing slots, including *coincidence* and *interference*, and thereby avoid correction (Diesing, 1985a). Nisbett and Ross's maxim, "Now look at the data from the vantage point of . . . " (1980, chap. 12) is meaningless to Friedman because he has only one vantage point. Nor do I claim that Friedman is unique or unusual in this respect; I just "happen" to know his work (availability bias).

In regard to histories of the Depression of the 1930s, we can contrast the single-frame history of Friedman and Schwartz (1963) with the flexible multiple-frame history of Kindelberger (1973). Friedman and Schwartz searched only for data about the variables listed in their quantity theory of money: money, price level, velocity, income, plus ratios and components and adjuncts to these variables such as interest rates. Their concern was to bring out relations among these variables, display the regularities that fit their theory, and puzzle over the exceptions such as the secular rise in velocity after 1946 (1963, chap. 12). Naturally, they conclude that their theory is empirically supported. For example, writing about the "Great Contraction" of 1929–33, so named by them because the quantity of money contracted in those years, Friedman and Schwartz assert, "The contraction is in fact a tragic testimonial to the importance of monetary forces" (p. 300). They note (p. 301) that other forces were also operative but write nothing about them.

Kindleberger is sensitive to the monetary variables, perhaps because he knows the work of Friedman and Schwartz (1963), but also because his Keynesian frame has places for monetary variables. But it also has subframes for consumer spending, stock market speculation, and the agricultural economy. On the latter topic, Kindleberger notes that farmers' tendency to increase production when the prices of their products fall produced a vicious circle of falling farm prices and overproduction in 1925–29, long before the quantity of money declined (1973, chap. 4). This in turn produced agricultural bankruptcy and bank failures in agricultural states, which fed into the monetary variables (pp. 186–89; cf. also Temin, 1976). Friedman and Schwartz list states in which bank failures were numerous (1963, p. 308), but do not notice that these are agricultural states: *agriculture* is not a monetary variable. They mention farm foreclosures in a footnote (p. 320) and refer vagely to poor bank loans (p. 355), but make no connections among these peripheral observations. Instead, they focus on Federal Reserve Board discussions (pp. 362–419).

Kindleberger also focuses on international-system factors such as trade and tariffs that are peripheral in the Keynesian conceptual framework; Friedman and Schwartz do not even mention the Smoot-Hawley tariff of 1930.

The AI people do not offer any therapy for the closed-mind single-frame theorist. However, one possibility is to maintain plural theoretical orientations in graduate departments. Plural orientations, two or three, can produce conflicting loyalties and ambivalent identifications in the growing cognitive program that might be maintained in later life. A strongly unified department tends to produce single-frame theorists. Rebels with oedipal tendencies can still reject the received theory and adopt a new one, but the rejection survives as a negative fixation that has its own defects, as in my own case. Plural orientations avoid both these weaknesses. However, this suggestion may be merely another case of my fitting the cognitivists' theories into the slots of my framework.

Finally, we must take seriously the cognitivists' frequent warnings that improvement of cognitive processes is slow and uncertain at best, and that some biases and errors seem hopeless. In particular, there is no cognitive therapy for overconfidence, self-esteem, which draws down an iron curtain against correction. This chapter should teach us humility;

but Merton's norm of humility will not correct overconfidence, since confidence is a matter of personality dynamics. And since people who are successful in the social science rat race tend to have a great deal of self-esteem, the outlook for improved objective knowledge is poor indeed. The prospect brightens only if we survey the obvious past progress of some field from the laughable errors of thirty years ago through the discoveries and improvements of our predecessors, culminating in our own brilliant illuminations and achievements.

10

Personality Influences in Social Science

DO SOCIAL SCIENTISTS' personalities find expression in their work? Yes, they do. Personality effects are a class of experimenter effects, and appear in all methods involving direct contact with people—experimentation, interviewing, survey research, clinical research, and ethnography (Rosenthal, 1966). "Experimenters who differ in anxiety, need for approval, hostility, authoritarianism, status, and warmth tend to obtain different responses from their experimental subjects" (Rosenthal, 1983, p. 91).

We can arbitrarily distinguish three kinds or levels of personality influences for study. First, there are the direct effects on other people, mentioned above. These include the extensively studied experimenter effects on subjects, interviewer effects on respondents, clinical and ethnographic effects on subjects, and the effects on other social scientists in discussion.

Personality effects are interferences to be systematically investigated and controlled; but they are also an essential resource in research. The researcher's personality should normally be nonthreatening, reassuring, to set the respondent at ease and prevent a defensive response. Thus the ethnographer studying a dependent, low-power or low-status group cannot appear to represent external or internal authority. In interviewing, the race of the interviewer should normally match that of the respondent. But sometimes a particular kind of personality effect is a tool for a more active probing method. Thus a somewhat authoritarian analyst can bring out the oedipal problems of an analysand for clinical study and working through, and matched female and male interviewers can be used to study how political opinions express attitudes toward gender (Hoag and Allerbeck, 1985).

Second, there are the influences of a researcher's personality on his concepts and values, and on the problems that attract his interest. Consider for example the concept of *authority*. What authority means to a person depends on what kinds of authority one has experienced and on

273

what sort of responses, coping mechanisms, and internalizations one has developed during these experiences. Thus Bruno Bettelheim, a fairly authoritarian person himself, used to say in class that Adorno et al., authors of *The Authoritarian Personality* (1950) had the wrong concept of authority. They thought only of bad authority, rigid, punitive, self-centered; but there was also good authority that maintains necessary order and direction, which they did not study at all. They gave *authority* a bad reputation. In addition concepts of authority are central for some writers such as Max Weber and Reinhard Bendix and peripheral for others, probably depending on the centrality of authority relations in their upbringing. Thus Namenwirth observes that in biology the concept of DNA as giving detailed orders to the cell as it develops is an authoritarian concept. An alternative concept would be the interaction or collaboration of several influences during development. Both concepts have some usefulness in understanding DNA (Bleier, 1986, pp. 25–28).

Or consider the concept of *nature*. For some, nature is neutral matter to be informed in Aristotle's sense, raw materials to be sorted out, transformed, cleared away, and used up. For others, nature is a wild and dangerous challenge—swamps, alligators, mountains—to be conquered, tamed, filled in and paved over. For still others, nature is a quiet, slow-moving place where one can escape the stresses and strains of city life. In some primitive cultures, nature was the source of all life, to be respected or even worshipped and not to be changed at all. More recently, nature has been regarded as the ecosystem that surrounds and sustains us; we, as the conscious part of the ecosystem, have the responsibility of maintaining and improving its complex functioning. These various concepts express personal and cultural differences.

Third, there are the ways in which researchers cope with data and concepts and problems, their cognitive style. Variables include the familiar Rorschach variables: focusing on wholes, parts, or details; emphasis on shape, color, or gray areas; motion; popular and animal responses; inability to perceive certain objects. Social science data are usually somewhat ambiguous, like the ink blots in a Rorschach test, so people with different cognitive styles will make different things of them.

PERSONALITY EFFECTS

I shall present two extreme, obvious examples of personality effects. The first example illustrates a good effect that uncovers otherwise hidden data; the second illustrates a bad effect that interferes with inquiry. In both cases, we do not inquire or speculate about the personality that produced these effects; we merely observe the effects on other people.

Neil Friedman cites a number of experiments with IQ tests that correlate tester-subject race with IQ scores. The results were that black subjects scored lower with white testers than with black testers, and white subjects scored lower with black testers than with white testers (1967, pp. 114–16). Here the race rather than the personality of the tester is the influence that either brings out or hides the subject's intelligence. Friedman observes, "It seems that Negroes learn very young to 'play Negro' with a white examiner " (p. 116). Note that Friedman focuses on the IQ of black children as the problem; he later taught at Tuskegee Institute in Alabama.

Friedman continues with a case report, quoted from Riessman (*The Culturally Deprived Child*, 1962, pp. 49–50) that shifts from race to personality: A few years ago a birthday party for a member of the staff at a well-known psychological clinic played a novel role in the test performance of a Negro child. Prior to the party this boy, whom we shall call James, had been described on the psychological record as "sullen, surly, slow, unresponsive, apathetic, unimaginative, lacking in inner life." This description was based on his behavior in the clinic interviews and on his performance on a number of psychological measures including an intelligence test and a personality test. His was not an unusual record; many culturally deprived children are similarly portrayed.

On the day of the birthday party, James was seated in an adjoining room waiting to go into the clinician's office. It was just after lunch hour and James had the first afternoon appointment. The conclusion of the lunch break on this particular day was used by the staff to present a surprise birthday cake to one of the clinicians who happened to be a Negro. The beautifully decorated cake was brought in and handed to the recipient by James' clinician who was white, as were all the other members of the staff. The Negro woman was deeply moved by the cake—and the entire surprise. In a moment of great feeling, she warmly embraced the giver of the cake. James inadvertently perceived all this from his vantage point in the outer office. That afternoon he showed amazing alacrity in taking the tests and responding in the interview. He was no longer sullen and dull. On the contrary, he seemed alive, enthusiastic, and he answered questions readily. His psychologist was astonished at the change and in the course of the next few weeks retested James on the tests on which he had done so poorly. He now showed marked improvement, and she quickly revised not only the test appraisal of him on the clinical record card, but her general personality description of him as well.

Here the white tester's act of love, and James's observation of its warm acceptance by a fellow Negro, overcame James's defensiveness and opened a deeper level of James's personality to clinical observation.

The second extreme example comes from philosophy. It consists of personality effects on other philosophers—that is, rhetoric. The example is Adolf Grünbaum's treatment of hermeneutics in *The Foundations of Psychoanalysis* (1984, pp. 1–94). Grünbaum's rhetoric begins mildly with such terms as "ludicrous" and "not a scintilla of evidence" (p. 14), "stone age physics" (p. 20), and gradually gets more sarcastic and scornful: "cognitive tribute to the patient" becomes "cognitive monopoly" (p. 21) and "truly formidable epistemic powers" (p. 30); "mutilation" becomes "ontological amputation" and "ontological stultification" based on an imported ideological objective (pp. 43–45); Grünbaum's comments run from "mirabile dictu!" (p. 48) to "fundamentally incoherent" (p. 49), "incongruous" and "pernicious myth" (p. 52), "guilty of legerdemain" (pp. 53, 65), "piece of philosophical malfeasance" (p. 53), "the entire hermeneutic enterprise is ill-conceived" (p. 54), "interpretive meaning—whatever that is" (pp. 59, 65), "my charge of utter emasculation" (p. 60), and "naive, if not smug, dismissal of the completely unsolved problem" (p. 65). And so on.

Grünbaum's sarcasm and scorn are a challenge to a fight, or debate, as philosophers call it. But in a fight the purpose is to beat up the adversary and cast him out, not to understand him. Consequently, the hostility expressed in his rhetoric interferes with his understanding of hermeneutics; he wants to fight, not to understand. It also dissuades others from discussing the topic with him, unless they too want to fight.

We turn now to the second kind or level of personality influences, influences on the scientist's concepts, values, and choice of problems.

A CASE STUDY: MAX WEBER

Arthur Mitzmann's study *The Iron Cage* (1970) is based on Marianne Weber's biography of her husband, Max Weber's autobiographical account of his years of nervous breakdown, letters of Weber and his relatives, interviews with survivors, official records, and all of Weber's writ ings published and unpublished. The method is historical case study, in which all available documents are checked against each other and pieced together like a jigsaw puzzle to form a coherent story of intertwined motives, themes, and influences.

Portis (1986, chap. 2) gives a somewhat different interpretation focusing on Weber's breakdown, which he describes as primarily an identity crisis. However, this topic does not concern us here.

According to Mitzmann, the family dynamics that imprisoned Max were the conflicting expectations of his father and mother plus the contradictory demands of his mother, as reinforced by the German culture of the time. Weber's writings expressed his successive interpretations of these demands and constituted *in part* an attempt to distance himself from them and overcome their grip on him. Portis emphasizes the strong internalized demands of the mother (1986, pp. 30ff.), but adds that some writings also were part of his search for a clear identity separate from the mother.

Weber's paternal ancestors were expelled from Salzburg by the Catholic archbishop for their Lutheran *Ketzerei* (as were some of my paternal ancestors); his grandfather became a rich capitalist and his father was a comfortable, authoritarian civil servant, an ally of Bismarck and the power structure. His mother's ancestors were expelled from France for their Calvinism, and his mother, who hated sex, urged her Calvinist morality of total asceticism, hard work, and compassion for the poor on Max.

Weber's early writings contain themes that express his interpretation of these demands: the conflict between political responsibility, power, and conscience (Mitzmann, 1970, pp. 37, 51); the argument that Bismarck (power, father's ally) ought to be limited by moral idealism (mother) (p. 35); and the argument that the East Prussian agricultural workers want to leave the patriarchal house at any price (pp. 95–96). Here the patriarchs are the Junkers, allies of the authoritarian father whose house Weber was then trying to leave literally and figuratively. The Protestant ethic represented Weber's own compulsive work—aimed, hopelessly, at gaining his mother's approval (pp. 171–74): "By identifying the work ethic of his mother's Calvinist ancestry as a device which formerly gave evidence of divine grace but now served only as a 'housing hard as steel,' Weber was focusing his intellect on his own experience in order . . . to liberate himself from it" (p. 173).

In the years after 1910, the main themes in Weber's writings are the functional rationalization of modern life, involving bureaucratization (father) and ascetic self-control (mother), opposed by the releasing force of charismatic leadership (p. 179). According to Mitzmann, charisma represented for Weber a feminine, erotic, emotional release from the iron cage of compulsive rationality, corresponding to a release Weber was then experiencing (pp. 299ff.). However, the liberating effect of charisma is doomed to gradually disappear in a new bureaucratic routine; bureaucratic and political rationalization will always overcome Eros. The same absolute opposition between Eros and authority (functional rationality) and the same pessimistic prognosis appeared in the German upper middle-class culture of the time, as expressed in Heinrich Mann's *Blue Angel* and Thomas Mann's *Buddenbrooks*, haunting and terrifying works.

What evidence does Mitzmann provide for his contention that the major themes in Weber's writings express his current libidinal experiences? First, the major concepts in his writings —bureaucracy, asceticism, rationality, charisma, authority, power, conscience—corresponded to the major interpersonal influences and conflicts in Weber's life (availability bias). One concept, tradition, is missing from Mitzmann's account. Other social science concepts of about 1900 such as anomy, collective conscience, conspicuous consumption, general market equilibrium, work as objectification and self-development, are foreign to Weber's experience and writings. For example, work for Weber was an exercise in asceticism, an endless struggle to control one's own desires, not a form of self-fulfillment.

Second, the changing treatment of these concepts, for instance in four successive drafts of Weber's study of East Prussian agriculture, corresponds in detail to changes in Weber's personal circumstances. Third, Weber's interpretation of these aspects of modern society and his stern and pessimistic prognoses correspond to their personal meaning for him. Contrast his treatment of rationality with that of Pareto, Walras, Veblen (the instinct of workmanship), or Marshall. In none of these contemporaries of Weber does rationality appear as deadening, compulsive bureaucratic authority.

Now, supposing that Mitzmann is more or less correct, can we judge Weber's sociological work to be defective insofar as it expressed his personal strivings and conflicts? Obviously not. The projection of his internalized parental identities on to his subject matter, German society, sensitized him to aspects of modern life that were hidden from sociologists like Durkheim, Pareto, and Veblen. In particular his understanding of the dynamics of (German) bureaucracy, the aloof authoritarian father, was an intellectual achievement that generations of sociologists with somewhat different personalities could build on. Conversely, since every focusing of attention, every sensitivity, negates other areas of attention and other sensitivities, Weber's personality excluded other aspects of modern society such as those studied by Veblen and Marshall.

What can we learn from Mitzmann's study? First, knowing Weber's family constellation, life history and identity crisis, and cultural milieu helps one to understand some otherwise puzzling concepts, pairings, contrasts, and omissions in his writings. Second, seeing how Weber's personality and culture expressed itself in his writings might help us recognize ourselves in the problems we pick to study, the tactics we use, the conclusions we try to reach or avoid.

For example, we can appreciate Weber's treatment of scientific method better when we read about the internalized demands his mother placed on him. Scientific method for Weber was an embodiment of those demands: scientists ought to practice total asceticism, self-denial, painstaking and compulsive concern with fact. Method demands complete control and repression of one's values, feelings, desires, imagination. No personality influences are allowed. Of course, the old Adam in us, our original sin, breaks through anyway and contaminates our research, but we must try to hold it back. If *you* think that way about research, notice it.

Third, we can generalize, superficially, from this one case by classifying the themes that appear in it and allowing for variations of each theme in other cases. Every personality is different, but most social scientists have a mother and a father, and usually also sisters and brothers. Brothers and sisters we cannot deal with, as they do not appear in Mitzmann's study.

German fathers are often authoritarian, like Bettelheim and like Weber's father, though the authoritative rules and expectations can vary greatly. Weber's identification of authority with bureaucratic rationality, national political responsibility, power, and agrarian patriarchy is a particular combination. Given this sort of father, a son can identify with authority; submit in hopes of receiving the benediction of masculinity; or rebel. Perhaps all German sons do all three, as Weber did, but in different combinations and circumstances. Weber's rather remote and limited empathy with the East Prussian peasants is a particularly weak example of rebellion, suitably displaced a good distance away. Mainly he submitted, fruitlessly; bureaucracy remained an external constraint for him.

With a nonauthoritarian father, one pattern is for the mother to devalue the father by contrast with her internalized authority figure, her own father. In that case, the son's task is to live up to the mother's internalized ideal, by endless achievement. Each success implies a devaluation of the real father, with resultant guilt, but no rebellion. Such a pattern may perhaps be found in some compulsive high achievers who publish continuously.

The demands of Weber's mother for (1) rebellion against the tyrannical father and (2) total sexual asceticism and compulsive work are an unusual maternal constellation, whose expression in Weber's thought has been discussed above. Such demands often come from the father, and can be rejected in part; that they came from the mother meant that Weber had no internal feminine alternative to counterpose against authority. Instead, love and temporary liberation came from outside Weber's marriage, just as charisma comes from outside the iron social order and brings temporary release. Weber had no concept of Mother Nature, the all-enveloping biosphere that sustains us, as it appears in the writings of ecologists like E. F. Schumacher. Indeed, he had no concept of nature at all. Nor did he have a concept of social totality, the central concept in Lukács's contemporaneous work (1923). Such "maternal" concepts are foreign to Weber's thought; instead, his mother gave him the Protestant ethic.

GENDER AND SCIENCE

Up to here we have looked at only half of the picture, the masculine half. All the categories and contrasts derivable from the Weber study apply only to men. We now call on feminist writers to lead us into the other half, and also to provide an external perspective on the masculine half. (The main references for this section are Gilligan, 1982, chap. 1; Harding and Hintikka, 1983; Keller, 1982, 1985; List, 1985; Belenky et al., 1986; and Kreisky, 1986.) Actually Maslow anticipated most of the feminist ideas, though vaguely and impressionistically (1966, p. 35, chap. 8–11). The feminist ideas are in an early stage of development, and are not to be taken as fixed and final. They are based on extensive interviews and on observation of children's play.

According to the feminist writers cited above, gender differences begin to develop in the first few years of life, from differences in the relation to the mother. Given adequate maternal care, babies at first experience a single undifferentiated process of living, and only gradually differentiate self and mother as two parts of this process. Later the father also becomes specified as the guardian and gateway to the outside world, the person who provides adventure, exploration, and protection against the unknown, and who has the skills to deal with things out there. The feminist writers do not approve of this type of child care, merely note it as fact.

Boys soon learn that they are different from the mother and more like the father. Thus they must manage a double separation from the mother, one in defining the self as a separate person and one in defining their gender as male. Separateness is the key to growing up, and separation involves giving up, denying, rejecting the infantile unity with the mother. Masculinity is an achievement, one that is always threatened by some surviving remnant of infantile habits, some unsuspected practice that can be shamefully exposed with the taunting cry, "Sissy!"

Girls in contrast learn that they are like the mother, so the infantile unity does not threaten their femaleness but on the contrary confirms it. Consequently, they do not need to reject and deny their infantile sense of selflessness. As a result for girls their femininity is relatively secure but their sense of separateness, of being a unique person with clear bound-aries, is more fragile. For girls the separation is rather from the world outside the family, and they need the *other*, the father, to lead them outside and protect them. The path to the outside world takes them away from themselves. For boys, in contrast, the outside world is their realm, the place where they find and assert themselves as masculine by showing their skills and independence.

These differences appear and are reinforced in children's play (Gilligan, 1982, chap. 1). Small girls tend to play indoors or near home in small groups or pairs, and play cooperative or take-turn games. Boys tend to play outdoors in larger groups, and their games are competitive and argumentative. Competition expresses and reinforces their sense of autonomy; and achievement, winning or playing well, demonstrates that they are skilful like the father and therefore masculine.

Competitive games, played by separate but equal individuals, require rules, and rules require a judicial process of argument and judgment. Thus boys learn to think in terms of rules and their application to cases by seemingly impartial arguments. They want to win, but win fairly by skill rather than by cheating.

Masculine science continues these childhood themes, plus others that appear later in life. For the male scientist, his subject matter is the outside world, the arena in which he must demonstrate his skills and thus his masculinity. He is not part of that world, but separate from it just as he is separate from other people, and just as his discipline is separate from other disciplines. The world is neutral material which he transforms by his work,or controls and organizes according to some plan of action. It must become familiar territory through which he can move confidently and whose changes he can predict and control according to his purposes. In order to do this he must focus his attention on the world, not on himself. His inner states are not part of the outside world, so attending to them is not science, not man's work, but daydreaming.

There are three kinds of masculine relations to other scientists. First, in order to demonstrate skills the male scientist must learn them and must learn his way around the world, so he needs a mentor or mentors to guide and train him. He also needs to receive the blessing of manhood, of equality, from this father figure. After that he can identify with the mentor by extending the mentor's theory and research, and/or can rebel and assert independence. In Weber's case the mentor, Hermann Baumgarten, came from the maternal side of the family and thus strengthened the maternal influence on Weber's thought and made bureaucracy an external phenomenon.

Second, with other scientists within his discipline he is competitive, either individually or cooperatively in teams, as in childhood games. The prize for winning can be individual recognition, citations, invitations; but it also includes acceptance and broader use of the theory or method that one's team is pushing. The most intense competition, Bourdieu reminds us, is with competitors for research funds.

Third, scientists from other disciplines are outsiders or even strangers, to be ignored or treated politely. However, if the outsiders pretend to know anything about the discipline, then they are politely but condescendingly put down. If they insist on horning in, they are put down more firmly. Extreme examples are Karl Brunner's repeated expressions of contempt for sociological (Keynesian) concepts in economics, plus his Popperian contempt for sociology in general. Nelson Polsby (1981) explains the total falsity of elitism by observing that the elitist theorists are sociologists who know nothing about politics and never will.

A female scientist can also take the masculine route, as in Eva Kreisky's case (1986): by finding a mentor (Josef Hindels) who can lead her into the outside world of men and their impersonal, factual discourse, away from the inner personal world of women, away from herself. But this route involves denying one's own feminine integrity and is unsatisfactory, as Kreisky found. A feminine social science, speaking abstractly, involves denying the sharp distinction between inner-personal and outside-impersonal world, and also the sharp distinction between the scientist and her object of study. Just as the slogan of the New Left women's movement, "The personal is the political," denied the separation between personal family life and outer, impersonal political life, so the slogan of feminist social science could be "The personal is the social." "Human beings are socially constituted, and have emotions, beliefs, and abilities only insofar as they are embedded in a web of interpretation that gives meaning to the bare data of inner experience" (Scheman, in Harding and Hintikka, 1983, p. 232).

In this kind of social science, the scientist becomes a part of her subject matter or relates closely to it, empathetically sharing its experiences. Instead of organizing and systematizing it according to her theories, she listens to its voices, "lets the material speak to her," "becomes part of the system," lets it tell her what to do next (Keller, 1982, p. 599). She accepts the other's views, patiently shares in gossip and small talk to get the feel of how the other thinks, watches or helps the other develop over time, watches her own participation, and learns about herself along with the other (Belenky et al., 1986, pp. 112–23).

Since her need is more to participate than to demonstrate individual prowess and achievement, her relations with other social scientists are primarily cooperative. Instead of pushing her own ideas, she is sensitive to other points of view and tries to include them in her own thinking.

Gilligan calls the feminine kind of knowing "connected" and the masculine kind "separate." Connected knowing is *kennen* and separate knowing is *wissen* (Belenky et al., 1986, pp. 100–01).

The weaknesses of both kinds of science express points of strain in the two paths of personal development. The characteristic weakness of the little girl is her fragile sense of self as a unique individual. Apart from overcompensation à la Ayn Rand, such weakness would express itself as a tendency to lose one's own point of view in the process of appreciating others' ideas. Elsewhere I have described this weakness as being good at losing arguments, because one gets interested in the opponent's line of reasoning, looks for presuppositions that would make it plausible, extends it to related topics, looks for its strong points and limitations, and in the process forgets or loses interest in one's own claim. Another version of this weakness would be a tendency to get pulled into various areas of research because there is no area or discipline that is one's own.

One characteristic masculine weakness is to overcompensate for the little boy's precarious sense of masculinity, that is, for one's fears about one's professional ability, by developing an egocentric self-esteem, a self-image of unfailing competence and infallible reasoning power, and scorn for everyone else. Such an attitude expresses itself in a lack of interest in others' ideas and research, emphatic and forthright statements of one's own ideas, rejection of any criticism of one's research, and insistent pushing of one's own work in all available forums. Examples here are abundant; one thinks of Mitroff's brutally masculine moon scientists, insisting on their own ideas and scornful of others'. (See also List, 1985, on masculinity in scientists.)

A closely related weakness is to get absorbed in the competitive aspect of science in order to affirm one's own masculinity and disparage that of others. This tendency is manifested in inconclusive disputes characterized by scorn and sarcasm for the opponent, misrepresentation of his position by taking some statement out of context or pushing his position to an extreme to "make it interesting" (Newton-Smith, 1981), or putting it into the context of one's own theory, and above all never admitting to any error of one's own. Team competition takes the form of attacking some other theory or research tradition again and again and exposing its longstanding errors, disconfirmations, and pseudo-scientific character.

Exaggerated competitiveness is even more prevalent in philosophy (cf. Moulton, "The Adversary Method in Philosophy," in Harding and Hintikka, 1983). In philosophy colloquia one sees people in the audience straining in excitement, eager to tear up the speaker's argument and expose its errors and non sequiturs. Nicholas Rescher begins his book on *The Strife of Systems* (1985) with this observation:

> The ranks of philosophy are in serious disarray. Theory confronts theory, school rivals school in implacable opposition. Disagreement and controversy prevail to such an extent in this discipline that one can safely endorse the quip: If two people agree, one of them isn't a philosopher.

Philosophers use another technique to separate themselves from their subject matter. They can claim to be unconcerned with the empirical details of their topic, because their concern as philosophers is only with its logic—for instance, the logic of theory testing or the logic of practical decisions. Thus they simultaneously claim separateness and superior status as the guardians of reason and logic.

A third masculine weakness mentioned by the feminists is the tendency to control or dominate one's experimental subjects and to use one's knowledge as an instrument of control (Keller, 1982, 1985, chaps. 5–6). Control is supposed to relieve the anxiety of separation by ensuring that the object of study remains in one's grasp, without giving up one's separateness. I'm afraid I have trouble understanding the argument on this point.

Enough on the subject of weaknesses.

If these abstract accounts of masculine and feminine science are correct, one would expect masculine types to feel comfortable with experimental and formal methods and aggregate data analysis, and feminine types to gravitate toward ethnographic participant observation and interviewing. Gilligan's research, for example, uses interviews organized as panel studies; Belenky et al. interviewed 135 women intensively over several years. Both interviewing and participant observation bring one into close relation with one's subject matter, and in the latter case even requires one to become part of it. Roe's study of anthropologists and clinical psychologists (1952) brings out "feminine" personality characteristics in people who chose participant observation as their method.

Formal methods and aggregate data—wholesale price index, percent change from trough of cycle—separate one from people and allow one instead to deal with numbers and mathematical objects by abstract, formal reasoning. Experimentation brings one into physical proximity with people, the S; but the emphasis in this method is on control. The S need not be experienced as whole people but as future numbers; and if the experimenter wants to reach out to them, he must worry about experimenter effects. Another more defensive type of control is theoretical, the construction of elaborate systems of classification and careful distinctions in the style of Talcott Parsons. A person in command of Parsons's theory can assign every event to its proper category and thereby understand it.

Having made a distinction between feminine and masculine science, let us be suspicious of it, as Whitehead advises. It is too neat and simple. The feminist writers themselves warn that they are not claiming that all or most men inevitably practice masculine science and all women, feminine science. There are large differences among both men and women scientists, and the association of gender with type of science is a very partial, empirical one. Gender has something to do with it. Nor do they claim that "masculine" science is bad and "feminine" science is good. Social science can be both an instrument of domination and control and a means of communion and self-transcendence. Gilligan writes of "the integrity of two disparate modes of experience that are in the end connected" (1982, p. 174).

In addition, they assert that the two kinds of science are blended, except in extreme cases. Gilligan writes of "the interplay of these voices within each sex" (1982, p. 2). She emphasizes that separation is only a stage in male development, a stage that is often followed by a return to the other and an empathetic appreciation of the other as subject. The masculine need to dominate and control can stay in the background except in cases of anxiety about competence. Conversely, girls can go through a stage of separation and difference in later life also. Bem (1974) has long asserted that *feminine* and *masculine* are separate dimensions, both present in everyone in varying degrees and combinations. Consequently, feminists would probably assert that the approach of the present chapter is itself masculine: it begins automatically with men, then turns to "the other half"—a separate but equal pretense. The idea of a purely feminine other half is a projection men make; women have as many sides to them as men do. Men and women are not that different.

Other feminist writers call for a revision of the connected-separate scheme. Belenky et al. (1986) ignore the first three years of life and study women's development from childhood to old age. They assert that in their cases connected knowing, when it occurs at all, is an achievement of adulthood or even late maturity. It appears sooner in families where the mother has independent views and expresses them in the family, where the relatively nonauthoritarian father listens to wife and even children, and where both parents can grow with their children. It does not appear until late in life, if at all, in cases of inadequate, authoritarian, hostile maternal and paternal care. For some women, motherhood is a challenge that develops more connected knowing in later life.

Westkott (1986) asserts that in at least one case, connected thinking was a result of the little girl's powerlessness. She was required to obey her father and take care emotionally of her mother, so she learned to be sensitive to her mother's feelings. This case suggests that separate thinking in science could express the power of the scientist over his subject matter; connected thinking, caring, and accepting, could express subordination. Hare-Mustin and Marecek agree: "Typically, those in power advocate rules, discipline, control, and rationality, while those without power espouse relatedness and compassion" (1988, p. 459). But Belenky et al. disagree; they argue that true connected thinking is appropriate for women's work, promoting human development, and does not express subordination (1986, pp. 188–89).

Still other feminist writers reject the connected-separate scheme in whole or in part. Some call for a science that is neither masculine nor feminine, and argue that the masculine-feminine distinction is itself sexist. Harding (1986, chap. 7) observes that African men and women are also raised by mothers, yet do not fit the Gilligan scheme; nor are all Africans alike. There are many kinds of men—northern and southern Italians, northern and southern Germans, etcetera—and many kinds of women, as the diversity of feminist thought attests. Spence rejects Bem's two-dimensional scheme and argues that a rapidly expanding body of data points to an incredibly complicated multidimensionality. There are many "masculinities" and "femininities" and many combinations (1981, pp. 144–47). Harding (1986, chap. 10) concludes that the current diversity and confusion of feminist thought is appropriate at this stage, since things are changing.

But let us resist the temptation Harding sets for us. Let us first learn what we can from the first group of feminist writers cited. Later we can return to enjoy the full complexity of feminist thought, one strand at a time.

What does the revised scheme tell us about social science? If we each have "masculine" and "feminine" sides, and if these sides also have many variations, then the issue is not two kinds of social science, but the interplay of two aspects of science. It may be that one aspect is normally dominant and the other subordinate, and in that case we could speak of "masculine" and "feminine" science; but we must remember that the other aspect is usually available as well. We need not call the two aspects *masculine* and *feminine*, if that sounds too sexist to some feminist writers. Nor need we insist on their presumed childhood origin, if early childhood is too psychoanalytic a topic for some readers. The two aspects of science in their many variations are obviously present all around us, wherever we look. Whether power is involved is another issue.

A masculine science is *predominantly* self-centered and externalizing, while a feminine science is *predominantly* other-centered and internalizing, in Roy Schafer's sense (1968). A self-centered scientist thinks his own thoughts, makes his own observations of fact, and has his own feelings; that is, he organizes his own experience. Then he puts or projects his thoughts and facts on to the *external* world in order to understand it. He treats the data he has created with his experimental or recording apparatus as news from the external world and applies his categories and theories to them to organize and adjust them. He also checks his ideas and hypotheses against his data for goodness of fit, hoping to eventually devise a theory that matches the data and therefore reveals the laws or structure of the world.

Similarly, to understand the work of another scientist he applies his categories and concepts to it; insofar as they do not fit, the work is objectively unclear or confused. He also applies his data to the hypotheses he has projected into the other's work; insofar as they do not match, the hypotheses are false. He treats his subsequent feelings of scorn as a response to objective characteristics of the work.

An other-centered scientist does not make so sharp a separation between herself and the people she is studying. Social science is social, and in social situations we share feelings and thoughts and experiences easily and naturally. But science tries to go beyond such everyday sharing to reach the more hidden thoughts and feelings of the other, to weaken the barriers of culture, social class, personality, history, even gender, that muffle and distort our communication. Insofar as we can reach others, we join them and become part of their world. We think their thoughts, share their feelings, take their values and self-presentations as our own, play the roles they provide for us. That is internalization. If we are successful, they will respond; otherwise they will correct us.

In this sort of science, data come from the other, from interviews and observed daily life and free associations and documents. But insofar as we have become part of the other, our reactions and experiences also become data, though imperfectly and unreliably.

Similarly, to understand the work of another scientist, an other-centered person tries to find her way into the world of that scientist, to think and feel and value like the other. However, this cannot be done intuitively and empathetically, since the work does not respond or correct us or cue us; instead, it involves intellectual, hermeneutic techniques.

In the present volume, the philosophies of chapter 1 and 2 emphasize externalization, and the philosophies of chapters 4 and 5 emphasize forms of internalization.

For an example of extreme externalization, consider Grünbaum's *Foundations of Psychoanalysis* (1984). Grünbaum has two logical schemes which he imposes on various writings to interpret and evaluate them.

Material that can be so interpreted he declares to be scientific; material that does not fit is incoherent, confused, naive, or "whatever that is," or is ignored. One scheme is the logic of science; this consists of testing causal hypotheses. We test a causal hypothesis by looking for evidence that confirms it and also disconfirms a plausible alternative hypothesis. If a critic can state a plausible alternative hypothesis that was not disconfirmed, the test is inconclusive. Scientists necessarily test causal hypotheses if they are scientists; whatever else they may do is of no particular interest and is classified as heuristics, confusion, or pseudo-science. To understand a theory, then, one must find the causal hypotheses it asserts and the tests they have undergone.

Grünbaum's second scheme is the logic of intentionality, which he takes from Kurt Baier, an OL philosopher. He applies this scheme to writings that claim to discuss intentional action, with the same results.

He also externalizes in discussions of his own work. In a 1986 symposium involving thirty-eight commentaries on his *Foundations of Psychoanalysis*, Grünbaum's awareness is limited entirely to his own ideas. He shows no interest in or awareness of any of the highly diverse and highly interesting lines of thought presented; his comments consist entirely of defenses of his 1984 work. He is quite clear about his own argument and quick to recognize any distortion of it, but quite muddy about opponents' views, when he mentions them at all. In other words he treats the discussion as an attack and defense of his ideas.[11]

Grünbaum's work also illustrates the positive contribution a consistently externalizing person can make to science. He projects his logic-of-science scheme onto Freud's writings consistently and clearly and thereby brings out that aspect of Freud's thought: Freud, the logical empiricist. Freud did in part think of his work as an exploratory neurology, a natural science that tries to discover the laws of the nervous system. He had other thoughts too, but Grünbaum is not attracted and distracted by them; he sees only what fits his scheme. The result is a clear demonstration that insofar as Freud thought he was conclusively testing a fundamental law of the mind, he was mistaken. Grünbaum's argument supports Habermas's claim that Freud's hypothesis-testing stance was a self-misunderstanding 1971, chap. 11). That is not what Freud was doing. A Lakatos or Stegmüller or Gadamer projection would give a different picture of what Freud was doing, and expand our understanding of Freud.

For internalization, I think of Clyde Kluckhohn, of whom his wife asserted, "He acts very differently when he's down there with the Navahos." I think of Robert Rietz, a thoroughly nonmilitary person to me, who when visiting the Fox Indians became a war veteran, a proud, patriotic legionnaire with helmet and uniform, because that was how his Indian friends saw him, for their own masculinity-affirming purposes. I think of Erving Goffman's *Presentation of Self in Everyday Life* (1959), based on a year's stay with Scottish islanders. Goffman describes life as his hosts saw it, from the inside of the home outward: the back rooms where the self is prepared and repaired, the front room or stage where the self is presented, and precarious encounters in the outside world. This book puzzled me for many years until, having met Goffman and watched him blend smoothly into the scene, I realized that s/he was describing primarily the presentation of the feminine Scottish self in this very family-centered society. How naive of me to have assumed that *self* meant *masculine self*!

Havens (1986, pp. 190–91) provides another example from case material by H. F. Searles. "Searles . . . describes having felt almost moribund while working with one patient. He first attributed this to fatigue, since he had been working hard, but said that gradually 'transference material emerged with made it clear he was reacting to me variously as his chronically depressed mother, and as a long-senile grandmother who had lived nearby, largely as a vegetable, during a considerable portion of his developmental years.' " Searles had simply taken the patient's cues without knowing it and had empathetically played the role assigned him—that of depressed vegetable.

Both externalizing and internalizing processes need to be corrected or supplemented at their weak points by the opposite process. An externalizing process, projecting a theoretical scheme onto a complex mass of data—say, a game model onto a diplomatic case history—can bring great clarity and order if the scheme is appropriate to the data. Insofar as it is inappropriate, it distorts or simply loses what is there. But to see whether it is appropriate, the modeler must get outside himself and his model, either by empathetically immersing himself in the case history or by hermeneutically studying some different treatment of the same material. Alternatively, the model builder could begin by moving into the case history, becoming other-centered, and seeing what models the actors in the case suggest to her. Then she can withdraw into herself, work out the model, and project it back into the case.

Internalizing the culture of the people one is studying enables one to participate and to give a vivid report of how they see themselves, but does not enable one to penetrate beyond their self-understanding and self-deception. For that, one needs to take some distance, skeptically, and project some theoretical scheme onto the material to see what order it imposes or exposes, and then test it by returning and trying to act according to the projected scheme. But this sort of skepticism requires a self separate from the other, a self into which one can withdraw and think one's own thoughts.

Another difficulty with excessive internalization is that the others can recruit the too-gullible scientist for their own purposes. Ned Polsky provides an example in his study of hustlers, beats, and others (1967). One shady character whom he had befriended suggested casually that Polsky might have a storage space for a gun he wouldn't be needing and didn't want to have to carry around all the time. More innocently, members of the Fox Project (Gearing, 1960) found themselves drawn into the political and economic problems of the Fox Indians and partici-pated in working out solutions, until some of us found ourselves peddling Indian paint kits to hobby stores. (I couldn't sell any.) Redfield (1960, p. 82) tells of the ethnographer who became so absorbed in the intricacies of Zuni ceremonial that he became a Zuni priest and stopped writing ethnography.

To avoid such weaknesses, each social science method should have its own blend of externalizing and internalizing processes. Participant observation, the most thoroughly internalizing method, should be a dialectic of attachment and detachment—joining in and then withdraw-ing to reflect and reorganize, alternating credulity and skepticism, appre-ciating particular features and then generalizing by comparison with other cases (Redfield, 1960). Havens (1986) prescribes the same bal-ance for client-centered therapy: "The language of empathy moves the therapist into the patient's space. . . . It is not the quintessential experi-ence, however, because empathy aims at merger or identification rather than a working distance" (p. 85). "Empathy is credulity operationalized: the goal is to be 'taken in' and in the process to locate another. Interper-sonal statements are skepticism operationalized: the idea is not to be taken in, not to allow the patient to settle assumptions or projections upon the therapist" (p. 91).

One could also add the reverse: the patient should not be taken in either, should not be induced to introject the analyst's diagnosis. Main-taining a working distance leaves room for the patient's skepticism, and allows the patient to withdraw and think his own thoughts.

The various kinds of interviewing and sample surveys range from semiclinical depth interviews, which yield small case histories, to voting surveys which yield essentially aggregate data; but they all maintain their own distinctive balance between research-centered and respondent-centered requirements. In ordinary attitude surveys, the balance is most nearly equal and the conflict the sharpest. A good interviewer must (1) phrase the questions in the respondent's language, empathetically catch the respondent's meanings, pursue the respondent's hinted qualifications and doubts and clarifications; but also (2) standardize the questions, control and standardize the interaction, firmly preserve the original variables that are being measured. The interviewer must (1) resemble the respondent in dress, speech, race, to set the respondent at ease; but (2) maintain role distance to avoid influencing the respondent. In depth interviewing, the standardization requirements nearly disappear, but are still present in the selection of respondents, the list of topics to be brought up at some appropriate time, and the controlled respondent-interviewer interaction. In voting surveys the respondent-centered requirements are weakest; they consist mainly of very careful phrasing of the standard questions ("Did you happen to vote . . . "). Here the empathy and sensitivity occurs mostly in the pilot test, where the interviewer tries out phrasings to see how they sound to the respondents. Once the right responses have been elicited, the questions and the nonverbal communication context are mostly locked into place for the actual survey. However, it is also desirable to select empathetic, nonthreatening interviewers who can notice and quietly manage the nonverbal context of the interview, smoothing the way for the respondent.

Oakley (in Roberts, 1981, chap. 2) describes her depth interviewing as an unstable, conflict-soaked experience. The methods textbooks she tried to follow pulled her toward a more impersonal, standardized relationship, while her respondents pulled her toward deeper personal involvement. For instance, they asked her questions, expressed anxiety and a need for information and support that she could provide. Those were not good methods texts that she cites; they were still dominated by the logical empiricist caricature of science. The Belenky et al. (1986) depth interviews show a better balance between standardization and rapport: standard questions, including some from earlier studies for comparison; free discussion of the answers and deep involvement in each case; quantitative treatment of some recurring variables; and qualitative study of the cases as wholes.

Experimentation is *usually* a primarily externalizing method, with its emphasis on the experimenter's hypotheses and variables and its concern with control of other variables. Yet the E must still be concerned with how the controls feel to the S and how the independent variable will be interpreted by the S. If experimenters mistakenly think they are in perfect control, as Clark Hull did, they will fail to see how their controls induce a response set in the S that biases the results (Bruner, 1973, pp. 137–39). The good E will realize the importance of an other-centered concern with how the experiment looks to the S. Experimenters might deal with this concern by taking a turn as S in pretesting. Or they may get absorbed during testing with "the experiment as a social occasion"—the tacit interpersonal exchanges that cluster around the official, impersonal process and affect the data. Even a formal modeler, say, one working out a model of optimal deterrence under uncertainty, may get absorbed in a case study, imaginatively taking various diplomatic roles, to clarify some obscure deductive implications. Conversely, a political scientist constructing a case study can use a formal model, in the "detachment" phase of construction, to interpret some obscure diplomatic or congressional interaction or to suggest new interview questions.

Note that we have now required a double balance of the researcher. The researcher should first find the method whose internalizing-externalizing or attachment-detachment requirements most nearly fit his or her own personal tendencies. Then within the method s/he must again find the right balance. It is doubtful that many will succeed perfectly at this double task.

The feminist writers could comment that all this discussion of balance is very nice in the abstract; but as methods are actually practiced, the "masculine" components are usually too strong for optimum results. They could also comment that research occurs in the "private" arena where some researchers can allow their "feminine" side to come out quietly. But little of this side appears in the written reports; and the public arena of publications and convention papers is still stridently and aggressively masculine.

COGNITIVE STYLES

Warning: do not get so fixated on the gender issue that you project it everywhere in social science. The externalization-internalization dimension is only one of several dimensions of cognitive style. In this section we briefly survey other dimensions to sketch a broader picture. Or rather, we survey other ways of conceptualizing the same material. Did you think psychologists of science agreed on the dimensions of cognitive style?

The term *cognitive style* refers to the characteristic ways in which individuals conceptually organize their environment (Goldstein and Blackman, 1978, p. 2). A masculine way of putting it.

One of the first styles to be studied systematically is the authoritarian or dogmatic personality (Adorno et al., 1950; Rokeach, 1960; Goldstein and Blackman, 1978, chaps. 1–2). Its main characteristics are (1) intolerance of ambiguity and (2) closed thinking—that is, rejection of ideas that differ from one's own. The dogmatic thinker has a set of clear and distinct categories, such as communism and democracy or market and planning or facts and values, which he imposes on ordinary fluid situations. These categories cut through the surface confusion and deception to reveal the clear underlying essentials. Usually one of a pair is good and the other is bad, or one is true and the other is false. There is no middle ground. Ideas that differ from one's own are either a confused variant of one's own truth, or they are false and deserving of scorn.

A closely related line of thought is Maslow's discussion of the pathology of cognition (1966, chaps. 3–4). He suggests that anxiety and defensiveness in some area can induce a researcher to be *too* controlled, rigorous, precise, neat, orderly, quantified. The need for certainty or reassurance in some area can lead to premature generalizations, rigid maintenance of a hypothesis against seemingly negative evidence, denial of doubt or ambiguity. The needs to conform, to appear powerful, to fight authority, and so forth, can produce other pathologies of thought. In contrast, the healthy or creative scientist balances caution and boldness, control and looseness, sobriety and playfulness, precision and ambiguity. The healthy scientist has the right degree of self-esteem, doubt, respect for authority, rigor, reasonableness, persistence, and so on. What is the right degree? If you're healthy, you'll know.

The discussions cited above treat cognitive style as characteristic of immature, poor scientists. Healthy or mature scientists also differ in cognitive style (Maslow, 1966, chaps. 8–11). Mature people are not all the same, after all. On the long path toward maturity, we carry our past with us, converting weaknesses to strengths, extending or refining old coping mechanisms, transferring old ways of relating to new situations. Whether or not anyone ever fully matures, the result is cognitive style.

The best and most thorough treatment of cognitive styles in "good" science is Mitroff and Kilmann, *Methodological Approaches to Social Science* (1978). Mitroff and Kilmann construct a two-dimensional space, based on concepts of Carl Jung, and show how several other treatments of cognitive style can be reduced to the Jungian dimensions. Instead of rushing through an abstract account of the two dimensions, I shall present one slice through them. For a more complete discussion of the dimensions the reader should consult the original text, which is itself quite condensed and abstract.

The slice to be presented is taken from Hudson (1966). Hudson studied a group of school*boys* aged fifteen to seventeen and induced two opposite types which he called *convergers* and *divergers*. These are actually dimensions rather than points on a scale, since a person could be high or low on each one. Also, the score defining each one is multidimensional.

Convergers approach a problem by distinguishing its component parts and decomposing each part into subparts. Then they study each subpart separately, seeking clarity in the small in order to put together a larger clarity step by step. Their creativity consists in being able to disassemble a complex, messy situation into clearly distinguishable parts and in avoiding distracting side issues and slippery analogies while analyzing a part. They prefer to collect impersonal, precise data about the part they are studying, and to draw implications from these data a step at a time. The preferred logic is mathematical rather than dialectical.

This style is most effective with well-defined problems, so convergers select such problems if possible and avoid vague, ill-defined situations. They are also uneasy with conflict and controversy, and either avoid studying such unclear topics or try to abstract a simplified version of them for study. One tactic is to construct a simpler version of some hopelessly complex situation and model that, then try to apply the model to the complex situation step by step, complicating it when differences appear. Emotional situations are particularly hopeless, and convergers prefer to assign such things to art rather than to science. Science, they feel, should deal with facts and laws, not feelings.

Divergers approach a problem by placing it in context, expecting the context to provide lines of study into the problem. For instance, they might try to understand a published article by reading previous articles by the same author so they can trace themes and concepts moving into the article. They also read the citations to find the sources of other ideas and to locate contrasts and controversies. This enables them to understand the article in contrast or opposition. Having located the controversy or issue that is the setting for this article, they study that by finding its context, the traditions of thought that went into it, the lines of publication that come together in the current situation.

In addition to locating larger and larger contexts in this fashion, divergers also locate multiple contexts. A diverger studying an international diplomatic statement, for example, the 1981 U.S. cancellation of the embargo on agricultural exports to the Soviet Union, initiated in 1979 in response to the Soviet invasion of Afghanistan, will first locate the international diplomatic contexts—previous relations between the countries, relations to allies over time, potential alliances and realignments—since the diplomatic statement may have been directed to any and all of these contexts. Then s/he locates the domestic politics contexts: the bureaucratic alignments, since the proposed statement is a move by one or more departments against or toward other departments; the party positions, since the statement is a pre-election maneuver or an attempt to establish a record to run on later; and executive-congressional relations. There is also the personal history and personality of the diplomat, which helps one interpret the nuances of his statement—as the diplomats in the other country well know. Next is the international trade context, since the grain embargo and its lifting affects other grain exporters, who are U.S. allies; and this must fit into the context of the international and domestic economic situation, which in turn impinges on government fiscal and tax policy. Bringing in the economy also forces one to bring in the lobbyists, who emphasize parts of the economic situation to the administration and thence to the diplomats; and so on.

Divergers like to play these multiple contexts against each other, since each throws a different light on the diplomatic statement. The result will often be to reveal ambiguities and dilemmas in what initially seemed to be a simple move. Thus divergers are skeptical of seemingly clear and simple situations, including clear and simple logic, and look for the complexities hidden beneath the surface simplicity. They feel more at home in the obviously complex and ambiguous situations that convergers shun. Also unlike convergers, divergers accept and emphasize the emotional aspects of reality as integral to it; the diplomatic exchange is a response to, and expression of, hostilities, suspicions, hopes, illusions, loyalties, and despair (the U.S. farmers, who went broke in 1980).

Students don't like divergent teaching, because it leaves them floundering, not knowing what the right answer is.

How would a converger deal with the U.S. cancellation of the Soviet grain embargo? If he was unable to escape the assignment, the converger would begin by breaking the problem into its basic parts and then proceed a step at a time. The U.S. action was partly domestic and partly international; let us begin with the international aspect. The two main countries involved were the United States and the Soviet Union; others can be brought in later. The U.S. move, cancellation, was either a response to some Soviet move or a new move. Search for previous Soviet moves and U.S. references to them. If none, the U.S. move either anticipated some Soviet response or it did not—for instance, if the domestic situation was primary. Search for reports of anticipated Soviet responses. Search also for reactions to the actual Soviet response, to see whether it was expected or not. And so on. Any positive data at any of these steps require further analysis and further data to clarify each substep.

Mitroff and Kilmann emphasize that we should not assign individual scientists to particular types or points on the two dimensions. People are mixtures of various things, as we observed in the masculine-feminine context. Thus a political scientist might feel divergent when constructing a case study of a diplomatic exchange, and shift to convergent when constructing a mathematical model of the same case piece by piece. The two styles can interact, as pieces of the model clarify the influence of some context, and as plural contexts demand complication of the model. Other researchers might be neither especially convergent nor divergent, but have other cognitive styles altogether.

However, some researchers may have developed one side of an opposition much more than the other, and their style would include rejection of research problems that require the other cognitive process. For example, a person might cultivate empathetic processes so much that problems requiring impersonal, formal reasoning, mathematical thought, become puzzling and insoluble. Such people, like the extreme convergers and divergers, will limit themselves to certain problems and concepts. They will also have difficulty perceiving the opposite components of problems they do study—for example, mathematical components of interpersonal relationships.

Another dimension that is hidden away in the Mitroff and Kilmann space is the ability to perceive movement or process (call it M). A person high on M will, for example, perceive a theory developing over time in a series of publications, or perceive the gradually increasing mobility of world capital after 1950 in balance-of-payments tables. The impetus to the development of theory will appear in the early publications as a pregnant metaphor or concept or model that must expand its range of applicability and work out its details; or a tension that pushes toward resolution through change of both poles. The impetus to the increased mobility of capital comes from familiar demand-supply contradictions: a postwar surplus of U.S. capital goods and a shortage of European capital goods, which turned of itself into a surplus pressing for outlet, accompanied by rising labor costs and shifts of finance capital, and so on.

The series of publications or trade tables are cross sections through the movement that reveal fluctuations and turning points; but the movement itself is already implicit in the tensions and contradictions of the initial situation.

A person low on M will be good at seeing distinctions and making classifications. Since everything is what it is and not something else, to perceive something clearly and distinctly is to perceive its difference from its context and from other things. Most differences are trivial, but the task of science is to find the important or relevant differences. The result is classes and categories and types: theoretical practice and practical practice, demand side and supply side, Chicken and Prisoner's Dilemma, firstness, secondness, and thirdness, high and low M. After that, one can establish causal connections, or stages in a sequence, or the essential structure or specificity of each type.

For the low-M thinker, a theory is a set of categories, concepts, and propositions, while for the high-M thinker it is a history. Thus for one person Keynesian theory is the doctrine appearing in the *General Theory*, perhaps as stated more carefully and systematically by Klein or Samuelson; for another person Keynesian theory is the whole Keynesian tradition. Consider for example Grünbaum's assertion (1984, chap. 7): if recent Freudians hold the same theory that Freud did, his objections to that theory apply to them too. But if their theory is different from Freud's, they are not Freudians. For a low-M thinker this statement is clear and correct, while for a high-M thinker it is ridiculous.

For a high-M thinker, the proper logic is dialectic, the logic of becoming; for a low M, logic is symbolic logic. Hermeneutic theorists like Gadamer are high M; logical empiricists like Ayer and Carnap are low M. The interplay of these two ways of thinking about logic has produced a continuing series of misunderstandings and ambiguities and fruitful ideas. Thus low-M Marxists like Engels and Kautsky have reduced *the* dialectic to exactly three laws of thought, or three kinds of science, or in Althusser's case have tried to remove it from *the* theory entirely.

The purpose of Mitroff and Kilmann's typology or space is not to classify particular scientists, but rather "to help us to see and to organize some of the complex patterns by which humans behave" (1978, p. 11). That is, they intend that their book should help us understand the particular cognitive style of some social scientist we are studying, including ourselves. That is also the aim of the present chapter.

CONCLUSION

The study of personality influences, the subjective side of science, helps us recognize how much we shape and construct what passes for objective knowledge. It may also help us accept or devise practices that do not fit some narrow definition of scientific method, and accept more of the pluralism of methods that actually exists. And since method expresses personality, it may help us accept parts of ourselves that we may have thought were irrelevant or even hindrances to good practice. In particular, many social scientists would do well to accept and use their "feminine" side more, at least in research if not in the aggressive and competitive public arena. To this end the study of the feminist writers would be helpful.

PUTTING IT
ALL TOGETHER

11

How Does Social Science Produce Knowledge?

IN PART III we begin to integrate the materials of parts I and II around our basic questions: (1) What sort of truth or knowledge does social science provide? (2) How does or should it do this? (3) What weaknesses and dangers appear, and how can they be avoided or corrected?

We begin in chapter 11 by taking answers from the philosophies summarized in part I. These philosophies provide answers aplenty for all three questions, but the answers conflict. By now we have several bases for evaluating the various answers: the internal difficulties and changes in the philosophies, the disagreements and agreements of different philosophies, and most important, the materials of part II. Part II tells us how social science actually works, socially, cognitively, and politically. A philosophical statement of how science should work and what its goal is should at least be compatible with an account of how it *does* work, since otherwise we cannot get from here to there. If cognitive psychology tells us that some recommended practice is impossible or very unusual, we would do well to look for a different recommendation. Or the part II materials may throw new light on some recommended practice or goal that clarifies it or raises questions about it.

Chapter 12 presents further answers to our basic questions, taken from the materials of part II. In general, the philosophical materials answer the questions: What is truth or knowledge, and how should social scientists operate to produce knowledge? The reflexive social science materials answer the questions: How do social scientists operate, what weaknesses and dangers appear, and how can they be avoided or corrected?

Chapter 11 will be organized around our basic questions rather than following the sequence of part I. However, we will begin with logical empiricism and bring in the other philosophies as needed.

Logical empiricism and ideal-language philosophy suggest that truth in social science consists of confirmed laws. Each law asserts a necessary or probable connection between two variables, an independent and a dependent one. For some philosophers, the laws should come in large packages, deductively connected in a theory; for others there can be little pieces of truth, separate laws that can be combined or not, as desired. Let us consider this proposal.

The material of chapter 10 tells us that this proposal is a strongly "masculine" one. First, it is not a proposal, it is an order. It comes down from the philosophers of science and the methodologists—the early Minnesota Studies, Nagel (1961), Rudner (1966), Campbell and Stanley, Kierlinger, etcetera—as a necessary goal for anyone claiming to be a scientist. It is not derived from social scientific practice, but from logic. If practice is different, practice is wrong, not logic. Abraham Kaplan (1964), has also pointed to the authority claim of philosophers, in his declaration of independence; he has argued that social scientists don't have to be told what science is because they have developed their own logics-in-use and their own goals. The issue here is whether philosophers can project their own conception of truth on to science, or whether like Kaplan they can internalize the implicit conception of truth that social scientists are already using.

Second, the proposal tells us that the real world must obey these laws. That is, society is determined by the laws of human nature and social processes. This conception of laws was not held by early logical empiricists such as Moritz Schlick, who regarded laws as empirical generalizations that describe what usually happens, never mind why.

Third, the laws are formulated by social scientists and then externalized onto society; they do not come from the Other, society. Scientists are supposed to be separate from society. The hypotheses become laws when they are tested and confirmed. Testing involves the exercise of power: samples taken from the real world are assigned to various control groups; instructions to the groups tell them what they should believe about the experiment or survey; the independent variable is administered according to the scientist's specifications; and responses are sorted out as useful or useless according to the scientist's categories. At the extreme, a philosopher might demand that psychotherapists randomly sort their patients into control and experimental groups, administering a placebo to one group and a standardized therapeutic dose to the other group.

Fourth, any laws that get confirmed in this way are themselves instruments of control. In a lawful world, knowledge of the causes of behavior can be used to control behavior, as in behavior modification. Knowledge of the causes of poverty, if we had such a thing, could be used by government agencies to control poverty—that is, reduce it to a desired level. Or, if the causes are out of reach, we could conclude that poverty is inevitable. Public opinion polls and attitude surveys can be used by politicians and campaign managers to control voting behavior. In this case there is also an illusion of countercontrol by the public, as Skinner observed long ago.[12]

The argument of chapter 10, and also the arguments of Habermas and Apel in chapter 5, assert that knowledge is in part an instrument of control and power over, but only in part. The logical empiricist conception of truth as laws has some validity; social process is in part lawlike, or can be treated as lawlike. Perhaps the most spectacular discovery of Skinner was the "law" that intermittent reinforcement would greatly increase the rate of response. He had discovered and explained gambling. Addiction is a similar behavioral process in which reinforcement is self-sustaining. Such processes are beyond the limits of theories that assume freedom or rational choice. Scientists who adopt, or are addicted to, a logical empiricist concept of truth deal with the nonrational, nonfree aspect of social process. Such truth can sometimes be used for control, by government or behavior therapists. Habermas reminds us that it can also possibly sometimes be used for self-control.

"Laws" in social science need not all take the ideal language form: "All A is B," "All crows are black." Causal models describe the multiple connections among several variables, and regression equations, like $C_t = a + bW_t + cN_t + dP_t + eA_t + fC_{t-1} + gL_{t-1}$ state how much one variable is affected by several other variables. Simultaneous regression equations describe a network of multiple influences.[13]

Causal laws take many forms depending on the various kinds of causes one recognizes (Wright, 1978, chap. 1). Thus an economy, by producing a certain distribution of occupational classes and class power, can *constrain*, limit the viable forms of government, as Aristotle observed in the *Politics*. One form of government can be *compatible* with the market *constraint* on corporations to accumulate capital; that is, the government is structurally able to facilitate capital accumulation. The compatibility may be quite limited, as with the empires that Eisenstadt (1963) describes, so that the two constraints conflict outside the narrow range of compatibility: the economic constraint to accumulate capital, and the political constraint to maintain imperial splendor and the dignity of the landed aristocracy. And so on. Philosophers have no right to impose any ideal causal language on social scientists.

The hermeneutic tradition and some ordinary-language philosophers recommend the opposite kind of truth, truth from the inside. The ethnographer or clinician gives us life as it is lived, a concrete universal. This kind of knowledge enables us to understand and even participate in that life; and by extension it helps us to understand our own life better. Thus a case study of poverty or adolescence or Elmtown enables us to make contact with these people, interpret their actions, and perhaps help with their problems as they define them. Goffman's *Presentation of Self in Everyday Life* (1959) shows us how we present ourselves in public, and how we prepare for it in private. Kluckhohn (1949) argued that the whole point of anthropology was to hold up a "mirror for man" so we could see ourselves better.

We need both kinds of truth, laws and mirrors.

Stegmüller and his structuralists point to a third kind of truth: abstract structural dynamics that can be exemplified in empirical cases. The simplest examples are mathematical models: games, Keynesian models, Poisson process models, Richardson process models, random walks, Hotelling-Downs spaces, and so forth. Stegmüller also mentions psychoanalytic theory, and Parsons's four-function model is another dynamic structure (see figure 2, p. 347).

Such structures, mathematical or nonmathematical, enable us to understand and predict the dynamics of some empirical system. They also enable us to participate in the dynamics, the game or neurosis or political system, to produce a desired outcome. Thus an administrator in an Eastonian political system can restructure gatekeepers to reduce input overload, and a Keynesian treasury official in a Keynesian closed economy can shift fiscal policy to reduce the unemployment rate.

On the issue of whether truth comes in small or large packages, separate laws or theories, the dominant answer of logical empiricists was "large packages," based on the practice of physicists. They observed that the variables in a law, for instance, U-238, were defined by other theoretical variables and laws, so that the theory had meaning as a whole, not as separate sentences. And since most of the variables were unobservable, the theory had to be tested as a whole, not as separate hypotheses.

This wholist conception of truth agrees with Stegmüller, and applies to the structural models that the Stegmüller people study. For example, in a game model the inequality $P < R$ is nothing by itself. It also applies to concatenated theories like those of Parsons and Freud. In a concatenated theory any lawlike connection must be qualified by other connections, constraints, and facilitations. During 1895–1920, Freud was building up a complex of concepts, lawlike connections, empirical indicators, and variant combinations in different cases. He was not testing a single fundamental hypothesis, as Grünbaum (1984) supposes, though he did make changes in it, as Grünbaum indicates.

The argument of chapter 9 reinforces this empirical observation. Frame theory and its various neighbors assert that cognition and perception, even of a crow, depend on the activation of complex multiply connected structures, and that these in turn depend on some kind of background knowledge. Indeed, one main thrust of artificial intelligence models in the last thirty years has been to move toward bigger and bigger structures, to locate meanings in bigger and bigger contexts—from bits to TOTE units (Miller et al., 1960) to chunks to schemas to frames to parallel distributed processing. This development cannot be brushed off by supposing that AI researchers have had a divergent personality style and were following their personality bent. Quite the contrary: the early cognitive modelers—Ashby, Simon, Miller as of 1960, Newell—were convergers, decomposers, meticulous and precise with details; but problems of construction—for instance, in machine translation—led them into bigger and bigger contexts. We return to this topic in chapter 12.

Popper's philosophy tells us more about the kind of knowledge we can hope to produce. Popper rejects the logical empiricist concept that a science needs some sort of foundation to get started—a proper language, a correct deductive logic, true axioms, some confirmed law, or whatever. Instead, he argues that we begin with defective instruments, false theories, mistaken or superficial observations, and gradually improve them. Science grows by correcting its errors rather than by building on secure foundations.

Popper's rejection of the need for a sound foundation agrees with recent speculations on how frames, cognitive structures, get developed. It also provides us with our only hope for a social science: we don't have any permanent, unquestionable foundations. Our foundations are Walras, Spencer, Wundt, Morgan, Marx, Ricardo, and they were wrong in many ways, though they gave us fruitful ideas and improvable methods. The truth we seek is therefore a truth for our time; it builds on past errors and will in turn be reconstructed in the future. Agassi puts it more bluntly: It's all partly false, and its successor truths will be false too; what part is false we don't know.

Nor does knowledge grow toward an ultimate unchanging truth. Popper's difficulty with verisimilitude shows us that we cannot measure progress toward any such timeless goal. We can sometimes see progress in retrospect, but even such judgments can be revised. All we have is truth for our time.

Abraham Kaplan (1964) has made the same point: truth is not the distant, ever receding horizon, but the ground beneath our feet as we move on. Merton too has made this point, in his discussion of the "fallacy of the latest word" (1984). The fallacy occurs when a scientist carefully exposes the errors of a predecessor: misinterpretation of an earlier theory, misreading of data sources, errors of method, etcetera. The fallacy consists of the scientist's belief that his criticism is progress, because he himself is free of the misinterpretations, data errors, and so on, he finds in his predecessor. How does he know that? Merton suggests that sociology seems to move in cycles; Kaplan's feet go in a circle. However, any such cycle can be later reinterpreted as a growth spiral.

For those readers who believe the concept of a changing truth is self-contradictory, since truth does not change, we can substitute Dewey's phrase "warranted assertibility" as the Popperian goal of science.

We turn next to the question of how these three kinds of truth for our time can be achieved. Here the logical empiricists are of no help at all, except to illustrate some wrong answers. Their basic answer is: You get a *confirmed* theory by *testing* a derived prediction against *observable* data. This answer is all wrong, even for the "law" kind of truth.

1. The argument of chapter 9 tells us that logical empiricists made a fundamental mistake when they sharply distinguished the contexts of discovery and testing. Cognitive processes do not operate that way. Testing occurs in a larger context of discovery and takes its character from that context. Thus a separate "logic" of testing is fundamentally misleading.

Let us review the general outline of a search or research program from chapter 9 to see how testing fits in, and how it varies at different stages of the process. There are of course a variety of search processes, so the following outline is necessarily sketchy. Suppose researchers are beginning to explore a new area—say, dreams as of 1890 or cognitive processes as of 1950 or Prisoner's Dilemma as of 1952.

Frame theory tells us that search is guided by a frame, which structures an area and provides questions to ask. When the field is new and no frame exists, an analogy or metaphor suggests a frame. In the case of Prisoner's Dilemma, the name itself is the analogy; in early cognitive experiments the behaviorist S-O-R or S-H-R scheme was the analogy. The analogy provides the initial questions that guide research: how does the "prisoner" solve the dilemma; if perception is a response to a stimulus, what cognitive variables intervene; if a dream is a "message" from the unconscious, how can we decode the message?

At this stage, no testing occurs at all, even though the experimenters may well have expectations and may state hypotheses in their published reports. The task is to produce data that answer the question. If the answer is negative, if the data say, "They don't solve the dilemma" (Scodel et al., 1959), nothing has been disconfirmed; rather, the experiment failed. We have learned something about how people deal with the dilemma in thirty trials, but the question remains unanswered. It is necessary to try again, about 1960, running 300 or even 1,000 trials and more carefully varying the obvious variables until an answer turns up (Rapoport and Chammah, 1965).

Once data that more or less fit expectations are available, a hypothesis can be induced from them by using a striking instance, availability, or other heuristic, and testing can begin. However, these new data can only confirm, not disconfirm; we mostly see what we expect to see. They can correct details of the hypothesis or suggest changes, but if they are entirely off the mark, the data are bad; something went wrong. The data may cue in a different frame, which finds a new pattern in them and produces a new hypothesis; but then there are two hypotheses to explore.

At a still later stage when a well-developed theory exists, tests can confirm or disconfirm details, direct the search process into more fruitful areas, and perhaps draw boundaries between the areas of relevance of two variants of a theory or two theories. They can also incidentally disconfirm hypotheses of rival theorists or schools, but the rivals of course reject such disconfirmations. Think for example of Suppes and Atkinson's total "disconfirmation" of game theory (1960), which was rightly ignored by game theorists.

As we know, some theories are eventually reclassified as "disconfirmed"—for example, the early hypothesis that there is a universal dream language. But this is the result of a long continued process in which other frames are cued in again and again and get developed successfully, while the original theory continually suffers from bad data, interferences, wrong techniques, and successes that cannot be replicated. No one test disconfirms a theory, except in retrospect—as Kuhn has observed.

Thus in the exploration of a field or topic over several decades, an early theory can gradually be completely changed through minor disconfirmations; supplementary or opposed theories or offshoots can appear and develop; an early variant can gradually be abandoned—all without any specific single tests of the logical empiricist or Popperian variety. A whole research program can be abandoned without any one specific disconfirmation. The most astounding example for me is the recent decline of behaviorism, except for behavior therapy. Who could have imagined such a possibility in the 1950s? Sigmund Koch, I suppose. Perhaps the decline is temporary.

A corollary is that we cannot expect the analytic philosophers to give up or revise their theory of hypothesis testing on the basis of such evidence. Human cognitive processes do not operate that way. The philosophers can ignore the "refutation," or ridicule it as "relativist," or argue that the data are bad—social studies are not yet real science—or were misinterpreted, or that their theory was misinterpreted or needs minor clarification.

The research summarized in chapter 7 agrees with this account of search processes, at least for laboratory experiments. The goal in those experiments was to get something to work; search consisted of trying one combination of variables after another until one worked. Various heuristics guided the search. Each experiment could be called a test, but only in the sense that the results told the researcher either to proceed farther in the same direction or try something else. Conceivably, continuous failure over several years might have induced the researchers to drop the whole project and start a different one—would that be disconfirmation?—but they would have been fired for incompetence long before that.

If tests can mainly only confirm, not disconfirm (except for details), is there any point in testing at all? The material on the public arena in chapter 7 provides an answer: the main point of confirmatory data is rhetorical. Here as elsewhere Donald McCloskey's work on the rhetoric of economics (1983, 1985) is highly illuminating. For the rhetoric of sociology, see Agger (1989). If the researcher is strongly committed to his theory, he will find confirmatory data and reinterpret or rework "puzzling" data. Data therefore add nothing to the researcher's knowledge. However, they serve to persuade other people, especially the uncommitted ones, that the theory should be taken seriously.

For an extreme example (oops! availability bias), Rayack (1987) has shown that Milton Friedman, in his numerous *Newsweek* articles, speeches, and books of propaganda, has consistently slanted and selected data, ignored or rejected negative data, given fanciful treatments of various national political economies, and even contradicted his earlier accounts to suit a later argument. The rhetoric is obvious. However, the same reworking of data to fit his theory occurs in his professional papers, in a more subdued fashion (Diesing, 1985a). Here the rhetoric is directed to a more discriminating audience.

If the researcher is not committed to a theory but is just trying it out, the confirmatory data serve to persuade *him* that the theory is worth developing; it works. Apart from rhetoric, however, the cognitive function of testing is not to confirm or disconfirm a theory, but to work on its details: correct wrong details, find areas of weakness or vagueness, try a new area of application or new variant, suggest supplementary hypotheses, find a better definition of some concept such as *money*, and so on.

2. The logical empiricist reduction of data to observables has had disastrous effects on the social sciences for decades. Deluded, submissive researchers thought that to be truly scientific and get philosophical approval they had to specify the observable, measurable phenomena that were relevant to their hypothesis. The result was decades of behaviorism in psychology and behavioralism in political science.

For example, Dahl's 1957 definition of power, "A has power over B to the extent that A can get B to do something he would not otherwise do" (cf. Dahl, 1963, pp. 40–53) seems like a plausible preliminary definition. However, Dahl the behavioralist then goes on to say, "It is one thing to define power and quite another to observe it" (p. 51) and continues by discussing operational definitions and operational tests. He is following the prescriptions of the logical empiricism of the 1950s: You can have a theory with its theoretical definitions, but to test a derived hypothesis you must operationally define the concepts by observables and then collect observations somehow.

Consequently, when the pluralists, following Dahl, did their case studies they focused on publicly observable political events. Two political groups, A and B, must make opposed policy demands; there is a contest, and A wins. The outcome is public, published, and recorded. In the decades after 1957, critics pointed out what this superficial operational definition omits. First, it ignores the resources that interest groups control, especially economic resources, which they can use or threaten to use in a contest. Recognition of these resources by other groups affects their decisions on whether and how to get involved in a political contest. Second, it omits nondecisions and unpolitics (Bachrach and Baratz, 1962; Crenson, 1971). Here nothing publically observable happens because: (1) B, C, . . . study A's resources and suspect that A would win or at least punish them severely, and so do not make a claim. (2) Control over the agenda by A or by constitutions and bylaws prevents B from bringing an issue up. (3) B does not know how and when to get a claim on the agenda, or does not have the resources to make a claim. (4) B cannot recognize its latent interests because it does not realize how the economic-political process affects it, perhaps because it has learned theories spread by A (Frey, 1971). In these cases, A has gotten B to do something B would not otherwise have done, namely, keep quiet, yet nothing observable has happened. Third, Stone (1986) describes still other kinds of power, including the ability to pass some costs of one's policies on to nonactive bystanders, and the ability to adjust the rules and structures of politics to benefit oneself. Here A can get B to do something, namely, die from environmental pollution; but this exercise of power is invisible to the pluralists. Emphasis on observable, behavioral data draws theory and search away from these kinds of power.

Observable data are of course indispensable; but social science can also use four other kinds of data. They are the following:

a. *Aggregate data* on local employment and unemployment, production, corporate wealth, investment, provide evidence of economic resources that can intimidate potential opposition. These are numbers reported by corporations and agencies rather than observable events.

b. *Conversations* with the subject being studied. Conversations use hermeneutic techniques to construct expressed and unexpressed meanings of the S. Sample surveys do not use conversation; they treat the respondent's utterances as observable behavior to be coded according to pre-set categories and then tabulated.

c. *Documents.* Some documents are records or traces of previous conversations, including the list of participants. Others provide evidence for the rules that constrain political action. Still others record the ideas that were current at a certain time. Organization membership lists, corporate board rosters (Schwartz, 1987), and even attendance records at weddings and debutante balls (Domhoff, 1978, pp. 14–16), provide evidence for communication networks that organize and activate the resources of the interest group.

d. *The researcher's own reactions* in a situation, insofar as s/he has become part of the situation being studied. Consider, for example, Reinharz's participant-observer study of how a frontier Israeli community adjusted to occasional bombing from across the border. Reinharz's own fears and adjustments to fear provided a sample data set that could sensitize her to others' adjustments (1979, pp. 341ff.). Even the difference between her terror and others' apparent but not quite perfect nonchalance raised questions for her to pursue.

None of these four kinds of data can be taken at face value, but neither can observable data. Even a public contest in which A wins over B by one vote could have been arranged by B, or by both together. All data can be questioned and corrected, and no one kind is more scientific than any other.

Nondecisions and unpolitics can be located by depth interviews, participant observation, and study of documents, as in Caro (1974) and Crenson (1971). The researcher can work out the thinking and agendas of various participants and nonparticipants, discover people's perceptions of others' power to reward and punish, locate channels of communication, and compare cases in which something happened with cases in which it didn't happen. For example, when Crenson heard the mayor of Gary, Indiana, comment that as long as he could see smoke coming from the U.S. Steel smokestacks he knew the city's economy was healthy, Crenson had located some of U.S. Steel's power.

3. The early logical empiricist assumption that observable data are there ready to collect, like crows in a corn patch, has long since been discarded, even by logical empiricists. Ludwik Fleck had already observed in 1935 that in the case of syphilis research, collective beliefs guided the production and perception of data (Fleck, 1979). In the late 1950s, Hanson and Kuhn argued that data are "theory-laden," so that different theories produce different data. Think for instance of the unemployment rate, the job creation rate, the deindustrialization rate. The observations of Fleck, Hanson, and Kuhn are reinforced by the materials of chapter 9.

But if data are in part a product of theory, the whole project of testing theory against data becomes more complex. The problem is not simply that observations might be mistaken and must be replicated, as Popper argued; the problem is that theory produces the data that test it. There are no true observations out there waiting to be picked up, no protocol sentences or sense data. Interpretation always mediates between scientists and the world (Gadamer, 1989).

What then does *test* mean? We are not testing a theory's correspondence with reality, but its ability to produce its own reflection in reality, in data. That's not easy to do; but success is only the beginning. It is necessary sometimes to test the data's robustness by producing them in different ways using other variables in the theory and other variants of the theory. Often it is necessary also to confront the data produced by other theories, and that means understanding the theories, and that means communication and interpretation of texts. Hermeneutic processes are a part of testing.

4. It may seem strange to assert that when we produce data that fit a theory we are not confirming the theory, except rhetorically. But remember Goodman's paradox: evidence that "confirms" one hypothesis also "confirms" an infinity of other hypotheses. Consequently, the degree of confirmation for any one of this infinite set is zero.

In other words, when we test a hypothesis experimentally or statistically and get confirming data, we have not actually confirmed the hypothesis. We have produced a regularity, but our interpretation of the regularity is one of an infinity of possible interpretations. Similarly, when we deduce a prediction from some theory and the predicted event occurs, the theory has not been confirmed. The same prediction could have been deduced from other theories known and unknown. But availability bias forcefully presents us our theory as the obvious explanation and blots out alternative theories, so we are reinforced in our belief. Popper too has made this point.

For example, the Witkin *field dependence* effect (see chapter 10) has been interpreted in several different ways since 1948 (Witkin, 1954; Haaken, 1988). Witkin's work was funded by ONR, which wanted a test for naval recruits.

In one of the Witkin experiments, the S sits in a dark room and views a lighted rod surrounded by a lighted frame. The frame is tilted, unknown to the S. The S is instructed to adjust the rod until it is upright. The S's score consists of the number of degrees of difference between the adjusted rod and true upright. If the rod is adjusted to the tilted frame, the score is large; if the frame is ignored, the score is small or zero. In another experiment, the S sits in a tilted chair in a tilted room and is instructed to sit upright. Scoring is the same. In another experiment the S is instructed to adjust the (tilted) room to the upright. Scoring is the same, and so on.

During the ensuing forty years, there were alternate interpretations of the percept itself and of the intervening psychological variable. Witkin saw the percept as the "perception of the upright." In a second interpretation, the perception is of a thing (rod), not a person. In an alternate experiment a human figure was substituted for the rod, and scores were different. A third interpretation refers to a "dark room" effect. The female S is led blindfolded into a dark room, is seated, and is instructed by the male E to view an illuminated upright rod and adjust it to her body.

These three interpretations should be understood as three intersecting (overlapping) sets of experiments. In Witkin's experiments there was always some sort of tilted field that interfered with the body's internal perception of the upright, and the S was instructed to ignore the field. Experiments focusing on differences between thing and person perceptions would be different, and "dark room" experiments different again. The rod and frame experiment could be included in all three sets and be part of three different, overlapping regularities.

Consider Witkin's frame of mind to see how he perceived the experimental setup. Witkin wanted to study a hypothetical personality construct, which he called *field dependence*. Field dependence was a dependence on external rather than internal cues. Since the construct was unobservable, one had to study it by finding an indicator whose value varied with the value of the construct. The value of the indicator could then stand for the hypothetical value of the hypothetical construct. To make sure that the indicator actually measured the hypothetical construct and not something else, one had to control all other variables that might influence the indicator. Then, having found a reliable indicator of the personality construct, one could start correlating the value of the indicator with the value of other variables and indicators.

Given this framework, Witkin's attention would have been focused on the indicator variable, the lighted rod, for example. In each experiment there would have to be some sort of rod, some sort of external cue like the frame, and the unobservable internal cue. *And nothing else.* What was the dark, then? The dark was *nothing*, the absence of interfering variables. No stimulus sampling allowed here. What was the experimenter? Silly question, as of 1950; the experimenter is not part of the experiment, by definition.

Having found a reliable indicator variable, Witkin proceeded to correlate it with various personality measures. He found that women are more field dependent than men (Witkin, 1954, pp. 44, 156; chap. 8). A typical female S used the tilted-field cues to determine the upright, rather than her own body sensations. She was unable to extract the rod from its context and relate it to her body (p. 25); she passively accepted the field (p. 36); she became dependent on it. After finding more correlations, Witkin renamed the field-dependent variable "ego strength" (male) versus submission to authority (female), or coping versus dependence, or active versus passive. The passive female needed environmental support, showed lack of awareness of inner life including body sensations, feared aggressive and sexual impulses, had poor impulse control and higher anxiety (chap. 21). In short, immature. All the above factors correlated positively with field dependence. There were also negative correlations (p. 470); also some mental patients scored low on field dependence; but Witkin could explain this away.

Asch, a social psychologist and Witkin collaborator, called the intervening variable *field relatedness*. He thought of it as the autonomous self (male) versus the socially involved self (female). In Asch's famous comparable experiment (1952, chap. 16), the "tilted frame" consisted of seven stooges—people, not wood.[14] Thus Asch's attention would have been focused on the people in the experiment (except the experimenter). The values of the variable might be seven people, one or two people, no people. The rod and frame experiment would be a "no people" variant. Darkness would be irrelevant; as long as there were no people, any sort of lighting would do.

Finally, in a "dark room" definition of the situation, the dark and the gender of the E would be crucial variables. A male E in a dark room would induce the female S to define the situation as external to and separate from her, and hopefully as impersonal, having nothing to do with her body.

The same variations in frame of mind would also produce different interpretations of the rod and frame data. Thus Bem reinterpreted Witkin's statistical data to find a variable she called rigidity versus sensitivity to subtle situational cues. Witkin too had noticed greater variation in task performance in women, correlated with differences in the task structure (1954, pp. 165–67); he explained this away as an incidental effect of women's passivity (p. 167). Haaken (1988) called the intervening variable *context stripping* versus seeing things in context. More theoretically, the variable was socioemotional isolation (men), denying social cues, versus sensitivity to social cues (women). Witkin too in 1979 suggested that the intervening variable was a lesser (male) or greater (female) capacity for interpreting social cues. Note that Witkin's original interpretation of the rod and frame experiment itself showed incapacity for interpreting the social cues in the "dark room" effect.

Obviously other interpretations are possible. Indeed, one could say that the observed sex differences were slight, a few degrees, and that men as well as women were affected by the tilted field. Similarly, in Asch's experiment nearly everybody was strongly affected by the "tilted" stooges. In short, Witkin's experiments discovered something, but not necessarily the regular connection of field dependence with gender, ego strength, or immaturity.

It does not help to use Popperian language and say we are not confirming anything, just disconfirming the null hypothesis. The null hypothesis says that the observed regularity was a coincidence, so disconfirming it says that the regularity was no coincidence. This is indeed something; we have found or produced a regularity. But this regularity can still be understood in any number of ways.

Nor does it help to use *eliminative induction*, that is, confirm our hypothesis and disconfirm one alternative hypothesis. That still leaves infinity-minus-one other possibilities.

The implication seems to be that we should focus on the discovered empirical regularity, not on the hypothesis that we mistakenly thought was confirmed. We should explore its scope, that is, the range of conditions that produce, intensify, weaken, nullify, change, redirect it. We should see whether it is itself a variant of some more general effect, and what produces the variant. Then we can look for alternate facilitating and modifying and blocking conditions, based on alternate theories.

Such a program is fairly common in experimental psychology. Indeed, Witkin and associates were carrying out exactly such a program, except for the "alternate theory" step. The program is typically described in terms of hypothesis testing in the journals; and such language is not entirely incorrect, since hypotheses, expectations, are involved at each stage. However, the "testing" language is misleading. It suggests that when a hypothesis has been confirmed to the .01 level some fixed, lasting truth has been discovered. Psychologists know that these truths don't last, especially the truths of their predecessors; but they like to hope that theirs will last a while. But this hope can slow down the search for more adequate theoretical interpretations of the produced regularity.

"More adequate" means more highly correlated and more robust, appearing in a greater variety of experimental setups and nonexperimental methods. In other words, more highly "confirmed." We are still "testing" hypotheses, still searching for laws; but Goodman's paradox reminds us that the search is endless. Let us therefore not spurn the outdated "confirmed" laws, such as the statistical association of field dependence with gender. There was some sort of truth in it, but not final truth.

The rejection of any philosophy that separates testing and discovery applies to Popper's philosophy as well. In addition, Popper's emphasis on falsification as the only engine of scientific progress is totally wrong. The arguments of chapters 7 and 9 agree that scientists do not think or act that way, any more than Popper did. Hands (1985, p. 322) observes that economic methodologists now agree on very few things, but they do agree that "economists seldom if ever practice a falsificationist methodology." Disconfirmation does occur in research, and is very useful, but it is a limited, peripheral process that leads to modification rather than total rejection of a theory.

By extension, it is illegitimate to require a scientist to specify what facts would totally refute his theory. I have found that this tactic is always applied to an opponent, not to oneself. It is always the opponent's theory that is unfalsifiable and therefore unscientific.

We turn next to Lakatos, Stegmüller, and Kuhn for three closely related versions of how science achieves knowledge. These versions were developed by reflecting on scientific practice, unlike Carnap and Popper, so they are quite compatible with practice.

In all three versions, science progresses by working out the implications of some founding theory, paradigm, metaphor, set of categories, or metaphysical idea. For example, Malinowski (1922) and Radcliffe-Brown (1922) developed the idea of a social system in which each part reinforces and fits into other parts, and in which supporting practices develop at points of strain. Keynes (1936) developed the idea of a closed system in which money and goods circulate irregularly at constantly changing rates due to multiple internal cross-influences and pervasive uncertainty. Rosenblueth et al. (1943) developed the idea of a process that stabilizes itself by feedback, a cybernetic process. Neumann and Morgenstern (1944) developed the idea of a game. Chomsky (1957) developed the idea of a deep syntactic structure that appears disguised in language. All these works could be called revolutionary or paradigmatic, and each founded a tradition.

For Lakatos such an initial theory sets up a long-term research program as the context in which particular hypotheses, models, and concepts are developed. The central concepts of the program provide the heuristic that guides research. Research aims at confirmation of hypotheses and especially at the discovery of new empirical phenomena; these are signs that the search is on the right track. Disconfirmation of peripheral parts of the program is allowed and leads to peripheral changes. But there is no way to disconfirm the central ideas or assumptions of the program; data that do not agree are reinterpreted, perhaps by making ad hoc assumptions about them or changing some peripheral theories or techniques. Multiple incompatible research programs are acceptable, even normal. A research program can be abandoned, but need not be, when it gets absorbed in explaining away or reinterpreting puzzling data, when its explanations get more and more ad hoc, and when few or no successes occur.

There is some difficulty with Lakatos's insistence that scientists working in a research program are rational. This seems to be the "hard core" of his theory, to be preserved by redefining rationality as much as necessary. The cognitive psychologists have long struggled with the concept of rationality; some of them have asserted that an introspective experience of calculation and choice is a rationalization, and others have worked out heuristic principles, satisficing techniques, or practical reasoning as more modest conceptions of rationality. This sort of reasoning occurs precisely where Popper thought it was absent, namely in the process of discovery. Perhaps followers of Lakatos might accept some such redefinitions of rationality, making it unconscious, simplified, and quite fallible.

For Stegmüller a tradition develops by applying an original model to new cases; if the model doesn't quite fit, one develops a variant. Or one can construct variants and look for cases that they might fit. In applying a model to a case one produces an interpretation that fits the model; that is, the theory produces the data. Insofar as the case objects, makes trouble, one develops a variant of the model.

The hermeneutic philosophers agree that a tradition develops by diversification, that is, by working out a plurality of interpretations of the original text and thereby enriching it. This theory, and Stegmüller's, is correct for Keynesianism, functionalism, behaviorism, institutional economics, Marxism, diffusionism in anthropology, game theory, neoclassical economics, and so on. In contrast, Kuhn's theory of scientific development is weaker. Kuhn has had only the concepts of normal science and revolution, and has had to deal with diversification within a tradition by positing smaller revolutions, each setting up a new disciplinary matrix and a new community. The result is perhaps too sharp a distinction between continuity and change within a tradition, and too fragmented a picture of traditions or research programs. However, in historical context Kuhn's distinction was fundamental in rejecting the older idea of linear progress in science; so the Kuhnian revolution set up a tradition of which Lakatos and Stegmüller are variants.

So far, these four accounts generally agree that social science achieves knowledge through the development and diversification of traditions or research programs. A number of traditions flourish simultaneously, each going its own way. This account leaves several gaps to be filled.

First, how does a tradition start? In 1962, Kuhn asserted that in natural science a revolution somehow occurs when an old tradition is in crisis, ready to die (1970a). He later allowed for exceptions. Moreover, the new paradigm usually includes the old one and goes beyond it— hence, progress. The social sciences haven't worked that way. Radcliffe-Brown invented functionalism because the diffusionist theory he took to the Andaman Islands didn't work well there; it left out too much of what was happening. Also he had read Durkheim and had an alternate frame available to deal with the happenings. However, the diffusionists didn't know of any crisis, and continued without him. Keynes did face an anomaly, British unemployment, but this anomaly certainly didn't convince neoclassicists at Chicago that there was any crisis; indeed, for some neoclassicists, Keynes was the crisis. The 1943 invention of feedback, from which computers and artificial intelligence developed, didn't come out of any crisis. Perhaps Norbert Wiener picked up some mathematical ideas from the people who were working on radar. And so on. But if old and new traditions continue side by side, acrimoniously, Kuhn's original conception of progress does not apply, and the issue of whether social science progresses or only changes remains open.

A second issue is: Is there a rational basis for choosing to join or abandon a research program? This issue was very important to Lakatos; his main point of disagreement with Kuhn, he claimed, was his insistence that the choice of a research program must somehow be rational. Otherwise there could be no progress in science. Critics such as Feyerabend and Blaug have observed that Lakatos did not succeed at this; nor have the cognitive psychologists and AI people provided any help. Their versions of rationality work in detailed research situations, not on a basic choice of theory. Some microsociologists (chapter 7) have suggested that the decision to join a research program (succession strategy) or abandon it and start a new one (subversion strategy) can be a rational choice of a perceived opportunity to accumulate intellectual capital—get published, get discussed, get research grants. However, this is not at all what Lakatos had in mind. Nor would he have liked Faust's suggestion that a research program captures the nonrational commitment of researchers just because it is there, through availability bias, socialization, nonrational internalization.

Perhaps we should accept Lakatos's problem as an important unsolved problem in philosophy of science. Can there be "rational" grounds for joining or leaving a scientific community? Here we mean rational in terms of the collective pursuit of truth, not rational in terms of individual advancement. Is there a scientific rationality in the large to supplement the heuristic, practical reasoning in the small that cognitive psychologists study? And if there is, is there evidence that scientists choose on this basis?

For example, was the abandonment of Hullian learning theory, the abandonment of Gestalt theory, the rapid rise of Estes's stimulus sampling theory, the abandonment of Skinnerian behaviorism including stimulus sampling, and the future return of neobehaviorism a rational process?

Feyerabend provides a perfect answer to this question. His answer is that rational theory choice is not necessary to the advance of science. Science is advanced by individual creativity, and the only problem is to maintain an atmosphere in which creativity can be stimulated and recognized. Lesser scientists can then build on the great discoveries, the Kuhnian exemplars, working out the implications and applications and details.

A pluralism of conflicting research programs provides the optimum stimulus for creativity, the optimum level of stress as Hans Selye–type psychologists would put it. The continuous conflict prevents the researcher from simply accepting any received dogma, and forces conflicting viewpoints into his consciousness as well. Some researchers cannot tolerate such stress and uncertainty; they withdraw into a comfortable dogma and do normal science. But a few will produce a creative synthesis or other solution and advance science.

If there is a homeostatic mechanism that can maintain a plurality of research programs in active contention, it makes no difference which one a new scientist picks, since he can be creative in any one. But the microsociological processes of chapter 7 provide just such a mechanism. The engine is the individual's need to accumulate symbolic capital, to get read and cited and discussed. The best opportunity to accumulate is to get into a new, small, rapidly expanding research program; or even better though risky, to start such a program. The worst tactic is to join a large, old, well-developed program as a follower of some third-generation loyal follower. In between these extremes, joining a recently established, moderately large program avoids the risk of getting stranded in an unsuccessful innovation but promises more recognition than joining a well-exploited old program that others are abandoning. Individuals will choose a research program according to expected payoff, given their own risk preference.

The general-equilibrium economists can deduce the aggregate consequences of these individual rational choices: a fluctuating plurality of research programs, the number of programs being a positive function of the level of funding. A new program will increase in size explosively, then continue to expand at an exponentially decreasing rate, and an old program will decrease at an exponentially increasing rate. The number of successful new programs is a function of the absolute rate of loss of old programs. New programs in excess of this number will fail to maintain exponential growth and will suddenly disappear.

The main alternative to this microsociological mechanism is the set of nonrational bases for choice: loyalty, identification with the mentor, rebellion, class identity, ethnic identity. In this case, plurality is maintained by variations in personality and by multiple class identifications.

Feyerabend's earlier (1962, 1965) argument for pluralism, for an "ocean of mutually incompatible alternatives," agrees exactly with frame theory (chapter 9). Feyerabend argues that researchers tend to interpret data in terms of their theory and use the data to confirm, develop, or modify the theory. If the data resist such interpretation, they can be adjusted and corrected until they fit the theory. If this is too difficult, they can be set aside as puzzling, a problem to be attacked later sometime maybe. A conflicting theory can interpret such data in its terms, thereby certifying them as good, well-produced data in no need of adjustment, and thereby asserting that the first theory needs adjustment or abandonment, not the data. Consequently, conficting theories are esential to progress, since each can expose the others' weakness by producing and certifying disconfirming data.

In frame theory, a frame has no slots labeled "disconfirming data." Input is sorted into existing slots or is not perceived. Frame changes occur when an input activates some other frame, and then only if the frames are connected so that the item can be transferred to the first frame as an addition or replacement.

This last step, a communication across theories that can induce the first theorist to accept disconfirming data as valid, eludes Feyerabend's attention. Perhaps he thought communication was no problem. But supporters of one program cannot force a second program into greater clarification, let alone creativity, if they cannot communicate. Even Galileo had to try to communicate with his Aristotelian audience. Remember Claxton's comments about the ocean of mutually incompatible alternatives in cognitive psychology (1980, p. 15, cited in chapter 9): "We are like the inhabitants of thousands of little islands, all in the same part of the ocean, yet totally out of touch with each other." Maybe Claxton was exaggerating. We all understand others' theories; it is their understanding of ours that is deficient.

Churchman's Hegelian inquirer is an attempt to solve this problem by designing both conflict and communication into the research process. Churchman agrees with Feyerabend and Agassi that effective research requires conflicting perspectives, each actively searching out the weaknesses of the other. But he agrees with Kuhn that communication based on some shared community structure is also essential to research. There is plenty of conflict in the social sciences, but it occurs between communities and therefore consists mostly of misrepresentation and shadow boxing. The Hegelian inquirer corrects this weakness by designing maximum conflict within a single research design, supervised by a neutral PI who maintains communication.

Unfortunately, I know of only two good examples of the Hegelian inquirer in action: Mitroff (1983, chap. 1) and the account by Mitroff et al. (1983) of the 1980 U.S. census—and the latter did not work out quite as intended, either. It's not easy to combine fundamental conflict and communication, even within a single research project.

In practice, Feyerabend has dealt with the problem of communication in the standard philosophical fashion, acrimonious argument. His articles are all directed against other philosophers of science, calling them incompetent (1978) and devoid of ideas (1981), or superficial readers, illiterates, and propagandists (1980, chap. 7); their writings are irrelevant to the practice of science (1970b). He describes one ridiculous attack on him as "a paste-job of stereotypes, uninterpreted facts, misread passages, and uncomprehended arguments" (1977). To be sure, his critics deserved what they got.

This sort of debate has nothing to do with rationality, communication, or truth. It is simply a verbal boxing match whose purpose is to demonstrate one's tough virility. Feyerabend shares this masculine approach to communication in the public arena with the other Popperians. Apparently, part of the Popperian heritage has been Popper's emphasis on criticism, refutation, debate, as well as his intolerance and scorn for opposing views.

Thus we come to another unsolved problem. If, according to Feyerabend, the conflicting traditions or communities need each others' criticisms to bring out their weak points, they must be able to communicate. What facilitates and maintains such communication?

Habermas and Kuhn have proposed answers, but they are insufficient. Habermas (1970) has observed that each tradition has its own language, so communication requires learning to translate. This in turn requires learning the other's language. One way to implement this proposal would be to deliberately maintain two opposed traditions within a graduate department, and require students to take several courses from each faction. That way they would learn both languages. This solution would soon collapse, and has, at various universities. Department politics, especially in tenure cases, would destroy communication between the factions, and the dean would move in to pick up the pieces. Or one faction would expel the other.

Kuhn has exemplified his solution in his own debating style. He has a position, but he is also sensitive to the other's position and to the problem of communicating with the other. He has always begun by trying to bring out areas of agreement, and has offered a translation of his concepts into the other's language. Then, having hopefully established communication and provided a shared starting point, he has moved to an area of disagreement and tried to state the issue in the other's language if possible. His purpose has not been to refute the other but to get the other to see it his way too, as a basis for discussing the disagreement. These tactics have always failed, in the cases known to me.

Probably Kuhn's theory of gestalt shifts in perception across paradigms have suggested this approach to communication; but the theory itself has come from his ability to recognize such shifts in the history of science, and that ability has involved an other-centered empathy. So we come back to personality characteristics in any case.

Kuhn's other-centered side has enabled him to learn from discussion and change his views accordingly. He does not have a fixed position, a

bastion on which he has defiantly planted his banner "Here I stand . . . ";
he has a growing theory which carries the traces of his various encounters
in it. For example, in the mid-1970s he began to incorporate hermeneutics
into his thinking (1977, p. xv).

This solution works between other-centered people like Kuhn, but
not otherwise. Are there social mechanisms, norms, or values that supplement personality factors in maintaining communication between different communities? We postpone this question to chapter 12.

In summary, the philosophers suggest that social science produces at
least three kinds of knowledge: (1) systems of laws which describe interconnected regularities in society; (2) descriptions, from the inside, of a
way of life, community, person, belief system, or scientific community's
beliefs; (3) structural models, mathematical or verbal, of dynamic processes exemplified in particular cases. The three kinds overlap, since
both life descriptions and structural models can include regularities, and a
system of laws can produce a characteristic dynamic or time path. Social
science does not produce another kind of knowledge, separate laws which
connect an independent and a dependent variable. This last point will be
developed further in chapter 12.

The truth that we produce is a temporary, changing truth for our
time, not an absolute truth. These truths build on past knowledge and
will in turn be discarded or forgotten or built on in the future. In retrospect, we can sometimes see signs of progress toward the present, or signs
of cyclical change without progress; but the philosophers provide no
guaranteed measure of progress or rules for how to advance science. We
return to this topic in chapter 12.

We do not produce knowledge by testing hypotheses or predictions
against observable data; such tests can neither confirm nor disconfirm
theories or hypotheses. There is no instant truth or falsity. Instead,
knowledge is produced by a community or tradition which develops the
possibilities of some initial text, paradigm, method, or concepts. Communities diversify, form branches, combine or intermingle, and disappear.
Community members develop their theory by using it to produce data
which then change the theory. They also develop theory by shifting to a
new area requiring a different interpretation of the theory.

There is apparently no rational rule for choosing the community that
best advances science. New communities or research programs do not
wait to appear until some older community is floundering in crisis; they
show up now and then, making a great commotion in getting started, and

later disappear for no good reason that we can see. Individuals may work in two or more communities, may shift communities, or go off on their own and be forgotten.

Multiple traditions or communities live side by side, more or less acrimoniously. The philosophers disagree on whether it is better to work steadfastly within a community and ignore the others (early Kuhn, Lakatos) or to actively engage other communities in dialogue, each community exposing others' weaknesses and learning about its own problems from the others (Feyerabend, Churchman). In the latter case, communication across communities is a problem. The hermeneutic philosophers provide techniques for communication, but not motivation. We return to this topic also in chapter 12.

12

Problems and Dangers on the Road of Knowledge

IN THIS CHAPTER we derive further answers to our basic questions from the materials of part II. We will focus on the second and third questions posed at the opening of chapter 11: (2) How do research programs or traditions develop knowledge; (3) What difficulties come up in this process and how can they be remedied? Under question 3, the philosophers have left two unanswered questions for us. One is a problem derived from Lakatos: there seems to be no rational basis for choosing to work in a particular research program or programs. By this we mean rational for the advancement of knowledge. What then influences the appearance of a program and the decisions to join it or abandon it? Is there any sign of progress in such processes, or is progress, if any, separate from the rise and fall of theories?

The second problem derives from Feyerabend: if the growth of knowledge requires criticism of one tradition by another, neoclassical economists by Marxist economists and vice versa, or cognitivists by behaviorists and vice versa, what makes communication between the traditions possible? If communication is a problem, and it certainly is, what remedies are available? If there are none, this conclusion would count against Feyerabend's recommended method of criticism and individuality, and it would count for the Lakatos-Kuhn recommendation to stick to one tradition and ignore the others.

RESEARCH PROCESSES

We begin with question 2: How do research programs or traditions or communities develop knowledge? The main conclusion from part II is that research is a process of search and discovery continuing over decades, and testing is a step in that process. Testing does not come after discovery as its culmination; it occurs within search. This means that it is not the conclusive step misdescribed by logical empiricists and by Popper, with its own fixed logic. Its character varies with its context. Nor does a test announce "Confirmed" or "Disconfirmed." Sometimes it says, "Promising" or "Unpromising"; that is, "Look farther in that direction or try something different." If that's what Hempel meant by epistemic utility he had a good idea. Sometimes it says, "Something is wrong"; or perhaps, "Here is something you didn't expect; look at it." Or it might say, "This case is a good (or poor) instance of your model; use it to develop the model." Those psychologists and sociologists who describe their research in logical empiricist terms simply don't know what they are doing. Like Freud, they misunderstand themselves.

The general characteristics of search processes have already been described in chapter 9. Search processes also vary according to their structural context, and we take up some of the variations in this section.

The chief sources of variation are the method: formal modeling, quantitative, case study, and all the intermediate variants; the type of interest or concern; and the stage of development of the research program. Another source of individual variation not considered here is cognitive style. For example, Bruner distinguishes a wholist and a partist strategy in the induction of hypotheses from a data set, and Mitroff and Kilmann distinguish, among other dimensions, between the tendency to see distinctions and clarify differences and the tendency to see similarities and analogies (1978, pp. 16–20).

We will consider two examples from the three types of method to illustrate variations in the search process. We begin with formal modeling.

Game theory was established as a research program by von Neumann and Morgenstern (1944, 2d ed. 1947). The community that gradually formed around game theory was a relatively diverse and loosely unified one, including different academic disciplines, different concerns, and different combinations of method. Kuhn might not want to call it a "community" because of its heterogeneity; but it certainly forms a hermeneutic tradition with its continual diversification.

The initial problem that concerned von Neumann and Morgenstern was a puzzle within neoclassical economics, that of deducing price and production curves for oligopoly. An oligopolistic market has from two to about six suppliers of a good. In perfect and imperfect competition there are so many suppliers that competition is impersonal; but in oligopoly the suppliers know each other and must take account of each other's price and production-quantity decisions in making their own decisions. They are interdependent.

In other words, the optimum price and production level for each supplier depends on the future price and production levels of all the other suppliers. If the others are going to charge $6, it would be disastrous for one supplier to charge $8. (It would seem to be advantageous to charge $5, but that turns out to be disastrous also.) Each supplier must therefore work through the calculations of all the other suppliers, including their calculations of what he will do and their calculations of what he will expect them to do, in order to determine his optimum price and production level. Remember that in neoclassical economics we are not concerned with what people will actually do but with what perfectly rational people would do, so the method must be mathematical and deductive.

Von Neumann and Morgenstern formalized this problem in the usual mathematical fashion by reducing it to its simplest terms: two players, each with two alternatives, choosing simultaneously. Each choice constituted one play of the game. Von Neumann and Morgenstern cut through the infinite regress of calculation by looking for equilibrium outcomes, that is, outcomes in which neither player could improve his payoff by choosing again.

Their initial problem, therefore, was to prove that any 2×2 game had an equilibrium solution, and to deduce the decision rules that a rational player would use to find this solution. They do not describe the search process that they went through to find the proof and the decision rule, but presumably they went through the kind of search described by George Polya in his *How to Solve It* (1945).

Their discoveries include the mixed strategy and the minimax rule. They proved that for any zero-sum game, that is a game in which A's winning exactly equal B's losses, there is always an equilibrium outcome. However, in many cases this outcome results from both players choosing a mixed strategy. A mixed strategy consists of choosing strategy 1 with probability p and strategy 2 with probability $1-p$. For example (Luce and Raiffa, 1957, pp. 68–74), if the payoffs to A are

	B1	B2
A1	3	1
A2	2	4

and the payoffs to B are the equivalent negative number, neither strategy yields an optimum payoff for either player. Thus if A consistently chooses 1, his payoff is 1, because B will catch on and play 2; and if A chooses 2 his payoff is 2 for the same reason. But there is a mixed strategy with an expected value of 2 1/2 for A. Similarly, pure strategies yield losses of 3 and 4 for B, while a mixed strategy holds the loss to 2 1/2. The minimax rule enables both A and B to find the optimum strategy.

The first stage in the development of game theory beyond von Neumann and Morgenstern was to extend their proofs to non-zero-sum games and games with uncertain payoffs (games against nature). This stage was purely mathematical and lasted about ten years. It produced several paradoxes and puzzles that made the concept of rational choice problematic. For example, in games against nature the minimax rule didn't work, and three other suggested decision rules did not work either (Milnor, 1954, RAND funding). Indeed, there was no satisfactory decision rule, so that the concept of rational choice in such situations had no clear meaning. In Hero and Leader there are two equilibria, neither of them minimax, and the minimax procedure does not produce any mixed-strategy equilibrium (Luce and Raiffa, 1957, ONR funding, pp. 89–93). Indeed, the minimax strategy produces an inferior payoff.

And worse, in Prisoner's Dilemma the minimax rule does produce an equilibrium outcome, but the payoffs are obviously inferior to a different outcome for both players. This means that "rational" choice produces a nonoptimum outcome, a self-contradictory assertion. There is apparently no rational way to get to the joint optimum outcome, just as in Hero and Leader there seems to be no rational way to choose between the two equilibria. These paradoxes are important because the four above games seem to model many common social and political situations.

The discovery of these mathematical paradoxes led directly into the second stage of game research about 1954. If pure mathematics had produced paradoxes, then perhaps empirical research would find solutions. People started to set up gaming experiments to see whether the players would solve the dilemma or find a good decision rule. Meanwhile, the mathematical thinkers continued their work, devising new decision rules and solutions and gradually systematizing the various games (for example, Shubik, 1959; Anatol Rapoport, 1967; Rapoport and Guyer, 1966).

Several types of game experiments may be distinguished (Goldhamer and Speier, 1959, RAND funding; Rapoport and Orwant, 1962). First, experiments with zero-sum games tested the hypothesis that players would use the minimax rule, that is, that players were $N + M$-rational at equilibrium. This was a Stegmüller-type hypothesis. Second, experiments with the dilemma games explored how players would deal with the dilemma (for example, Scodel et al., 1959; Edwards, 1961), and then searched for variables that would correlate with the various outcomes (for example, Morton Deutsch, 1966; Deutsch and Krauss, 1962). Here the basic aim was to search for solutions to common social and political dilemmas, solutions the mathematicians had been unable to find. Third, there were exploratory experiments with n-person and other complex games. "The interest in such experiments is not primarily to test specific mathematical models (since the extant mathematical models make hardly any specific predictions). Rather, the interest is akin to that of the naturalist who is beginning to explore a new area" (Rapoport and Orwant, 1962, p. 292). Some of the experiments, such as Vinacke and Arkoff (1957), began with the intent of testing specific coalition predictions, but then focused on new phenomena that unexpectedly appeared, such as trust (Lieberman, 1964), sex differences (Vinacke, 1959), and coalitions against the experimenter (Riker, 1962, pp. 50–51).

Fourth, some gaming experiments simulated international political situations (Guetzkow, 1959; Schelling, 1961). The purpose here was to use both game models and experimental results to produce insights into international bargaining and conflict. The game model was used to represent the underlying structure of the situation, and the simulation produced suggestions as to how diplomats might act in such a situation, in comparison to how they actually did act.

Note that the search process in these experiments varied according to the questions provided by the theory. A specific question: Do they use the minimax rule? focused on whether a specific outcome appeared, and could be answered by yes or no. A more general question: How do they solve the dilemma? involved comparing a process of solution over many plays with the mathematical constraints of the game. An exploratory question: What happens in such games? required variations in the experimental setup, plus a willingness to pick up and explore new phenomena as they appeared.

Of the research programs that got started in this second, experimental stage, I shall concentrate on programs in international politics. There were two, based on two different concerns.

One concern was about presumed Soviet aggressiveness, and the problem was: "How can we counter Soviet aggressive moves without war?" This program centered at the RAND Corporation and included Ellsberg, Iklé, Helmer, and Wohlstetter among others, and also Schelling, who spent a year at RAND (1960, p. vi). The nature of Soviet aggressiveness defined the problem. The Soviets *had to know* that the territory they were trying to grab, such as West Berlin, did not belong to them. Therefore they were testing our resolve, our willingness to risk war to protect our property against brazen thievery. But the property itself was not worth atomic war to them; therefore they were bluffing. These characteristics showed that the appropriate formal model was Chicken. Accordingly, the research program consisted of (1) studying the formal characteristics of Chicken, (2) applying the model to some situation, (3) interpreting the situation by means of the game, and (4) complicating the game model to fit the situation.

The third step, interpreting the situation as Chicken, required a study of U.S.-Soviet diplomatic moves in the 1950s, the Soviets trying to grab something of ours and the United States trying to protect it or perhaps foolishly letting it be stolen. The fourth step, complicating the model, involved finding tactics that could produce a win for the United States. This step continued the mathematicians' early interest in finding winning strategies, except that now empirical situations were used heuristically to suggest tactics. The result was articles and books by the above authors on Chicken dynamics and tactics.

A second, opposite concern was to prevent nuclear war. The problem was: What strategies can the United States use to prevent U.S.-Soviet conflicts from degenerating into war as in 1914? Obviously, both sides preferred peace through some kind of compromise resolution of conflicts to war; but mutual suspicion might lead each side to strengthen its defenses in ways that the other side might mistakenly regard as aggressive, until one side because convinced that the other was planning war, and might attack to protect itself. The appropriate model therefore was Prisoner's Dilemma or sometimes Leader (Deutsch and Krauss, 1962), and the research question was; How do they solve the dilemma and learn to cooperate?

This research program proceeded through experiments. The search process was similar to that described by Latour (1981a) for his biology lab: vary one plausible variable at a time until the desired solution appeared, then continue the variations to see what variables would counteract or confirm the solution (Rapoport and Chammah, 1965, NIH funding; Morton Deutsch, 1966, 1973, NSF funding). Other researchers used a formal search process, looking for new models that would resolve the dilemma. The result was the supergame (Amnon Rapoport, 1967) and the metagame (Howard, 1971).

No testing of any kind occurred in the RAND program—there was indeed nothing to test—though the formal tactics and models constructed were regarded as signs of success. The only testing that occurred in the second program was to try one experimental variable after another until one worked. Nor apparently did members of either program contribute to the other, though they did meet in February 1964, argued, and knew each other's work (Archibald, 1966). Their social concerns were too different.

The third stage of research got under way in the mid-1960s. Several research groups began to study historical cases of diplomatic crises in detail (George et al., 1971, 1974; Snyder et al., 1977; Lebow, 1981). The questions they asked were: How frequently do the games studied in the second stage—Chicken, PD, and Leader—actually occur in international politics? What empirical characteristics go with each game? Specifically, in Chicken games are Schelling's tactics used, or different tactics? In Prisoner's Dilemma, does Rapoport's solution appear or do the players find a different solution? Are the supergame and the metagame useful in clarifying the situation? Finally, what are good tactics in such games? In what sort of game does deterrence work? There were also quantitative studies of much the same questions, such as Leng and Wheeler (1979), which continue to appear.

Since this stage of research built on the two opposite research programs of the second stage, we could have an instance of Churchman's Hegelian inquirer. The difference is that in the Hegelian inquirer the two opposed positions argue and criticize, while in game research they ignored each other. Their concerns were too different.

The search process took a still different form in third-stage research. Instead of studying one model such as Chicken, the basic question always was: What game model best fits this case? Answering this question involved identifying each component of a game in the case and comparing alternate games on specific points to see which gave the best fit. Since there are seventy-eight possible 2 × 2 games, one of them was bound to fit. The result was a Stegmüller-type hypothesis, such as: The 1958 Berlin crisis was a PD game. The hypotheses were tested in intensive group discussion in which the supporter of the hypothesis had to defend his interpretation of the historical events, and opponents tried to fit an alternate model by interpreting the events differently. In other words, this testing process was hermeneutic, based on memoirs and archives and historians' reports. It also included much unexpected conflict over the interpretation of cases. Snyder had inadvertently set up an adversary model or Hegelian inquirer.

Once the S-theses for each crisis were agreed on, sometimes by negotiation and compromise, the original questions could be answered: How often do Chicken and PD games occur? Rarely. When they occur, are the Schelling and Rapoport tactics used to solve the dilemma? Not exactly. Are the supergame and metagame useful? Not in these cases. When does deterrence work? Answer: in very special situations (George et al., 1971). Is anything left of second-stage deterrence theory? Very little; its errors and omissions are numerous (Jervis, 1979, reviewing the third-stage case studies).

Another development at this stage was the construction of supplementary formal models. The need for such models was brought out by finding persistent discrepancies between cases and models. For example, in case after case the researchers found that one characteristic of a game, known payoffs, was missing in the case. The next step was to construct a cybernetic model of the process by which players discovered, and changed, payoffs. Other researchers found payoffs that were known, but only probabilistically, and constructed models that included uncertain payoffs.

Thus, in the third stage of game theory, some testing did occur. However, it was Stegmüller-type testing, not that discussed by logical empiricists, Popper, Agassi, Lakatos, or even Churchman. Moreover, the testing was incidental to the construction of new models and the search for the empirical relevance of old models.

The fourth stage, beginning about 1980, returned to the primarily formal approach of the first stage. The researchers used the interpreted case materials of the third stage heuristically to suggest new formal models that solved some of the puzzles of the first stage. The main recent example is the Brams-Wittman theory of moves (1981; Zagare, 1987, pp. 42–52; Kugler and Zagare, 1987). This theory uses game trees in conjunction with 2×2 matrices. Some researchers in the third stage regarded game trees as too elementary to be useful, somewhat like counting on one's fingers for arithmetic, but Brams and Wittman derived some new theorems from those simple trees. Another result was the demonstration that the ideal deterrence game was Prisoner's Dilemma, not Chicken; the deterrence theorists of the second stage, except Wohlstetter, were barking up the wrong model (Zagare, 1987, chap. 2). This error of the deterrence theorists has important consequences for their theory, especially as regards escalation, which is disastrous in Prisoner's Dilemma. Some theorist should soon point this out, and Kugler probably will. The theory of moves also has been worked out for a larger subset of the seventy-eight possible games.

Nigel Howard's "metagame" has also recently returned in the form of a computer program code-named CONAN, which searches game trees for equilibrium outcomes. The game trees are based on empirical case studies.

There are several indicators of progress in this history. First, the number of 2×2 games studied has expanded from two or three in the late 1950s to about ten in the early 1970s to about twenty in the 1980s. Second, the mathematical and empirical characteristics of the four central games have been explored more and more thoroughly, including the solution of one or two early puzzles and the correction of one or two early errors. Third, a variety of supplementary models such as the supergame and the expanded game have been invented and studied and applied empirically. Fourth, "tacit knowledge" of how to apply a model to a case has accumulated, enough to make the applications and theoretical interpretations of the 1950s look terribly crude. Fifth, the historical understanding of international diplomatic and crisis behavior has been enriched by game thinking and case studies.

We turn next to an example from the experimental literature, where lots of hypothesis testing is claimed to occur. The example is a research program within the larger program of behaviorism in psychology, as reported by Travis (1981). This example comes from the middle to late stages of behaviorism, when the basic theory had already been established and attention had shifted to working out further implications and applications. Also in this case no social interests are in evidence.

The program began with experiments reported by Thompson and McConnell in 1955. They believed basic Skinnerian learning theory to be already established, and wished to extend the theory a bit. The theory says that when an unconditioned stimulus (UCS) is paired with a neutral event a number of times, the response (R) to UCS becomes associated with the neutral event. That is, R will occur shortly after the neutral event, even when UCS does not occur. In other words, the neutral event becomes a conditioned stimulus (CS) for R. The first sequence, CS—UCS—R, is replaced by a second sequence, CS—R.

Thompson and McConnell hypothesized that such conditioning consisted of some change in the nervous system. The change must consist of new connections between nerves excited by CS, and nerves that produced R. But since synaptic connections involve the presence of certain chemicals at the synapses, the changes must be chemical.

From this hypothesis Thompson and McConnell deduced the rather flimsy prediction that if an untrained animal would eat the brain and hence the learning chemicals of a trained animal, the chemicals would go right to the untrained brain and make a connection between CS and R in the new animal. Popper would have called that a bold prediction and praised it. To test this prediction they had to find a cannibalistic animal, and they found flatworms, which wiggle aimlessly along the bottom of a pond and eat anything they bump into.

The experimental task then was to condition a flatworm under controlled conditions, then grind it up and feed the head (brain) or tail (control) half to a new flatworm, then see whether the meal had conditioned the new worm. The first step, conditioning a flatworm, added nothing to behaviorist theory; it was merely preparatory.

They set up a twelve-inch plastic trough, semicircular in cross section, with electrodes on each end, filled with familiar pond water. As the worm crawled along the bottom a light (CS) went on, then 2 seconds later a shock (UCS) caused the poor worm to scrunch up in pain and wiggle a bit (R). If the worm regularly scrunched up as soon as the light went on, even without the shock, it had been conditioned. Then it got ground up and fed to the next worm.

There were three control groups. (1) Some lucky worms got to crawl back and forth all day without getting any shocks; the number of times they scrunched up from other troubles like upset stomach provided a statistical baseline for measuring additional scrunchings by shocked animals. (2) Some animals got lights (CS) only (sensitization control group). This controlled for the possibility that the CS itself would eventually get annoying enough to produce R. (3) Some animals got both UCS and CS but unconnected in time; this controlled for the possibility that they were scrunching up out of general annoyance with the whole setup (pseudo-conditioning). The R rate of the test animals after CS had to be significantly higher than the R rate of the three control groups.

Thompson and McConnell reported in 1956 that they had produced learning, the first step in their program. In 1961 McConnell et al. reported that they had also produced learning by feeding *either* head or tail half of conditioned worms to unconditioned worms. This second claim aroused some interest.

Other experimenters disputed the first claim, asserting that the worm runner group had produced only sensitization (Halas et al., 1961). Halas et al. used a brighter light without an UCS and recorded some wiggling; they inferred that a light was a weak UCS that could eventually produce R all by itself. McConnell et al. replied that the Halas experiments were not true replications. They had massed trials, giving the poor worms no rest, and in other ways had bothered the worms enough to make them wiggle around impatiently. They argued that a true replication would have to proceed exactly like the original experiment.

But what does "exactly" mean? Does it mean the same time of day, phase of the moon, planetary positions, magnetic field, floor of a building? It means that the interferences with learning have to be removed—tiredness, distraction, illness, excessive hunger, and so on. It also means that the facilitating conditions for learning have to be present—a real UCS, a real CS, a close enough pairing in time of UCS and CS, the right amount of hunger, pond water temperature, and so on. But since flatworms, unlike rats, had not yet been used in learning experiments, the facilitating and interfering conditions were not yet known.

This means that a search for the conditions to be controlled was an essential part of the test replication process. That is, the experimenters had to discover all the factors that affected flatworm learning, in order to control them. If the R rate was too low in some experiment, this could mean that another interfering factor had been discovered; and a high R rate would suggest the presence of a new facilitating condition. These possibilities could be tested by removing or controlling some suspected interference and comparing the new R rate with the old. During the four hundred or so experiments conducted up to 1976, McConnell's group noted some seventy factors that supposedly influenced planarian behavior. They included of course age and size of worms, number of trials per day (as with rats), but also the strength, color, and duration of the light, parameters of the shock, barometric pressure, time of day and feeding schedule, phase of the moon. Flatworms are very sensitive creatures.

For example, during the search for interferences McConnell suspected that trained worms might leave some learning chemicals behind in the slime that worms, like snails, deposit. Then the next worm might slurp up these chemicals and learn before it was supposed to. So he tried washing out the trough after each worm. Unexpectedly, the R rate increased. Other experimenters suggested that the clean, hard plastic was scratching the sensitive stomachs of the poor worms, causing them to scrunch up in pain. This idea was tested by letting a new, naive worm slime up the trough before each experiment. Sure enough, the worms now scrunched at the proper rate.

This in turn means that the rule to replicate exactly is a mistake. A replication is a test; but it is also part of a larger search and discovery process. *We cannot test one hypothesis* about flatworms, or students, or therapy patients, or small groups, until we have learned many things about the interacting factors affecting their behavior in an experimental situation. The tests for each of these factors in turn depend on knowing something about the others. Until we have accumulated some plausible knowledge about many contextual factors, we cannot even specify what an exact replication is. Lester Thurow has made the same point for econometrics (1983, pp. 106–08). Recent dream research illustrates the same problem (Haskell, 1986).

For testing, a replication should be the same; but for search it should be different. Both are necessary. In the early stages of a project, sameness is not even possible, or it occurs by accident; later, both search and testing can be more systematic. In the early stages, failure to get the expected results is not a falsification but a step in the discovery of some limiting or interfering factor (Brinberg and McGrath, 1985, p. 127) or a sign of experimenter error (H. Collins, 1985, pp. 30–33, chap. 5). Falsification, in the later stages, consists of finding that some other combination of factors was producing the predicted outcome.

The end result of such a research program is not a single generalization but a cluster of generalizations. Some state the limits of validity of a major generalization; others state facilitating or interfering factors. Some state conditions for variations in a process; others describe the variations (Brinberg and McGrath, 1985, pp. 116–27). One of these generalizations can be singled out in publications as the central one—for instance, "Flatworms can be conditioned to respond to a light." In that case, the other knowledge, such as "Flatworms respond to barometric pressure" is treated as tacit or background knowledge, part of the experimenter's know-how. Or a cluster of mutually limiting or facilitating factors can be described in a model or theory about how flatworms behave.

In practice, experimenters have assumed background knowledge of human beings in order to pick out factors to be controlled. Thus we assume that college sophomores are not affected by phases of the moon, so it is not necessary to control for that. But flatworms are so affected! We used to assume that experimenters' knees, like the moon's phases, are irrelevant—until Rosenthal discovered that knees can convey the experimenter's expectations! (1966, p. 258). Since then, experimenters have had to be aware of kinesic communication in the experimental situation.

In any case, our experimental knowledge about a given area, whether flatworms or human learning or human neuroses, is built up gradually on a broad front involving the interrelation of many factors. It is not built up piece by piece by testing and confirming individual hypotheses without reference to "general" knowledge of the whole area. Truth comes in big packages, not little pieces.

COMMUNITIES

Next we take up the topic of how communities, traditions, or research programs maintain themselves. This is part of question 3, since a research program must be maintained if it is to produce its quota of truth. Maintenance includes the recruitment and retention of members, communication among members, and a willingness to use and build on each other's work to produce a shared truth. Several weaknesses and difficulties show up here, including the two from chapter 11, the problem of communication and the problem of finding progress in the succession of programs.

Communities exist at several levels. At the most general level, there is social science, which is not a community but an institution or institutions within society—universities, research institutes, funding agencies, R & D departments, and so on. Second, there are disciplines like sociology, which are the Mertonian communities. Disciplines are unified by a weak government and by socialization structures (sociology departments), and indeed have all four AGIL subsystems (see figure 2, p. 347). Third, there are the Kuhnian communities within or across disciplines, like the symbolic interactionists and the functionalists. Each of these is unified by Kuhn's "disciplinary matrix" or Lakatos's "research program" or Gadamer's "tradition." Fourth, most Kuhnian communities contain schools or "invisible colleges" or Claxton's "islands in the ocean," networks of researchers who share a more specific dialect and disciplinary matrix and who communicate frequently and build on each other's work. The Mertonian functionalists are a school, as were the Almond-Apter functionalists, the Luhmann functionalists, and the British anthropological functionalists; also the Iowa and Chicago schools in symbolic interactionism; and in AI, the Stanford, Carnegie Mellon, Yale, MIT schools, one or more British schools, and probably others. The schools or colleges or communication networks do not have sharp boundaries; they are clusters of intensive communication surrounded by many weaker communication links, including links to others schools within a tradition, plus silent followers. Some of the links are to schools in other disciplines; and indeed Kuhnian communities can maintain communication links across disciplines and develop a partly unified research program, like the cognitive psychologists, AI people, cognitive anthropologists, and structural linguists. In this case the quasi-research program, quasi-discipline is called "cognitive science."

One would suppose that communication would not be a problem within a school or network; there is a shared language, fairly cooperative work, and a shared truth. Nor should it be much of a problem within the Kuhnian communities, since there is still a shared language with slightly different dialects, a shared tradition, and shared disciplinary matrix. The problem would presumably occur across Kuhnian communities. Is there communication and shared research activity within a discipline or other large grouping, and if so, what maintains it?

We consider the answers of three groups of sociologists from chapters 6 and 7: the Mertonians, the externalist sociologists like Mannheim and the Edinburgh people, and the microsociologists. We will begin with the Mertonian-anti-Mertonian consensus and dissensus. Here we are fortunate in having a well-developed theory of scientific communities, the fruit of some forty years of development. The Mertonian truth still lives, as part of a still active community of interpretation in Gadamer's and Josiah Royce's sense. When that community will have decayed, fragmented, or disappeared in fifteen years, its truth will have died and become unusable. That is, it will have been rigidified, reduced by later theorists to a few seemingly dogmatic doctrines whose context has been forgotten, a few concepts and categories and classifications of no evident purpose, and many superseded empirical studies. Its descendants, however, will live on.

The Mertonians describe three sources of community maintenance: norms, government (G function), and socialization (L function).

The Mertonian norms of science maintain conflict within unity, dissensus within consensus. Consider the following four pairs of norms and counternorms:

WE	THEY
Original achievement	Humble appreciation of others' achievement
Interestedness, commitment to self-promotion	Disinterestedness, impersonality, self-skepticism
Secrecy, possessiveness about one's work	Communism, sharing ideas
Value commitment	Value neutrality

In this table, the first column applies to oneself and provides the standards that *we* have to follow in research. The second column applies to others (and in principle to oneself as well) and provides the standards that permit achievements to be accepted by others and diffused throughout the community.

Original achievement means publishing results that other people will accept as new and important and will use in their own thinking and research. Merton has emphasized that subsidiary norms are involved here governing the means for achievement, such as no plagiarism, no data massaging, no dishonest reporting of data and research techniques; each of these forbidden means is a tempting shortcut to original achievement, but the result is not objective knowledge and so does not achieve the goal of the community. The implication is that each of these means is used more or less frequently and covered up, and one tactic in competition is to uncover the suspected dishonesty of others.

The other three norms, and others, are subsidiary to original achievement. *Interestedness* means being committed to one's own ideas, contacts, techniques, because these are the materials one is using to achieve results. Results are usually not easy to achieve, and to get them quickly one must make the most of one's materials, tinkering, pushing, adjusting, reinterpreting, but mostly staying within the rules. *Secrecy* prevents others from stealing one's ideas and getting credit for them; it is comparable to locking one's doors at night. *Value commitment* means being ideologically involved in one's research, such as diagnosing a social problem to facilitate its solution, sympathetically describing the life style of deviants, expounding the social benefits of free markets, or promoting the good society that will result from proper use of conditioning techniques. Such commitment provides further urgency to research, inducing one to search for the idea or technique or data adjustment that will get the results.

By itself, this set of norms encourages competition and dissensus; it produces a collection of quarreling egotists (individuals or schools), each proclaiming the greatness of his own achievement and disparaging or ignoring everyone else except those who use his ideas. Such an anomy would be futile for individuals because they get no recognition and reward for achievement, and for science since little cumulation of knowledge would result.

According to Staats (1983), this is the present situation in psychology. Everyone is busy developing his own theory, and ignores all other theories including those very similar to his own. Each theorist invents a unique terminology and avoids any attempt to translate his terms into those of other theories (chap. 6). He cites Thorndike, Watson, Skinner, and Hull as examples. The result is fads, research topics like group cohesion that get experimented on vigorously for ten or twenty years by many self-isolating theorists and then die out without yielding any cumulative knowledge (chap. 4). From Staats's examples (chap. 6 and *passim*), we conclude that what mainly bothers him is others' failure to cite his work and acknowledge his priority in achievement.

Similarly, Denzin (1970, p. 40) cites a study of sociology journals that finds that between 1954 and 1965 some 2,080 scales and indices were described and used. Of these, forty-seven were used more than five times.

The second set of norms is supposed to prevent this cacophony by encouraging people to be humble, tolerant, and unbiased in considering others' publications. In practice, this means that each researcher wants *others* to be humble, tolerant, and unbiased in evaluating *his* achievements. The implication is that this set of norms is less likely to be followed than the first set, if at all, and therefore that government and socialization must emphasize and strengthen this second set. In game terms, the situation is an n-person Prisoner's Dilemma. Of course, the second set by itself would not achieve the goal of science either; if everybody were humble, tolerant, and unbiased they would all read each other's publications with enthusiasm and agreement but there would be little original achievement; it would not be necessary. That would be a unity, not a community.

Government accordingly has two basic system-maintenance functions: supporting the second set of norms, and providing rewards for achievement to keep the first set operative. These two functions require expressive (emotional) and instrumental (task specialist) leadership in Parsons and Bales's (1955) sense. Expressive leadership (GL function) consists in proclaiming the norms of universalism, communism, disinterestedness, humility, and value neutrality—for example, in articles by Merton, in public statements by the scientific elite, and in empirical studies by Merton's students. These expressive statements proclaim that true scientists are humble and so forth, single out examples of humility for praise, and thereby touch the conscience of scientists.

Instrumental leadership is identical with Parsons's GA function, providing investment capital. Capital here consists of research grants, publication in prestige journals, and various awards at conventions, such as control of a convention session. These rewards simultaneously encourage individual achievement and direct the community's resources to their most promising uses.

The institutions of government exist at the discipline level, not in the Kuhnian communities and research networks. They consist, instrumentally, of advisory committees at NSF, SSRC, and other funding agencies; the editorial boards of official disciplinary journals, such as the *AER*, *APSR*, *ASR*; and convention program committees. Expressively, they include the discipline's president and elder statesmen, who are expected to make ceremonial speeches about the norms of science.

Since government exists at the discipline level and research occurs at lower levels in schools and communication networks, government has a third, GI function of ensuring that different research programs (politically, interest groups) are represented on the various advisory bodies and convention program committees. In the 1970s there was much politicking about the status of the Caucus for New Political Science within the American Political Science Association, the Union for Radical Political Economics within the American Economic Association, and the world system people in sociology, with fairly effective democratic outcomes.

My impression is that in political science government has been very weak in performing the first two functions. Expressively, the president tends to prefer summarizing the state of his own research area in the annual presidential address, rather than praising the norms of science. Instrumentally, the various Kuhnian communities have their own journals, so publication in the *APSR* is not much of an honor; and there are various funding agencies and sources. As a result, the discipline has little or no unity; the real communities are the research networks at the fourth level.

Does socialization internalize the norms in graduate students? I know of no Mertonian study of graduate students, so the question is unanswered. It is plausible to suppose that students learn that a good sociologist does not massage or fudge data too much, ought to read other sociologists' works in studying for comprehensive exams, and so forth.

I do find that graduate school produces a disciplinary identity in job-hunting students. Not having any disciplinary identity myself, I have again and again (Oops! small sample bias) been astounded by the depth and solidity of disciplinary identity in others, the confident "I'm a sociologist" expressed implicitly in speeches and conversation and in the polite treatment accorded visiting foreigners, nonsociologists; also in the urgent way they ask, "What are *you*?" People do not communicate the self-concept "I'm a causal modeler" or "I'm a public choicer" in at all the same way; they let you find that out yourself. A psychologist can shift from a behaviorist research program to a cognitivist program without becoming a different person.

However, disciplinary identity does not include the norm of humility; quite the reverse—people communicate the sense that their discipline is better than other disciplines. They are proud of their discipline. Does it maintain communication and even understanding within a discipline? Not much. New classical and Marxist economists can go to the same convention and perhaps feel a kinship as economists, but that does not induce them to discuss research problems, actually read each other's work, or even attend the same convention sessions. Nor would they understand each other's work if they did read it. Psychology is not one discipline but many: social, behavioral, educational, cognitive, clinical, developmental social, organizational. Staats (1983) writes of psychology; but his main concern and most numerous examples come from his own tradition, behaviorism. Apparently there is little communication even within behavioral psychology.

Note that disciplinary identity is a "masculine" identity in the sense of the feminist writers. It implies a clear separation of self and not-self, economist and noneconomist, and bases identity on one's work. A "feminine" or "connected" identity would be grounded more in close friends and colleagues and would not sharply distinguish self from others. Both kinds of identity occur in social scientists, often mixed.

It seems that neither disciplinary identity nor Mertonian norms maintain much shared research even in traditions, research programs, let alone whole disciplines. If researchers followed the norms and especially the second set, there would indeed be cumulative, shared knowledge, with no Matthew effects and fallacies of the latest word; but they don't. Shared knowledge occurs in schools and networks; but beyond that the norms remain an ought, not an is. Perhaps Randall Collins was right when he called early Mertonian sociology of science "neosaintly science"—an idealized account of a smooth-running, problem-free cumulative science.

We turn next to the microsociological perspective on communities and community structures, and especially to the work of Bourdieu and his followers. This perspective comes from the bottom, from the individual researcher, and thus supplements Merton's macro or community-oriented perspective.

The Bourdieu people recognize only the first set of norms in the above table, if indeed they can make sense of norms at all. They recognize *original achievement* not as an ought but as a must. The researcher must achieve to survive, and this "must" brings with it the need for secrecy, commitment to one's materials, sometimes a bit of trickery and rhetoric, and so on. The researcher is caught in the investment cycle: survival requires achievement, which requires a position and research funds, which requires achievement or at least promise of achievement, and so on back to graduate school. The force of the "must" comes from competition, for a job, for tenure, for research funds, for journal space. Nor can the researcher rest on past achievements, short of retirement; if he does so, the competition will move past him. Others' latest publications will be cited and his older ones will be gradually forgotten; he will not be drawn into new research projects but will find himself doing routine committee work; and new problems, techniques, data, disputes will occupy journal space and current research. In short, his accumulated symbolic capital will gradually lose its value. The analogy is with an inflationary economy, in which money must be immediately reinvested to maintain its value. Thus the Mertonian norm "To be a scientist, you ought to do some original research" becomes the Marxist imperative, "Accumulate! Accumulate!"

Bourdieu's theory does not contradict Merton's, however; it supplements it. The Bourdieu people are describing the A-system or economy of science, the part devoted to converting resources into symbolic capital. They show us a capitalist, free-enterprise economy, governed by market forces. There are multiple sources of investment capital, and anyone who can show promise of marketable achievement to a funding agency or publisher can get some resources and start producing. Some succeed in getting published and cited, others fail; those who succeed can continue, gradually establishing a reputation, regular readers, and reliable sources of capital. Those who fail can try again, but must eventually make a profit or lose out. The effect of market forces is presumably, by definition, to eliminate the inefficient and reward the efficient with more capital; in the aggregate, we observe the Matthew effect, the accumulation and centralization of capital in a few leaders like Merton. The Mertonians would add that this market is not perfectly or imperfectly competitive; it is highly controlled. Control is exercised by the elites who control a discipline's investment capital—research funds, journal space, and convention programs (GA function). For example, the Columbia Bureau of Applied Social Research was long controlled by Lazarsfeld and Merton; in the 1950s SSRC was dominated by behavioralists and functionalists; Dean Rusk was head of Rockefeller in the 1950s and McGeorge Bundy was head of Ford in the late 1960s. In the early 1950s RAND scouts were out looking for Ph.D.s to do systems analysis on topics selected by RAND, at good pay. In the journals Austin Ranney and then Nelson Polsby were long-term managing editors of the *APSR*; and so on.

The disciplinary elites try to allocate the discipline's capital to the most promising and socially desirable research areas, just as banks and corporate boards do in the larger economy. In doing so, the elites determine what will count as mainstream social science, and how much off-beat or extremist research will be encouraged. Standing behind the elite are the corporate and government funders with their own research priorities, priorities which they push in negotiations with the elites on their boards.

This treatment of the A-system of science explains its dynamics, while the approach through norms and counternorms focuses our attention on the community-anomy dimension. The normative approach says that a scientific community exists *insofar as* its members share the second set of norms—humility, self-skepticism, tolerance, impartiality, etcetera. It also says that such a community maintains itself *if* it can get new members to internalize these values. However, community self-maintenance remains an "ought" which is scarcely implemented by socialization and government. Competition for capital is a "must." The actual dynamics, therefore, consist of the circulation and accumulation of capital.

The dynamics of a free-enterprise economy derive from individual rationality, that is, from researchers' decisions on what research is most likely to be published and cited. Shifts in perceived opportunities, such as new foundation programs, will produce rapid and massive shifts of research and publication in the direction of those opportunities, plus intense competition, as researchers move to exploit them. As the opportunities get exploited, researchers search for, and move to, other opportunities.

The result is the fluctuating process discussed in chapter 11 in the section on Feyerabend, and in chapter 7 under the heading "scientific communities." This process produces exponential growth and gradually increasing decline among a plurality of Kuhnian communities within each discipline, plus a succession of "new paradigms" that never get off the ground. What it does not produce is cumulative, shared knowledge. In a free-enterprise economy, each producer must try to individualize his product to attract and hold customers. The customers, who are also competitors (this is the Althusserian specificity of the scientific field according to Bourdieu), can adopt ideas and techniques from their suppliers, but then try to give them a new wrinkle, a new trademark. Thus each idea or technique develops many variants over time. The result is Staats's and Denzin's crisis of disunity—that is, imperfect, monopolistic competition.

According to Bergin and Strupp (1970), the same situation exists in psychotherapy, where new therapies proliferate, clinicians and experimenters ignore each other's knowledge, and different therapies ignore each other. "To characterize the field as chaotic is hardly an exaggeration" (p. 21).

Figure 2 summarizes the discussion of the structures of science up to here.

We return now to the macro perspective, this time bringing in an external factor, the ideological commitments of researchers. The Bourdieu people describe a research process that is carried on by Ravetz's pure professionals, interested only in getting results and publishing. They have no substantive interests that prevent them from getting involved in

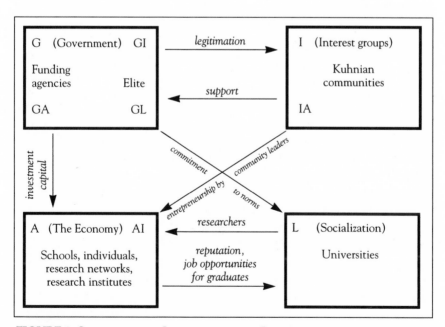

FIGURE 2. STRUCTURES AND INTERCHANGES OF A DISCIPLINE

whatever topic is hot and using the latest technique to study it. Nor do they care about truth; or rather, they care only about this year's truths and ignore the outdated opinions of the past. One may call their work "alienated" in the sense that they care more about the extrinsic payoffs— publication, grants, promotion—than the subject they are researching. This is the picture about which Latour comments, "If that's science, we don't want it." Katouzian (1980, chap. 5) gives a good account of the dangers of exaggerated professionalism.

But the picture is one-sided. It leaves out the real interests that most scientists have and that motivate their research. Concerned social scientists are not primarily interested in their own original achievement; they wish rather to promote and preserve a shared truth relevant to their concern. Thus the second set of Mertonian norms is more binding on them than the first set, except for *value commitment* from the first set. That is, a shared truth excludes secrecy and commitment to one's private research materials; one wishes rather to share ideas and materials from the start. The shared concern maintains a community more effectively than either Mertonian norms or disciplinary socialization. Concerned researchers will not shift their research to join the latest research program or use the latest techniques, but will continue exploring the areas relevant to their concerns. Instead of publishing in the main disciplinary journals, they will start their own journals, such as *Economic Development and Cultural Change* for the ex-colonial country research program. If the funding agencies decline to fund research on how to promote socialist revolution, they will seek other funds or do without. Nor are they interested only in the latest findings; quite the contrary, they try to preserve and extend the achievements of their tradition and even return to the ancient founders to recover their wisdom, the wisdom of Marx, Veblen, Keynes. The result is an element of stability that counteracts the restless changes of the professionals.

For example, the economics department at the University of Chicago lived through the time of the Keynesian revolution without changing a word in its courses or research projects, at a time when Harvard, MIT, Yale, Illinois, and Pennsylvania were shifting rapidly or involved in turmoil. I never heard the name Keynes mentioned in any of my undergraduate and graduate courses, let alone any Keynesian ideas or followers of Keynes. Our price theory text was Stigler, not Samuelson. Oskar Lange or Paul Douglas might have discussed Keynes, but they had left long before my time and had not been replaced. Nor did I get the vaguest notion of what or who institutional economics was, even though I took a course entitled "Neoclassical versus Institutional Economics." Schumpeter was mentioned just once, as the opposing view; I had to go to the library to find out about Schumpeter. In other words, the Chicago free-market vision prevented them from joining the latest Keynesian fad. The effect of this encapsulation was to preserve a research tradition out of which monetarist theory could emerge to enrich (?) economic theory.

My impression is that visions and interests have been strongest in economics and weakest in psychology where, conversely, professionalization has been strongest. However, according to Colander and Klamer (1987), professionalism is now strongly inculcated in economics graduate students at several leading U.S. universities. The students come to graduate school with an interest in public policy, but learn that skill in mathematical puzzle solving is what counts toward a career. "There was a strong sense that economics was a game and that . . . devising relevant models that demonstrated a deep understanding of institutions would have a lower payoff than devising models that were analytically neat" (p. 100). Apparently the social concerns have become latent or implicit as concern with mathematical dexterity has increased. In contrast, anthropology has exhibited a more moderate level of professionalization, combined with strong social concerns: the Marxist world system theory was started by specialists in African cultures, and social concerns are obvious in late Malinowski, Redfield, Mead, Gluckman, Eric Wolf, our Fox project director and hero Sol Tax, and many others.

Social concerns, like professionalism, can become too strong for scientific integrity. That point is reached when the scientist's vision, of the free market or the self-managing society or responsible democratic government is treated as the essence of social reality. All interferences or blemishes are temporary accidents. The scientist's task them is to reveal this essence to all, and to encourage the removal of the interferences.

The signs that this has happened include: (1) The theory is presented in heavily rhetorical terms (cf. D. McClosky, 1983) and associated with values like freedom, democracy, starvation, torture, communism, always vaguely defined. (2) The reader's attention is focused forcefully on certain phenomena and quietly away from other phenomena. (3) The adjustment and selection of data that we all practice is deliberately extended to create a desired effect. Interpretation and explanation are connected by availability bias to the propagandist's focus of concern: the communists are behind it, the Fed did it, rent control or federal regulation did it, the welfare program did it. (4) Vivid examples are presented, out of context. The vivid examples that occur to me are naturally all conservative: Jean E. Smith, *The Defense of Berlin* (1963); Klaus P. Schultz, *Berlin Zwischen Freiheit und Diktatur* (1963); James L. Payne, *The American Threat* (1970); Richard McKenzie, *Fugitive Industry* (1984); here the data are slanted by attributing all of a company's labor force to the state in which its headquarters are located, not where production occurs, and the con-clusion is that deindustrialization is a myth. And, McKenzie adds, all those laid-off workers were already compensated in advance for the risk of unemployment by higher wages (1984, p. 87; the market knows all); Milton Friedman's news magazine columns, reprinted as *Dollars and Defi-cits* (1968) and later volumes; *Free to Choose* (1980); and Charles Mur-ray's *Losing Ground* (1984). Here the vivid example is a fairy tale about a young Horatio Alger couple living in a truly free-enterprise economy where hard work as a waitress or dry cleaning helper will propel one up the ladder of success (pp. 156–62, 176–77). The welfare program, Mur-ray argues, has ruined all that (availability bias once again). Murray's data charts are pure propaganda—for example, his index of "latent pov-erty" is designed to show that the unemployed would have found *some* kind of work if welfare had not been available to make them lazy.

We have been witnessing the degeneration of a good portion of eco-nomics into propaganda and even pseudo-science in recent years. The Austrian School, deriving from von Mises and Hayek, have provided some of the impetus in this direction. The concern in this case has been to stop the descent into serfdom by preaching the virtues of the free market. The focus is on the ideal market, not on actual imperfect mar-kets, and the assumption is that the ideal automatically appears as govern-ment hindrances are removed. The ideal is the essence of the real. Similarly, von Mises proved long ago that individual rational choice is an a priori truth, so no empirical investigations into actual choices are necessary. Instead, it is necessary to deduce the characteristics and conse-quences of individual rational choice, and to show the bad consequences of interfering with the market. Empirical materials are used only as illus-tration; there is indeed nothing to test, since the basics of the theory are true a priori. Vision/fantasy and reality coincide. For another example, consider the Laffer curve, another a priori fantasy. To be sure, good ideas and illuminating empirical work can be built even on this rotten founda-tion, as Popper reminds us.

Social science exists between two opposite kinds of degeneration, a value-free professionalism that lives only for publications that show off the latest techniques and concepts, and a deep social concern that uses science for propaganda. A healthy science maintains some social interests and some connection to political actors, plus personal interests and a pure desire to know, but also maintains some political detachment and some connections with research groups having different but compatible interests. It also pays some minimum respect to the tenure-publication-convention rat race without becoming a complete society of Grant Swingers.

Klamer's conversations with economists (1984) provide examples of these two kinds of degeneration, plus the healthier middle ground. For professionalism, Robert Townsend: "New classical economics means a modeling strategy which allows for a variety of results; . . . it is, ideally, writing down the model at the level of the tastes or preferences of the decision-makers, the technology available, whatever wealth or endowment decision-makers have, and then imposing some additional structure" (Klamer, 1984, p. 85). "These models can be solved now because we know so much more about dynamic programming and we know a lot about statistical decision theory" (p. 83). "I always wish that I had taken more math" (p. 82). Townsend's math is the kind used in the latest economics program of the mid-1970s, rational expectations theory. For propaganda: "I believe that Friedman had a crusade that he was pushing all over the world, not just in the profession. He saw the big picture. . . . He didn't really want to be bothered by these little technical problems" (p. 106). "As far as Friedman's arguments are concerned, I always thought that he sang two tunes. In the economics profession, he was absolutely reasonable . . . but in writing for *Newsweek*, he argued a hard monetarism. . . . In hard monetarism, velocity is constant and *nothing* but the money supply matters for nominal GNP" (p. 135).

The middle ground, James Tobin: "A neo-Keynesian seems to be more concerned about employment, jobs, and producing goods than people who have a great faith in market processes. [Neo-Keynesians] think that demand management policy can assist the economy to stay close to its equilibrium track" (p. 101). Referring to Lucas, a new classical economist: "I criticized him but also praised him. I really thought that it was a neat piece of theory and very interesting. . . . Rational expectations is an innovation in model building. It exposes the problem in other models. . . . Once you assume rational expectations, there are all kinds of technical problems. I, personally, do not find them interesting. I might, if I took the time to go into them . . . . I understand, though, why it is exciting for young people in the profession. It is challenging; it provides new mathematical problems" (pp. 106–08).

A radical social science is always pulled in these two opposite directions. On the one hand there is a desire to be accepted as a true professional; this leads one to demonstrate technical expertise, publish in the "reputable" journals, use the latest citations and techniques such as Okishio's theorem, demonstrate bourgeois respectability. But there is also a very justified fear of getting accepted into the system and becoming another aimless critical thinker, cut off from the vision and the social movement that justifies one's work. David Perry (1984) has especially emphasized the danger of losing contact with current proletarian social movements, and consequently getting lost in theoretical and technical abstractions. Studying the demands of the striking Soviet and U.S. miners and of Polish Solidarity should keep one's thought focused on real problems.

The healthy middle ground looks like an Aristotelian golden mean between two opposite extremes, but it's not quite that simple. One cannot simply counteract one extreme by adding more of the other extreme. For one thing, none of the three sociological approaches discussed above has focused on personality factors. Yet personality is obviously important. A high need for achievement will force the researcher to feel the pressures of Bourdieu's investment cycle as urgent. He wants not only to survive, but to win big. Such pressures will force him to develop his own unique product and promote it at every opportunity. In addition, a primarily "masculine," externalizing person will project his own categories onto others' works and, finding as a result logical errors, conflations, omissions, and incoherence in their work, will be convinced that his is far superior and deserves promotion. Such personality factors strengthen the influence of the investment cycle and produce an exaggerated professionalism.

A person with a more moderate need for achievement and an ability to empathize with others' ways of thinking will not feel the same pressure to develop an individualized theory product. In such cases, the pressures to individualized achievement can indeed by counteracted by a shared interest and a shared vision. A community can develop around the interest, a community with a common language and a collective achievement.

For another thing, it is doubtful that anything can counteract an exaggerated social concern. The propagandist is so absorbed in the urgency of his vision/fantasy that he does not care about publishing in the reputable journals and using the proper citations and techniques. He has more important work to do. However, social changes over time do reduce the urgency of a concern and could possibly also reduce the output of propaganda. When the concern is new and socially prominent, one gets the largest propaganda output.

For example, now that the cold war is over, we can hope for a reduction in the alarming reports of communist menace and scheming in El Salvador, Guatemala, Grenada, South Yemen, and so forth. In 1970 many New Left Marxists saw the revolution as imminent or at most coming within thirty years, so it was a matter of urgency to organize and indoctrinate the workers. Now that the revolution has been relocated to the distant, unknown future, we have plenty of time to try to understand the complex dynamics of our own time; organizing can wait. The 1960s liberal vision of a responsible, sensitive, fine-tuning government (or of a selfless, wise, modernizing elite in the LDCs) has been complicated by studies of bureaucratic politics and organizational dynamics, and this should enable liberals to produce more realistic diagnoses and policy proposals.

How can a community maintain the middle ground? The basis for a healthy science is (1) a definite social interest and commitment, including political action, plus (2) some detachment and self-skepticism, as indicated in chapter 6, and (3) some moderate professionalism. Self-skepticism implies a willingness to doubt one's own theory, a willingness to look at the data from some other perspective and even to study the data coming from other concerns to see where they might lead. It also implies trying to understand the theories coming from those concerns, in their own terms. Moderate professionalism implies a willingness to use some technical concepts and mathematics and to appreciate others' techniques, as Tobin does, above. It also requires arranging research and publication and conference opportunities for newer members of the community, so they get some recognition and symbolic capital. But, conversely, shared interests require *slowing down* one's own publication rate: avoiding multiple articles on the same topic, working out an idea thoroughly and discussing it broadly before publishing it, using others' ideas and terminology instead of producing another unique brand-name product. The objective here is to slow down the competitive market process. A community with a shared concern maintains itself by emphasizing a collective research process: reading and discussing more and writing less, developing a common theory rather than individualized ideas. Competition for symbolic capital and appropriation of surplus value from newcomers will still occur, but at a reduced rate. In game theoretic terms, the shared concern counteracts the competitive pressure of the n-person Prisoner's Dilemma.

I conclude that research programs are primarily maintained by a shared interest and by personality, not by norms-counternorms or disciplinary identity. When a research program includes two or more concerns, it will diversify by concern, as in the case of game theory discussed above. When social commitment is weak as in much of psychology, the competition for symbolic capital will be important, and there will be much surface diversity of product. In this latter case, research will occur mainly in schools or networks, each with its own brand-name product. The professional reads intensively but narrowly, staying within his own school. As for personality, even a program that is unified by a single concern can exhibit diversification of dialects and weakening of communication due to egocentric insistence on one's own categories. An example is New Left Marxism in the 1980s.

Communication and collaboration are also possible between schools that have fairly similar concerns. Within radical social science, for example, left Keynesians, left institutionalists, and Marxists have worked together at times, including mutual criticism and debate. The December 1988 convention of the Union of Radical Political Economists included sessions on the work of Eichner and of Kaldor, two Keynesians, and a session on game theory. There were also many non-Marxist economists delivering papers, commenting, and presiding. Another example in urban politics is occasional collaboration between elitists and Marxists (Domhoff, 1980; Schwartz, 1987).

However, when social concerns are very different, communication becomes impossible. Writings coming from a very different perspective are ideological, slanted, narrow, overlooking the obvious, using suspect data and probably hidden trickery. They can be read to provide illustrations of the errors one wishes to expose, but not as sources of ideas for one's own research. For example, the two social-concerns communities within international relations game theory have not, to my knowledge, used each other's ideas, though they knew each other's work. The anticommunists probably regarded the Rapoport-type peace researchers as naive about communism and blind to the communist menace, dupes of communist trickery. Their case studies use suspect historical materials to produce naive accounts of Soviet aims and payoffs, and their formal models are correct but irrelevant. Conversely, the peace researchers regarded the anticommunists as paranoid, deluded about actual U.S. aims, and blind to the effect of U.S. strategies on Soviet thinking. The case studies use suspect historical materials like the Penkovsky papers, read official U.S. documents uncritically, and thus produce weird, paranoid accounts; the formal materials are interesting but irrelevant to real politics. Conferences combining the two groups have produced, at best, a clarification of the unbridgeable differences. (Cf. Wohlstetter, 1966, on Rapoport, and Rapoport's rejoinder.) For a similarly fruitless political science conference combining pluralists and elitists, see Waste (1986).

The implication seems to be that Feyerabend's and Churchman's proposal to advance science by mutual criticism works only within a unifying shared concern, or at most, precariously, between two very similar concerns. It would be pointless to urge neoclassicists and Marxists to criticize each other constructively, or pluralists and elitists in political science, or Parsons and Homans followers (functionalists and rational choice microsociologists). They would have no motive to begin the difficult task of learning the other language and slowly translating texts; the truth they aim at is too different.

For most of us, therefore, most of the time, the Kuhn-Lakatos advice to work within a research program and ignore the others is the relevant advice. If we feel moved to broaden our outlook and seek criticism by outsiders, we should look to schools with similar concerns. Then we can use hermeneutic techniques and learn to translate.

Yet a broader communication would be useful to the advance of science. In areas like cognitive psychology where several schools are working in the same area with fairly similar theories, better communication would broaden one's understanding of a new experimental finding or new concept, because the divergent approaches would provide better depth perception of it. Also the modeling ideas—say, in PDP—would give the frame or schema people hints that they could use in their modeling. Also the problem of discrepant experimental results could be attacked more intensively, to perhaps produce more reliable data. Here the barrier to communication seems to be excessive professionalism: each school wants credit for its own original achievements, and so maintains its own terminology.

In many areas of economics, sociology, and political science, differences of interest and vision are the main barriers to communication. Yet here too, some communication across interests would be useful. Frequently researchers with different interests study the same area with different results: poverty, the labor market, international trade, diplomatic crisis bargaining, policy making, the business cycle, urban politics, class structure and stratification, and so on. It would be useful, sometimes, to really understand a different treatment of one's area of research; not to disconfirm, but to broaden one's perception. Remember Nisbett and Ross's maxim (1980): Now look at the data from the vantage point of . . . . A broader perception would enable a school to find weak points in its own treatment of a topic. It might also prevent the more dogmatic members of a school from pushing a good theory to an absurd extreme where it explains everything, as the rational choice people are now doing.

Thus Susan Strange observes that "the Marxist literature . . . is neither extensive nor well known outside leftwing bookshops and journals" (in Tsoukalis, 1985, p. 25). Then she advises her fellow mainstreamers to look at it; some of it isn't all that bad. The literature, that is. Similarly, the anticommunist game theorists could learn from the peace researchers that there could be misperception by both U.S. and Soviet diplomats; that U.S. diplomacy is not necessarily always honest and defensive, and Soviet diplomacy not always the reverse; and that bureaucratic politics occurs in both countries. The peace researchers could consider the problem of how to recognize genuinely aggressive behavior or dishonesty, which they admit exists, in the abstract. Thus the two schools might learn from each other without actually agreeing on anything.

Schools with different interests can also correct each other's fundamental attribution errors. If two schools study poverty, one from the inside and one from the outside, each one will produce a partial account that could be supplemented by its opposite. If one school treats government as a rational problem solver performing the G-function of overall system maintenance, and another school treats it as a bureaucracy concerned only with self-maintenance, each could learn from the other.

Nevertheless, I fear that such communication is likely to develop only between similar concerns. The peace researchers and anticommunists are unlikely to learn from each other, because their concerns are so different. For example it is not possible for Undersecretary of Defense Fred Iklé, one of the anticommunist researchers of the 1960s, to admit the possibility that U.S. diplomacy could be aggressive or dishonest or threatening.

Had he come to that belief in the 1960s, as Ellsberg did, he would have shifted to a peace research concern and severed his connection with RAND and the government, as Ellsberg did. That is, the differences of social concern between the two schools of game theorists leads them to reject each other as immoral.

How can communication across similar social concerns and across similar research programs be improved? This is obviously a situation requiring hermeneutic techniques. A norm of self-skepticism or value tolerance can provide some impetus, but cannot solve the problem of communication. For similar schools within a larger research program, as in cognitive science, the problem is to translate and learn to use the other language. For similar concerns, it is necessarily to empathetically take on the alien concern and gradually develop an other-schema. This in turn requires an other-centered, internalizing component in one's personality. One develops an other-schema through personal conversation over an extended period, involving conscious attention to misunderstanding, making one's assumptions about the other explicit, and correcting errors. After that, one can read the texts and learn to translate.

Extended personal conversation can occur in informal settings such as lunch, or within a research group. For example, Barry Commoner (1976, p. 299) reports that he regularly had lunch with Hyman Minsky (a Keynesian) and Murray Weidenbaum (a neoclassicist). The two disagreed constantly, about everything, but in the process Commoner learned something about neoclassical and Keynesian ways of thinking.

Communication will not be improved by arranging public debates between representatives of different interests (for example, Waste, 1986). In public one is expected to be confident, decisive, unruffled by irrelevant and confused criticism, and gentle only with those critics who confess their errors. Communication, like negotiation, is a private affair.

A sign that one has developed an other-schema is one's ability to read a work as part of a living, flowing development of thought. Some parts of a theory are fundamental, others peripheral and expendable. Some statements repeat ideas from the past, thought to be firmly established, while other statements move into new territory, perhaps tentatively and unclearly. Some arguments are part of a continuing attempt to deal with an old problem, perhaps by revising a previous solution, while others outline a new problem. All statements get their meaning from this large historical context. We all understand this about our own writings and writings within a familiar tradition. We can see the implicit references to old ideas and theories, notice the new departures, distinguish the well thought-out and the tentative. We can dismiss, or appreciate, one section as a clumsy initial sketch and accept another part as a refinement of previous work. But when we read a work from an unfamiliar tradition, we do not have the context, so the work appears self-contained, even arbitrary and flat. The danger then is that we will focus on some puzzling argument or error of detail and dismiss the whole work, as the early reviewers of Keynes's *General Theory* did. Or we will tacitly read the work in the context of our own theories and concepts and find the work muddled and misguided.

CONCLUSION

It is quite clear that there is no possibility of anything remotely like a unified theory of society in the foreseeable future. The small improvements in communication and community that are possible will not reduce the plurality of interests, Kuhnian communities, and schools. A plurality of mutually incompatible theories and unrelated communities exists and will continue to exist; misunderstanding and useless disputes will continue. Feyerabend need not worry about the good health of the social sciences.

We can attribute this state of affairs either to the limited, partial nature of human cognition or to the complex multifaceted nature of human society. Indeed, these are two ways of saying the same thing. On human cognition: interests and visions are inevitably partial because they focus on one aspect of society, one set of actual and possible changes. Each cognitive process of focusing on one aspect of society makes it cognitively difficult to attend persistently to the opposite aspect. As Barnes comments, "These interests acted as a filter upon experience; they intensified the investigation of some aspects of social and economic relationships and led to others being ignored" (1977, p. 28).

For example, the New Institutional Economics (such as Nabli and Nugent, 1989) focuses meticulously on how institutions are established, maintained, and changed by myriad individual rational choices. This approach makes it difficult to be cognitively sensitive to the internal dynamics of institutions: how their functional requirements are being met or not met, their internal contradictions, limits of functional compatibility, developmental tendencies. If a NIE researcher were to raise one of these questions, his attention would always shift to the opposite question, "How does this look to an individual in the institution?" or "Who is making these changes and why?" He also has a residual category into which he can dump empirical instances of institutional dynamics: Unintended consequences of rational actions. Nothing more need be said about such puzzling data. Conversely, various types of functionalists can study institutional dynamics empirically and theoretically, but in the process the individuals in these institutions become vague and amorphous.

Costello et al. (1989) can describe the rather poor performance of the British market economy in recent years—unstable and fluctuating financial markets, poor information flows, uncoordinated production, environmental damage—*in contrast to* what a rational, flexible and decentralized planning process could accomplish. The vision or idealized possibility of government planning reveals the deficiencies and inefficiencies of actual market processes. Planning is a real possibility, not a fantasy, Costello et al. emphasize, by pointing to actual cases of efficient Japanese and French planning. Conversely, Bates (1981) can describe the terrible performance of government agricultural planning in various African states—exploitation of peasants, subsidies to rich farmers, declining productivity, use of resources for political patronage and enrichment—*in contrast to* what a free market could do. The idealized market vision reveals the ineradicable deficiencies of actual government planning. This market is not a fantasy; Bates shows how market processes such as smuggling are continually intruding to ameliorate the worst effects of planning.

The various concerns and visions usually conflict: plan versus market as in the Costello-Bates example, a concern for labor versus a concern for capital, a concern for economic growth versus ecological balance, and the anticommunists versus the peace researchers. Each of these concerns encompasses possibility as well as actuality, and the possibilities conflict. It is possible for some markets to become more free, for some workers to become socially conscious enough to manage their own work collectively, for some governments to actually manage some social problems effectively, and so on. But the possibilities conflict, so that actual changes that facilitate one possibility hinder another. Freeing capital markets and thereby facilitating the worldwide movement of capital strengthens capital against labor and thereby blocks labor's moves toward greater self-management. Faster economic growth will speed the use of natural resources, increase pollution during manufacturing, and increase the need for garbage dumps. Consequently, accounts—even true accounts—based on one vision will conflict with those based on other visions, as in Studdert-Kennedy's example (chapter 6, above).

Cognition is also partial in other ways. Personal concerns, which project personality components onto society, as with Max Weber's Protestant ethic, produce differing results. Cognitive styles, which also reflect personality, are a third source of one-sidedness. Differences of method are a fourth source.

But the fact that all these partial approaches to society can get results, can develop theories and produce data, shows that society itself, our subject matter, is a many-faceted, complex manifold that contains different possibilities, different futures, within itself, and responds to many different approaches. Arithmetic does not respond that way; it comes out the same no matter who is doing the adding and subtracting. It is impervious to personal and social differences. Higher mathematics already shows some traces of cognitive differences: the mind that invented cusp or catastrophe theory must have been different from the mind that first imagined Boolean algebra. (A cusp is a point at which a quantitative change becomes qualitative).

Consider for example human cognitive processes. Experimentalists study them from the outside, using simple artificial tasks, controlling the subjects and enforcing passivity on them. Artificial intelligence formal modelers study them from the inside, constructing active programs that deal with complex tasks and hold conversations. Data for the models can come from verbal protocols, participant observation, or experiments. Both approaches get results, different but not incompatible. People can be both passive and active, obedient and independent. Both approaches together are still partial because they ignore the cultural differences studied by cultural linguists and cognitive anthropologists; nor do they consider personality influences on cognition, or class differences. Human cognitive processes respond to all these approaches because they are complex and multifaceted. As Sigmund Koch asserts, psychological events are multiply determined, ambiguous, polymorphous, contextual, evanescent, and labile (1981, p. 268). So there.

Consequently, the truth that we seek will be plural and multifaceted, even seemingly contradictory or incompatible, for the foreseeable future. Some facets are probably more fundamental or general, but we can expect that even these can be approached from different angles or expressed in different ways—models, flow charts, diagrams, laws, or case studies. Each research program has its own angle of vision on society; some angles are similar, some very different. Over the decades the categories, problems, and angles of vision shift as research programs come and go.

This conclusion returns us to Lakatos's unsolved problem: What rule can we suggest for rationally choosing a research program? And, having chosen, at what point ought one abandon a degenerating program and join a progressive program? By now it is clear that any such rule would be pointless. Scientists do not join a research community to advance knowledge in general; they join either to advance their own careers or to advance some social or personal interest, or both.

Instead, we can ask: What influences the appearance of a program and the decision to join it or abandon it? Can we discern any sign of progress in the coexistence and succession of research programs? It is clear that programs like game theory exhibit progress internally as they mature; is there similar progress in the succession of programs? Or, if not progress, is there at least some discernible pattern other than the recurring cycles that Merton fears he sees?

There are at least three causes for the appearance and flourishing of communities or research programs. (1) Striking developments in the world system have awakened a strong social concern in an age cohort of social scientists, who have then founded a research program. Some of these programs get their initial ideas from a striking book appearing at just the right time, like Keynes's *General Theory*; others like New Left Marxism pick up their initial ideas more piecemeal. Some theories, like game theory and ethnomethodology, get their start entirely from some striking book, without a shared interest. These programs diversify rapidly.

(2) Funding agencies select, narrowly or broadly, some programs for research support. The heavily funded programs, like behavioralism in the 1950s and AI in the 1970s, have attracted more members and have flourished; nonfunded programs, such as the ecological "Small is beautiful" intermediate technology, have stayed small or have died out. The funding agencies attract those who share the agency's interests; they also attract the pure professionals, who thus unwittingly become servants of power.

(3) Government, corporations, or other social groups use certain types of research and thus provide field experiments, practical tests of external validity. The result is an enriched, relevant theory, plus social encouragement to continue that line of research.

The effect of the funding agencies is to support and strengthen right-liberal and conservative concerns. Government agencies and the corporate liberal foundations emphasize liberal research, while military agencies like RAND and the conservative foundations emphasize conservative research. Radicals can also get funding—for instance, from NSF—occasionally. Thus the funding agencies help define "mainstream" social science plus the tolerated offbeat programs.

Government utilization of research has a still narrower emphasis. The administrative agencies like HUD still used liberal research, though at a rapidly declining rate in the early 1980s. But in foreign and economic policy, government has used conservative research from the 1970s on, with a few exceptions in 1977–78 (Destler et al., 1984, pp. 116ff.). The peace researchers were wasting their time, even in the 1960s, if they thought they were providing policy-relevant knowledge of how the U.S. government could reduce tensions in its relations with the Soviet Union. The third, more eclectic school of researchers have also been irrelevant to government policy (a bitter realization for me).

Only the anticommunist researchers have been taken seriously. The RAND researchers and their university counterparts have always had close government connections, with Undersecretary Iklé only the most recent example. Dean Rusk of the Rockefeller Foundation, secretary of state 1961–69, was as conservative an anticommunist as any. The U.S. ambassador to Cambodia in the Lon Nol years, after the U.S. carpet bombing of Cambodia and overthrow of the Sihanouk government, was not Boulding or Rapoport; it was William Kintner of the Orbis group. The U.S. ambassador to Brazil in 1964, when the Brazilian military were discussing the alarming leftward drift of the electorate, was not Paul Baran; it was Gen. Vernon Walters. In economic policy the monetarists have dominated policy making since 1969, and in the 1980s even supply-siders have provided policy advice and propaganda.

Traditions last for perhaps twenty to forty years, then peter out as the social concern gets discredited. For example, the cold war is now over. Research programs that have little sustaining social concern are weakened by the appearance of exciting new programs supported by new research funds. For example, funding for drug therapy and more recently neurology has drawn some researchers away from psychoanalytic research, and increasing funding for cognitive experiments drew some researchers away from behaviorist experiments around 1970.

Is there any sign of progress here? Some researchers will perceive definite progress since at least 1970: the decline of Keynesian fantasies, of functionalism, welfare state and peace research, and the rise of monetarism, public choice, microsociology, rational expectations, and supply-side and new institutional and Austrian economics. Others will find progress in the 1950s and 1960s, with pluralist behavioralism, Keynesianism, functionalism, institutionalism, symbolic interactionism, modernization theory, ethnomethodology, and all the poverty and civil rights and community and unemployment and deviance studies. Who is right? Let him whose thought is uninfluenced by personality or social factors make the first judgment.

In any case, the professionals remind us that there is unquestionable progress in techniques and methods. Rational expectations models are a definite advance over earlier Keynesian models such as Tobin's, as Tobin has observed. Ethnography and qualitative methods have become more sophisticated in the 1980s. Survey researchers and experimenters have steadily improved their awareness and control of interfering factors for many decades. Statistical techniques developed in the 1960s and continue to develop. We are slowly learning to learn.

Perhaps future generations will build on these technical achievements and look back with amusement at the clumsy research and theorizing of our time.

Would it be too presumptuous to suggest that social science can also progress by self-study, by increasing awareness of the pitfalls and the nonrational influences on research? Perhaps increased awareness, selfawareness, of these factors can make possible some control of them, or even an adjustment that makes some of them aids rather than hindrances to research.

I have now finished answering our three questions. Question 2, How do or should social scientists operate to produce knowledge, has been answered in chapter 11: Researchers work within a research program or community or tradition to develop the potentialities of some "new paradigm," some creative and exemplary work that relates to their interests. Chapter 12 has added two examples to illustrate some variations in how research programs work. The main contribution of this chapter has been to address question 3. We have dealt with two subquestions: (a) What maintains community and communication within and across programs? and (b) What sorts of degeneration occur in research programs?

(3a) Community and communication within the social sciences are not maintained by norms and counternorms. This implies that knowledge is not developed within the Mertonian disciplines, such as sociology, but within research programs or traditions, as we have already observed. Communication within a tradition is facilitated in part by the shared exemplar and disciplinary matrix; however, this source of commu nity gets ever weaker as the tradition diversifies and absorbs parts of other traditions. Most traditions or branches of a tradition are also unified by a shared social concern, which mutes the egocentric striving for recognition and promotes a desire to communicate and share ideas. Where a shared concern is latent or absent, as in cognitive psychology or psychotherapy, there is much brand-name differentiation. If a shared concern dies down, the same diversification will gradually appear.

(3b) Research programs are susceptible to two opposite kinds of degeneration. (1) When a shared concern is muted or absent, the egocentric desire for recognition is unchecked and brand-name differentiation runs wild. Each new index or scale or concept rapidly becomes obsolete and forgotten because few others use it; they are busy developing their own. (2) When the vision/fantasy and the shared concern become urgent and political action becomes central, the theory and examples are used as propaganda to support and guide some political program. The theory becomes rigidified into dogma, as with orthodox Marxism-Leninism or free-market individualism, and empirical research is devoted to finding vivid examples to move people to action.

As for question 1: Social science produces a multiple, contradictory truth for our time—that is, a set of diversified perspectives and diagnoses of our changing, tangled, and contradictory society. These truths live in the practices and understandings of a research community, not in particular laws, and when that community peters out, its truth passes into history along with the society it tried to understand.

TECHNICAL NOTES

REFERENCES

INDEX

TECHNICAL NOTES

These notes explain the more technical examples and concepts for readers who wish to understand the examples in more detail. They are not necessary for understanding the main argument.

1. This ugly term was used by the logical empiricists as a sign of scorn for those who dabble in metaphysics. The dabblers call themselves *metaphysicians*, a much more suave and dignified term.

2. Friedman defines *permanent income* (Y_p) as that income which a person expects to receive, on the average, for some time ahead. Permanent consumption is similar. Since Friedman doesn't know how people calculate their permanent income, he has to estimate Y_p from the data for actual aggregate income. To do this, he defines Y_p operationally as a weighted average of income over the last three years, or the last seventeen, or whatever number of years works better. He could vary the weights so they decline linearly, or exponentially, into the past; could exclude extreme points as accidents which consumers ignore in forming their expectations; could fit a curve through the data rather than using weights; could reject some puzzling data as unreliable; and so on (Friedman, 1957). Perhaps he is looking for the way consumers estimate their Y_p, or perhaps he is looking for that definition of Y_p that will fit the data to his theory.

3. According to Keynes, businessmen know that the present economic expansion cannot continue indefinitely, but are uncertain about when the downturn will start. They want to invest and expand production as long as the expansion lasts, because demand is strong; but they don't want to be caught by the downturn. Since an expansion program takes months or years to complete, they have to slow down investment months or years before the downturn starts. But they can't predict when it will start. So they anxiously look for advance indicators such as lower interest rates or some competitor's slowdown in investment. When a few producers spot some such indicator and reduce their investment, the others notice that and follow suit, and the downturn begins.

Knight distinguishes individual decisions under risk and under uncertainty. "Risk" means that the probabilities of the various possible outcomes are known, so the rational decision maker can simply calculate the best choice. "Uncertainty" means that the probabilities are not known even vaguely, so rational decision is not possible. If there are businessmen who nevertheless manage to make the right decision somehow, perhaps by sensitivity to subtle cues, they deserve the profits they make as a result.

Keynes deals with uncertainty in a whole economy, while Knight deals with individual choice.

4. A reduced-form equation describes only the ultimate effect of a change in one variable such as money supply on another variable such as GNP, at equilibrium. It omits all the "intermediate" interactions and feedbacks among many variables that interest Keynesians. Several reduced form equations can be combined to deduce the ultimate effect of one changed variable on a number of other variables. Keynesians observe that we never get to ultimate equilibrium, so the equations are rather fictitious. They want to describe the multiple short-run interactions occurring in a real economy which never is in equilibrium, and the reduced-form equations cannot express such interactions.

5. Blau was studying a government agency. The manager assigned him a desk near the office doorway, while all the office workers watched. From his desk he could watch everybody working, and write down what he saw. He promptly took out pencil and paper and started looking. The remark about the bathroom told Blau that he was thought to be a spy for management, keeping track of how hard people worked. "Going to the bathroom" was the text, "You're a spy" was the subtext (Blau, 1964).

6. Here is an example of how idealization works in practice. The Federal Reserve has recently considered adopting a new variable, P^*-P, as a predictor of the inflation rate 2–3 years ahead (Christiano, 1989; Carlson, 1989). P is the actual price level, P^* is the equilibrium price level. The assumption, based on monetarist theory, is that P will return to P^* in 2–3 years via a shift in the inflation rate, unless government interferes. P^* is calculated from V^*, equilibrium velocity of money, assumed to be a constant (despite the puzzling Friedman and Schwartz (1963) data), divided by Q^*, the equilibrium rate of growth. Money is defined as whatever M has a constant velocity. When the velocity of M_1 recently fluctuated wildly, the Fed shifted to M_2 as the measure of money. Thus the calculation of P^* is based on the quantity equation $MV=PQ$. Q^* is calculated by taking the average change in GNP for a number of years and extrapolating; the result is a smooth curve, rising at 2.5 percent per year since 1980.

The idealization is located in the monetarist concept of long-run equilibrium. This concept asserts that the economy is always close to long-run equilibrium and that it tends automatically and rapidly to return after some external shock such as oil-price change has knocked it off equilibrium. Equilibrium includes the rate of growth, price level, and the velocity of money. The ideal is the essence of the real, and fluctuations are trivial or unpredictable. Contrast this with the Keynesian Harrod-Domar concept *equilibrium rate of growth,* a target for an idealized government to aim at as it manages a balky, inherently unstable economy.

7. The law of comparative advantage says that at equilibrium countries will export those goods and raw materials that they can produce more cheaply than other countries. Leontief showed in 1956 that U.S. exports did not fit that scheme at all. The law of one price says that at equilibrium relative prices in two countries that trade together a lot will be quite similar. Another fiction.

8. Parsonian functionalism can be summarized most simply as an agenda for an organization or family or society, a list of things the organization has to do to keep going. The list is the set of functional prerequisites, or in Marion Levy's version, functional requisites and prerequisites. For instance, an organization has to take in members and resources. The members have to be trained to do what the organization does, and the resources have to be used effectively, not wasted. In Almond's functionalism, a political system has to aggregate interests in interest groups, among other things.

If the prerequisite is performed poorly, a distinctive trouble results. For instance, if some interests are not aggregated the politicians will not find out about them and probably will not take them into account in their policies. This could lead to apathy, dissatisfaction, poor performance, or revolt. Failure to take in enough members or new resources leads to different troubles.

Organizations develop routines for doing the things they have to do; these are their subsystems, institutions, bureaus, structures. Each subsystem is sensitive to how well it is doing its job; or, alternatively, the control subsystem (government) is sensitive to how well they are doing it. If the job is not being done adequately, for instance if new members are not being adequately trained or interests are not being adequately aggregated, trouble results. Then either the subsystem redoubles its efforts or the trouble gets worse. Stinchcombe's feedback model assumes that organizations automatically, mechanically respond to trouble. This is a caricature of Parsons' or Almond's or Merton's functionalism.

The subsystem may not respond adequately to signs of trouble because it is caught up in its own internal difficulties; maintaining the subsystems in working order is another set of functional prerequisites. In Almond's functionalism it becomes apparent that the political subsystems in developing countries cannot possibly respond effectively to the signs of trouble, because everything is going wrong simultaneously. Eventually there is an army coup, and things go from worse to terrible.

Another reason the control subsystem may not respond adequately is that the functional prerequisites conflict. Merton especially emphasizes this problem. Thus the more one subsystem is egged on to do its job, the worse some other trouble gets. For example, the resource-producing subsystem may, in its pursuit of productive efficiency, so successfully mold members to perform their production tasks that it damages their ability to perform other tasks such as socialization. Interests can be so effectively aggregated that the government flounders in an excess of conflicting demands. Such conflicts among functional requirements do not appear in Stinchcombe's mechanical feedback model.

Radcliffe-Brown's functionalism, which G. A. Cohen cites, is a quite different, earlier version of functionalism. This version *must* be understood in contrast to the diffusionist theory that Radcliffe-Brown took with him to the Andaman Islands and which he found inadequate there. That version of diffusionism was micro and historical: it told the ethnographer to focus on one culture trait at a time, and to compare each trait with similar traits in neighboring or contacting cultures. The ethnographer's task was to reconstruct the history of a trait, such as the Indian Ghost Dance in the western United States, as it diffused to one culture after another over time. Differences in the trait in different cultures provided clues as to which cultures had it earlier and which got it later.

Radcliffe-Brown was impressed by the systematic interconnection of the parts of Andaman culture: each part fit into other parts, supporting or fulfilling or providing materials for other cultural activities. The unity was not perfect, but at each point of strain there were myths and ceremonies that seemed to reduce the strain, like a bandage or antibodies. Accordingly, he rejected the diffusionist microhistorical project: his functionalism was macro and antihistorical. It told him to describe how the parts of the culture fit together; it did not tell him to inquire how the myths and ceremonies developed or where they came from. That would have returned him to the diffusionist program he had rejected.

9. Lou Schneider spent many years studying Karl Menger's forgotten century-old ideas in order to recover them for current sociology. Now, apparently, Schneider himself is forgotten.

10. It was rumored that Miller thought up the idea, Galanter worked it out, and Pribram *actually believes it.*

11. For discussion of Grünbaum's argument, see Ferguson (1988).

12. In Skinner's account, one rat in a cage is bragging to the other: "Boy, have I got this guy conditioned! Every time I press this bar he drops a pellet of food down for me!" That is, the campaigner tells the public what it wants to hear, each time it moves toward the voting lever.

13. This example is from the Klein-Goldberger model of a Keynesian economy.

14. You never heard of the Asch experiment? Eight people are seated in a row, viewing three upright bars on a blackboard or wall chart: a long one, a short one, and a middle-sized one. The E announces, "This is a perception experiment. I want each of you to report which of the three bars looks the longest to

you. You first." The first seven people report that number two (the short one) is the longest. They are all stooges, but the eighth does not know this. They provide the "tilted frame" for number eight, the sucker (S for *sucker*). The experiment can be repeated many times and also varied, using number three (the middle-sized one) as the tilted answer.

REFERENCES

Aaron, Henry J. 1978. *Politics and the Professors*. Washington, D.C.: Brookings.

Achinstein, Peter, and Stephen Barker, eds. 1969. *The Legacy of Logical Positivism*. Baltimore: Johns Hopkins Press.

Ackoff, Russell, S. Gupta, and J. Sayer Minas. 1962. *Scientific Method: Optimizing Applied Research Decisions*. New York: Wiley.

Adorno, Theodor, et al. 1950. *The Authoritarian Personality*. New York: Harper.

Agar, Michael. 1986. *Speaking of Ethnography*. Beverly Hills, Calif.: Sage.

Agassi, Joseph. 1975. *Science in Flux*. Boston Studies no. 28. Dordrecht: Reidel.

———. 1976. Review of Paul Feyerabend, *Against Method*. *Philosophia* 6: 165–91.

———. 1981. *Science and Society*. Boston Studies no. 65. Boston: Reidel.

Agger, Ben. 1989. *Reading Science*. New York: General Hall.

Albertini, Luigi. 1942. *The Origins of the War of 1914*. London: Oxford University Press.

Alcaly, Roger, and D. Mermelstein, eds. 1976. *The Fiscal Crisis of American Cities*. New York: Random House.

Alexander, Franz, and T. M. French. 1946. *Psychoanalytic Therapy*. New York: Ronald.

Almond, Gabriel. 1970. *Political Development*. Boston: Little, Brown.

Anderson, Martin. 1978. *Welfare: The Political Economy of Welfare in the United States*. Stanford, Calif.: Hoover Institution Press.

Andersson, Gunnar. 1978. "The Problem of Verisimilitude." In *Progress and Rationality in Science*, ed. G. Radnitzky and G. Andersson. Boston: Reidel.

Apel, Karl Otto. 1970. "Szientismus oder Transzendentale Hermeneutik?" In *Hermeneutik und Dialektik. Festschrift für H. G. Gadamer*, ed. Rüdiger Bubner. Tübingen: Mohr.

———. 1977 (orig. publ. 1972). "The a Priori of Communication and the Foundation of the Humanities." In *Understanding and Social Inquiry*, ed. Fred Dallmyer and T. McCarthy. Notre Dame, Ind.: University of Notre Dame Press.

———. 1980. *Toward a Transformation of Philosophy*. London: Routledge and Paul.

373

———. 1981. "Intentions, Conventions, and References to Things." In *Meaning and Understanding*, ed. H. Parret and J. Bouveresse. New York: de Gruyter.

Archibald, Kathleen, ed. 1966. *Strategic Interaction and Conflict*. Berkeley and Los Angeles: University of California Press.

Argyris, Chris. 1980. *Inner Contradictions of Rigorous Research*. New York: Academic Press.

Arnove, Robert F., ed. 1980. *Philanthropy and Cultural Imperialism*. Boston: G. K. Hall.

Asch, Solomon. 1952. *Social Psychology*. Englewood Cliffs, N.J.: Prentice-Hall.

Ashby, W. Ross. 1952. *Design For a Brain*. New York: Wiley.

Ayer, Alfred J. 1949 (orig. publ. 1936). *Language, Truth, and Logic*. 2d ed. New York: Dover Publications.

———. 1987. "Reflections on *Language, Truth, and Logic*." In *Logical Positivism in Perspective*, ed. Barry Gower, 23–34. London: Croom Helm.

Bach, Robert. 1980. "On the Holism of a World-systems Perspective." In *Processes of the World-System*, ed. T. Hopkins and I. Wallerstein. World System Annuals, vol. 3. Beverly Hills, Calif.: Sage.

Bachrach, Peter, and Morton Baratz. 1962. "Two Faces of Power." *American Political Science Review* 56:947–52.

Banfield, Edward. 1974. *The Unheavenly City Revisited*. Boston: Little, Brown.

Barber, Bernard. 1982. Review of Barnes, *T. S. Kuhn and Social Science*. *4S Review* 7, no. 4:49–51.

Barber, Theodore X. 1976. *Pitfalls in Human Research*. New York: Pergamon.

Barnes, Barry. 1977. *Interests and the Growth of Knowledge*. London: Routledge.

———. 1982. *T. S. Kuhn and Social Science*. London: Macmillan.

Bates, Robert. 1981. *Markets and States in Tropical Africa*. Berkeley and Los Angeles: University of California Press.

Bauer, Henry. 1984. "Velikovsky and Social Studies of Science." *4S Review* 2, no. 4:2–8.

Bauman, Zygmunt. 1978. *Hermeneutics and Social Science*. London: Hutchinson.

Becker, Howard, and B. Geer. 1960. *Boys in White*. Chicago: University of Chicago Press.

Belenky, Mary, et al. 1986. *Women's Ways of Knowing*. New York: Basic Books.

Bem, Sandra. 1974. "The Measurement of Psychological Androgyny." *Journal of Consulting and Clinical Psychology* 42:155–62.

Ben-David, Joseph. 1978. "Emergence of National Traditions in the Sociology of Science." *Sociological Inquiry* 48:197–218.

Bentley, Arthur F. 1908. *The Process of Government*. Chicago: University of Chicago Press.

———. 1954. *Inquiry into Inquiries*, ed. J. Ratner. Boston: Beacon Press.

Berger, Johannes. 1982. "Die Versprachlichung des Sakralen und die Entsprach-lichung der Ökonomie." *Zeitschrift für Soziologie* 11:353–65.

Berger, Susanne, ed. 1980. *Utilisation of the Social Sciences in Policy Making in the United States*. Paris: OECD.

Bergin, Allen, and Hans Strupp. 1970. "New Directions in Psychotherapy." *Journal of Abnormal Psychology* 76:13–26.

Bergmann, Gustav. 1954. *The Metaphysics of Logical Positivism*. New York: Long-mans, Green.

Berkowitz, L. 1971. "Reporting an Experiment: A Case Study in Leveling, Sharpening, and Assimilation." *Journal of Experimental Social Psychology* 7:237–43.

Berman, Edward. 1983. "The Influence of the Carnegie, Ford, and Rockefeller Foundations on American Foreign Policy." *The Ideology of Philanthropy*. Albany, N.Y.: SUNY Press.

Bernstein, Michael. 1987. *The Great Depression*. Cambridge: Cambridge University Press.

Bernstein, Richard, ed. 1960. *John Dewey on Experience, Nature, and Freedom*. New York: Liberal Arts Press.

Blau, Peter. 1964. "Dynamics of Bureaucracy." In *Sociologists at Work*, ed. Phillip Hammond. New York: Basic Books.

Blaug, Mark. 1976. "Paradigms vs. Research Programmes." In *Method and Appraisal in Economics*, ed. Spiro J. Latsis, 149–80. Cambridge: Cambridge University Press.

———. 1980. *The Methodology of Economics*. New York: Cornell University Press.

———. 1985. "Comment on D. Wade Hands, 'Karl Popper and Economic Methodology: A New Look.' " *Economics and Philosophy* 1, no. 2:286–89.

Bleicher, Josef. 1982. *The Hermeneutic Imagination*. London: Routledge and Paul.

Bleier, Ruth, ed. 1986. *Feminist Approaches to Science*. New York: Pergamon Press.

Blight, James G. 1981. "Must Psychoanalysts Retreat to Hermeneutics?" *Psychoanalysis and Contemporary Thought* 4:147–206.

Blissett, Marlan. 1972. *Politics in Science*. Boston: Little, Brown.

Block, Fred. 1977. *The Origins of International Economic Disorder*. Berkeley and Los Angeles: University of California Press.

———. 1985. "Postindustrial Development and the Obsolescence of Economic Categories." *Politics and Society* 14:71–104.

Bluestone, Barry, and Bennett Harrison. 1980. *Capital and Communities: The Causes of Private Disinvestment*. Washington, D.C.: Progressive Alliance.

———. 1982. *The Deindustrialization of America*. New York: Basic Books.

Bobrow, Daniel, and Terry Winograd. 1977. "An Overview of KRL, a Knowledge Representation Language." *Cognitive Science* 1:3–46.

Boehme, Gernot, et al. 1983. *Finalization in Science*. Trans. Peter Burgess, ed. Wolf Schafer. Boston Studies no. 77. Dordrecht: Reidel.

Bourdieu, Pierre. 1975. "The Specificity of the Scientific Field and the Social Conditions of the Progress of Reason," trans. R. Nice. *Social Science Information* 14, no. 6:19–47.

———. 1977. *Outline of a Theory of Practice*. Trans. R. Nice. Cambridge: Cambridge University Press.

Bowles, Samuel, and Herbert Gintis. 1976. *Schooling in Capitalist America*. New York: Basic Books.

Brams, Steven J., and D. Wittman. 1981. "Nonmyopic Equilibria in 2 × 2 Games." *Journal of Conflict Management and Peace Science* 6:39–62.

Brinberg, David, and J. E. McGrath. 1985. *Validity and the Research Process*. Beverly Hills, Calif.: Sage.

Brooks, Harvey. 1968. *The Government of Science*. Cambridge, Mass.: Harvard University Press.

Brown, Robert. 1960. *Explanation in Social Science*. New York: Aldine.

Bruner, Jerome S., 1973. *Beyond the Information Given*. New York: Norton.

———. 1979. *On Knowing. Essays for the Left Hand*. Cambridge, Mass.: Harvard University Press.

———. 1983. *In Search of Mind*. New York: Harper.

Bruner, Jerome S., and C. D. Goodman. 1947. "Value and Need as Organizing Factors in Perception." *Journal of Abnormal and Social Psychology* 42:33–44.

Bruner, Jerome S., and L. Postman. 1949. "On the Perception of Incongruity: A Paradigm." *Journal of Personality* 18:206–23.

Bruner, Jerome S., J. Goodnow, and G. Austin. 1956. *A Study of Thinking*. New York: Wiley.

Bryant, Christopher. 1983. "Who Now Reads Parsons?" *Sociological Review* 31, no. 1:337–50.

Buck, Roger. 1956. "On the Logic of General Behavior Systems Theory." In *Minnesota Studies in the Philosophy of Science*, ed. Herbert Feigl and Michael Scriven, 1:223–38. Minneapolis: University of Minnesota Press.

Cannon, James P. 1975 (orig. publ. 1953). *America's Road to Socialism*. New York: Pathfinder Press.

Carlson, John P. 1989. "The Indicator P-star; Just What Does It Indicate?" Federal Reserve Bank of Cleveland, *Economic Commentary*, Sept. 15, 1989.

Carnap, Rudolf. 1928 (2d ed. 1961). *Der Logische Aufbau der Welt*. Trans. Rolf George. Hamburg: Meiner.

———. 1929. *Abriss der Logistik*. Wien: Springer.

———. 1935. *Philosophy and Logical Syntax*. London: Kegan Paul.

———. 1937. *Logical Syntax of Language*. London: Kegan Paul.

———. 1956. "The Methodological Character of Theoretical Concepts." In *The Foundations of Science and the Concepts of Psychology and Psychoanalysis*, ed. Herbert Feigl and Michael Scriven. Minnesota Studies in the Philosophy of Science, vol. 1. Minneapolis: University of Minnesota Press.

———. 1963. "Intellectual Autobiography." In *The Philosophy of Rudolph Carnap*, ed. Paul Schilpp, 3–84. LaSalle: Open Court.

Carnoy, Martin, and Derek Shearer. 1980. *Economic Democracy*. White Plains, N.Y.: M. E. Sharpe.

Caro, Robert. 1974. *The Power Broker*. New York: Random House.

Casper, Jay. 1984. "The Crimininal Justice System." Presented at a Colloquium on Law and the Social Sciences, Buffalo, N.Y.

Chabot, Barry. 1982. *Freud on Schreber*. Amherst: University of Massachusetts Press.

Chandler, Alfred. 1990. *Scale and Scope: The Dynamics of Industrial Capitalism*. Cambridge, Mass.: Harvard University Press.

Cherniak, Christopher. 1986. *Minimal Rationality*. Cambridge, Mass.: MIT Press.

Chomsky, Noam. 1957. *Syntactic Structures*. The Hague: Mouton.

Christiano, Lawrence J. 1989. "P*: Not the Inflation Forecaster's Holy Grail." Federal Reserve Bank of Minneapolis, *Quarterly Review*, December, 3–18.

Churchman, C. West. 1963. "An Analysis of the Concept of Simulation." In *Symposium on Simulation Models*, ed. Austin C. Hoggatt and F. E. Balderston. Cincinnati: Southwestern Publishing Co.

———. 1968a. *Challenge to Reason*. New York: McGraw-Hill.

———. 1968b. *The Systems Approach*. New York: Dell.

———. 1971. *The Design of Inquiring Systems*. New York: Basic Books.

Cicourel, Aaron. 1964. *Method and Measurement in Sociology*. New York: Free Press.

Claxton, Guy, et al., 1980. *Cognitive Psychology*. London: Routledge.

Coddington, Alan, 1976. "Keynesian Economics: The Search for First Principles." *Journal of Economic Literature* 14:1258–73.

Cohen, G. A., 1978. *Karl Marx's Theory of History: A Defense*. Princeton, N.J.: Princeton University Press.

Colander, David, and A. Klamer. 1987. "The Making of an Economist." *Journal of Economic Perspectives* 1:95–112.

Cole, Jonathan, and S. Cole. 1967. "Scientific Output and Recognition: A Study of the Operation of the Reward System in Science." *American Sociological Review* 32:377–90.

———. 1973. *Social Stratification in Science*. Chicago: University of Chicago Press.

Cole, Jonathan, and H. Zuckerman. 1975. "The Emergence of a Specialty: The

Self-Exemplifying Case of the Sociology of Science." *The Idea of Social Structure.* Papers in Honor of R. K. Merton, ed. Lewis Coser, 139–74. New York: Harcourt, Brace.

Collins, Allan. 1977. "Why Cognitive Science?" *Cognitive Science* 1:2.

Collins, Harry. 1985. *Changing Order.* London: Sage.

Collins, Randall. 1975. *Conflict Sociology.* New York: Academic Press.

———. 1989. "Toward a Theory of Intellectual Change: The Social Causes of Philosophies." *Science, Technology, and Human Values* 14:107–40.

Colvin, Ian. 1971. *The Chamberlain Cabinet.* New York: Taplinger.

Commoner, Barry. 1971. *The Closing Circle.* New York: Knopf.

———. 1976. *The Poverty of Power.* New York: Knopf.

Converse, Jean. 1987. *Survey Research in the U.S.* Berkeley and Los Angeles: University of California Press.

Coser, Lewis. 1956. *The Functions of Social Conflict.* New York: Free Press.

———, ed. 1975. *The Idea of Social Structure.* Papers in Honor of R. K. Merton. New York: Harcourt, Brace.

Coser, Rose. 1975. "The Complexity of Roles as a Seedbed of Individual Autonomy." In L. Coser, *The Idea of Social Structure,* 237–63.

Costello, Nicholas, et al. 1989. *Beyond the Casino Economy: Planning for the 1990s.* London: Verso.

Crane, Diana. 1965. "Scientists at Major and Minor Universities: A Study of Productivity and Recognition." *American Sociological Review* 30: 699–714.

———. 1972. *Invisible Colleges.* Chicago: University of Chicago Press.

Crenson, Matthew. 1971. *The Unpolitics of Air Pollution: a Study of Non-decisionmaking.* Baltimore: Johns Hopkins University Press.

Cunningham, Frank. 1972. *Objectivity in Social Science.* Toronto: University of Toronto Press.

Dahl, Robert. 1957. "The Concept of Power." *Behavioral Science* 2:201–15.

———. 1961. "The Behavioral Approach to Political Science: Epitaph for a Movement to a Successful Protest." *American Political Science Review* 55:765–66.

———. 1963. *Modern Political Analysis.* Englewood Cliffs, N.J.: Prentice-Hall.

Davidson, Paul. 1978. *Money and the Real World.* New York: Wiley.

De Mey, Marc. 1982. *The Cognitive Paradigm.* Boston: Reidel.

Denzin, Norman. 1970. *The Research Act.* New York: McGraw-Hill.

Destler, I. M., L. Gelb, and A. Lake. 1984. *Our Own Worst Enemy.* New York: Simon and Schuster.

Deutsch, Morton. 1966. "Bargaining, Threat, and Communication: Some Experimental Studies." In *Strategic Interaction and Conflict,* ed. Archibald.

———. 1973. *The Resolution of Conflict: Constructive and Destructive Processes.* New Haven, Conn.: Yale University Press.

Deutsch, Morton, and R. Krauss. 1962. "Studies of Interpersonal Bargaining." *Journal of Conflict Resolution* 6:52–76.

Dewey, John. 1916. *Essays in Experimental Logic.* New York: Dover.

———. 1922 (rpt. 1930). *Human Nature and Conduct.* New York: Random House.

———. 1927. *The Public and Its Problems.* New York: Holt.

———. 1939. *Theory of Valuation.* Chicago: University of Chicago Press.

Dewey, John, and A. F. Bentley. 1949. *Knowing and the Known.* Boston: Beacon Press.

Dickson, David. 1984. *The New Politics of Science.* New York: Pantheon.

Dickson, Paul. 1971. *Think Tanks.* New York: Athenaeum.

Diesing, Paul. 1966. "Objectivism and Subjectivism in the Social Sciences." *Philosophy of Science* 33:124–33.

———. 1971. *Patterns of Discovery in the Social Sciences.* New York: Aldine.

———. 1982. *Science and Ideology in the Policy Sciences.* Hawthorne, N.Y.: Aldine.

———. 1985a. "Hypothesis Testing and Data Interpretation: The Case of Milton Friedman." In *Research in the History of Economic Thought and Methodology,* ed. Warren Samuels. New York: JAI Press.

———. 1985b. "Comments on 'Why Freud's Research Methodology Was Unscientific' by Von Eckhardt." *Psychoanalysis and Contemporary Thought* 8:551–66.

———. 1986. Review of Edwin Wallace, *Historiography and Causation in Psychoanalysis. Contemporary Psychology* 31:417–18.

Dixon, N., 1971. *Subliminal Perception: The Nature of a Controversy.* New York: McGraw-Hill.

Doeringer, Peter, and Michael Piore. 1969. *Internal Labor Markets and Manpower Analysis.* Lexington, Mass.: Heath.

Domhoff, G. W., 1978. *Who Really Rules?* New Brunswick, N.J.: Transaction Books.

Domhoff, G. W., ed. 1980. *Power Structure Research.* Beverly Hills, Calif.: Sage.

Donovan, John C. 1967. *The Politics of Poverty.* New York: Pegasus.

Douglas, Jack D. 1976. *Investigative Social Research.* Beverly Hills, Calif.: Sage.

Dreyfus, Hubert. 1979 (orig. publ. 1972). *What Computers Can't Do.* New York: Harper and Row.

Eagle, Morris. 1983. "The Epistemological Status of Recent Developments in Psychoanalytic Theory." In *Physics, Philosophy, and Psychoanalysis,* ed. R. S. Cohen and L. Laudan. Boston Studies no. 76. Boston: Reidel.

Edelman, Murray. 1962. *The Symbolic Uses of Politics.* Urbana: University of Illinois Press.

Edelson, Marshall. 1988. *Psychoanalysis: A Theory in Crisis.* Chicago: University of Chicago Press.

Edwards, Ward. 1961. "Probability Learning in 1000 Trials." *Journal of Experimental Psychology* 62:385–94.

Eichner, Alfred. 1978. *A Guide to Post-Keynesian Economics.* White Plains, N.Y.: M. E. Sharpe.

Eisenstadt, S. N. 1963. *The Political System of Empires.* New York: Free Press.

Eisner, Robert. 1958. "The Permanent Income Hypothesis: Comment." *American Economic Review* 48:972–90.

Elkana, Yehuda. 1976. Review of Merton, *The Sociology of Science. American Journal of Sociology* 81:906–10.

Ellsberg, Daniel. 1956. "Theory of the Reluctant Duelist." *American Economic Review* 46, no. 2:909–23.

———. 1972. *Papers on the War.* New York: Simon and Schuster.

Elster, Jon. 1979. *Ulysses and the Sirens.* New York: Cambridge University Press.

Erikson, Erik. 1950. *Childhood and Society.* New York: Norton.

———. 1964. *Insight and Responsibility.* New York: Norton.

Evans, J. St. B. T. 1980. "Thinking: Experimental and Information Processing Approaches." In Claxton et al., *Cognitive Psychology.*

———. 1982. *Psychology of Deductive Reasoning.* London: Routledge.

Eysenck, Michael. 1984. *Handbook of Cognitive Psychology.* London: Erlbaum.

Fainsod, Merle. 1958. *Smolensk Under Soviet Rule.* Cambridge, Mass.: Harvard University Press.

Fainstein, Susan, and Norman Fainstein. 1983. *Restructuring the City.* New York: Longman.

Faust, David. 1984. *The Limits of Scientific Reasoning.* Minneapolis: University of Minnesota Press.

Fay, Brian. 1975. *Social Theory and Political Practice.* London: Allen and Unwin.

Feigl, Herbert. 1956. "Some Major Issues and Developments in the Philosophy of Science of Logical Empiricism." In *The Foundations of Science and the Concepts of Psychology and Psychoanalysis,* ed. Feigl and Michael Scriven. Minnesota Studies in the Philosophy of Science, vol. 1. Minneapolis: University of Minnesota Press.

———. 1971. "Research Programs and Induction." In *PSA 1970,* ed. Roger Buck and R. S. Cohen. Boston Studies no. 8. Boston: Reidel.

Fellner, William. 1946. *Monetary Policies and Full Employment.* Hamden, Conn.: Anchor Books.

———. 1957. "Keynesian Economics after Twenty Years: What Is Surviving?" *American Economic Review* 47, no. 1:67–76.

Ferguson, Michael. 1988. "The Clinical Situation and Epistemological Problems in Psychoanalysis: A Response to Grunbaum." *Psychoanalysis and Contemporary Thought* 11:535–61.

Ferguson, Thomas, and Joel Rogers. 1987. *Right Turn: The Decline of the Democrats and the Future of American Politics.* New York: Hill and Wang.

Feuer, Lewis. 1960. "The Standpoints of Dewey and Freud: A Contrast and Analysis." *Journal of Individual Psychology* 16:119–36.

Feyerabend, Paul. 1962. "Explanation, Reduction, and Empiricism." In *Scientific Explanation, Space, and Time,* ed. Herbert Feigl and Grover Maxwell. Minnesota Studies in the Philosophy of Science 3:28–97. Minneapolis: University of Minnesota Press.

———. 1965. "Problems of Empiricism." In *Beyond the Edge of Certainty. Pittsburgh Symposium,* ed. Robert Colodny. Englewood Cliffs, N.J.: Prentice-Hall.

———. 1969. "Linguistic Arguments and Scientific Method." *Telos* 3:43–63.

———. 1970a. "Consolations for the Specialist." In *Criticism and the Growth of Knowledge,* ed. Imre Lakatos and A. Musgrave. Cambridge: Cambridge University Press.

———. 1970b. "Philosophy of Science: A Subject with a Great Past." In *Minnesota Studies in the Philosophy of Science,* ed. R. Stuewer, 5:172–81. Minneapolis: University of Minnesota Press.

———. 1974. "Popper's 'Objective Knowledge.' " *Inquiry* 17:475–507.

———. 1975. *Against Method.* London: New Left Books.

———. 1976. *Wider Den Methodenzwang.* Frankfurt-am-Main: Suhrkamp.

———. 1977. "Marxist Fairy Tales from Australia." *Inquiry* 20:372–97.

———. 1978. "From Incompetent Professionalism to Professionalized Incompetence." *Philosophy of Social Science* 8:37–54.

———. 1979. "Dialogue on Method." In *The Structure and Development of Science,* ed. Gerard Radnitzky and Gunnar Andersson, 63–132. Dordrecht: Reidel.

———. 1980a. "Democracy, Elitism, and Scientific Method." *Inquiry* 23:3–18.

———. 1980b. *Erkenntnis für Freie Menschen.* Frankfurt-am Main: Suhrkamp.

———. 1981. "More Clothes from the Emperor's Bargain Basement." *British Journal for Philosophy of Science* 32:57–94.

———. 1987. "Creativity—A Dangerous Myth." *Critical Inquiry* 13:700–11.

Field, M. 1955. "Former Soviet Citizens' Attitudes Toward the Soviet, the German, and the American Medical Systems." *American Sociological Review* 20:674–79.

Fisch, Max, ed. 1951. *Classic American Philosophers.* New York: Appleton-Century Crofts.

Fischer, Fritz. 1967. *Germany's Aims in the First World War.* New York: Norton.

———. 1974. *World Power or Decline.* New York: Norton.

Fleck, Ludwik. 1979 (orig. publ. 1935). *Genesis and Development of a Scientific Fact.* Trans. Bradley and Trenn, ed. Trenn and Merton, pref. by T. S. Kuhn. Chicago: University of Chicago Press.

———. 1983. *Erfahrung und Tatsache.* Ed. Lothar Schäfer and Thomas Schnelle. Frankfurt: Suhrkamp.

Fleisig, H. 1976. "Reparations and Depression." *American Economic Review*, May.

Flew, Antony. 1956. "Motives and the Unconscious." In *Foundations of Science and the Concepts of Psychology and Psychoanalysis*, ed. Herbert Feigl and Michael Scriven. Minnesota Studies in the Philosophy of Science, 1:155–73. Minneapolis: University of Minnesota Press.

Fodor, Jerry. 1982. *The Modularity of Mind*. Cambridge, Mass.: MIT Press.

Freudenthal, Gad. 1984. "The Role of Shared Knowledge in Science: The Failure of the Constructivist Program in Science." *Social Studies of Science* 14:285–96.

Frey, Fred. 1971. "Comment: On Issues and Nonissues in the Study of Power." *American Political Science Review* 65:1081–1101.

Freyd, Jennifer. 1983. "Shareability: The Social Psychology of Epistemology." *Cognitive Science* 7:191–210.

Friedman, Milton. 1953. *Essays in Positive Economics*. Chicago: University of Chicago Press.

———. 1957. *A Theory of the Consumption Function*. Princeton, N.J.: Princeton University Press.

———. 1968. *Dollars and Deficits*. Englewood Cliffs, N.J.: Prentice-Hall.

Friedman, Milton, and Rose Friedman. 1980. *Free to Choose*. New York: Harcourt Brace.

Friedman, Milton, and Simon Kuznets. 1945. *Income From Independent Professional Practice*. New York: NBER.

Friedman, Milton, and David Meiselman. 1963. "The Relative Stability of Monetary Velocity and the Investment Multiplier in the U.S., 1897–1958." In *Stabilization Policies*. Englewood Cliffs, N.J.: Prentice-Hall.

Friedman, Milton, and L. J. Savage. 1948. "The Utility Analysis of Choices Involving Risk." *Journal of Political Economy* 56:279–304.

Friedman, Milton, and Anna Schwartz. 1963. *A Monetary History of the United States*. Princeton, N.J.: Princeton University Press for the NBER.

Friedman, Milton, and Anna Schwartz. 1982. *Monetary Trends in the U.S. and the U.K.* Princeton, N.J.: Princeton University Press for the NBER.

Friedman, Neil. 1967. *The Social Nature of Psychological Research: The Psychological Experiment as a Social Interaction*. New York: Basic Books.

Fuller, Steve. 1988. *Social Epistemology*. Bloomington: Indiana University Press.

Gadamer, Hans Georg. 1975 (orig. publ. 1960). *Truth and Method*. New York: Seabury.

———. 1984. "The Hermeneutics of Suspicion." In *Hermeneutics*, ed. Gary Shapiro and Alan Sica, 54–65. Amherst: University of Massachusetts Press.

————. 1989. "Text and Interpretation." In *Dialogue and Deconstruction*, ed. Diane Michelfelder and Richard Palmer, pp. 21–51. Albany: SUNY Press.

Galbraith, John K. 1955. *The Great Crash*. Boston: Houghton Mifflin.

————. 1973. *Economics and the Public Purpose*. Boston: Houghton Mifflin.

Gardner, Howard. 1985. *The Mind's New Science*. New York: Basic Books.

Garfinkel, Herbert, et al. 1981. "The Work of a Discovering Science Construed with Materials from the Optically Discovered Pulsar." *Philosophy of the Social Sciences* 11:131–58.

Gaston, Jerry. 1970. "The Reward System in British Science." *American Sociological Review* 35:718–32.

Gearing, Fred, et al., eds. 1960. *Documentary History of the Fox Project*. Chicago: University of Chicago Department of Anthropology.

Geertz, Clifford. 1973. *The Interpretation of Culture*. New York: Basic Books.

George, Alexander, D. Hall, and W. Simons. 1971. *The Limits of Coercive Diplomacy*. Boston: Little, Brown.

George, Alexander, and R. Smoke. 1974. *Deterrence in American Foreign Policy*. New York: Columbia University Press.

Gergen, Kenneth J. 1982. *Towards Transformation in Social Knowledge*. New York: Springer.

Gilbert, Nigel, and M. Mulkay. 1981. "Contexts of Scientific Discourse: Social Accounting in Experimental Papers." In *The Social Process of Scientific Investigation*, ed. K. Knorr et al., 269–94. Dordrecht: Reidel.

Gilligan, Carol. 1982. *In a Different Voice*. Cambridge, Mass.: Harvard University Press.

Gilpin, Robert, and Christopher Wright, eds., 1964. *Scientists and National Policymaking*. New York: Columbia University Press.

Goffman, Erving. 1959. *Presentation of Self in Everyday Life*. Garden City, N.Y.: Doubleday.

Goldhamer, H., and Hans Speier. 1959. "Some Observations on Political Gaming." In Shubik, 1964.

Goldstein, Ira, and Seymour Papert. 1977. "AI, Language, and the Study of Knowledge." *Cognitive Science* 1:84–123.

Goldstein, Kenneth, and Sheldon Blackman. 1978. *Cognitive Style*. New York: Wiley.

Goldstein, Richard, and Stephen Sachs, eds. 1983. *Applied Poverty Research*. Totowa, N.J.: Rowman and Allenheld.

Goodman, Nelson. 1955. *Fact, Fiction, and Forecast*. Indianapolis: Bobbs Merrill.

Gouldner, Alvin W. 1970. *The Coming Crisis of Western Sociology*. New York: Basic Books.

————. 1976. "Revolutionary Intellectuals." *Telos* 26:3–36.

————. 1979. *The Future of Intellectuals and the Rise of the New Class*. New York: Seabury.

Graesser, Arthur C., and John Black, eds. 1985. *The Psychology of Questions*. Hillsdale, N.Y.: Erlbaum.

Graham, Loren, et al., eds. 1983. *Functions and Uses of Disciplinary Histories*. Boston: Reidel.

Greenberg, Daniel S. 1967. *The Politics of Pure Science*. New York: New American Library.

Griggs, Richard, and Sarah Ransdell. 1986. "Scientists and the Selection Task." *Social Studies of Science* 16:319–30.

Grünbaum, Adolf. 1984. *The Foundations of Psychoanalysis*. Berkeley and Los Angeles: University of California Press.

————. 1986. "Précis of *The Foundations of Psychoanalysis: A Philosophical Critique*, with Commentary." *Behavioral and Brain Sciences* 9, no. 2: 217–84.

Guetzkow, Harold, ed. 1951. *Groups, Leadership, and Men*. Pittsburgh, Pa.: Carnegie Institute of Technology.

————. 1959. "Uses of Simulation in the Study of International Relations." In Shubik, 1964.

Gusfield, Joseph. 1976. "The Literary Rhetoric of Science: Comedy and Pathos in Drinking Driver Research." *American Sociological Review* 41:16–34.

Haaken, Janice. 1988. "Field Dependence Research: A Historical Analysis of a Psychological Construct." *Signs* 13:700–11.

Habermas, Jürgen. 1967. *Zur Logik der Sozialwissenschaften*. Tübingen: Mohr.

————. 1970. "Der Universalitätsanspruch der Hermeneutik." In Rüdiger Bubner et al., eds., *Hermeneutik und Dialektik*, 73–104. Tübingen: Mohr.

————. 1971 (orig. publ. 1968). *Knowledge and Human Interests*. Trans. Shapiro. Boston: Beacon Press.

————. 1977. Review of Gadamer, *Truth and Method*. In *Understanding and Social Inquiry*, ed. Fred Dallmyer and T. McCarthy. Notre Dame, Ind.: University of Notre Dame Press.

Hafer, R. W., ed., 1986. *The Monetary vs. Fiscal Policy Debate*. Totowa, N.J.: Rowman and Allanheld.

Hagstrom, Warren. 1965. *The Scientific Community*. New York: Basic Books.

————. 1974. "Competition in Science." *American Sociological Review* 39:1–18.

Halas, E. S., et al. 1961. "Types of Response Elicited in Planaria by Light." *Journal of Comparative and Physiological Psychology* 54:302–05.

Hammond, Phillip, ed. 1964. *Sociologists at Work*. New York: Basic Books.

Hands, D. Wade. 1985. "The Structuralist View of Economic Theories." *Economics and Philosophy* 1, no. 2:303–35.

Handy, Rollo. 1964. *Methodology of the Behavioral Sciences*. Springfield, Ill.: C. C. Thomas.

Hanson, Norwood. 1958. *Patterns of Discovery*. Cambridge: Cambridge University Press.

Harding, Sandra. 1986. *The Science Question in Feminism*. Ithaca, N.Y.: Cornell University Press.

Harding, Sandra, and Merrill Hintikka, eds. 1983. *Discovering Reality: Feminist Perspectives on Epistemology, Metaphysics, Methodology, and Philosophy of Science*. Dordrecht: Reidel.

Hare-Mustin, Rachel, and Jeanne Marecek. 1988. "The Meaning of Difference. Gender Theory, Postmodernism, and Psychology." *American Psychologist* 43:455–64.

Hargens, Lowell. 1978. "Theory and Method in the Sociology of Science." *Sociological Inquiry* 48:121–39.

Harré, Rom. 1978. "Accounts, Actions, and Meanings." In *The Social Context of Method*, ed. Michael Brenner, P. Marsh, and M. Brenner, 44–66. New York: St. Martins.

Harré, Rom, and P. Secord. 1972. *The Explanation of Social Behavior*. Totowa, N.J.: Bedminster.

Harris, Errol. 1970. *Hypothesis and Perception*. London: Allen & Unwin.

———. 1972. "Epicyclic Popperism." *British Journal of the Philosophy of Science* 23:55–67.

Harris, Seymour, ed., 1947. *The New Economics*. New York: Knopf.

Harrod, Roy. 1937. "Mr. Keynes and Traditional Theory." *Economica* 5:74–86.

———. 1939. "An Essay in Dynamic Theory." *Economic Journal* 61:261–75.

Harvey, Bill. 1981. "The Effects of Social Context on the Process of Scientific Investigation: Experimental Tests of Quantum Mechanics." In *The Social Process of Scientific Investigation*, ed. K. Knorr et al., 139–64. Dordrecht: Reidel.

Harvey, David. 1985a. *Consciousness and the Urban Experience*. Baltimore: Johns Hopkins University Press.

———. 1985b. *The Urbanization of Capital*. Baltimore: Johns Hopkins University Press.

Haskell, Robert, ed. 1986. *Cognition and Dream Research*. New York: Journal of Mind and Behavior.

Haugeland, John, ed. 1981. *Mind Design*. Montgomery, Vt.: Bradford.

Haveman, Robert. 1986. "Social Science and Social Policy: Who Uses Whom?" In Frank Heller, ed., 1986.

———. 1987. *Poverty Policy and Poverty Research*. Madison: University of Wisconsin Press.

Havens, Leston. 1986. *Making Contact: Uses of Language in Psychotherapy*. Cambridge, Mass.: Harvard University Press.

Haworth, L., and J. Sayer Minas. 1954. "Concerning Value Science." *Philosophy of Science* 21:54–61.

Hechter, Michael. 1983. *Microfoundations of Macrosociology*. Philadelphia: Temple University Press.

———. 1987. *Principles of Group Solidarity*. Berkeley and Los Angeles: University of California Press.

Heijdra, Ben, Anton Lowenberg, and Robert Mallick. 1988. "Marxism, Methodological Individualism, and the New Institutional Economics." *Journal of Institutional and Theoretical Economics* 144:296–317.

Heller, Frank, ed. 1986. *The Use and Abuse of Social Science*. London: Sage.

Heller, Walter. 1967. *New Dimensions in Political Economy*. Cambridge, Mass.: Harvard University Press.

Hempel, Carl. 1965. *Aspects of Scientific Explanation*. New York: Free Press.

Hicks, John R. 1937. "Mr. Keynes and the Classics: A Suggested Interpretation." *Econometrica* 5:147–59.

———. 1939. *Value and Capital*. London: Oxford University Press.

———. 1974. *The Crisis in Keynesian Economics*. New York: Basic Books.

Higgins, E. Tory, et al., eds. 1981. *Social Cognition*. Hillsdale, N.Y.: Erlbaum.

Hintikka, Jaakko, ed. 1975. *Rudolph Carnap, Logical Empiricist*. Synthese Library no. 73. Boston: Reidel.

Hirsch, Abraham, and Neil de Marchi. 1986. "Making a Case When Theory is Unfalsifiable: Friedman's Monetary History." *Economics and Philosophy* 2:1–22.

Hirsch, E. D. 1976. *The Aims of Interpretation*. Chicago: University of Chicago Press.

Hoag, Wendy, and Klaus Allerbeck. 1985. "Interviewer-und Situations-effekte in Umfragen: eine log-lineare Analyse." *Zeitschrift für Soziologie* 10, no. 4:413–26.

Hodgson, Geoffrey. 1974. "The Theory of the Falling Rate of Profit." *New Left Review* 8:55–82.

Holland, Norman. 1982. "Why, This Is Transference, nor Am I Out of It." *Psychoanalysis and Contemporary Thought* 5:27–34.

Hollinger, David. 1983. "The Defense of Democracy and Robert K. Merton's Formulation of the Scientific Ethos." In *Knowledge and Society*, ed. Henrika Kuklick and R. Jones, annual vol. 4:1–16. Greenwich, Conn.: JAI Press.

Hook, Sidney, ed. 1959. *Psychoanalysis, Scientific Method, and Philosophy*. New York: NYU Press.

Hoos, Ida. 1972. *Systems Analysis in Public Policy: A Critique*. Berkeley and Los Angeles: University of California Press.

Horelick, Arnold, and Myron Rush. 1966. *Strategic Power and Soviet Foreign Policy*. Chicago: University of Chicago Press.

Horowitz, Irving Louis. 1970 (orig. publ. 1965). "The Life and Death of Project

Camelot." In *The Values of Social Science*, 2d ed., ed. Norman K. Denzin, 241–66. New Brunswick, N.J.: Transaction Books.

Howard, Nigel. 1971. *Paradoxes of Rationality*. Cambridge, Mass.: MIT Press.

Hübner, K. 1978. *Kritik der Wissenschaftlichen Vernunft*. Freiburg/Munich: Alber.

Hübner, K., et al., eds. 1976. *Die Politische Herausforderung der Wissenschaft: Gegen eine Ideologisch Verplante Forschung*. Hamburg: Hoffman und Campe.

Hudson, Liam. 1966. *Contrary Imaginations*. New York: Schocken.

Hull, Clark, et al. 1940. *Mathematico-deductive Theory of Rote Learning*. New Haven, Conn.: Yale University Press.

Hunter, Floyd. 1953. *Community Power Structure*. Chapel Hill: University of North Carolina Press.

———. 1959. *Top Leadership, USA*. Chapel Hill: University of North Carolina Press.

Huntington, Samuel P. 1968. *Political Order in Changing Societies*. New Haven, Conn.: Yale University Press.

Huntington, Samuel P., and Joan Nelson, 1976. *No Easy Choice*. Cambridge, Mass.: Harvard University Press.

Isaak, Alan. 1975 (orig. publ. 1969). *Scope and Method of Political Science*. 2d ed. Homewood, Ill.: Dorsey Press.

Jervis, Robert. 1976. *Perception and Misperception in International Politics*. Princeton, N.J.: Princeton University Press.

———. 1979. "Deterrence Theory Revisited." *World Politics* 31:289–324.

Johnson, Paul E., et al. 1981. "Expertise and Error in Diagnostic Reasoning." *Cognitive Science* 5:235–83.

Kahn, Herman. 1965. *On Escalation*. Westport, Conn.: Greenwood Press.

Kahneman, D., P. Slovic, and A. Tversky. 1982. *Judgments Under Uncertainty: Heuristics and Biases*. Cambridge: Cambridge University Press.

Kalecki, Michal. 1939. *Essays in the Theory of Economic Fluctuations*. New York: Farrar and Rinehart.

Kaplan, Abraham. 1964. *The Conduct of Inquiry*. San Francisco: Chandler.

Kaplan, Morton. 1954. "Balance of Power, Bipolarity, and Other Models of International Systems." *American Political Science Review* 48:684–95.

Katouzian, Homa. 1980. *Ideology and Method in Economics*. New York: NYU Press.

Keller, Evelyn Fox. 1982. "Feminism and Science." *Signs* 7:589–602.

———. 1985. *Reflections on Gender and Science*. New Haven, Conn.: Yale University Press.

Kelley, Harold H. 1973. "The Processes of Causal Attribution." *American Psychologist* 28:107–28.

Kemeny, John, and L. Snell. 1962. *Mathematical Models in the Social Sciences*. Boston: Ginn.

Kern, Leslie, H. Mirels, and V. Hinshaw. 1983. "Scientists' Understanding of

Propositional Logic: An Experimental Investigation." *Social Studies of Science* 13, no. 1:131–46.

Keynes, John M. 1936. *The General Theory of Employment, Interest, and Money.* New York: Harcourt, Brace.

———. 1937. "The General Theory of Employment." *Quarterly Journal of Economics* 51:209–23.

Kharasch, Robert. 1973. *The Institutional Imperative.* New York: Charterhouse Books.

Kindleberger, Charles P. 1973. *The World in Depression. 1929–1939.* Berkeley and Los Angeles: University of California Press.

Kintsch, Walter, James R. Miller, and Peter Polson, eds. 1984. *Method and Tactics in Cognitive Science.* Hillsdale, N.Y.: Erlbaum.

Klahr, David, and K. Dunbar. 1988. "Dual Space Search During Scientific Reasoning." *Cognitive Science* 12:1–48.

Klamer, Arjo. 1984. *Conversations with Economists.* Totowa, N.J.: Rowman and Allanheld.

Klein, Lawrence. 1947. *The Keynesian Revolution.* New York: Macmillan.

Kluckhohn, Clyde. 1949. *Mirror For Man.* New York: Whittlesey House.

Knight, Frank H. 1921. *Risk, Uncertainty, and Profit.* New York: Kelley and Millman.

Knorr, Karin. 1977. "Producing or Reproducing Knowledge." *Social Science Information* 16:669–96.

Knorr-Cetina, Karin. 1981. *The Manufacture of Knowledge.* Oxford: Pergamon.

———. 1988. "Das naturwissenschaftliche Labor als Ort der Verdichtung der Gesellschaft." *Zeitschrift für Soziologie* 17:85–101.

Knorr-Cetina, Karin, and M. Mulkay, eds. 1983. *Science Observed.* London: Sage.

Koch, Sigmund. 1981. "Nature and Limits of Psychological Knowledge." *American Psychologist* 36:257–69.

Kosslyn, Stephen. 1983. *Ghosts in the Mind's Machine.* New York: Norton.

Kosslyn, Stephen, and James R. Pomerantz. 1977. "Imagery, Propositions, and Internal Representations." *Cognitive Psychology* 9:52–76.

Kovel, Joel. 1978. "Things and Words." *Psychoanalysis and Contemporary Thought* 1:21–88.

Kraft, Victor. 1968 (orig. publ. 1950). *Der Wiener Kreis.* Vienna: Springer.

Kramer, Ralph. 1969. *Participation of the Poor.* Englewood Cliffs, N.J.: Prentice-Hall.

Kreisky, Eva. 1986. Guten Tag, Frau Marx!" In *Gegen den Strom. Festschrift für Josef Hindels,* ed. M. Häupl et al. Vienna.

Kugler, Jacek, and Frank Zagare, eds. 1987. *Exploring the Stability of Deterrence.* Boulder, Colo.: Lynne Rienner.

Kuhn, Thomas. 1970a (orig. publ. 1962). *The Structure of Scientific Revolutions.*

2d ed. Encyclopedia of Unified Science, vol. 2, no. 2. Chicago: University of Chicago Press.

———. 1970b. "Logic of Discovery or Psychology of Research?" In *Criticism and the Growth of Knowledge*, ed. I. Lakatos and A. Musgrave. Cambridge: Cambridge University Press.

———. 1971. "Notes on Lakatos." In *PSA 1970*, ed. Roger Buck and R. S. Cohen, 137–46. Boston Studies no. 8. Boston: Reidel.

———. 1977. *The Essential Tension*. Chicago: University of Chicago Press.

Ladd, Everett, and Seymour Lipset. 1975. *The Divided Academy: Professors and Politics*. New York: McGraw-Hill.

Lakatos, Imre. 1970. "Falsification and the Methodology of Scientific Research Programmes." In Lakatos and Musgrave, 1970, 91–196.

Lakatos, Imre, and Alan Musgrave, eds. 1970. *Criticism and the Growth of Knowledge*. Cambridge: Cambridge University Press.

Landsberger, Michael. 1970. "The Life-Cycle Hypothesis: A Reinterpretation and Empirical Test." *American Economic Review*, 60 no. 1:175–83.

Lang, S. 1981. *The File*. New York: Springer.

Langley, Pat, Herbert Simon, Gary Bradshaw, and Jan Zytkow. 1987. *Scientific Discovery*. Cambridge, Mass.: MIT Press.

Latour, Bruno. 1981a. "Is It Possible to Reconstruct the Research Process? Sociology of a Brain Peptide." In *The Social Process of Scientific Investigation*, ed. Karin Knorr et al., 53–73. Dordrecht: Reidel.

———. 1981b. "Insiders and Outsiders in the Sociology of Science; Or, How Can We Foster Agnosticism?" In *Knowledge and Society*, ed. Robert A. Jones and Henrika Kuklick, 3:199–216. Greenwich, Conn.: JAI Press.

———. 1982. Review of Karin Knorr, *The Manufacture of Knowledge*. 4S Review 7, no. 4:30–35.

Latour, Bruno, and Steve Woolgar. 1979. *Laboratory Life: The Social Construction of Scientific Facts*. Beverly Hills, Calif.: Sage.

Laudan, Larry. 1981. "The Pseudo-Science of Science?" *Philosophy of the Social Sciences* 11:173–98.

Lavoie, Don. 1985. *National Economic Planning: What is Left?* Cambridge, Mass.: Ballinger.

Law, John, and David French. 1974. "Normative and Interpretive Sociologies of Science." *Sociological Review* 20:581–95.

Lebow, Richard. 1981. *Between Peace and War*. Baltimore: Johns Hopkins University Press.

Leijonhufvud, Axel. 1968. *On Keynesian Economics and the Economics of Keynes*. New York: Oxford University Press.

———. 1976. "Schools, Revolutions, and Research Programmes." In *Method and Appraisal in Economics*, ed. Spiro J. Latsis, 149–80. Cambridge: Cambridge University Press.

Leinfellner, Werner. 1983. "Marxian Paradigms vs. Microeconomic Structures." In *Epistemology, Methodology, and the Social Sciences*, ed. Robert S. Cohen and Marx Wartofsky, 153–202. Boston Studies no. 71. Boston: Reidel.

Leng, Russell, and H. Wheeler. 1979. "Influence Strategies, Success, and War." *Journal of Conflict Resolution* 23:655–84.

Leontief, Wassily. 1936. "Mr. Keynes' Monetary Theory of Unemployment." *Quarterly Journal of Economics* 51, no. 1. Rpt. in *Essays in Economics*. New York: Oxford University Press, 1966.

Lepley, Ray, ed. 1945. *Value: a Co-operative Inquiry*. New York: Columbia University Press.

Levine, Murray. 1974. "Scientific Method and the Adversary Model." *American Psychologist* 29:661–77.

Levy, Marion. 1952. *The Structure of Society*. Princeton, N.J.: Princeton University Press.

Leys, Wayne. 1952. *Ethics For Policy Decisions*. New York: Prentice-Hall.

Lichten, Eric. 1986. *Class, Power, and Austerity*. South Hadley, Mass.: Bergin and Garvey.

Lieberman, Bernhardt. 1964. "i-trust." *Journal of Conflict Resolution* 8:271–80.

Lipset, Seymour. 1960. *Political Man*. Garden City, N.Y.: Doubleday.

List, Elisabeth. 1985. "Die Männliche Stimme der Vernunft." *Österreichische Zeitschrift für Politikwissenschaft*, 185–96.

Luce, R. Duncan, and H. Raiffa. 1957. *Games and Decisions*. New York: Wiley.

Lukács, Georg. 1923. *Geschichte und Klassenbewusstsein*. Berlin: Malik. Trans. 1971 by Rodney Livingstone as *History and Class-consciousness*. Cambridge, Mass.: MIT Press.

Lynch, Michael. 1985. *Art and Artifact in Laboratory Science*. London: Routledge and Kegal Paul.

Lynch, Michael, A. Livingston, and H. Garfinkel. 1983. "Temporal Order in Lab Work." In Knorr-Cetina and Mulkay, eds., 1983.

Lyons, Gene M. 1969. *The Uneasy Partnership*. New York: Russell Sage.

Lyons, Gene M., and Louis Morton. 1965. *Schools for Strategy*. New York: Praeger.

McClelland, James, and Jeffrey Elman. 1986. "The TRACE Model of Speech Perception." *Cognitive Psychology* 18:1–86.

McCloskey, Donald. 1983. "The Rhetoric of Economics." *Journal of Economic Literature* 21:481–517.

———. 1985. *The Rhetoric of Economics*. Madison: University of Wisconsin Press.

McClosky, Herbert. 1964. "Consensus and Ideology in American Politics." *American Political Science Review* 58:361–82.

McConnell, J., et al. 1961. "The Effects of Ingestion of Conditioned Planaria on the Response Level of Naive Planaria: A Pilot Study." *Worm Runner's Digest* 3:41–47.

McCorquodale, K., and P. Meehl. 1948. "On a Distinction Between Hypothetical Constructs and Intervening Variables." *Psychological Review* 55:95–107.

McGrath, Joseph. 1981. "Dilemmatics: The Study of Research Choices and Dilemmas." *American Behavioral Scientist* 25, no. 2:179–210.

McHoul, A. W. 1982. *Telling How Texts Talk: Essays on Reading and Ethnomethodology.* London: Routledge.

MacIntyre, Alasdair. 1977. "Epistemological Crises, Dramatic Narrative, and the Philosophy of Science." *Monist* 60:453–72.

McKenzie, Richard. 1984. *Fugitive Industry.* San Francisco: Pacific Institute for Public Policy Research.

Magat, Richard. 1979. *The Ford Foundation at Work.* New York: Plenum Press.

Mahoney, Michael J. 1976. *Scientist as Subject: The Psychological Imperative.* Cambridge, Mass.: Ballinger.

Malinowski, Bronislaw. 1922. *Argonauts of the Western Pacific.* London: Routledge.

Manicas, Peter. 1987. *History and Philosophy of the Social Sciences.* New York: Blackwell.

Marris, Peter, and Martin Rein. 1967. *Dilemmas of Social Reform.* New York: Atherton.

Maslow, Abraham H. 1966. *The Psychology of Science.* New York: Harper.

Meade, James E. 1937. "A Simplified Model of Mr. Keynes' System." *Review of Economic Studies* 4:98–107.

Meehl, Paul. 1954. *Clinical vs. Statistical Prediction.* Minneapolis: University of Minnesota Press.

Meissner, W. W. 1981. *Internalization in Psychoanalysis.* New York: International Universities Press.

Melman, Seymour. 1970. *Pentagon Capitalism.* New York: McGraw Hill.

Meltzer, Allan. 1981. "Keynes' *General Theory*: A Different Perspective." *Journal of Economic Literature* 19:34–64.

Mendelsohn, Everett, et al., eds. 1977. *The Social Production of Scientific Knowledge.* Boston: Reidel.

Merton, Robert. 1938. "Social Structure and Anomie." *American Sociological Review* 3:672–82.

———. 1949. *Social Theory and Social Structure.* New York: Free Press.

———. 1973. *The Sociology of Science.* Chicago: University of Chicago Press.

———. 1976. *Sociological Ambivalence and Other Essays.* New York: Free Press.

———. 1977. "The Sociology of Science, an Episodic Memoir." In *The Sociol-*

ogy of Science in Europe, ed. Merton and Gaston, 3–141. Carbondale: Southern Illinois University Press.

———. 1984. "The Fallacy of the Latest Word: The Case of 'Pietism and Science.'" *American Journal of Sociology* 89:1091–1121.

Merton, Robert, et al. 1957. *The Student-Physician: Introductory Studies in the Sociology of Medical Education.* Cambridge, Mass.: Harvard University Press.

Middlemas, Keith. 1973. *Diplomacy of Illusion.* London: Weidenfeld and Nicholson.

Miller, David. 1974. "Popper's Qualitative Theory of Verisimilitude." *British Journal of the Philosophy of Science* 25:160–66.

———. 1975. "The Accuracy of Predictions." *Synthese* 30, no. 1:159–91.

Miller, George A. 1956. "The Magic Number 7 ± 2." *Psychological Review* 63:81–97.

Miller, George A., E. Galanter, and K. Pribram. 1960. *Plans and the Structure of Behavior.* New York: Holt.

Mills, C. Wright. 1951. *White Collar.* New York: Oxford University Press.

———. 1956. *the Power Elite.* New York: Oxford University Press.

Milnor, J. 1954. "Games against Nature." Rpt. in Shubik, 1964.

Minsky, Hyman. 1975. *Keynes.* New York: Columbia University Press.

———. 1986. *Stabilizing an Unstable Economy.* New Haven, Conn.: Yale University Press.

Minsky, Marvin. 1975. "A Framework for Representing Knowledge." In *The Psychology of Computer Vision*, ed. Patrick Winston. New York: McGraw-Hill.

———. 1981. Appendix to "A Framework for Representing Knowledge." In *Mind Design*, ed. John Haugeland, chap 3. Montgomery, Vt.: Bradford.

———. 1983. "Jokes and the Logic of the Collective Unconscious." In *Methods of Heuristics* ed. Rudolf Groner et al., 171–93. Hillsdale, N.Y.: Erlbaum.

Minsky, Marvin, and Seymour Papert. 1972. "Progress Report on Artificial Intelligence." MIT AI Lab, Memo 252.

Mitroff, Ian. 1974a. *The Subjective Side of Science.* New York: Elsevier.

———. 1974b. "Norms and Counternorms . . . A Case Study of the Ambivalence of Scientists." *American Sociological Review* 30:579–95.

———. 1983. *Stakeholders of the Organization Mind.* San Francisco: Jossey-Bass.

Mitroff, Ian, and Ralph Kilmann. 1978. *Methodological Approaches to Social Science.* San Francisco: Jossey-Bass.

Mitroff, Ian, R. Mason, and V. Barabba. 1983. *The 1980 Census: Policymaking Amid Turbulence.* Lexington, Mass.: Heath.

Mitzmann, Arthur. 1970. *The Iron Cage.* New York: Knopf.

Modigliani, Franco. 1984. In *Conservations with Economists*, pp. 114–26. Totowa, N.J.: Rowman and Allenheld.

Morgan, Brian. 1978. *Monetarists and Keynesians*. New York: Wiley.

Moynihan, Daniel Patrick. 1969. *Maximum Feasible Misunderstanding*. New York: Free Press.

Mulkay, Michael. 1969. "Some Aspects of Cultural Growth in the Natural Sciences." *Sociological Research* 36:22–52.

———. 1975. "Three Models of Scientific Development." *Sociological Review* 23:509–37.

———. 1976a. "Methodology in the Sociology of Science." In *Perspectives on the Emergence of Scientific Disciplines*, ed. R. MacLeod and G. Lemaine, 207–20. The Hague: Mouton.

———. 1976b. "Norms and Ideology in Science." *Social Science Information* 15:637–56.

———. 1979. *Science and the Sociology of Knowledge*. London: Allen and Unwin.

———. 1980. "Sociology of Science in the West." *Current Sociology* 28, no. 3:1–116.

Mulkay, Michael, and David Edge. "Cognitive, Technical, and Social Factors in the Growth of Radio Astronomy." *Social Science Information* 12, no. 6:25–62.

Mullins, Nicholas. 1973. *Theories and Theory Groups in Contemporary American Sociology*. New York: Harper.

———. 1983. "Theories and Theory Groups Revisited." In *Sociological Theory 1983*, ed. Randall Collins, 319–37. San Francisco: Jossey-Bass.

Murphy, Arthur E. 1927. "Objective Relativism in Dewey and Whitehead." *Philosophical Review* 36:121–44.

Murray, Charles. 1984. *Losing Ground*. New York: Basic Books.

Nabli, Mustapha, and Jeffrey Nugent, eds. 1989. *The New Institutional Economics and Development*. Amsterdam: North-Holland.

Nagel, Ernest. 1949. "The Meaning of Reduction in the Natural Sciences." *Science and Civilization*, ed. R. C. Stauffer, 99–145. Madison: University of Wisconsin Press.

———. 1961. *The Structure of Science*. New York: Harcourt, Brace.

Neisser, Ulric. 1976. *Cognition and Reality*. San Francisco: Freeman.

Nelkin, Dorothy, ed. 1984. *Controversy: The Politics of Technical Decisions*. 2d ed. Beverly Hills, Calif.: Sage.

Neumann, John von, and Oskar Morgenstern. 1944 (2d ed. 1947). *Theory of Games and Economic Behavior*. Princeton, N.J.: Princeton University Press.

Newton-Smith, W. H. 1981. *The Rationality of Science*. Boston: Routledge and Kegan Paul.

Nielsen, Waldemar A. 1972. *The Big Foundations*. 20th Century Fund study. New York: Columbia University Press.

———. 1985. *The Golden Donors*. New York: Dutton.

Nisbett, Richard, and Lee Ross. 1980. *Human Inference: Strategies and Shortcomings of Social Judgment.* Englewood Cliffs, N.J.: Prentice-Hall.

Norman, Donald A., ed. 1981. *Perspectives in Cognitive Science.* (Rpt. of *Cognitive Science*, vol. 4.) Hillsdale, N.Y.: Erlbaum.

OECD. 1980. *The Utilisation of the Social Sciences in Policymaking in the U.S.* Paris: OECD.

Orlans, Harold. 1973. *Contracting For Knowledge.* San Francisco: Jossey-Bass.

Orren, Karen. 1974. *Corporate Power and Social Change.* Baltimore: Johns Hopkins Press.

Pap, Arthur. 1949. *Elements of Analytic Philosophy.* New York: Macmillan.

Parijs, Phillipe van. 1980. "The Falling-Rate-of-Profit Theory of Crisis: A Rational Reconstruction by Way of Obituary." *Review of Radical Political Economics* 12:1–16.

Parsons, Talcott. 1960. *Structure and Process in Modern Societies.* New York: Free Press.

———. 1967. *Sociological Theory and Modern Society.* New York: Free Press.

———. 1969. *Politics and Social Structure.* New York: Free Press.

Parsons, Talcott, and R. F. Bales. 1955. *Family, Socialization and Interaction Process.* New York: Free Press.

Parsons, Talcott, and Neil Smelser. 1956. *Economy and Society.* New York: Free Press.

Patel, Vimla, and Guy Groen. 1986. "Knowledge Based Solution Strategies in Medical Reasoning." *Cognitive Science* 10:91–116.

Patinkin, Don. 1956. *Money, Interest, and Prices.* Evanston, Ill.: Row, Peterson.

———. 1976. *Keynes' Monetary Thought: A Study of Its Development.* Durham, N.C.: Duke University Press.

Payer, Cheryl. 1974. *The Debt Trap: The IMF and the Third World.* New York: Monthly Review Press.

Payne, James L. 1970. *The American Threat.* Chicago: Markham.

———. 1975. *Principles of Social Science Measurement.* College Station, Tex.: Lytton.

Penick, James, et al., eds. 1972. *The Politics of American Science*, rev. ed. Cambridge, Mass.: MIT Press.

Pepper, Stephen. 1938. *World Hypotheses.* Berkeley: University of California Press.

Perry, David C. 1984. "Structuralism, Class Conflict, and Urban Reality." In *Cities in Transformation*, ed. Michael P. Smith, 219–34. Urban Affairs Annual Reviews, vol. 26. Beverly Hills, Calif.: Sage.

Peschek, Joseph. 1987. *Policy-planning Organizations, Elite Agendas, and America's Rightward Turn.* Philadelphia: Temple University Press.

Peterfreund, Emanuel. 1983. *The Process of Psychoanalytic Therapy.* Hillsdale, N.Y.: Erlbaum.

———. 1986. "Reply to Eagle and Wolitzky." *Psychoanalysis and Contemporary Thought* 9:103–24.

Pickering, Andrew. 1981. "The Role of Interests in High-Energy Physics." In *The Social Process of Scientific Investigation*, ed. Karin Knorr et al., 107–38. Dordrecht: Reidel.

———. 1985. "Constructing Consensus: World Views, Institutional Structures, and Policy Making in Recent High Energy Physics." Presented at 4S Society meeting, Troy, N.Y., Oct. 25.

Pigou, A. C. 1936. "Mr. J. M. Keynes' General Theory of Employment, Interest, and Money." *Economica* 3:115–32.

———. 1952. *Keynes' General Theory: A Retrospective View*. London: Macmillan.

Piven, Frances F., and Richard Cloward. 1971. *Regulating the Poor*. New York: Random House.

Polsby, Nelson. 1981. *Community Power and Political Theory*, 2d ed. New Haven, Conn.: Yale University Press.

Polsky, Ned. 1967. *Hustlers, Beats, and Others*. New York: Aldine.

Polya, George. 1945 (2d ed. 1957). *How To Solve It*. Princeton, N.J.: Princeton University Press.

Popper, Karl. 1935. *Logik der Forschung*. Trans. 1959 as *The Logic of Scientific Discovery*. New York: Harper.

———. 1945. *The Open Society and Its Enemies*. London: Routledge and Paul.

———. 1962. *Conjectures and Refutations*. New York: Harper.

———. 1963. "The Demarcation Between Science and Metaphysics." In Schilpp, 1963, 183–226.

———. 1970. "Normal Science and Its Dangers." In *Criticism and the Growth of Knowledge*, ed. I. Lakatos and A. Musgrave. Cambridge: Cambridge University Press.

———. 1972. *Objective Knowledge*. London: Oxford University Press.

———. 1976. "A Note on Verisimilitude." *British Journal for the Philosophy of Science* 27:147–59.

Portis, Edward B. 1986. *Max Weber and Political Commitment*. Philadelphia: Temple University Press.

Possony, Stephen. 1967. "Mao's Strategic Initiative of 1965 and the U.S. Response." *Orbis* 11:149–81.

Postman, Leo. 1953. "On the Problem of Perceptual Defense." *Psychological Review* 60:298–306.

Price, Don. 1967. *The Scientific Estate*. Cambridge, Mass.: Harvard University Press.

Putnam, Hilary. 1962. "The Analytic and the Synthetic." In *Minnesota Studies in the Philosophy of Science*, ed. Herbert Feigl and Grover Maxwell, 3:358–97. Minneapolis: University of Minnesota Press.

Pylyshyn, Zenon, ed. 1987. *The Robot's Dilemma: The Frame Problem in AI.* Norwood, N.J.: Ablex.

Quade, E. S., ed. 1964. *Analysis For Military Decisions.* Chicago: Rand McNally.

Quarles, Susan. 1986. *Guide To Federal Funding For Social Scientists.* New York: Russell Sage.

Quine, Willard V. 1953. "Two Dogmas of Empiricism." In *From a Logical Point of View*, chap. 2. Cambridge, Mass.: Harvard University Press.

Radcliffe-Brown, A. R. 1922. *The Andaman Islanders.* New York: Free Press.

Radnitzky, Gerard. 1970. *Contemporary Schools of Metascience.* 2 vols. Goteborg: Akademiforlaget.

———. 1979. "On Justifying a Theory." In *Structure and Development of Science*, ed. G. Radnitzky and G. Andersson. Boston: Reidel.

———. 1981. "Analytic Philosophy as the Confrontation Between Wittgensteinians and Popper." In *Scientific Philosophy Today*, ed. J. Agassi and R. S. Cohen, 239–86. Boston: Reidel.

Rapoport, Amnon. 1967. "Optimal Policies for the Prisoner's Dilemma." *Psychological Review* 74:136–48.

Rapoport, Anatol. 1960. *Fights, Games, and Debates.* Ann Arbor: University of Michigan Press.

———. 1964. *Strategy and Conscience.* New York: Harper.

———. 1967. "Exploiter, Leader, Hero, and Martyr: The Four Archetypes of the 2 × 2 Game." *Behavioral Science* 12, no. 2:81–84.

Rapoport, Anatol, and A. Chammah. 1965. *Prisoner's Dilemma.* Ann Arbor: University of Michigan Press.

Rapoport, Anatol, and M. Guyer. 1966. "A Taxonomy of 2 × 2 Games." In *General Systems*, vol. 11, ed. L. von Bertalanffy and A. Rapoport.

Rapoport, Anatol, and C. Orwant. 1962. "Experimental Games: A Review." Rpt. in Shubik, 1964.

Ravetz, Jerome. 1971. *Scientific Knowledge and Its Social Problems.* New York: Oxford.

Rayack, Elton. 1987. *Not So Free to Choose.* New York: Praeger.

Reagan, Michael. 1969. *Science and the Federal Patron.* New York: Oxford University Press.

Redfield, Robert. 1960. *The Little Community.* Chicago: University of Chicago Press.

Reichenbach, Hans. 1938. *Experience and Prediction.* Chicago: University of Chicago Press.

Reinharz, Shulamit. 1979. *On Becoming a Social Scientist.* San Francisco: Jossey-Bass.

Rescher, Nicholas. 1985. *The Strife of Systems.* Pittsburgh, Pa.: University of Pittsburgh Press.

Restivo, Sal. 1983. "The Myth of the Kuhnian Revolution." In *Sociological Theory 1983*, ed. Randall Collins, 293–305. San Francisco: Jossey-Bass.

———. 1984. Review of Böhme, *Finalization in Science. 4S Review* 2, no. 4:14–20.

Ricoeur, Paul. 1970. *Freud and Philosophy: An Essay in Interpretation.* New Haven, Conn.: Yale University Press. Trans. of *De l'Interpretation: Essai sur Freud* (1965).

———. 1977 (orig. publ. 1971). "The Model of the Text: Meaningful Action Considered as a Text." In *Understanding and Social Inquiry*, ed. Fred Dallmyer and T. McCarthy. Notre Dame, Ind.: University of Notre Dame Press.

Riessman, Frank. 1962. *The Culturally Deprived Child.* New York: Harper.

Riker, William. 1962. *The Theory of Political Coalitions.* New Haven, Conn.: Yale University Press.

Ritzer, George. 1975. *Sociology: A Multiple Paradigm Science.* Boston: Allyn and Bacon.

Roberts, Helen, ed. 1981. *Doing Feminist Research.* London: Routledge.

Robinson, Joan. 1951. *Collected Papers*, vol. 1. New York: Kelley.

———. 1965. *Collected Economic Papers*, vol. 3. Oxford: Blackwell.

———. 1973. *After Keynes.* Oxford: Blackwell.

———. 1978. *Contributions to Modern Economics.* Oxford: Blackwell.

———. 1979. *The Generalization of the General Theory and Other Essays.* New York: St. Martin's Press.

———. 1981. *What Are the Questions?* Armonk, N.Y.: M.E. Sharpe.

Rock, I. 1957. "The Role of Repetition in Associative Learning." *American Journal of Psychology* 70:186–93.

Roe, Anne. 1952. "A Psychological Study of Eminent Psychologists and Anthropologists, and a Comparison with Biological and Physical Scientists." *Psychological Monographs* 67:1–55.

Roemer, John. 1981. *Analytical Foundations of Marxian Economic Theory.* New York: Cambridge University Press.

———, ed. 1986. *Analytical Marxism.* Cambridge: Cambridge University Press.

Rogers, Carl. 1961. *Client-Centered Therapy.* New York: Houghton Mifflin.

Rokeach, Milton. 1960. *The Open and Closed Mind.* New York: Harper.

Röpke, Wilhelm. 1937 (rpt. 1963). *Economics of the Free Society.* Trans. P. Boarman. Chicago: Regnery.

Rorty, Richard. 1979. *Philosophy and the Mirror of Nature.* Princeton, N.J.: Princeton University Press.

Rose, Hilary, and Stephen Rose. 1976. *Ideology of/in the Natural Sciences.* Rochester, Vt.: Schenkman.

Rosenberg, Alexander. 1980. *Sociobiology and the Preemption of Social Science.* Baltimore: Johns Hopkins University Press.

Rosenblueth, A., N. Wiener, and J. Bigelow. 1943. "Behavior, Purpose, Teleology." *Philosophy of Science* 10:18–24.

Rosenthal, Robert. 1966. *Experimenter Effects in Behavioral Research.* New York: Appleton-Century.

———. 1983. "Experimenter Effects in Laboratories, Classrooms, and Clinics." In *Bias in Psychotherapy*, ed. Joan Murray and Paul Abramson, 84–102. New York: Praeger.

Roth, Michael. 1987. *Psychoanalysis as History.* Ithaca, N.Y.: Cornell University Press.

Rozeboom, William. 1962. "The Factual Content of Theoretical Concepts." In *Minnesota Studies in the Philosophy of Science*, ed. Herbert Feigl and Grover Maxwell, 3:273–57. Minneapolis: University of Minnesota Press.

Rubinstein, Benjamin. 1980. "On the Psychoanalytic Theory of Unconscious Motivation and the Problem of its Confirmation." *Psychoanalysis and Contemporary Thought* 3:3–20.

———. 1983. "Freud's Early Theories of Hysteria." In *Physics, Philosophy, and Psychoanalysis*, ed. Robert S. Cohen and L. Laudan. Boston: Reidel.

Rubinstein, Robert, Charles Laughlin, and John McManus. 1984. *Science As Cognitive Process.* Philadelphia: University of Pennsylvania Press.

Rubovitz-Seitz, Philip. 1986. "Clinical Interpretation, Hermeneutics, and the Problem of Validation." *Psychoanalysis and Contemporary Thought* 9:3–42.

Rudner, Richard. 1966. *Philosophy of Social Science.* Englewood Cliffs, N.J.: Prentice-Hall.

Rumelhart, David, James McClelland, et al. 1986. *Parallel Distributed Processing: Explorations in the Microstructure of Cognition*, vols. 1–2. Cambridge, Mass.: MIT Press.

Runkel, B. J., and J. McGrath. 1972. *Research on Human Behavior: A Systematic Guide to Method.* New York: Holt.

Ryan, William. 1976 (orig. publ. 1971). *Blaming the Victim.* New York: Random House.

Sahner, Heinz. 1979. "Veröffentlichte empirische Sozialforschung: eine Kumulation von Artefakten?" *Zeitschrift für Soziologie* 8:267–78.

Salmon, Wesley, R. Jeffery, and J. Greeno. 1971. *Statistical Explanation and Statistical Relevance.* Pittsburgh, Pa.: University of Pittsburgh Press.

Salomon, J.-J. 1977. "Science Policy Studies and the Development of Science Policy." In *Science; Technology, and Society*, ed. Ina Spiegel-Rösing and Derek Price. London: Sage.

Samuelson, Paul. 1947. *Foundations of Economic Analysis.* Cambridge, Mass.: Harvard University Press.

———. 1948. *Economics*, 1st ed. New York: McGraw-Hill.

Schafer, Roy. 1968. *Aspects of Internalization.* New York: International Universities Press.

————. 1976. *A New Language for Psychoanalysis*. New Haven, Conn.: Yale University Press.

————. 1983. *The Analytic Attitude*. New York: Basic Books.

————. 1984. "The Pursuit of Failure and the Idealization of Unhappiness." *American Psychologist* 39:398–405.

Schank, Roger. 1980. "Language and Memory." *Cognitive Science* 4:243–84.

————. 1986. *Explanation Patterns*. Hillsdale, N.Y.: Erlbaum.

Schank, Roger, and R. Abelson. 1977. *Scripts, Plans, Goals, and Understanding*. Hillsdale, N.Y.: Erlbaum.

Schank, Roger, and P. Childers. 1984. *The Cognitive Computer*. Reading, Mass.: Addison-Wesley.

Scheffler, Israel. 1963. *TheAnatomy of Inquiry*. New York: Knopf.

————. 1967. *Science and Subjectivity*. Indianapolis: Bobbs Merrill.

Schelling, Thomas. 1960. *The Strategy of Conflict*. New York: Oxford.

————. 1961. "Experimental Games and Bargaining Theory." Rpt. in Shubik, 1964.

Schlick, Moritz. 1925. *Allgemeine Erkenntnislehre*. Berlin: Springer. Rpt. Suhrkamp, 1979.

————. 1987 (orig. publ. 1933–34). *The Problems of Philosophy in Their Interconnection*. Trans. Peter Heath, ed. H. Mulder et al. Boston: Reidel.

————. 1938. *Gesammelte Aufsätze. 1926–1936*. Vienna: Gerold & Co.

Schmitt, Bernadotte. 1930. *The Coming of the War, 1914*. New York: Scribner's.

Schneider, David, and G. C. Homans. 1955. "Kinship Terminology and the American Kinship System." *American Anthropologist* 57, no. 6:1194–1208.

Schoenfeld, Alan H. 1983. "Beyond the Purely Cognitive: Belief Systems, Social Cognition, and Metacognitions as Driving Forces in Intellectual Performance." *Cognitive Science* 7:329–63.

Schulman, Jay, Carol Brown, and Roger Kahn. 1972. "Report on the Russell Sage Foundation." *Insurgent Sociologist* 2, no. 4:2–34.

Schultz, Klaus P. 1963. *Berlin Zwischen Freiheit und Diktatur*. Berlin: Staneck.

Schumpeter, Joseph. 1939. *Business Cycles*. New York: McGraw-Hill.

————. 1949. "Science and Ideology." *American Economic Review* 39:345–59.

Schuon, Karl. 1972. *Wissenschaft, Politik, und Wissenschaftliche Politik*. Cologne: Pahl-Rugenstein.

Schurmann, Franz. 1974. *The Logic of World Power*. New York: Random House.

Schwartz, Michael, ed. 1987. *The Structure of Power in America*. New York: Holmes and Meier.

Scodel, A., et al. 1959. "Some Descriptive Aspects of Two-Person Non-Zero-Sum Games." *Journal of Conflict Resolution* 3:114–19.

Searle, John R. 1969. *Speech Acts*. London: Cambridge University Press.

Seybold, Peter. 1987. "The Ford Foundation and the Transformation of Political

Science." In *The Structure of Power in America*, ed. Michael Schwartz, chap. 12. New York: Holmes and Meier.

Shackle, G.L.S. 1968. *Expectations, Investment, and Income*. Oxford: Oxford University Press.

Shapere, Dudley. 1984. *Reason and the Search for Knowledge*. Boston: Reidel.

Sherwood, Michael. 1969. *The Logic of Explanation in Psychoanalysis*. New York: Academic Press.

Shonfeld, Andrew. 1972. "The Social Sciences in the Great Debate on Science Policy. *Minerva* 10, no. 3:426–38.

Shubik, Martin. 1959. *Strategy and Market Structure*. New York: Wiley.

———, ed. 1964. *Game Theory and Related Approaches to Social Behavior*. New York: Wiley.

Silk, Leonard, and David Vogel. 1976. *Ethics and Profits: The Crisis of Confidence in American Business*. New York: Simon and Schuster.

Simon, Herbert. 1977. *Models of Discovery*. Dordrecht: Reidel.

Slusser, Robert. 1973. *The Berlin Crisis of 1961*. Baltimore: Johns Hopkins University Press.

Smith, Barry. 1987. "The Austrian Origins of Logical Positivism." In *Logical Positivism in Perspective*, ed. Barry Gower, 35–68. London: Croom Helm.

Smith, Jean E. 1963. *The Defense of Berlin*. Baltimore: Johns Hopkins Press.

Snyder, Glenn H., and P. Diesing. 1977. *Conflict Among Nations: Bargaining, Decision-Making, and System Structure in International Crises*. Princeton, N.J.: Princeton University Press.

Spence, Janet. 1981. "Changing Conceptions of Men and Women." In *The Feminist Perspective in the Academy*, ed. Elizabeth Langland and Walter Gove, 130–48. Chicago: University of Chicago Press.

Spiro, Alan. 1979. "A Philosophical Appraisal of Roy Schafer's *A New Language for Psychoanalysis*." *Psychoanalysis and Contemporary Thought* 2:253–91.

Staats, Arthur W. 1983. *Psychology's Crisis of Disunity: Philosophy and a Unified Science*. New York: Praeger.

Stegmüller, Wolfgang. 1976. *Structure and Dynamics of Theories*, Trans. Wohlhueter. New York: Springer.

———. 1977. *Collected Papers*, vol. 2. Dordrecht: Reidel.

———. 1979. *The Structuralist View of Theories*. New York: Springer.

———. 1986. *Theorie und Erfahrung*, vol. 3. New York: Springer.

Stegmüller, Wolfgang, W. Balzer, and W. Spohn, eds. 1982. *Philosophy of Economics*. New York: Springer.

Stevenson, Charles. 1938. *Ethics and Language*. New Haven, Conn.: Yale University Press.

Stinchcombe, Arthur L. 1968. *Constructing Social Theories*. New York: Harcourt, Brace.

———. 1978. *Theoretical Methods in Social History*. New York: Academic Press.

———. 1983. *Economic Sociology*. New York: Academic Press.

————. 1985. "The Functional Theory of Social Insurance." *Politics and Society* 14:411–30.

Stockman, Norman. 1983. *Antipositivist Theories of the Sciences.* Dordrecht: Reidel.

Stone, Clarence. 1986. "Power and Social Complexity." In *Community Power,* ed. Robert J. Waste, pp. 77–113. Beverly Hills, Calif.: Sage.

Storer, Norman. 1973. Introduction to Robert Merton. *The Sociology of Science.* Chicago: University of Chicago Press.

Stouffer, Samuel, et al. 1949. *The American Soldier.* Princeton, N.J.: Princeton University Press.

————. 1950. *Measurement and Prediction.* Princeton, N.J.: Princeton University Press.

Stretton, Hugh. 1969. *The Political Sciences.* New York: Basic Books.

Studdert-Kennedy, Gerald. 1975. *Evidence and Explanation in Social Science.* London: Routledge.

Suppe, Frederick, ed. 1977. *The Structure of Scientific Theories.* 2d ed. Urbana: University of Illinois Press.

Suppes, Patrick, and R. Atkinson. 1960. *Markov Learning Models for Multiperson Interactions.* Stanford, Calif.: Stanford University Press.

Suttles, Gerald. 1970. *The Social Order of the Slum.* Chicago: University of Chicago Press.

Sylvan, David, and Barry Glassner. 1985. *A Rationalist Methodology for the Social Sciences.* New York: Blackwell.

Sztompka, Piotr. 1974. *System and Function.* New York: Academic Press.

————. 1986. *Robert K. Merton, An Intellectual Profile.* London: Macmillan.

Tarski, Alfred. 1944. "The Semantic Conception of Truth." *Philosophy and Phenomenological Research* 4:341ff.

Temin, Peter. 1976. *Did Monetary Forces Cause the Great Depression?* New York: Norton.

Thompson, R., and J. McConnell. 1955. "Classical Conditioning in the Planarian." *Journal of Comparative and Physiological Psychology* 48:65–68.

Thurow, Lester. 1983. *Dangerous Currents.* New York: Random House.

Tichy, Pavel. 1974. "On Popper's Definition of Verisimilitude." *British Journal for the Philosophy of Science* 25:155–60.

Tobin, James. 1971. *Essays in Economics,* vol 1. Chicago: Markham.

Tomkins, Silvan, and Samuel Messick, eds. 1963. *Computer Simulation of Personality.* New York: Wiley.

Toulmin, Stephen. 1961. *Foresight and Understanding.* New York: Harper.

————. 1972. *Human Understanding.* Princeton, N.J.: Princeton University Press.

Travis, G. D. 1981. "Replicating Replication? Aspects of the Social Construction of Learning in Planarian Worms." *Social Studies of Science* 11:11–32.

Truman, David. 1951. *The Governmental Process.* Westport, Conn.: Greenwood.

Tsoukalis, Loukas, ed. 1985. *The Political Economy of International Money.* London: Sage.

Turner, L.C.F. 1973. *Origins of the First World War.* New York: Norton.

Turner, Merle. 1967. *Psychology and the Philosophy of Science.* New York: Appleton-Century.

Tversky, Amos, and D. Kahneman. 1973. "Availability: A Heuristic for Judging Frequency and Probability." *Cognitive Psychology* 5:207–32.

———. 1974. "Judgment under Ucertainty: Heuristics and Biases." *Science* 185:1124–31.

Useem, Michael. 1976a. "Government Influence on the Social Science Paradigm." *Sociological Quarterly* 17:146–61.

———. 1976b. "State Production of Social Knowledge: Patterns in Government Financing of Academic Research." *American Sociological Review* 41:613–29.

Van den Daele, Wolfgang. 1977. "The Social Construction of Science." In *The Social Production of Scientific Knowledge,* ed. Everett Mendelsohn, 27–54. Boston: Reidel.

Van Fraassen, Bas. 1980. *The Scientific Image.* New York: Oxford.

Vinacke, W. E. 1959. "Sex Roles in the Three-person Game." *Sociometry* 22:343–60.

Vinacke, W. E., and A. Arkoff. 1957. "An Experimental Study of Coalitions in the Triad." *American Sociological Review* 22:406–14.

Viner, Jacob. 1937. "Mr. Keynes on the Causes of Unemployment." *Quarterly Journal of Economics* 51:147–67.

———. 1964. "Comments on My 1936 Review." In *Keynes' General Theory: Reports of Three Decades,* ed. Robert Lekachman, 253–66. New York: St. Martin's Press.

Von Eckhardt, B. 1982. "Why Freud's Research Methodology Was Unscientific." *Psychoanalysis and Contemporary Thought* 5:549ff.

Wallerstein, Immanuel. 1979. *The Capitalist World-Economy.* Cambridge: Cambridge University Press.

Walter, Oliver, ed. 1971. *Political Scientists at Work.* Belmont, Calif.: Duxbury.

Ward, Benjamin. 1973. *What's Wrong with Economics?* New York: Basic Books.

Warner, W. Lloyd, and P. Lunt. 1973 (orig. publ. 1941). *The Social Life of a Modern Community.* Westport, Conn.: Greenwood.

Wason, P. C., and P. N. Johnson-Laird. 1972. *Psychology of Reasoning.* Cambridge, Mass.: Harvard University Press.

Waste, Robert J., ed. 1986. *Community Power.* Beverly Hills, Calif.: Sage.

Watkins, John. 1978. "Corroboration and the Problem of Content Comparison." In *Progress and Rationality in Science,* ed. G. Radnitzky and G. Andersson. Boston: Reidel.

Wax, Murray. 1967. "On Misunderstanding Verstehen: A Reply to Abel. *Sociology and Social Research* 5:323–33.

Weingart, Peter. 1983. "Verwissenschaftlichung der Gesellschaft— Politisierung der Wissenschaft." *Zeitschrift für Soziologie* 12:225–41.

Weinstein, James. 1968. *The Corporate Ideal in the Liberal State*. Boston: Beacon Press.

Weiss, Carol, ed. 1977. *Using Social Research in Public Policy Making*. Lexington, Mass.: Heath.

Weizenbaum, J. 1976. *Computer Power and Human Reason*. San Francisco: Freeman.

Wellman, David. 1969. "Wrong Way to Find Jobs for Negroes." *Transaction* 5:9–18; 6:2–3.

West, James. 1945. *Plainville, USA*. New York: Columbia University Press.

Westkott, Marcia. 1986. *The Feminist Legacy of Karen Horney*. New Haven, Conn.: Yale University Press.

Whitaker, Ben. 1974. *The Philanthropoids*. New York: William Morrow.

Whitehead, Alfred North, and Bertrand Russell. 1915. *Principia Mathematica*. Cambridge: Cambridge University Press.

Whyte, William F. 1956 (orig. publ. 1943). *Street Corner Society*. Chicago: University of Chicago Press.

Wilber, Charles, and R. Harrison. 1978. "The Methodological Basis of Institutional Economics: Pattern Model, Storytelling, and Holism." *Journal of Economic Issues* 12:61–89.

Wilensky, Harold. 1967. *Organizational Intelligence*. New York: Basic Books.

Williams, Robin. 1951. *American Society, a Sociological Interpretation*. New York: Knopf.

Winograd, Terry. 1980. "What Does It Mean to Understand Language?" *Cognitive Science* 4:209–41. Rpt. in Norman, ed., 1981.

Winson, Patrick. 1985. *Brain and Psyche: The Biology of the Unconscious*. Garden City, N.Y.: Doubleday.

Winston, Patrick H., ed. 1975. *The Psychology of Computer Vision*. New York: McGraw-Hill.

———. 1979. *AI: The MIT Perspective*. Reading, Mass.: Addison Wesley.

Witkin, H. A. 1954. *Personality Through Perception*. New York: Harper.

Wittgenstein, Ludwig. 1922. *Tractatus Logico-Philosophicus*. Trans. Pears and McGuiness. London: Routledge and Kegan Paul.

Wohlstetter, Albert. 1966. "The Non-strategic and the Non-existent." In Archibald, ed., 1966, 107–26. Rejoinder by Rapoport, 126–34.

Wright, Erik O. 1978. *Class, Crisis, and the State*. London: Verso.

Young, Warren. 1987. *Interpreting Mr. Keynes: The IS-LM Enigma*. Boulder, Colo.: Westview Press.

Yovits, Marshall, et al., eds. 1962. *Self-Organizing Systems*. Washington, D.C.: Spartan Books.

Zagare, Frank. 1987. *The Dynamics of Deterrence*. Chicago: University of Chicago Press.

INDEX

Pitt Series in Policy and Institutional Studies
Bert A. Rockman, Editor